Lecture Notes in Computer Science   11565

Commenced Publication in 1973
Founding and Former Series Editors:
Gerhard Goos, Juris Hartmanis, and Jan van Leeuwen

More information about this series at http://www.springer.com/series/7410

Joshua D. Guttman · Carl E. Landwehr ·
José Meseguer · Dusko Pavlovic (Eds.)

Foundations of Security, Protocols, and Equational Reasoning

Essays Dedicated to Catherine A. Meadows

Editors
Joshua D. Guttman
Worcester Polytechnic Institute
Worcester, MA, USA

Carl E. Landwehr
George Washington University
Washington, DC, USA

José Meseguer
University of Illinois
Urbana, IL, USA

Dusko Pavlovic
University of Hawai'i
Honolulu, HI, USA

ISSN 0302-9743   ISSN 1611-3349 (electronic)
Lecture Notes in Computer Science
ISBN 978-3-030-19051-4   ISBN 978-3-030-19052-1 (eBook)
https://doi.org/10.1007/978-3-030-19052-1

LNCS Sublibrary: SL4 – Security and Cryptology

Cover illustration: Composite Privacy Protocol: Social Networking (SNet), p. 184

This Springer imprint is published by the registered company Springer Nature Switzerland AG
The registered company address is: Gewerbestrasse 11, 6330 Cham, Switzerland

Catherine A. Meadows

Preface

This volume contains the papers presented at the Catherine Meadows Festschrift Symposium held during May 22–23, 2019, in Fredericksburg, Virginia.

Dr. Catherine A. Meadows, Head of the Formal Methods Group at the US Naval Research Laboratory (NRL) in Washington, D.C., has been—since the very inception of the field—a key leading researcher in formal specification and verification of cryptographic protocols. Her research ideas continue to have immense influence in shaping and advancing it.

The pervasiveness of cryptographic protocols in a massively interconnected world makes their security a direct concern, not just for governments and businesses, but also for the lives of billions of people worldwide. Formal approaches to cryptographic protocol verification are important, since even rigorous review and testing of these protocols has repeatedly failed to reveal significant vulnerabilities. The key technical point is that, even under the optimistic assumption that the cryptographic primitives used by a communication protocol cannot be broken, the protocol itself can be broken. That is, a malicious attacker can still sometimes obtain the secret information sent by an honest user without violating the protocol's specification. This subversion is typically achieved by a so-called man-in-the-middle attack. Since communication—for example, wireless or Internet communication—can often be intercepted, an attacker can listen to various communications and maliciously participate in them, impersonating various participants at various times. In this way, the attacker can obtain correctly encrypted pieces of information, combine and use them in clever ways, and reveal protected information or obtain unauthorized capabilities. Well-tested protocols have fallen victim to subtle attacks after years of practical use, dramatically demonstrating that testing by itself is not a reliable method to ensure security. Some of Dr. Meadows's most important contributions have been precisely in the development of formal specification and verification methods and tools that can uncover such subtle attacks by a systematic formal analysis that exhaustively considers all the possible malicious actions of an attacker.

This kind of formal verification is quite challenging for at least three reasons: (1) the number of actions an attacker can perform is unbounded; (2) the number of protocol sessions an attacker can participate in to obtain and combine information from various users to mount an attack is likewise unbounded; and (3) the algebraic properties of the cryptographic functions employed by the protocol can also be used by an intruder to mount even more subtle attacks. What is challenging about issues (1)–(3) is that they make it difficult to automatically verify protocols by standard model checking methods, since standard model checkers assume a finite set of reachable states, which is ruled out by both (1) and (2).

Dr. Meadows has been a pioneer in developing symbolic formal verification methods and tools that are automatic and overcome the above difficulties. Her methods can be described as a novel form of symbolic model checking of infinite-state systems that exploits the specific properties of cryptographic protocols. By using a symbolic expression to stand for a typically infinite set of concrete protocol states, both difficulties (1) and (2) can be overcome. And by reasoning symbolically about the algebraic properties of the protocol's cryptographic functions using equational unification and narrowing methods, difficulty (3) can likewise be overcome. In the 1990s, Dr. Meadows first embodied these symbolic model checking techniques in her NRL Protocol Analyzer, a tool and methodology that has been fruitfully applied to the analysis of many protocols and protocol standards and has had an enormous influence in the field. Although protocol security is an undecidable problem, by using very powerful state reduction techniques based on grammars, the NRL Protocol Analyzer was able in a good number of cases to terminate its exhaustive symbolic analysis of a given protocol security property with either an actual attack or an absence of attacks that, by the exhaustive nature of the analysis, proved the desired property.

The NRL Protocol Analyzer could reason modulo some algebraic properties of cryptographic functions, but a variety of other such properties were outside its scope. In her more recent research on the Maude-NPA tool, she and her collaborators have made key contributions to overcoming challenge (3) by endowing such a tool with powerful symbolic methods to reason modulo the algebraic properties of a wide variety of cryptographic functions. Maude-NPA has been highly innovative in enabling analysis for cryptographic protocols whose primitive operators satisfy quite a general range of algebraic properties. Actually, algebraic theories in Maude-NPA are user-definable, so new ones can be defined and combined by the user under quite general assumptions. In particular, Maude-NPA has been used to analyze a wide variety of cryptographic protocols whose algebraic properties, besides the usual theories for encryption and decryption, can include and combine complex algebraic theories such as exclusive or, Diffie–Hellman exponentiation, homomorphic encryption, and associativity of string concatenation. Furthermore, besides verifying secrecy and authentication properties, Maude-NPA has also been used to analyze protocol indistinguishability properties, and to reason not just about protocols, but also about protocol compositions and cryptographic APIs.

Dr. Meadows's research contributions go far beyond the brief outline sketched out here. She has, for example, developed a new temporal logic to specify protocol properties as well as new methods for analyzing various kinds of properties beyond secrecy, such as authentication and resilience under denial of service (DoS) attacks. Similarly, she has also developed compositional methods to specify and reason about larger protocols obtained by composing smaller ones, and has made important contributions in other areas such as wireless protocol security, intrusion detection, and the relationship between computational and symbolic approaches to cryptography. Her early cryptography work on rank schemes has also had a great impact and is very highly cited.

In advancing these and various other research directions, she has successfully enlisted the collaboration of many other colleagues in both the US and Europe. Such collaborations, many of them ongoing, have widened the depth and breadth of her contributions, multiplying the impact of her ideas. In particular, under her leadership for more than 20 years, researchers at NRL's Formal Methods Group have made pioneering research contributions to security in a wide range of topics. Given her international stature in the field, she is constantly asked to chair or serve on program committees of many international scientific conferences in her area, and also to serve in an advisory capacity in many US and international research organizations.

For us it has been a great pleasure not only to work with Dr. Meadows, but to edit this Festschrift volume and, with the collaboration of Dr. Andrew Marshall at the University of Mary Washington, to organize this symposium in Fredericksburg, Virginia, to honor Dr. Meadows. We would like to thank UMW for their excellent hospitality at the event. We deeply appreciate Andrew Marshall's work arranging the event.

We are grateful to the National Security Agency and to the National Science Foundation (SFS grant number 1662487), for providing the funding that made this event possible.

Thanks to all the researchers from Europe and North America who have contributed research papers for this volume and will present them at the symposium, as well as all other researchers participating in it; this Festschrift volume and the symposium itself will be important scientific events providing a unique opportunity for serious reflection on the long-term evolution and future prospects of research in cryptographic protocol specification and verification that Dr. Meadows has done so much to advance.

March 2019

Joshua Guttman
Carl Landwehr
José Meseguer
Dusko Pavlovic

Contents

Cathy Meadows: A Central Figure in Protocol Analysis

Sylvan Pinsky[✉]

SRI International, Menlo Park, CA 94025, USA
sylvan.pinsky@sri.com

Abstract. This anecdotal note describes Cathy Meadow's leadership role in formal specification and verification of cryptographic protocols. Cathy has been a central figure in protocol analysis through her significant research and successful efforts to bring researchers together to form a unified, cohesive, and effective community to design and evaluate cryptographic protocols.

1 Computer Security at NSA

The National Security Agency (NSA) started an initiative in computer security by establishing the National Computer Security Center (NCSC) in 1981. I came to NSA in the summer of 1984 when I joined the Office of Research and Development in the National Computer Security Center. Our office had the responsibility to oversee all computer security research conducted within the Department of Defense (DOD). For NSA to manage the coordinated research effort within the DOD, our office chief, George Jelen, formed subgroups in Operating Systems, Networks, Databases, and Formal Methods. As the subgroup chairman for Formal Methods, I worked with all subgroup chairmen and representatives from the Army, Navy, and Air Force to understand the efforts in computer security and identify the leading researchers in industry, government, and academia. Cathy Meadows was quickly named as one of the leading researchers in formal methods.

As the NCSC manager of the MITRE Corporation's contract for computer security support, I first learned about protocol analysis through Jonathan Millen and his Interrogator tool [1] for protocol analysis. He introduced me to Cathy Meadow's NRL Protocol Analyzer [2]. These tools and studies by Kemmerer and Meadows [3,4] generated interest in applying formal methods to the design and analysis of cryptographic protocols. These seminal papers were presented at the well-established IEEE Symposium on Security and Privacy and the newly formed Computer Security Foundations Workshop (started in 1988). Cathy and Jon inspired colleagues such as Guttman, Fábrega and Herzog [5] to introduce the concept of strand spaces, and Cervesato, Durgin, Lincoln, Mitchell, Scedrov and Syverson [6,7] to contribute to the foundations of protocol analysis.

© Springer Nature Switzerland AG 2019
J. D. Guttman et al. (Eds.): Meadows Festschrift, LNCS 11565, pp. 1–5, 2019.
https://doi.org/10.1007/978-3-030-19052-1_1

2   The Protocol eXchange: Historical Perspective

Formal methods activities were spread over several organizations at NSA. Protocol analysis was one of the major areas of common interest when I moved to the evaluation organization to work with Ed Zieglar and Al Maneki. Our Advanced Protocol Analysis Group also sponsored the MITRE research effort in strand spaces. We arranged to have Cathy and her NRL colleagues join us when Joshua Guttman and his team visited us to discuss protocol analysis. These meetings were so productive that we scheduled future gatherings when other researchers, such as Carolyn Talcott and George Dinolt, were in the area. We occasionally used the Cryptologic Museum at NSA to host meetings when other members of the computer security community were available or other agency's groups, such as Brad Martin's formal methods team, wanted to participate.

Ed Zieglar was working on his PhD at the University of Maryland Baltimore County (UMBC). He arranged to have UMBC host our meetings. By 2002 about a half dozen ad-hoc meetings were held. In 2003, Ed and I scheduled the meetings on a quarterly basis and expanded our group to include Mark-Oliver Stehr, José Meseguer, Santiago Escobar, Grit Denker, Andre Scedrov, John Mitchell, Dusko Pavlovic, and other researchers active in protocol analysis. That year we hosted meetings at UMBC and Illiano Cervesato initiated the first Protocol eXchange website which is now hosted by George Dinolt at the Naval Postgraduate School (NPS). George suggested that we hold meetings on both the East and West coasts.

Fig. 1. Hosted by George Dinolt, Naval Postgraduate School

These meetings were designed to provide a forum for discussing work in progress, generating input from peers, and introducing new ideas. Andre Scedrov would frequently have his PhD students present their work in order to gain experience in interacting with researchers in their field. We typically scheduled the meetings over two days and hosted a dinner the night before at a restaurant in the area. One of our favorite locations served the best Maryland crab cakes. Andre ordered oysters stuffed with crab and even he was surprised by the size of the portion.

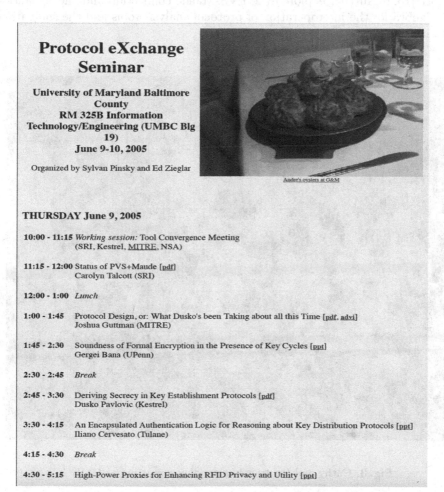

Fig. 2. Dinner at G&M the night before our meetings

The schedule shows our informality (look at Joshua Guttman's talk).

The maturing of strand space theory and multiset rewriting for protocol analysis developed by Cervesato, Durgin, Lincoln, Mitchell and Scedrov [8] and the introduction of the Protocol Derivation Assistant (PDA) by Pavlovic [9] prompted a unified approach to protocol analysis. The Protocol eXchange Seminars provided an excellent forum to get a common framework and methodology for developing and enhancing automated tools. Meadows, Talcott [10,11], and José Meseguer played key roles in defining how to use the best features of PVS [12] and Maude [13] as an underlying framework for the MITRE Cryptographic Protocol Shape Analyzer (CPSA), the Kestrel Protocol Derivation Assistant, and the NRL Protocol Analyzer written in Maude (Maude-NPA). Owre [14] and Talcott [15,16] further explored the PVS-Maude connection and the semantics and algebra for the interoperation of protocol analysis tools and the simulation and analysis of protocol specifications.

Fig. 3. Cathy and her friends attending a meeting at UMBC

3   Concluding Remarks

Cathy Meadows has played a central role in protocol analysis through her continuing research contributions and leadership in building and nurturing a successful and effective research community. She is highly respected by both her peers and the managers of computer security research. I was particularly impressed when I heard praises about Cathy from program managers such as Ralph Wachter (Office of Naval Research), H.O. Lubbes (NRL), and her researcher/manager contemporaries Carl Landwehr and John McLean (NRL), Pete Tasker of MITRE Corporation, Pat Lincoln (SRI), any many, many more. The only thing that tops this praise is to have the opportunity to work with or learn from her. Just talk to José Meseguer, Santiago Escobar, Joshua Guttman, Carolyn Talcott, George Dinolt, Paul Syverson, Illiano Cervesato, Grit Denker, Dusko Pavlovic, Jonathan Millen, Andre Scedrov, Ed Zieglar, me, or many, many others. It has been a pleasure and honor to work with Cathy and I look forward to celebrating her achievements with everyone.

References

1. Millen, J.: The interrogator: a tool for cryptographic protocol security. In: Proceedings 1984 Symposium on Security and Privacy. IEEE Computer Security Society (1984)
2. Meadows, C.: The NRL protocol analyzer: an overview. J. Log. Program. **26**, 113–131 (1996)
3. Kemmerer, R.: Analyzing encryption protocols using formal verification techniques. IEEE J. Sel. Areas Commun. **7**(4), 448–457 (1989)
4. Meadows, C.: Applying formal methods to the analysis of a key management protocol. J. Comput. Secur. **1**(1), 5–35 (1992)
5. Fábrega, J.T., Herzog, J., Guttman, J.: Strand spaces: why is a security protocol correct? In: The IEEE Symposium on Security and Privacy (1998)
6. Syverson, P.: Formal semantics for logics of cryptographic protocols. In: The Computer Security Foundations Workshop (1990)
7. Cervesato, I., Durgin, N., Lincoln, P., Mitchell, J., Scedrov, A.: Relating strands and multiset rewriting for security protocol analysis. In: The Computer Security Foundations Workshop (2000)
8. Cervesato, I., Durgin, N., Lincoln, P., Mitchell, J., Scedrov, A.: A comparison between strand spaces and multiset rewriting for security protocol analysis. In: Okada, M., Pierce, B.C., Scedrov, A., Tokuda, H., Yonezawa, A. (eds.) ISSS 2002. LNCS, vol. 2609, pp. 356–383. Springer, Heidelberg (2003). https://doi.org/10.1007/3-540-36532-X_22
9. Anlauff, M., Pavlovic, D., Waldinger, R., Westfold, S.: Proving authentication properties in the protocol derivation assistant. Kestrel Institute (2006)
10. Talcott, C.: A Maude-PVS tool for Strand Spaces. Protocol eXchange (2004)
11. Talcott, C., Owre, S.: CPSA + Maude + PDA + PVS. Protocol eXchange (2005)
12. Owre, S., Rushby, J.M., Shankar, N.: PVS: a prototype verification system. In: Kapur, D. (ed.) CADE 1992. LNCS, vol. 607, pp. 748–752. Springer, Heidelberg (1992). https://doi.org/10.1007/3-540-55602-8_217
13. Clavel, M., et al.: All About Maude: A High-Performance Logical Framework. Springer, Heidelberg (2007). https://doi.org/10.1007/978-3-540-71999-1
14. Owre, S.: Maude2PVS. Protocol eXchange (2007)
15. Talcott, C.: TOOLIP Semantics & TOOLIP - Maude NPA. Protocol eXchange (2007)
16. Talcott, C.: TOOLIP Semantics & Interoperation. Protocol eXchange (2008)

A Long, Slow Conversation

Jon Millen(✉)

Rockport, MA, USA
j.millen@computer.org
http://jonmillen.com

Abstract. Cathy has always been an inspiration for me, because of the
example she has set for quality in her research work, and more personally for her interest in my own attempts in the same area. In all her
professional activities, I admire her humility, energy, constructive ideas,
and commitment to serving the research community.

Cathy Meadows and I have had a long-time interest in symbolic methods for
cryptographic protocol analysis. We were co-authors on one paper, along with
Dick Kemmerer: Three systems for cryptographic protocol analysis, in *J. Cryptology* in 1994 [1]. That paper compared the NRL Protocol Analyzer, the Interrogator, and Inatest, the tool used by Kemmerer. As a bonus of that, I gained
the Erdös number of 3, since Cathy was a 2. Since then, we have influenced one
another over many years in another way, one which might be described as a long,
thoughtful theoretical conversation. Here are three examples of that.

Cathy wrote a paper called "Using Narrowing in the Analysis of Key Management Protocols" in 1989 [2]. Narrowing is a form of term rewriting that allows
substitutions for variables. Cathy realized its applicability for symbolic protocol
analysis, in the NRL tool. I saw this as potentially useful in the Interrogator,
which did something similar, but more *ad hoc*. I had been having a problem with
search termination in the Interrogator at the time. Cathy's paper led me and
a co-author at MITRE to write "Narrowing terminates for encryption" in 1996
[3]; this paper assured termination for my adjusted algorithm and rules.

Another example of how a paper by Cathy influenced my own work involved
a connection between multilevel databases and survivability. Cathy's paper was
"Extending the Brewer-Nash Model to a Multilevel Context" in 1990 [4], about
the aggregation problem: combining data available at a low sensitivity level could
sometimes lead to a higher-level result. The "NSA phone book" was a simple
popular example of that - individual phone numbers were considered unclassified,
but the book was classified. When aggregation is possible, security levels must
be assigned to all sets of "datasets" (security-marked data objects), since one
cannot assume that the maximum or lattice join of the individual levels will
suffice. Cathy proved that there was a maximum flow policy between datasets
that respected the given level assignments.

In a survivability context, I noticed an analogy between a set of datasets and
a set of system components, such that the "security level" of a component set

J. D. Guttman et al. (Eds.): Meadows Festschrift, LNCS 11565, pp. 6–7, 2019.
https://doi.org/10.1007/978-3-030-19052-1_2

could be taken as the set of system services supported by those components. The current set of supported services should be preserved when the system is reconfigured by reallocating components to services, as a result of the failure of some components. This condition turned out to match the flow policy condition abstractly, so Cathy's result implied the existence of an optimal "Local reconfiguration policy" strategy in 1999 [5].

One more example, this one going in the opposite direction: I published a paper with a partial result that left a question open, and Cathy responded with a paper that answered the open question and extended the result. This was "On the freedom of decryption" in 2003 [6]. Some protocol analysis techniques modeled symbolic encryption without an explicit decryption operator. They assumed that decryption was not useful, even for an attacker, unless it was applied to an encrypted term, so that decryption was simply a matter of stripping off the encryption operator. This is not true in general – my paper had a counterexample – but it was a safe assumption as long as encryptions in the protocol were protected by combining the secret with a recognizable data item. This is normally done in real protocols. However, I could prove my result only for symmetric encryption, and left the public key case open. But then Cathy and Christopher Lynch came out with "On the Relative Soundness of the Free Algebra Model for Public Key Encryption" in 2005 [7], which wrapped up the result for public key protocols as well.

Everyone who does research would like to know that their results are read and appreciated by at least a few people, and even better, that they stimulated further thought and progress. In our long slow-motion tennis game of ideas, Cathy has always been an inspiration for me because of the example she has set for rigor and thoroughness in her research work, and more personally for her interest in my own attempts in the same area. It has also been my pleasure and privilege to have worked with her in other professional activities, where I admired her humility, her energy, her constructive ideas, and her commitment to serving the research community.

References

1. Kemmerer, R., Meadows, C., Millen, J.: Three systems for cryptographic protocol analysis. J. Cryptol. **7**(2), 79–130 (1994)
2. Meadows, C.: Using narrowing in the analysis of key management protocols. In: IEEE Symposium on Security and Privacy, pp. 138–147. IEEE Computer Society (1989)
3. Millen, J., Ko, H.-P.: Narrowing terminates for encryption. In: IEEE Computer Security Foundations, pp. 39–49. IEEE Computer Society (1996)
4. Meadows, C.: Extending the Brewer-Nash model to a multilevel context. In: IEEE Symposium on Security and Privacy, pp. 95–102. IEEE Computer Society (1990)
5. Millen, J.: Local reconfiguration policies. In: IEEE Symposium on Security and Privacy, pp. 48–56. IEEE Computer Society (1999)
6. Millen, J.: On the freedom of decryption. Inf. Process. Lett. **86**(6), 329–333 (2003)
7. Lynch, C., Meadows, C.: On the relative soundness of the free agebra model for public key encryption. Electron. Notes Theor. Comput. Sci. **125**(1), 43–54 (2005)

Key Reminiscences

Paul Syverson[✉]

U.S. Naval Research Laboratory, Washington, D.C., USA
paul.syverson@nrl.navy.mil

Abstract. I offer some reminiscences about work by Cathy Meadows as
well as about working with and for Cathy Meadows. I also recall cryptographic protocol properties introduced in our work in the 1990s and
show their applicability to analyzing novel protocols today. Specifically,
I describe a recent protocol [8] for anonymous proof of account ownership
using the novel primitive of secure channel injection (SCI). And I describe
how the claim of transcript privacy for a specific SCI protocol depends on
an implicit and not necessarily justified assumption of key virginity. I also
discuss ways to modify the protocol to achieve intended goals.

1 Reminiscences

I came to the U.S. Naval Research Laboratory (NRL) in 1989 to work in the
Formal Methods Section. I had not yet completed my dissertation and expected
to stay at NRL just until I was done with it and then seek a position at a
university. Three decades later I'm still at NRL, in no small part because of
Cathy Meadows. Despite all the things on her plate (more on that below) she
has persistently been open to a knock on her door asking if she has a moment—
then taking far more than a moment to give really helpful feedback on research
questions or ideas, as well as how to approach collaborations, funding, bureaucratic hurdles, etc. Many times I approached her with an idea that I thought
was roughly there, only to have it completely revised or even upended—always
for the better. Cathy has steered me towards much success and away from many
disasters over the years.

16 Memories

In the early days, other than our then section head, John McLean, she and the
rest of our section were in one room in Building 16 (now a parking lot). We
rigged up ad hoc dividers at various angles to make individual office spaces for
ourselves. In a wire cage in the hallway was the motor for what we guessed to be
Thomas Edison's first automatic elevator at NRL. When someone pushed the
call button we could hear the relays trip from the office. If you were in the hall,
you could catch a whiff of ozone. A year or so after Cathy became section head,
she was rewarded with her own office, previously occupied by the copy machine

J. D. Guttman et al. (Eds.): Meadows Festschrift, LNCS 11565, pp. 8–14, 2019.
https://doi.org/10.1007/978-3-030-19052-1_3

and overlooking the "Grit Chamber" building situated on Thickening Court, according to the signs at the sewage treatment plant next door and visible from her then office window.

Though not as brash as myself and some of the other more bombastic members of our section, she was nonetheless an active participant in our strange little in jokes. For example, for a few years after a mistaken comment involving polymorphic types that one of us had made in the office, any of us might respond to an apparent error by another section member (whether about research or a trivial error about the time of an upcoming meeting) with, "Well all I can say is, 'Thank God Luca Cardelli isn't here.'" (At the time, I'm not sure any of us had met Luca Cardelli or knew anything about him other than his published work.) Another time in the nineties, Cathy and I were attending a meeting in California and were surprised when we went to pick up our rental car to see that they had upgraded us to a metallic-aqua-blue Mustang. She quickly dubbed it the Attack Sub.

Working

I haven't actually checked, but I wouldn't be surprised if Cathy has chaired a record number of conferences, symposia, workshops, etc. Certainly she has done so more than anyone else I know of. Plus, she has served a gazillion more times on program committees or doing journal reviews. Plus of course, she has handled all the bureaucratic overhead joy that comes from being a manager for nearly three decades, and in a way that, to quote one of my section colleagues, makes her "the kind of boss you wish for but didn't know was possible". Besides all that and much more I'm skipping over, she still manages to contribute an amount and quality of research that would be impressive for someone who wasn't doing all those other things. In short, she's someone that I suspect might not really be human. It's hard to come up with a more plausible explanation.

NRL Protocol Analyzer

What I was initially assigned to when I arrived at NRL in 1989 was helping Cathy with her project in the largely unexplored field of formal techniques and tools for cryptographic protocol analysis. She had been working just a little while on what was to become the NRL Protocol Analyzer (NPA).

My skills with Prolog being nonexistent when I arrived and slow to develop, I was never any help with the code development of NPA—or honestly very much help with the large amount of theory development that underlies it. Cathy did most of that essentially on her own. Early work on automated analysis of security protocols built off of theorem provers, which would *sometimes* show a protocol secure given enough assumptions and development of supporting lemmas. Alternatively, automated support used model checkers, which would explore state spaces looking for insecure states that indicated a potential protocol flaw. But at the time, these were basically disparate approaches: symbolic model checking and SAT solvers had yet to develop. NPA was an early instance of a bridge between these approaches. It worked backwards, allowing a user to specify an insecure state and then search through the prior states from which it could be reached. However, it also supported proofs about unreachability or properties of classes of states. In many cases, this allowed reduction from infinitely many states to a finite and manageable set that could then support a protocol security proof.

NPA (now Maude-NPA) remains in active use and development. I do not intend to more than touch on the general history and state of research problems and solutions for formal security protocol analysis. Cathy herself published a helpful guide to the developments and problems facing formal cryptographic protocol analysis in the early days [5], as well as a collaborative comparison of NPA with two other early approaches, Millen's Interrogator and Kemmerer's use of Ina Jo [2]. She has also been giving us a summary of where things stand at roughly decadal intervals [3,4].

I would not want to give the impression that Cathy is inclined against collaborative research, which she has done extensively. And, despite my shortcomings, she did figure out a way I could usefully contribute to NPA. Together, we created the NRL Protocol Analyzer Temporal Requirements Language (NPATRL). We also explored many protocol properties together. I now turn to an example of the continued relevance of one of them.

2   Research About Remembered Keys (Recalled from a Reminiscence Venue) Remains Fresh

In a forthcoming paper [8], Wang et al. introduce anonymous proofs of account ownership (PAO). Numerous systems for anonymous or blinded credentials exist, but PAO is designed to minimally add to normal email interaction with a domain to prove that the client has an account on that domain, while *not* revealing which account that is. PAO uses a novel primitive, secure channel injection (SCI). An SCI protocol allows a prover and verifier "to jointly generate a sequence of encrypted messages sent to a server, with the ability of the verifier to insert a private message at a designated point in the sequence." (The paper also introduces and describes blind certificate authorities that issue certificates without knowing the identity to which they are binding a public key. But this will not concern us for present purposes.)

Wang et al. target SCI construction at TLS interactions with a mail server. The basic idea is to have the verifier act as a proxy for all protocol messages between the prover and a mail server on which the prover has an account, and to which the prover establishes a TLS connection. Once the prover has a session key with the server, she sends a message comprised of a sequence of cipher blocks using this key. The twist is that the verifier is able to inject into this sequence one or a few cipher blocks that encrypt a nonce unknown to the prover. The resulting email message is sent to another throw-away email account that the prover has. The prover is able to read the nonce in that message, send it to the verifier, and thus show possession of account ownership.

Amongst other things, the authors prove SCI provides transcript privacy for TLS using AES-CBC with HMAC-SHA256, which means that, "The proxy does not learn anything about messages other than M^*." ("Messages" are the plaintext inputs into cipher blocks, and "M^*" is the nonce injected by the proxy.) This should imply that the proxy cannot tell if the client is sending the same message as in a previous protocol run. We show below that, though this appears to be true, it depends on properties of TLS not covered in the paper or security proof. And, it is based on an implicit assumption that session keys chosen uniformly and hidden from the proxy have other properties that they do not necessarily have.

In a paper that Cathy and I published in a 1996 special issue of *Designs, Codes and Cryptography* dedicated to Gus Simmons [7], we discussed (and formally analyzed) various properties for the timely and appropriate use of keys—that they be previously unused or recently authenticated, etc. As we shall see freshly illustrated below, these can be especially important in protocols that support repeated authentication with the same session key, such as TLS.

To see how, we should recall some features of cipher block chaining (CBC mode). As the name implies, CBC uses the previous cipher block as input to generating the next. SCI starts with the client producing the first blocks of the ciphertext as normal. It then has the proxy and client use general-purpose multiparty computation (MPC) to take the last cipher block produced thus far by the client and a plaintext nonce produced by the proxy as input to produce the next cipher block(s) in the chain, which are output to the proxy. The proxy sends to the client the last of the MPC-produced cipher blocks encoding the nonce. The client uses this as input along with the next block of remaining plaintext and then proceeds to produce the rest of the message, which is then sent to the server via the proxy. So that the whole message, including the nonce, is integrity protected, a similar construction injects the appropriate block(s) into the HMAC, although MPC is not needed to produce them.

Content of the email message in a PAO are not discussed by Wang et al. It is reasonable to assume, however, that all or much of the text of email messages in PAOs from the same client might be the same. Suppose further, that a proxy suspects that the session keys (K_{aes} and K_{hmac}) being used in the current protocol run are the same as in some previous run (and thus presumably that the same client is participating). Because of the initialization vector, the first cipher blocks he receives from the client will not look the same even if they are for the same plaintext. He can, nonetheless, replay his cipher block(s) from the previous run regardless of the current input cipher block he has received and regardless of the result of the current MPC. If the subsequent blocks produced by the client are the same, then the same key must be being used to produce them. This violates transcript privacy. Because the nonce should be unknown to the client and uniformly random, it is possible that the cipher blocks produced by the MPC in different protocol runs could be the same even if the session keys are different.

Thus, the outcome will still yield a valid message to send to the server even if the proxy will not know the value of the nonce that has been injected into it.

The authors had assumed that different runs of their TLS protocols used different keys, and they assumed that session keys being chosen uniformly and remaining unknown to the proxy was sufficient. (Personal communication.) But that is not quite the case. To reduce overhead, both TLS 1.2 and 1.3 allow "session resumption" based on previously exchanged keys, though with a wrinkle as we shall see.

There has been much published work analyzing security protocols for guarantees that the keys used or established by them cannot be used in unintended ways, such as through some sort of unauthorized reuse. In [7], Cathy and I set out three properties that can be relevant to the just-noted assumptions: "*Freshness* is the property of having been generated or sent after the start of the present epoch. *Currency* is the property of being part of the present protocol run. (Currency usually implies freshness, but it may not.) *Virginity* is the property of not having been accepted for use previously (accept [sic] possibly by other principals in the protocol)." Freshness is not sufficient to preclude the attack just described. For example, interleaved runs of a protocol might still have problems. To ground the assumption they wish to make, Wang et al. would have to assume that keys are virgin. This would rule out the reuse of keys in different runs of the protocol.

Of course, proscribing the overhead savings of session resumption might conflict with a goal of making minimal additions or changes to TLS usage by mail servers. Fortunately, it is not necessary. The primary reason is that session resumption in both TLS 1.2 and TLS 1.3 does provide virgin session keys. When resuming a session, the session "master secret" key is hashed with virgin nonces [1,6]. This consciously does not provide perfect forward secrecy. It does, however, guarantee that K_{aes} and K_{hmac} for each TLS session will be virgin, even if the master secret key underlying them might not be and whether or not it is a resumption session.

A revised proof of transcript privacy including the assumption of virgin keys would then be consistent with TLS. However, since SCI is intended to be more general, it is worth considering whether it is possible for a protocol to achieve secure channel injection without assuming virginity of keys.

One way to avoid the specific attack introduced above would be to not allow the proxy to use the protocol as an oracle in this way. Simply include the encrypted proxy nonce in the last blocks of the ciphertext rather than permitting the client to add more cipher blocks after that. This would reduce the generality of the current construction, which was the intended purpose of having the injected nonce occur in the midst of the ciphertext. (Personal communication.) One could also imagine, however, that letting the proxy provide the last blocks of the ciphertext, even via MPC, could facilitate some flavor of padding oracle. Injecting the nonce in the middle thus also provides some intuitive resistance against such potential attack.

Another simple and cheap mechanism to avoid our attack would be to have the proxy send the client a secure hash of the injected nonce when returning the cipher block at the end of the MPC. When the nonce is later uncovered in the message sent to the throw-away email address for PAO, it will be trivial to check that it matches the hashed nonce sent to the client during the SCI construction. This would then avoid the need to assume virginity of keys, provided that detection of proxy misbehavior after the fact is sufficient. A somewhat less cheap variant that could allow the client to stop the protocol and prevent the attack would have the proxy send to the client a zero-knowledge proof that he knows the injected nonce.

Wang et al. say only that the two parties use a generic MPC to compute the block(s) constituting the encrypted nonce portion of the encrypted message. They do, however, specify that the output of the MPC is sent to the proxy. Another way to avoid the attack without assuming virgin keys would be to have the output sent to the client rather than the proxy. For example, if garbled circuits are used (as in the analysis they do of expected SCI overhead) then the garbler and evaluator roles could be reversed. This might also be slightly more efficient in communication overhead since the client needs this output to produce the remainder of the ciphertext in any case.

The attack we introduced is precluded by the key-format requirements of session resumption in TLS. Nonetheless, our analysis indicates that a proof of SCI for TLS (using the construction in [8]) must specifically make use of the virginity of TLS session keys. Modified SCI constructions we raised would seem to allow avoiding an assumption of virgin session keys, but these constructions would still require a new security proof. If the computational capabilities of client and proxy are different, even if the protocol simply switches the output of the MPC to the client rather than the proxy, there is a performance consideration as well.

We leave such proofs for future work. Nonetheless, we have in this example an illustration that lessons from Cathy's work of decades ago remain freshly applicable to today's protocols.

Thanks to the authors of [8] and to my Formal Methods Section colleagues, Aaron Jaggard and Aaron Johnson, for helpful comments and discussion. This work supported by ONR.

References

1. Dierks, T., Rescorla, E.: The Transport Layer Security (TLS) Protocol Version 1.2, August 2008. https://tools.ietf.org/html/rfc5246
2. Kemmerer, R., Meadows, C., Millen, J.: Three systems for cryptographic protocol analysis. J. Cryptol. **7**(2), 79–130 (1994)
3. Meadows, C.: Formal methods for cryptographic protocol analysis: emerging issues and trends. IEEE J. Sel. Areas Commun. **21**(1), 44–54 (2003)
4. Meadows, C.: Emerging issues and trends in formal methods in cryptographic protocol analysis: twelve years later. In: Martí-Oliet, N., Ölveczky, P.C., Talcott, C. (eds.) Logic, Rewriting, and Concurrency. LNCS, vol. 9200, pp. 475–492. Springer, Cham (2015). https://doi.org/10.1007/978-3-319-23165-5_22

5. Meadows, C.A.: Formal verification of cryptographic protocols: a survey. In: Pieprzyk, J., Safavi-Naini, R. (eds.) ASIACRYPT 1994. LNCS, vol. 917, pp. 133–150. Springer, Heidelberg (1995). https://doi.org/10.1007/BFb0000430
6. Rescorla, E.: The Transport Layer Security (TLS) Protocol Version 1.3, August 2018. https://tools.ietf.org/html/rfc8446
7. Syverson, P., Meadows, C.: A formal language for cryptographic protocol requirements. Des. Codes Crypt. **7**(1/2), 27–59 (1996)
8. Wang, L., Asharov, G., Pass, R., Ristenpart, T., shelat, a.: Blind certificate authorities. In: Proceedings of the 40th IEEE Symposium on Security and Privacy (S&P 2019), May 2019. https://eprint.iacr.org/2018/1022

Canonical Narrowing with Irreducibility Constraints as a Symbolic Protocol Analysis Method

Santiago Escobar[1]($\boxtimes$) and José Meseguer[2]

[1] DSIC-ELP, Universitat Politècnica de València, Valencia, Spain
`sescobar@dsic.upv.es`
[2] University of Illinois at Urbana-Champaign, Urbana, IL, USA
`meseguer@illinois.edu`

Abstract. This work proposes *canonical constrained narrowing*, a new symbolic reachability analysis technique applicable to topmost rewrite theories where the equational theory has the finite variant property. Our experiments suggest that canonical constrained narrowing is more efficient than both standard narrowing and the previously studied contextual narrowing. These results are relevant not only for Maude-NPA, but also for symbolically analyzing many other concurrent systems specified by means of rewrite theories.

1 Introduction

Formal analysis of cryptographic protocols has become one of the most successful applications of rewriting to security, with a vast literature (see [4,12] for surveys) and a number of tools: NRL Protocol Analyzer [30], FDR [29], ProVerif [6], AVISPA [2], Maude-NPA [18], Scyther [11], AKISS [1], and Tamarin [31]. There has been a growing body of research in extending these tools to reason about different types of cryptographic properties (aka equational theories).

On the one hand, many protocols are known to be secure if cryptographic properties are not exploited, but can be broken if they are. For example, the recursive authentication protocol proposed by Bull [7], broken by Ryan and Schneider [40] by exploiting the properties of the exclusive-or operation, and a group key protocol based on group Diffie-Hellman [3], broken by Pereira and Quisquater [38] using associative-commutative properties of modular exponentiation. On the other hand, modern cryptographic protocols are so complex that they require sophisticated cryptographic properties to secure applications such as video-conferencing and electronic voting. For example, exclusive-or is necessary in RFID protocols [13] and mobile protocols such as 5G [5].

This work has been partially supported by the EU (FEDER) and the Spanish MINECO under grant TIN 2015-69175-C4-1-R, by Generalitat Valenciana under grants PROME-TEOII/2015/013 and PROMETEO/2019/098, by the US Air Force Office of Scientific Research under award number FA9550-17-1-0286, and by NRL under contract number N00173-17-1-G002.

J. D. Guttman et al. (Eds.): Meadows Festschrift, LNCS 11565, pp. 15–38, 2019.
https://doi.org/10.1007/978-3-030-19052-1_4

There are different ways of addressing automated reasoning w.r.t. cryptographic properties in the literature [4]. A prominent one can be described as *unification-based symbolic reachability analysis*. The key idea is that to make sure that analysis will not miss security attacks where the attacker takes advantage of the protocol's algebraic properties described, say, as an equational theory G, one describes typically infinite sets of states by *symbolic patterns* with logical variables, and characterizes protocol transitions between such symbolically-represented sets of states by performing G-unification (i.e., solving of equations modulo the equational theory G) before applying protocol transition rules.

Catherine Meadows research on the *NRL Protocol Analyzer* [30] opened up this line of research by relying on the Prolog-based support for patterns with logical variables and unification. Furthermore, unification modulo an equational theory G was also supported for some theories, such as cancellation of encryption and decryption, where narrowing with such equations was guaranteed to terminate and would therefore provide an G-unification algorithm.

We have had the great fortune of working closely with Catherine on a very fruitful long-term collaboration to extend the original NRL Protocol Analyzer's insights about unification-based symbolic reachability analysis to be able to handle a much wider range of protocols and of algebraic properties. The tool resulting from this collaboration is the Maude-NPA [18]. The great generality provided by Maude-NPA to symbolically analyze the security properties of a protocol $\mathcal{P}$ *modulo* its algebraic properties is based on the following foundational ideas:

1. Both the algebraic properties of $\mathcal{P}$ and its transitions are formally specified by means of a rewrite theory [32] of the form: $\mathcal{P} = (\Sigma, E \cup B, R)$, where:
   - Σ describes the syntax of the cryptographic functions and of state constructors,
   - the protocol's algebraic properties G decompose as a (disjoint) union $G = E \uplus B$, with B commonly occurring axioms such as associativity and/or commutativity and/or identity of some symbols and the oriented equations $\overrightarrow{E}$ are confluent, coherent, and terminating modulo B, and
   - $\mathcal{P}$'s transition rules are described by a set R of *rewrite rules*.
2. $E \uplus B$-unification is performed by *folding variant narrowing* [23] using the oriented equations $\overrightarrow{E}$ modulo B, assuming that $E \uplus B$ has the so-called *finite variant property* [10].
3. A sound and complete method for symbolic reachability analysis of the security properties of $\mathcal{P}$ is achieved by *narrowing* symbolic states [37] with the transition rules R *modulo* $E \uplus B$.

In this way, security properties for a wide range of protocols modulo many sophisticated algebraic properties and their combinations have been analyzed in Maude-NPA [19–22, 25–27, 41, 42, 45–47].

To honor Catherine in this occasion, in this paper we present the theoretical foundations of, and some experimental results for, a new *theory-generic* narrowing technique, that we call *canonical constrained narrowing* that can be used not only for symbolically analyzing protocols modulo algebraic properties, but for any concurrent system specifiable as a so-called topmost rewrite theory $\mathcal{R} = (\Sigma, E \cup B, R)$ where the equations $E \cup B$ have the finite variant property. Our initial experiments suggest that this new technique is more efficient—both in the size of the symbolic state space that needs to be explored and in execution time—than previous narrowing-based reachability techniques. Furthermore, it is directly relevant not just for analyzing protocols in Maude-NPA, but also for analyzing many other concurrent systems in Maude [8, 15]. Intuitively, the key idea of this new symbolic method is to always keep the symbolic patterns with logical variables, describing infinite sets of states, in *irreducible form* by the equations E modulo B, and to carry along such irreducibility requirements in the reachability analysis as a set of global *irreducibility constraints*. In this way, many symbolically reachable states can be safely discarded because such constraints are violated.

Let us motivate the main issues in unification-based symbolic reachability analysis with an example.

Example 1. Let us consider a very simple protocol [16] using an exclusive-or operator $\oplus$, which is associative and commutative (AC) and self-canceling with identity 0. Alice and Bob exchange nonces, denoted by N_A or N_B, encrypted using a function pk, where $pk(A, X)$ stands for encryption of message X with $A's$ (standing for Alice's) public key; below, B stands for Bob. Upon receiving the final message, Alice verifies that she received $N_A \oplus N_B$ for some nonce N_B received in the first message.

$$\text{Alice and Bob}$$
$$1. \ B \rightarrow A : pk(A, N_B)$$
$$2. \ A \rightarrow B : pk(B, N_A)$$
$$3. \ B \rightarrow A : N_A \oplus N_B$$

The protocol is seen differently by Bob and Alice, as shown below using variables X and Y for blobs that Alice and Bob cannot identify.

Bob	Alice
1. $B \rightarrow A : pk(A, N_B)$	1. $B \rightarrow A : pk(A, Y)$
2. $A \rightarrow B : pk(B, X)$	2. $A \rightarrow B : pk(B, N_A)$
3. $B \rightarrow A : X \oplus N_B$	3. $B \rightarrow A : N_A \oplus Y$

If we see these two as role specifications, we can ask whether an instance of Alice's specification can be executed. Using an automated analysis tool, we may find an instance obtained by applying the substitution $Y \mapsto N_A \oplus Z$ (or simply $Y \mapsto N_A$) modulo the exclusive-or properties.

$$\text{Alice after } Y \mapsto N_A \oplus Z$$
$$1. \ B \rightarrow A : pk(A, N_A \oplus Z)$$
$$2. \ A \rightarrow B : pk(B, N_A)$$
$$3. \ B \rightarrow A : N_A \oplus N_A \oplus Z = Z$$

However, many automated analysis tools would identify this instance as unfeasible and discard it, since Alice cannot receive a message $N_A \oplus Z$ before she generates the nonce N_A in the second step.

Protocol analysis modulo cryptographic properties must be done very carefully to avoid incompleteness problems, as shown in the following example.

Example 2. If the instance of the previous example is discarded, a protocol analysis tool may lose the possibility of a regular, valid execution, e.g., by further instantiating Z by the substitution $Z \mapsto N_A \oplus N_B$

Alice after $Z \mapsto N_A \oplus N_B$.
1. $B \to A : pk(A, N_A \oplus N_A \oplus N_B) = pk(A, N_B)$
2. $A \to B : pk(B, N_A)$
3. $B \to A : N_A \oplus N_A \oplus N_A \oplus N_B = N_A \oplus N_B$

This is the intended legal execution of the protocol! Thus, a protocol analysis tool could inadvertently have ruled out a legal execution. Note that the same intended execution could have been produced by an initial substitution $Y \mapsto N_B$ but an automated tool may not know it a priori.

These problems have been addressed in the literature as follows. We first decompose the equational theory $(\Sigma, E \cup B)$ associated to the exclusive-or operator $\oplus$ into $(\Sigma, B, \overrightarrow{E})$, where B is the AC theory and $\overrightarrow{E}$ is a set of oriented equations for the self-canceling ($X \oplus X = 0$) and identity ($X \oplus 0 = X$) properties. Then, one could consider all the possible most general instantiations (*variants*) of Alice's role $\{pk(A, Y), pk(B, N_A), N_A \oplus Y\}$ normalized by using the oriented equations modulo AC. There are four such cases:

(i) $\{pk(A, Y), pk(B, N_A), N_A \oplus Y\}$ where no oriented equation is ever applied,
(ii) $\{pk(A, 0), pk(B, N_A), N_A\}$ where the identity oriented equation is applied with the substitution $Y \mapsto 0$,
(iii) $\{pk(A, N_A), pk(B, N_A), 0\}$ where the self-cancelling oriented equation is applied with the substitution $Y \mapsto N_A$, and
(iv) $\{pk(A, Z \oplus N_A), pk(B, N_A), Z\}$ where the self-cancelling oriented equation is applied with the substitution $Y \mapsto Z \oplus N_A$ (see Footnote 1 below).

Any other normalization using the two oriented equations modulo AC of a substitution instance of Alice's role is subsumed by these three. For instance, applying the substitution $Z \mapsto N_A \oplus N_B$ to case (iii) yields an instance of case (i), or applying the substitution $Z \mapsto N_A$ to case (iii) yields an instance of case (ii); in both cases without the need to apply the self cancelling oriented equation. However, considering a decomposition (Σ, B, E) of an equational theory $(\Sigma, E \cup B)$ raises two important questions:

How can we capture all the possible most general, normalized instantiations (*variants*)?
And how can we propagate the information that the results are already *normalized*, so that no further normalization will be needed in the future (*irreducibility constraints*)?

In [16], we provided an answer to these two questions in the context of narrowing-based symbolic reachability analysis of cryptographic protocols: (i) generate all the possible variants of the term being symbolically executed by narrowing, (ii) associate an irreducibility constraint to each generated variant, and (iii) propagate those irreducibility constraints along a narrowing sequence. In this paper, we reconsider such approach and conclude that: (i) it is considerably more efficient not to generate the variants of the term being narrowed (see Sect. 7), (ii) can associate an irreducibility constraint to the lefthand side of the transition rule being applied instead of computing the variants of the term being narrowed, and (iii) can keep those irreducibility constraints along a narrowing sequence as before. Note that both the narrowing-based reachability framework of [16] and the new framework proposed in this paper make use of the notion of *asymmetric unification* developed in [17]. Note that the new framework proposed here is not related to how variants are computed, using the folding variant narrowing [23], or how asymmetric unification is performed, which are connected to the equational theory $E \uplus B$, but how transition rules R are applied modulo $E \uplus B$ for reachability analysis.

On the other hand, a very satisfactory answer to these two questions is given in [34,35] but under some extra conditions: the equational theory must be a *constructor finite variant theory*. In this paper, we provide a symbolic reachability analysis framework modulo equational theories without such restrictions and focus on the exclusive-or theory and the Abelian Group for illustration purposes.

The rest of the paper is organized as follows. After some preliminaries in Sect. 2, we introduce the Maude-NPA tool in Sect. 3. We redefine the narrowing-based reachability framework of [16] in Sect. 4. We present in Sect. 5 how rewriting modulo an equational theory could be simplified when we have a finite variant theory, called *canonical rewriting*, and define the new *canonical narrowing* in Sect. 6. Finally, we demonstrate in Sect. 7 that the canonical narrowing is more efficient than standard narrowing and the narrowing relation defined in [16]. And we conclude in Sect. 8.

2 Preliminaries

We follow the classical notation and terminology from [43] for term rewriting, and from [32] for rewriting logic and order-sorted notions.

We assume an order-sorted signature $\Sigma = (S, \leq, \Sigma)$ with a poset of sorts $(S, \leq)$. The poset $(\mathsf{S}, \leq)$ of sorts for Σ is partitioned into equivalence classes, called *connected components*, by the equivalence relation $(\leq \cup \geq)^+$. We assume that each connected component $[s]$ has a *top element* under $\leq$, denoted $\top_{[s]}$ and called the *top sort* of $[s]$. This involves no real loss of generality, since if $[s]$ lacks a top sort, it can be easily added.

We assume an S-sorted family $\mathcal{X} = \{\mathcal{X}_s\}_{s \in S}$ of disjoint variable sets with each $\mathcal{X}_s$ countably infinite. $\mathcal{T}_\Sigma(\mathcal{X})_s$ is the set of terms of sort s, and $\mathcal{T}_{\Sigma,s}$ is the set of ground terms of sort s. We write $\mathcal{T}_\Sigma(\mathcal{X})$ and $\mathcal{T}_\Sigma$ for the corresponding order-sorted term algebras. Given a term t, $Var(t)$ denotes the set of variables in t.

A *substitution* $\sigma \in \mathcal{S}ubst(\Sigma, \mathcal{X})$ is a sorted mapping from a finite subset of $\mathcal{X}$ to $\mathcal{T}_{\Sigma}(\mathcal{X})$. Substitutions are written as $\sigma = \{X_1 \mapsto t_1, \ldots, X_n \mapsto t_n\}$ where the domain of σ is $Dom(\sigma) = \{X_1, \ldots, X_n\}$ and the set of variables introduced by terms $t_1, \ldots, t_n$ is written $Ran(\sigma)$. The identity substitution is id. Substitutions are homomorphically extended to $\mathcal{T}_{\Sigma}(\mathcal{X})$. The application of a substitution σ to a term t is denoted by $t\sigma$ or $\sigma(t)$.

A Σ-*equation* is an unoriented pair $t = t'$, where $t, t' \in \mathcal{T}_{\Sigma}(\mathcal{X})_{\mathsf{s}}$ for some sort $\mathsf{s} \in \mathsf{S}$. Given Σ and a set E of Σ-equations, order-sorted equational logic induces a congruence relation $=_E$ on terms $t, t' \in \mathcal{T}_{\Sigma}(\mathcal{X})$ (see [33]). Throughout this paper we assume that $\mathcal{T}_{\Sigma,\mathsf{s}} \neq \emptyset$ for every sort s, because this affords a simpler deduction system. We write $\mathcal{T}_{\Sigma/E}(\mathcal{X})$ and $\mathcal{T}_{\Sigma/E}$ for the corresponding order-sorted term algebras modulo the congruence closure $=_E$, denoting the equivalence class of a term $t \in \mathcal{T}_{\Sigma}(\mathcal{X})$ as $[t]_E \in \mathcal{T}_{\Sigma/E}(\mathcal{X})$.

An *equational theory* (Σ, E) is a pair with Σ an order-sorted signature and E a set of Σ-equations. An equational theory (Σ, E) is *regular* if for each $t = t'$ in E, we have $Var(t) = Var(t')$. An equational theory (Σ, E) is *linear* if for each $t = t'$ in E, each variable occurs only once in t and in t'. An equational theory (Σ, E) is *sort-preserving* if for each $t = t'$ in E, each sort s, and each substitution σ, we have $t\sigma \in \mathcal{T}_{\Sigma}(\mathcal{X})_{\mathsf{s}}$ iff $t'\sigma \in \mathcal{T}_{\Sigma}(\mathcal{X})_{\mathsf{s}}$. An equational theory (Σ, E) is *defined using top sorts* if for each equation $t = t'$ in E, all variables in $Var(t)$ and $Var(t')$ have a top sort.

An *E-unifier* for a Σ-equation $t = t'$ is a substitution σ such that $t\sigma =_E t'\sigma$. For $Var(t) \cup Var(t') \subseteq W$, a set of substitutions $CSU_E^W(t = t')$ is said to be a *complete* set of unifiers for the equality $t = t'$ modulo E away from W iff: (i) each $\sigma \in CSU_E^W(t = t')$ is an E-unifier of $t = t'$; (ii) for any E-unifier ρ of $t = t'$ there is a $\sigma \in CSU_E^W(t = t')$ such that $\sigma|_W \sqsupseteq_E \rho|_W$ (i.e., there is a substitution η such that $(\sigma\eta)|_W =_E \rho|_W$); and (iii) for all $\sigma \in CSU_E^W(t = t')$, $Dom(\sigma) \subseteq (Var(t) \cup Var(t'))$ and $Ran(\sigma) \cap W = \emptyset$.

A *rewrite rule* is an oriented pair $l \to r$, where $l \notin \mathcal{X}$ and $l, r \in \mathcal{T}_{\Sigma}(\mathcal{X})_{\mathsf{s}}$ for some sort $\mathsf{s} \in \mathsf{S}$. An *(unconditional) order-sorted rewrite theory* is a triple (Σ, E, R) with Σ an order-sorted signature, E a set of Σ-equations, and R a set of rewrite rules. The set R of rules is *sort-decreasing* if for each $t \to t'$ in R, each $\mathsf{s} \in \mathsf{S}$, and each substitution σ, $t'\sigma \in \mathcal{T}_{\Sigma}(\mathcal{X})_{\mathsf{s}}$ implies $t\sigma \in \mathcal{T}_{\Sigma}(\mathcal{X})_{\mathsf{s}}$.

The rewriting relation on $\mathcal{T}_{\Sigma}(\mathcal{X})$, written $t \to_R t'$ or $t \to_{p,R} t'$ holds between t and t' iff there exist $p \in Pos_{\Sigma}(t)$, $l \to r \in R$ and a substitution σ, such that $t|_p = l\sigma$, and $t' = t[r\sigma]_p$. The relation $\to_{R/E}$ on $\mathcal{T}_{\Sigma}(\mathcal{X})$ is $=_E; \to_R; =_E$. The transitive (resp. transitive and reflexive) closure of $\to_{R/E}$ is denoted $\to_{R/E}^+$ (resp. $\to_{R/E}^*$). A term t is called $\to_{R/E}$-irreducible (or just R/E-irreducible) if there is no term t' such that $t \to_{R/E} t'$. For $\to_{R/E}$ confluent and terminating, the irreducible version of a term t is denoted by $t\downarrow_{R/E}$.

A relation $\to_{R,E}$ on $\mathcal{T}_{\Sigma}(\mathcal{X})$ is defined as: $t \to_{p,R,E} t'$ (or just $t \to_{R,E} t'$) iff there is a non-variable position $p \in Pos_{\Sigma}(t)$, a rule $l \to r$ in R, and a substitution σ such that $t|_p =_E l\sigma$ and $t' = t[r\sigma]_p$. Reducibility of $\to_{R/E}$ is undecidable in general since E-congruence classes can be arbitrarily large. Therefore,

R/E-rewriting is usually implemented [28] by R, E-rewriting under some conditions on R and E such as confluence, termination, and coherence (see [28]).

We call (Σ, B, E) a *decomposition* of an order-sorted equational theory $(\Sigma, E \cup B)$ if B is regular, linear, sort-preserving, defined using top sorts, and has a finitary and complete unification algorithm, which implies that B-matching is decidable, and the equations E oriented into rewrite rules $\overrightarrow{E}$ are *convergent*, i.e., confluent, terminating, and strictly coherent modulo B, and sort-decreasing.

Given a decomposition (Σ, B, E) of an equational theory, (t', θ) is an E, B-*variant* [10,23] (or just a variant) of term t if $t\theta{\downarrow}_{E,B} =_E t'$ and $\theta{\downarrow}_{E,B} =_E \theta$. A *complete set of E, B-variants* [23] (up to renaming) of a term t is a subset, denoted by $[\![t]\!]_{E,B}$, of the set of all E, B-variants of t such that, for each E, B-variant (t', σ) of t, there is an E, B-variant $(t'', \theta) \in [\![t]\!]_{E,B}$ such that $(t'', \theta) \sqsupseteq_{E,B} (t', \sigma)$, i.e., there is a substitution ρ such that $t' =_B t''\rho$ and $\sigma|_{Var(t)} =_B (\theta\rho)|_{Var(t)}$. A decomposition (Σ, B, E) has the *finite variant property* (FVP) [23] (also called a *finite variant decomposition*) iff for each Σ-term t, a complete set $[\![t]\!]_{E,B}$ of its most general variants is finite.

2.1 Symbolic Reachability Analysis by Narrowing

Since we are performing reachability analysis for protocol analysis, we recall basic notions on reachability goals. In what follows, the set G of equations will in practice be $G = E \uplus B$ and will have a decomposition (Σ, B, E).

Definition 1 (Reachability goal). [37] *Given an order-sorted rewrite theory (Σ, G, R), a reachability goal is defined as a pair $t \xrightarrow[R/G]{?}{}^{*} t'$, where $t, t' \in \mathcal{T}_{\Sigma}(\mathcal{X})_{\mathsf{s}}$. It is abbreviated as $t \xrightarrow{?}{}^{*} t'$ when the theory is clear from the context; t is the source of the goal and t' is the target. A substitution σ is a R/G-solution of the reachability goal (or just a solution for short) iff there is a sequence $\sigma(t) \rightarrow_{R/G} \sigma(u_1) \rightarrow_{R/G} \cdots \rightarrow_{R/G} \sigma(u_{k-1}) \rightarrow_{R/G} \sigma(t')$.*

A set Γ of substitutions is said to be a complete set of solutions *of $t \xrightarrow[R/G]{?}{}^{*} t'$ iff (i) every substitution $\sigma \in \Gamma$ is a solution of $t \xrightarrow[R/G]{?}{}^{*} t'$, and (ii) for any solution ρ of $t \xrightarrow[R/G]{?}{}^{*} t'$, there is a substitution $\sigma \in \Gamma$ more general than ρ modulo G, i.e., $\sigma|_{Var(t) \cup Var(t')} \sqsupseteq_G \rho|_{Var(t) \cup Var(t')}$.*

This provides a tool-independent semantic framework for symbolic reachability analysis of protocols under algebraic properties. Note that we have removed the condition $Var(r) \subseteq Var(l)$ for rewrite rules $l \rightarrow r \in R$ and thus a solution of a reachability goal must be applied to all terms in the rewrite sequence. If the terms t and t' in a goal $t \xrightarrow[T/G]{?}{}^{*} t'$ are ground and rules have no extra variables in their righthand sides, then goal solving becomes a standard rewriting reachability problem. However, since we allow terms t, t' with variables, we need a mechanism more general than standard rewriting to find solutions of reachability goals. *Narrowing* with R modulo G generalizes rewriting by performing *unification* at non-variable positions instead of the usual matching modulo G.

Specifically, narrowing instantiates the variables in a term by a G-unifier that enables a rewrite modulo G with a given rule of R and a term position.

Definition 2 (Narrowing modulo G). [37] *Given an order-sorted rewrite theory (Σ, G, R), the narrowing relation on $\mathcal{T}_{\Sigma}(\mathcal{X})$ modulo G is defined as $t \leadsto_{\sigma, R, G} t'$ (or $\overset{\sigma}{\leadsto}$ if R, G is understood) iff there is $p \in Pos_{\Sigma}(t)$, a rule $l \to r$ in R such that $Var(t) \cap (Var(l) \cup Var(r)) = \emptyset$, and $\sigma \in CSU_G^V(t|_p = l)$ for a set V of variables containing $Var(t)$, $Var(l)$, and $Var(r)$, such that $t' = \sigma(t[r]_p)$.*

The reflexive and transitive closure of narrowing is defined as $t \leadsto_{\sigma, R, G}^* t'$ iff either $t = t'$ and $\sigma = id$, or there are terms $u_1, \ldots, u_n$, $n \geq 1$, and substitutions $\sigma_1, \ldots, \sigma_{n+1}$ s.t. $t \leadsto_{\sigma_1, R, G} u_1 \leadsto_{\sigma_2, R, G} u_2 \cdots u_n \leadsto_{\sigma_{n+1}, R, G} t'$ and $\sigma = \sigma_1 \cdots \sigma_{n+1}$.

Soundness and completeness of narrowing with rules R modulo the equational theory G for solving reachability goals is proved in [28,37] for order-sorted *topmost* rewrite theories, i.e., rewrite theories were all the rewrite steps happen at the top of the term.

3   Overview of Maude-NPA

Here we give a high-level summary of Maude-NPA. For further details see [18].

Given a protocol $\mathcal{P}$, we define its specification in the strand space model as a rewrite theory of the form $(\Sigma_{SS_\mathcal{P}}, E_{SS_\mathcal{P}}, R_\mathcal{P}^{-1})$, where (i) the signature $\Sigma_{SS_\mathcal{P}}$ is split into predefined symbols Σ_{SS} for strand syntax and user-definable symbols $\Sigma_\mathcal{P}$ based on a parametric sort Msg of messages, (ii) the algebraic properties $E_{SS_\mathcal{P}}$ are also split into the algebraic properties of the strand notation E_{SS} and the user-definable algebraic properties $E_\mathcal{P}$ for the cryptographic functions, and (iii) the transition rules $R_\mathcal{P}^{-1}$ are defined on states, i.e., terms of a predefined sort State. They are *reversed* for backwards execution.

Example 3. For the protocol of Example 1, the equational theory $(\Sigma_{SS_\mathcal{P}}, E_{SS_\mathcal{P}})$ for exclusive-or is decomposed into $(\Sigma, B, \overrightarrow{E})$ where B is the associativity and commutativity axioms for $\oplus$ and $\overrightarrow{E}$ is as follows:[1]

$$X \oplus 0 \to X \quad X \oplus X \to 0 \quad X \oplus X \oplus Y \to Y$$

In Maude-NPA states are modeled as elements of an initial algebra $\mathcal{T}_{\Sigma_{SS_\mathcal{P}}/E_{SS_\mathcal{P}}}$, i.e., an $E_{SS_\mathcal{P}}$-equivalence class $[t]_{E_{SS_\mathcal{P}}} \in \mathcal{T}_{\Sigma_{SS_\mathcal{P}}/E_{SS_\mathcal{P}}}$ with t a ground $\Sigma_{SS_\mathcal{P}}$-term. A state has the form $\{S_1 \& \cdots \& S_n \& \{IK\}\}$ where $\&$ is an associative-commutative union operator with identity symbol $\emptyset$. Each element in the set is either a *strand* S_i or the *intruder knowledge* $\{IK\}$ at that state.

The *intruder knowledge* $\{IK\}$ belongs to the state and is represented as a set of facts using the comma as an associative-commutative union operator with

---

[1] Note that the two first equations are not AC-coherent, but adding the last equation is sufficient to recover that property (see [44]).

identity element *empty*. There are two kinds of intruder facts: *positive* knowledge facts (the intruder knows message m, i.e., $m \in \mathcal{I}$), and *negative* knowledge facts (the intruder *does not yet know* m but *will know it in a future state*, i.e., $m \notin \mathcal{I}$), where m is a message expression.

A *strand* [24] specifies the sequence of messages sent and received by a principal executing a given role in the protocol and is represented as a sequence of messages $[msg_1^{\pm}, msg_2^{\pm}, msg_3^{\pm}, \ldots, msg_{k-1}^{\pm}, msg_k^{\pm}]$ with $msg_i^{\pm}$ either msg_i^{-} (also written $-msg_i$) representing an input message, or msg_i^{+} (also written $+msg_i$) representing an output message. Note that each msg_i is a term of a special sort Msg.

Variables of sort Fresh are unique for each instance of a strand schema, i.e., if we compare two strands for Alice or a strand for Alice and a strand for Bob, they will always have different, unique, fresh variables associated with them. We make them explicit by writing $:: r_1, \ldots, r_k :: [m_1^{\pm}, \ldots, m_n^{\pm}]$, where each r_i first appears in an output message $m_{j_i}^{+}$ and can later appear in any input and output message of $m_{j_i+1}^{\pm}, \ldots, m_n^{\pm}$. If there are no Fresh variables, we write $:: nil :: [m_1^{\pm}, \ldots, m_n^{\pm}]$.

Strands are used to represent both the actions of honest principals (with a strand specified for each protocol role) and the actions of an intruder (with a strand for each action an intruder is able to perform on messages). In Maude-NPA strands evolve over time; the symbol | is used to divide past and future. That is, given a strand $[\ msg_1^{\pm}, \ \ldots, \ msg_i^{\pm} \ | \ msg_{i+1}^{\pm}, \ \ldots, \ msg_k^{\pm} \ ]$, messages $msg_1^{\pm}, \ldots, msg_i^{\pm}$ are the *past messages*, and messages $msg_{i+1}^{+}, \ldots, msg_k^{\pm}$ are the *future messages* ($msg_{i+1}^{\pm}$ is the immediate future message). A strand $[msg_1^{\pm}, \ldots, msg_k^{\pm}]$ is shorthand for $[nil \ | \ msg_1^{\pm}, \ldots, msg_k^{\pm}, nil]$. An *initial state* is a state where the bar is at the beginning for all strands in the state, and the intruder knowledge has no fact of the form $m \in \mathcal{I}$. A *final state* is a state where the bar is at the end for all strands in the state and there is no intruder fact of the form $m \notin \mathcal{I}$.

Example 4. For the protocol of Example 1, the strand specification of the protocol is as follows:

(Bob) $:: r_1 :: [\ +(pk(A, n(B, r_1))), -(pk(B, Y)), \quad +(Y \oplus n(B, r_1))\ ]$
(Alice) $:: r_2 :: [\ -(pk(A, X)), \quad +(pk(B, n(A, r_2))), -(n(A, r_2) \oplus X)\ ]$

Since the number of states $T_{\Sigma_{SS_{\mathcal{P}}}/E_{SS_{\mathcal{P}}}}$ is in general infinite, rather than exploring concrete protocol states $[t]_{E_{SS_{\mathcal{P}}}} \in T_{\Sigma_{SS_{\mathcal{P}}}/E_{SS_{\mathcal{P}}}}$ Maude-NPA explores *symbolic strand state patterns* $[t(x_1, \ldots, x_n)]_{E_{SS_{\mathcal{P}}}} \in T_{\Sigma_{SS_{\mathcal{P}}}/E_{SS_{\mathcal{P}}}}(\mathcal{X})$ on the free $(\Sigma_{SS_{\mathcal{P}}}, E_{SS_{\mathcal{P}}})$-algebra over a set of variables $\mathcal{X}$. In this way, a state pattern $[t(x_1, \ldots, x_n)]_{E_{SS_{\mathcal{P}}}}$ represents not a single concrete state but a possibly infinite set of such states, namely all the *instances* of the pattern $[t(x_1, \ldots, x_n)]_{E_{SS_{\mathcal{P}}}}$ where the variables $x_1, \ldots, x_n$ have been instantiated by concrete ground terms.

The semantics of Maude-NPA is expressed in terms of the following *forward rewrite rules* that describe how a protocol moves from one state to another via the intruder's interaction with it.

$$\{SS \,\&\, [L \mid M^-, L'] \,\&\, \{M \in \mathcal{I}, IK\}\} \rightarrow \{SS \,\&\, [L, M^- \mid L'] \,\&\, \{M \in \mathcal{I}, IK\}\} \quad (1)$$

$$\{SS \,\&\, [L \mid M^+, L'] \,\&\, \{IK\}\} \rightarrow \{SS \,\&\, [L, M^+ \mid L'] \,\&\, \{IK\}\} \quad (2)$$

$$\{SS \,\&\, [L \mid M^+, L'] \,\&\, \{M \notin \mathcal{I}, IK\}\} \rightarrow \{SS \,\&\, [L, M^+ \mid L'] \,\&\, \{M \in \mathcal{I}, IK\}\} \quad (3)$$

$$\forall \, [l_1, u^+, l_2] \in \mathcal{P} : \{SS \,\&\, [l_1 \mid u^+] \,\&\, \{u \notin \mathcal{I}, IK\}\} \rightarrow \{SS \,\&\, \{u \in \mathcal{I}, IK\}\} \quad (4)$$

where L and L' are variables denoting a list of strand messages, IK is a variable for a set of intruder facts ($m \in \mathcal{I}$ or $m \notin \mathcal{I}$), SS is a variable denoting a set of strands, and l_1, l_2 denote a list of strand messages. The set R_p^{-1} of *backwards* state transition rules is defined by reversing the direction of the above set of rules $\{(1), (2), (3)\} \cup (4)$. In the backwards executions of (3) and (4), $u \notin \mathcal{I}$ marks when the intruder learnt u.

For example, the protocol of Example 1 can be modeled as a rewrite theory (Σ, G, T) where T is the reversed version of the generic rewrite rules (1)–(3) plus the following rewrite rules for introducing new strands.

$$\{SS \,\&\, :: r_1 :: [\, +(pk(A, n(B, r_1))), \; -(pk(B, Y)) \mid \, +(Y \oplus n(B, r_1)) \,]$$
$$\&\, \{Y \oplus n(B, r_1) \notin \mathcal{I}, IK\}\}$$
$$\rightarrow \{SS \,\&\, \{Y \oplus n(B, r_1) \in \mathcal{I}, IK\}\}$$
$$\{SS \,\&\, :: r_1 :: [\, nil \mid \, +(pk(A, n(B, r_1))) \,]$$
$$\&\, \{pk(A, n(B, r_1)) \notin \mathcal{I}, IK\}\}$$
$$\rightarrow \{SS \,\&\, \{pk(A, n(B, r_1)) \in \mathcal{I}, IK\}\}$$
$$\{SS \,\&\, :: r_2 :: [\, -(pk(A, X)) \mid \, +(pk(B, n(A, r_2))) \,]$$
$$\&\, \{pk(B, n(A, r_2)) \notin \mathcal{I}, IK\}\}$$
$$\rightarrow \{SS \,\&\, \{pk(B, n(A, r_2)) \in \mathcal{I}, IK\}\}$$

One uses Maude-NPA to find an attack by specifying an insecure state pattern called an *attack pattern*. Maude-NPA attempts to find a path from an initial state to the attack pattern via backwards narrowing (narrowing using the rewrite rules with the orientation reversed). That is, a narrowing sequence from an initial state to an attack state is searched *in reverse* as a *backwards path* from the attack state to the initial state. Maude-NPA attempts to find paths until it can no longer form any backwards narrowing steps, at which point it terminates. If at that point it has not found an initial state, the attack pattern is shown to be *unreachable* modulo $E_{SS_{\mathcal{P}}}$. Note that Maude-NPA places *no bound on the number of sessions*, so reachability is undecidable in general. Note also that Maude-NPA does not perform any data abstraction such as a bounded number of nonces. However, the tool makes use of a number of sound and complete state space reduction techniques that help to identify unreachable and redundant states [21], and thus make termination more likely.

Example 5. The final pattern used as an input to the backwards symbolic reachability analysis of Example 1 could, for example, be as follows:

$\{ :: r_2 :: [nil, -(pk(A, X)), +(pk(B, n(A, r_2))), -(X \oplus n(A, r_2)) \mid nil]$ &
$:: r_1 :: [nil, +(pk(A, n(B, r_1))), -(pk(B, Y)), +(Y \oplus n(B, r_1)) \mid nil]$ & SS & $\{IK\}\}$

This pattern does not require the intruder to have learnt anything, so it is very general and could lead to a regular execution and to an attack. Indeed, this protocol has the following attack reachable from that final pattern, where the intruder starts a protocol session with B but uses B's nonce to start a protocol session with A, so finally the intruder is able to learn both B's nonce and A's nonce:

1. $B \to I : pk(i, N_B)$ 3. $A \to B : pk(B, N_A)$
2. $I \to A : pk(a, N_B)$ 4. $B \to A, I : N_A \oplus N_B$

4   Contextual Narrowing

In [16], we provided a symbolic reachability analysis framework called *contextual symbolic reachability analysis* that we summarize here.

The first step is to consider how to represent the information that *no more oriented equations should be applicable to a term*. A term $t(x_1{:}s_1, \ldots, x_n{:}s_n)$ can be viewed as a symbolic, effective method to describe a (typically infinite) set of terms, namely the set

$$\lceil t(x_1{:}s_1, \ldots, x_n{:}s_n) \rceil = \{t(u_1, \ldots, u_n) \mid u_i \in \mathcal{T}_\Sigma(\mathcal{X})_{s_i}\} = \{t\theta \mid \theta \in \mathcal{S}ubst(\Sigma, \mathcal{X})\}.$$

We think as t as a *pattern*, which symbolically describes all its *instances* (including non-ground). However, since (Σ, B, E) is a decomposition of an equational theory $(\Sigma, E \cup B)$, we can consider only normalized instances of t

$$\lceil t \rceil_{\overrightarrow{E}, B} = \{(t\theta)\!\downarrow_{\overrightarrow{E}, B} \mid \theta \in \mathcal{S}ubst(\Sigma, \mathcal{X})\}$$

However, since we are interested in terms that may satisfy some irreducibility conditions, we can obtain a more expressive symbolic pattern language where patterns are *constrained by irreducibility constraints*. That is, we consider constrained patterns of the form $\langle t, \Pi \rangle$ where Π is a finite set of normalized terms. Then we can define:

$$\lceil \langle t, (u_1, \ldots, u_k) \rangle \rceil_{\overrightarrow{E}, B} = \{(t\theta)\!\downarrow_{\overrightarrow{E}, B} \mid u_1\theta, \ldots, u_k\theta \text{ are } \overrightarrow{E}, B\text{-normalized}\}.$$

Second, the paper [16] introduced two new notions: *contextual rewrite theory* and *contextual reachability goal* that differed from the notion of a rewrite theory and a reachability goal given in Sect. 2 only in the addition of a function ϕ, called the *irreducibility requirements*, which is a function mapping each $f \in \Sigma$ to a set of its arguments, i.e., $\phi(f) \subseteq \{1, \ldots, ar(f)\}$, where $ar(f)$ is the number of arguments of f. In this section, we completely disregard such a function ϕ, since it is irrelevant for this work.

Narrowing of patterns with irreducibility constraints requires a special unification algorithm, *asymmetric unification*, already developed in [17] for the contextual narrowing [16].

Definition 3 (Asymmetric Unification). [17] *Given a decomposition (Σ, B, E) of an equational theory $(\Sigma, E \cup B)$, a substitution σ is an asymmetric $\overrightarrow{E}, B$-unifier of a set P of asymmetric equations $\{t_1 =_\downarrow t'_1, \ldots, t_n =_\downarrow t'_n\}$ iff for every asymmetric equation $t_i =_\downarrow t'_i$ in P, σ is an $(E \cup B)$-unifier of the equation $t_i = t'_i$ and $(t'_i \downarrow_{\overrightarrow{E},B})\sigma$ is in $\overrightarrow{E}, B$-normal form.*

A set of substitutions Ω is a complete set of asymmetric $\overrightarrow{E}, B$-unifiers of P iff: (i) every member of Ω is an asymmetric $\overrightarrow{E}, B$-unifier of P, and (ii) for every asymmetric $\overrightarrow{E}, B$-unifier θ of P there exists a $\sigma \in \Omega$ such that $\sigma \sqsupseteq_B \theta$ (over $Var(P)$).

Example 6. Consider the protocol of Example 1. The asymmetric unification problem found by backwards narrowing-based reachability in Maude-NPA is $t =_\downarrow t'$ where t is $\{SS \mathbin{\&} [L, M^+ \mid L'] \mathbin{\&} \{M \in \mathcal{I}, IK\}\}$, i.e., the righthand side of Rule (3), and t' is the following state, found by Maude-NPA after one backwards narrowing step using Rule (1) from the state pattern of Example 5:

$$\{ :: r_2 :: [nil, -(pk(A, X)), +(pk(B, n(A, r_2)))] \mid -(X \oplus n(A, r_2)), nil] \mathbin{\&}$$
$$:: r_1 :: [nil, +(pk(A, n(B, r_1))), -(pk(B, Y)), +(Y \oplus n(B, r_1)) \mid nil] \mathbin{\&}$$
$$SS \mathbin{\&} \{(X \oplus n(A, r_2)) \in \mathcal{I}, IK\}\}$$

The two key terms are $+(Y \oplus n(B, r_1))$ and $(X \oplus n(A, r_2)) \in \mathcal{I}$. An asymmetric unifier is $\sigma_1 = \{Y \mapsto n(A, r_2), X \mapsto n(B, r_1)\}$, whereas the substitutions $\sigma_2 = \{Y \mapsto X \oplus n(B, r_1) \oplus n(A, r_2)\}$ and $\sigma_3 = \{X \mapsto Y \oplus n(B, r_1) \oplus n(A, r_2)\}$ are *not* valid asymmetric unifiers: σ_2 makes term $Y \oplus n(B, r_1)$ reducible and σ_3 makes term $X \oplus n(A, r_2)$ reducible.

A special-purpose asymmetric unification algorithm for exclusive-or was developed in [17]. In general, however, an asymmetric variant-based unification algorithm can be easily defined by just freezing one side of a unification problem [16].

Using an asymmetric unification algorithm, we can modify the standard notion of narrowing as follows. Note that the following definition differs from Definition 2 only in using contextual unification $CSU_{E \cup B}(l =_{\downarrow_\phi} t|_p)$ instead of regular unification $CSU_{E \cup B}(l = t|_p)$ and carrying along a set of irreducible terms Π passed on to the contextual unification algorithm, where Π is the set of irreducible terms that have been computed earlier in the narrowing sequence. Note also that the following definition differs, essentially, from the contextual narrowing in [16] by removing the function ϕ.

Definition 4 (Contextual Constrained Narrowing). *Given an order-sorted rewrite theory $(\Sigma, E \cup B, R)$ such that (Σ, B, E) is a decomposition of $(\Sigma, E \cup B)$, the contextual constrained narrowing relation modulo R, E, B on pairs $\langle t, \Pi \rangle$ for t a Σ-term and Π a set of $\overrightarrow{E}, B$-irreducible Σ-terms is defined as $t \leadsto_{\sigma, R, E, B} t'$ (or $\stackrel{\sigma}{\leadsto}$ if R, E, B is understood) iff there is $p \in Pos_\Sigma(t)$, a rule $l \to r$ in R such that $Var(t) \cap (Var(l) \cup Var(r)) = \emptyset$, and $\sigma \in CSU_{E \cup B}^V(P)$ for*

$P = \{l =_\downarrow t|_p\} \cup \{u =_{\downarrow_\phi} u \mid u \in \Pi\}$ *and a set V of variables containing $Var(t)$,*
$Var(l)$, and $Var(r)$, such that $t' = \sigma(t[r]_p)$.

Let us motivate the issues involved with this narrowing relation by an example.

Example 7. Let us consider the state pattern shown in Example 5 with the extra
requirement that the intruder learns $n(A, r_2)$:

$$\{ :: r_2 :: [nil, -(pk(A, X)), +(pk(B, n(A, r_2))), -(X \oplus n(A, r_2)) \mid nil] \ \& $$
$$:: r_1 :: [nil, +(pk(A, n(B, r_1))), -(pk(B, Y)), +(Y \oplus n(B, r_1)) \mid nil] \ \& $$
$$SS \ \& \ \{n(A, r_2) \in \mathcal{I}, IK\}\}$$

This term does have a backwards narrowing step in Maude-NPA by just applying
the substitution $X \mapsto 0$, where 0 is the identity symbol of $\oplus$. However, the
term $X \oplus n(A, r_2)$ becomes reducible under such substitution and the attack
would not be reachable because of our irreducibility condition on $X \oplus n(A, r_2)$.
To solve this problem, the key idea is that the pattern $X \oplus n(A, r_2)$ should
be replaced by its *variants* before each contextual narrowing step, i.e., by the
possible instance patterns of it which are irreducible, namely: (i) the pattern
$X \oplus n(A, r_2)$ itself, (ii) the pattern Y, which is the normal form after applying
substitution $X \mapsto Y \oplus n(A, r_2)$, (iii) the pattern 0, which is the normal form
after applying substitution $X \mapsto n(A, r_2)$, and (iv) the pattern $n(A, r_2)$, which
is the normal form after applying substitution $X \mapsto 0$. Only after replacement of
the original term by these variants, can we impose the irreducibility conditions
for reducing the search space. That is, for contextual reachability analysis, we
first need to compute what we call the $\overrightarrow{E}, B$-*variants* of a term.

Definition 5 ($\overrightarrow{E}, B$-variants). *Given an order-sorted rewrite theory $(\Sigma, E \cup B, R)$ such that (Σ, B, E) is a decomposition of $(\Sigma, E \cup B)$, the set of $\overrightarrow{E}, B$-variants of a pair $\langle t, \Pi \rangle$ for t a term and Π a set of irreducible terms is defined as $[\![\langle t, \Pi \rangle]\!]_{E,B} = \{(t', \sigma) \mid (t', \sigma) \in [\![t]\!]_{E,B} \wedge \forall u \in \Pi : \sigma(u) \text{ is } \overrightarrow{E}, B\text{-irreducible}\}$. For readability, we write $\langle t, \Pi \rangle \twoheadrightarrow_{\theta, \overrightarrow{E}, B} \langle w, \overline{\Pi} \rangle$ to denote that $(w, \theta) \in [\![\langle t, \Pi \rangle]\!]_{E,B}$ and $\overline{\Pi} = \theta(\Pi) \cup \{w\}$.*

Example 8. Let us consider the state t' shown in Example 6:

$$\{ :: r_2 :: [nil, -(pk(A, X)), +(pk(B, n(A, r_2))) \mid - (X \oplus n(A, r_2)), nil] \ \& $$
$$:: r_1 :: [nil, +(pk(A, n(B, r_1))), -(pk(B, Y)), +(Y \oplus n(B, r_1)) \mid nil] \ \& $$
$$SS \ \& \ \{(X \oplus n(A, r_2)) \in \mathcal{I}, IK\}\}$$

We generate the three variants associated to $X \oplus n(A, r_2)$ and the three variants
associated to $Y \oplus n(B, r_1)$, with a total of eight new terms.

The key idea to achieve the desired semantic equivalence between contextual
constrained narrowing and ordinary narrowing is to precede each contextual
constrained narrowing step by a variant computation step. The proof of this
theorem is immediate from [16, Theorem 1].

Theorem 1 (Soundness and Completeness of Contextual Constrained Narrowing). *Given a topmost order-sorted rewrite theory* $(\Sigma, E \cup B, R)$ *such that* (Σ, B, E) *is a decomposition of* $(\Sigma, E \cup B)$ *and* B *has a finitary* B-*unification algorithm, a reachability goal* $t \xrightarrow{?}^* t'$ *has a solution iff there is a substitution* σ, *a sequence of terms* $u_1, \ldots, u_n, w_1, \ldots, w_{n+1}, t''$ *and a sequence of substitutions* $\theta_1, \ldots, \theta_{n+1}, \theta'_1, \ldots, \theta'_{n+1}$ *such that:*

$$
\begin{aligned}
\langle t, \Pi_0 \rangle &\twoheadrightarrow_{\theta_1, \vec{E}, B} \langle w_1, \Pi_1 \rangle \quad \rightsquigarrow_{\theta'_1, R, \vec{E}, B} \langle u_1, \overline{\Pi_1} \rangle \\
&\twoheadrightarrow_{\theta_2, \vec{E}, B} \langle w_2, \Pi_2 \rangle \quad \rightsquigarrow_{\theta'_2, R, \vec{E}, B} \langle u_2, \overline{\Pi_2} \rangle \\
&\quad\quad\quad \vdots \\
&\twoheadrightarrow_{\theta_n, \vec{E}, B} \langle w_n, \Pi_n \rangle \quad \rightsquigarrow_{\theta'_n, R, \vec{E}, B} \langle u_n, \overline{\Pi_n} \rangle \\
&\twoheadrightarrow_{\theta_{n+1}, \vec{E}, B} \langle w_{n+1}, \Pi_{n+1} \rangle \rightsquigarrow_{\theta'_{n+1}, R, \vec{E}, B} \langle t'', \overline{\Pi_{n+1}} \rangle
\end{aligned}
$$

and also:

1. $\Pi_0 = \emptyset$, $\Pi_1 = \{w_1\}$, $\overline{\Pi_1} = \theta'_1(\Pi_1)$, $\Pi_2 = \theta_2(\overline{\Pi_1}) \cup \{w_2\}$, $\overline{\Pi_2} = \theta'_2(\Pi_2)$, ..., $\Pi_{n+1} = \overline{\Pi_n} \cup \{w_{n+1}\}$, $\overline{\Pi_{n+1}} = \theta'_{n+1}(\Pi_{n+1})$,
2. *for each* $i \in \{1, \ldots, n+1\}$, *the term* $w_i \theta'_i \theta_{i+1} \theta'_{i+1} \cdots \theta_{n+1} \theta'_{n+1}$ *is* R, E-*irreducible,*
3. *there is a substitution* τ *such that* $\sigma =_E \theta_1 \theta'_1 \theta_2 \theta'_2 \cdots \theta_{n+1} \theta'_{n+1} \tau$, *and*
4. $t' =_{E \cup B} t'' \tau$.

Furthermore, such a substitution σ *is a solution of the reachability goal. Conversely, for any solution* γ *of the above reachability goal, there is a substitution* α *and a substitution* σ *satisfying the above conditions such that* $\gamma =_{E \cup B} \sigma \alpha$.

Example 9. Continuing Example 8, we have sixteen state patterns after variant generation. The legal execution of the protocol follows from the following generated variant, where everything is labeled as irreducible.

$$
\begin{aligned}
\{ &:: r_2 :: [nil, -(pk(A, X)), +(pk(B, n(A, r_2))) \mid -(X \oplus n(A, r_2)), nil] \ \& \\
&:: r_1 :: [nil, +(pk(A, n(B, r_1))), -(pk(B, Y)), +(Y \oplus n(B, r_1)) \mid nil] \ \& \\
&SS \ \& \ \{(X \oplus n(A, r_2)) \in \mathcal{I}, IK\}\}
\end{aligned}
$$

Some other variants will be discarded by Maude-NPA, such as

$$
\begin{aligned}
\{ &:: r_2 :: [nil, -(pk(A, Z \oplus n(A, r_2))), +(pk(B, n(A, r_2))) \mid -(Z), nil] \ \& \\
&:: r_1 :: [nil, +(pk(A, n(B, r_1))), -(pk(B, Y)), +(Y \oplus n(B, r_1)) \mid nil] \ \& \\
&SS \ \& \ \{Z \in \mathcal{I}, IK\}\}
\end{aligned}
$$

As shown in [16], the state space reduction achieved in Maude-NPA is huge by using the irreducibility conditions and, especially, the state space reduction techniques [21] based on such irreducibility conditions. Indeed, condition (2) in Theorem 1 for terms w_i to be irreducible after substitution application ensures that variants are not computed more than once for each irreducible subterm in term t or irreducible subterms introduced by righthand sides of rules. However, we present in this paper a constrained narrowing algorithm that has an even better performance. The first step is to redefine the concept of rewriting in an order-sorted rewrite theory.

5   Canonical Rewriting

A topmost rewrite theory $\mathcal{R} = (\Sigma, E \cup B, R)$ specifies a concurrent system whose states are $E \cup B$-equivalence classes $[t]_{E \cup B} \in T_{\Sigma/E \cup B,\text{State}}$ of the topmost sort State, and whose concurrent transitions are rewrite steps

$$[t]_{E \cup B} \to_{R/E \cup B} [t']_{E \cup B}$$

induced by the $R/E \cup B$ rewriting relation.

Without additional conditions on $E \cup B$, the relation $\to_{R/E \cup B}$ is *undecidable*, see Sect. 2. However, if $(\Sigma, E \cup B)$ has a finite variant decomposition (Σ, B, E) and B has a finitary B-unification algorithm, this relation becomes *decidable* when R is finite, B has a finitary unification algorithm, and a substitution for the variables $\overrightarrow{y} = Var(r) - Var(l)$ of each rule $l \to r \in R$ is provided. This decidability is achieved by the following notion of *canonical rewriting*, for which the notion of the *canonical term algebra*, and the *free canonical term algebra* are worth recalling.

When $(\Sigma, E \cup B)$ has a decomposition as (Σ, B, E), then the initial algebra $T_{\Sigma/E \cup B}$ is isomorphic to the canonical term algebra $C_{\Sigma/E \cup B} = (C_{\Sigma/E \cup B}, \to_{R/E \cup B})$, where $C_{\Sigma/E \cup B} = \{C_{\Sigma/E \cup B,\text{s}}\}_{\text{s} \in \text{S}}$ and $C_{\Sigma/E \cup B,\text{s}} = \{[t\downarrow_{\overrightarrow{E},B}]_B \in T_{\Sigma/B} \mid t\downarrow_{\overrightarrow{E},B} \in T_{\Sigma,\text{s}}\}$ and where for each $f \in \Sigma$, $f_{C_{\Sigma/E \cup B}}([t_1]_B, \ldots, [t_n]_B) = [f(t_1, \ldots, t_n)\downarrow_{\overrightarrow{E},B}]_B$.

We have an isomorphism of initial algebras $T_{\Sigma/E \cup B} \cong C_{\Sigma/E \cup B}$. Likewise, we have an isomorphism of free $(\Sigma, E \cup B)$-algebras $T_{\Sigma/E \cup B}(\mathcal{X}) \cong C_{\Sigma/E \cup B}(\mathcal{X})$, where $C_{\Sigma/E \cup B}(\mathcal{X}) = (C_{\Sigma/E \cup B}(\mathcal{X}), \to_{R/E \cup B})$ and

$$C_{\Sigma/E \cup B,\text{s}}(\mathcal{X}) = \{[t\downarrow_{\overrightarrow{E},B}]_B \in T_{\Sigma/B}(\mathcal{X}) \mid t\downarrow_{\overrightarrow{E},B} \in T_{\Sigma}(\mathcal{X})_\text{s}\}.$$

The key point of canonical rewriting is that we can simulate rewritings $[t]_{E \cup B}$ $\to_{R/E \cup B} [t']_{E \cup B}$ by corresponding rewritings $[t\downarrow_{\overrightarrow{E},B}]_B \to_{R/E \cup B} [t'\downarrow_{\overrightarrow{E},B}]_B$ and make rewriting decidable when $(\Sigma, B, \overrightarrow{E})$ is FVP.

Definition 6 (Canonical Rewriting). *Let $\mathcal{R} = (\Sigma, E \cup B, R)$ be a topmost rewrite theory such that $(\Sigma, E \cup B)$ has an FVP decomposition (Σ, B, E). Let $C^{\circ}_{\Sigma/E \cup B}(\mathcal{X})_{\text{State}} = \bigcup C_{\Sigma/E \cup B}(\mathcal{X})_{\text{State}}$, i.e., $C^{\circ}_{\Sigma/E \cup B}(\mathcal{X})_{\text{State}} = \{t\downarrow_{\overrightarrow{E},B} \mid t\downarrow_{\overrightarrow{E},B} \in T_{\Sigma}(\mathcal{X})_{\text{State}}\}$, so that $C^{\circ}_{\Sigma/E \cup B}(\mathcal{X})_{\text{State}} \subseteq T_{\Sigma}(\mathcal{X})_{\text{State}}$. We then define the $\to_{R/E,B}$ canonical rewrite relation with rules R modulo $E \cup B$ as the following binary relation $\to_{R/E,B} \subseteq C^{\circ}_{\Sigma/E \cup B}(\mathcal{X})_{\text{State}} \times C^{\circ}_{\Sigma/E \cup B}(\mathcal{X})_{\text{State}}$, where $t \to_{R/E,B} t'$ iff $\exists l \to r \in R$ and $\exists \theta$ with $Dom(\theta) \subseteq Var(l) \cup Var(r)$ and $\theta = \theta\downarrow_{\overrightarrow{E},B}$ such that: (i) $(l\theta)\downarrow_{\overrightarrow{E},B} =_{E \cup B} t$, and (ii) $t' =_B (r\theta)\downarrow_{\overrightarrow{E},B}$.*

The claim that $\to_{R/E,B}$ exactly captures/bisimulates the $\to_{R/E\cup B}$ rewrite relation is justified by the following result.

Theorem 2. *For each* $t, t' \in T_\Sigma(\mathcal{X})_{\text{State}}$, $t \to_{R/E\cup B} t'$ *iff* $t\downarrow_{\vec{E},B} \to_{R/E,B} t'\downarrow_{\vec{E},B}$.

Proof. Since $\to_{R/E,B} \subseteq \to_{R/E\cup B}$, we only need to prove the $(\Rightarrow)$ direction. If $t \to_{R/E\cup B} t'$, we have a substitution θ and a rule $l \to r \in R$ such that $t =_{E\cup B} l\theta$ and $t' =_{E\cup B} r\theta$. But then, of course, we also have $t =_{E\cup B} l(\theta\downarrow_{\vec{E},B})$ and $t' =_{E\cup B} r(\theta\downarrow_{\vec{E},B})$. By the Church-Rosser Theorem modulo B [36, Theorem 3], we then have

$$
\begin{array}{ccccc}
t & =_{E\cup B} \; l(\theta\downarrow_{\vec{E},B}) & \to_R & r(\theta\downarrow_{\vec{E},B}) & =_{E\cup B} \; t' \\
\downarrow_{\vec{E},B} & \downarrow_{\vec{E},B} & & \downarrow_{\vec{E},B} & \downarrow_{\vec{E},B} \\
t\downarrow_{\vec{E},B} =_B & l(\theta\downarrow_{\vec{E},B})\downarrow_{\vec{E},B} \to_{R/E,B} & r(\theta\downarrow_{\vec{E},B})\downarrow_{\vec{E},B} =_B & t'\downarrow_{\vec{E},B}
\end{array}
$$

as desired. □

In fact, when considering the induced relation $[u]_B \to_{R/E,B} [v]_B$ on $C_{\Sigma/E,B}$ we get an *isomorphism of binary relations*

$$
(C_{\Sigma/E,B}(\mathcal{X})_{\text{State}}, \to_{R/E,B}) \simeq (T_{\Sigma/E,B}(\mathcal{X})_{\text{State}}, \to_{R/E\cup B})
$$

induced by the isomorphism $T_{\Sigma/E,B}(\mathcal{X}) \simeq C_{\Sigma/E,B}(\mathcal{X})$:

$$
\begin{array}{ccc}
[t]_{E\cup B} & \to_{R/E\cup B} & [t']_{E\cup B} \\
\downarrow_{\vec{E},B} & & \downarrow_{\vec{E},B} \\
[t\downarrow_{\vec{E},B}]_B & \to_{R/E,B} & [t'\downarrow_{\vec{E},B}]_B
\end{array}
$$

The claim that when $Var(r) \subseteq Var(l)$, or we provide a substitution for the variables $\vec{y} = Var(r) - Var(l)$, the rewrite relation $t \to_{R/E\cup B} t'$ becomes *decidable* is also easy to justify assuming a finite set $\vec{E}$ of rules and a finitary B-unification algorithm.

Note that by (Σ, B, E) being a FVP and B-unification finitary, we get an $E \cup B$-*matching algorithm* $Match_{E\cup B}(u, v) = \{\theta \mid \bar{\theta} \in CSU_{E\cup B}(u = \bar{v})\}$ where $\bar{v}$ is obtained from v by turning its variables $x_1, \ldots, x_n$ into fresh constants $\bar{x}_1, \ldots, \bar{x}_n$, and θ is obtained from $\bar{\theta}$ by, given a binding $x \mapsto \bar{t} \in \bar{\theta}$, adding the binding $x \mapsto t$ to θ; the term t is easily obtained from $\bar{t}$ by replacing every occurrence of a fresh constant $\bar{x}_1, \ldots, \bar{x}_n$ by its original.

This means that we can *decide* whether $t \to_{R/E\cup B} t'$ as follows: (i) compute all the matching substitutions, i.e., $M = \bigcup_{l \to r \in R} Match_{E\cup B}(l, t)$, and (ii) test whether $t'\downarrow_{\vec{E},B} =_B (r\theta)\downarrow_{\vec{E},B}$ for each $\theta \in M$ (assuming $Var(r) \subseteq Var(l)$ or otherwise use $\theta \uplus \rho$ for a substitution ρ instantiating $Var(r) - Var(l)$ such that $\rho = \rho\downarrow_{\vec{E},B}$).

Note that, since all $\vec{E}, B$-variant unifiers are $\vec{E}, B$-normalized by construction, in particular any $\alpha \in CSU_{E\cup B}(u = v)$ is such that $\alpha = \alpha\downarrow_{\vec{E},B}$ and we get $(\theta \uplus \rho)\downarrow_{\vec{E},B} = \theta \uplus \rho$.

6   Canonical Constrained Narrowing

Although the contextual narrowing relation of Sect. 4 is very useful to reduce the state search space of a protocol analysis tool such as Maude-NPA by carrying along irreducibility constraints, it is not clear that computing the variants of a term before performing narrowing is very efficient. For this reason, it seems worth making explicit the alternative possibility of defining and using instead a canonical narrowing relation $\leadsto_{R/E,B}$ with irreducibility constraints only for the lefthand sides of the rules.

Definition 7 (Canonical Constrained Narrowing). *Given an order-sorted rewrite theory* $(\Sigma, E \cup B, R)$ *such that* (Σ, B, E) *is a decomposition of* $(\Sigma, E \cup B)$, *the* canonical narrowing relation with irreducibility constraints *holds between* $\langle t, \Pi \rangle$ *and* $\langle t', \Pi' \rangle$, *denoted*

$$\langle t, \Pi \rangle \leadsto_{\alpha, R/E,B} \langle t', \Pi' \rangle$$

iff there exists $l \to r \in R$, *which we always assume renamed, so that* $Var(\langle t, \Pi \rangle) \cap (Var(r) \cup Var(l)) = \emptyset$, *and a unifier* $\alpha \in CSU_{E \cup B}^{W}(t = l)$, *where* $W = Var(\langle t, \Pi \rangle) \cup Var(r) \cup Var(l)$, *and*

1. $\langle t', \Pi' \rangle = \langle r\alpha, \Pi\alpha \cup \{(l\alpha)\downarrow_{\overrightarrow{E},B}\}\rangle$, *and*
2. $\Pi\alpha \cup \{(l\alpha)\downarrow_{\overrightarrow{E},B}\}$ *are* $\overrightarrow{E}, B$-*normalized.*

Note that we do not require a narrowing step to compute $CSU_{E \cup B}(t =_\downarrow l)$ anymore, we perform regular equational unification but impose an irreducibility constraint on the normal form of the instantiated lefthand side, which can be handled by using asymmetric unification.

The key completeness property about this relation is the following.

Lemma 1 (Lifting Lemma). *Given* $\langle t, \Pi \rangle$, *a* $\overrightarrow{E}, B$-*normalized substitution* θ, *and terms* $u, v \in \mathcal{C}_{\Sigma/E,B}^{\circ}(\mathcal{X})$ *such that* $u = (t\theta)\downarrow_{\overrightarrow{E},B}$ *and* $\Pi\theta$ *are* $\overrightarrow{E}, B$-*normalized and* $u \to_{R/E,B} v$, *there is a canonical narrowing step with irreducibility constraints*

$$\langle t, \Pi \rangle \leadsto_{\alpha, R/E,B} \langle r\alpha, \Pi\alpha \cup \{(l\alpha)\downarrow_{\overrightarrow{E},B}\}\rangle$$

and a $\overrightarrow{E}, B$-*normalized substitution* γ *such that*

$$
\begin{array}{ccc}
\langle t, \Pi \rangle & \leadsto_{\alpha, R/E,B} & \langle r'\alpha, \Pi\alpha \cup \{(l\alpha)\downarrow_{\overrightarrow{E},B}\}\rangle \\
\downarrow\theta & & \downarrow\gamma \\
\lceil\langle t, \Pi \rangle\rceil_{\overrightarrow{E},B} & \to_{R/E,B} & v
\end{array}
$$

(i) $\theta =_B (\alpha\gamma)|_{Var(\langle t, \Pi \rangle)}$,
(ii) $(r\alpha\gamma)\downarrow_{\overrightarrow{E},B} =_B v$,
(iii) $\Pi\alpha\gamma \cup \{((l\alpha)\downarrow_{\overrightarrow{E},B})\gamma\}$ *are* $\overrightarrow{E}, B$-*normalized*

Note that this shows that $v \in \lceil\langle r\alpha, \Pi\alpha \cup \{(l\alpha)\downarrow_{\overrightarrow{E},B}\}\rangle\rceil_{\overrightarrow{E},B}$.

Proof. The rewriting step $u \to_{R/E,B} v$ exactly means that there is $l \to r \in R$ and a $\vec{E}, B$-normalized substitution β with $Dom(\beta) = Var(l) \cup Var(r)$ for a rule $l \to r \in R$ such that $u =_B (l\beta)\downarrow_{\vec{E},B}$ and $v = (r\beta)\downarrow_{\vec{E},B}$. But, since $Var(\langle t, \Pi \rangle) \cap (Var(l) \cup Var(r)) = \emptyset$ by the rule renaming assumption, this exactly means that $\theta \uplus \beta$ is a $E \cup B$-unifier of the unification problem $t = l$. Therefore, thanks to [36, Theorem 4], there is an $E \cup B$-unifier $\alpha \in CSU_{E \cup B}(t = l)$ and a $\vec{E}, B$-normalized substitution γ such that

$$\theta \uplus \beta =_B (\alpha\gamma)|_W$$

which gives (i). But the proof of [36, Theorem 4] shows that

$$((t\alpha)\downarrow_{\vec{E},B}^{\bullet} = (l\alpha)\downarrow_{\vec{E},B}, \alpha) \sqsupseteq_{\vec{E},B} ((t\theta)\downarrow_{\vec{E},B} = (l\beta)\downarrow_{\vec{E},B}, (\theta \uplus \beta)|_{Var(t=l)})$$

and this means that $(\Pi\alpha \cup \{(l\alpha)\downarrow_{\vec{E},B}\}\gamma) =_B \Pi\theta \cup \{(l\alpha)\downarrow_{\vec{E},B}\gamma\} = \Pi\theta \cup \{(l\beta)\downarrow_{\vec{E},B}\}$ which proves (iii) by the assumption that $\Pi\theta$ is $\vec{E}, B$-normalized. Finally we also get $(r\alpha\gamma)\downarrow_{\vec{E},B} =_B (r\beta)\downarrow_{\vec{E},B} = v$, proving (ii). $\qquad\square$

Example 10. The equational unification problem found by backwards narrowing-based reachability in Maude-NPA is $t = t'$ (instead of the asymmetric $t =_\downarrow t'$ of Example 6) where t is $\{SS \ \& \ [L, M^+ \ | \ L'] \ \& \ \{M \in \mathcal{I}, IK\}\}$ i.e., the righthand side of Rule (3), and t' is the following state of Example 6:

$$\{ :: r_2 :: [nil, -(pk(A, X)), +(pk(B, n(A, r_2))) \ | \ -(X \oplus n(A, r_2)), nil] \ \&$$
$$:: r_1 :: [nil, +(pk(A, n(B, r_1))), -(pk(B, Y)), +(Y \oplus n(B, r_1)) \ | \ nil] \ \&$$
$$SS \ \& \ \{(X \oplus n(A, r_2)) \in \mathcal{I}, IK\}\}$$

During variant-based unification, the eight variants of t' are internally generated by Maude and no variant is generated for the lefthand side because it does not have the exclusive-or symbol. The variant-based unification algorithm (see [9] for details on the variant unification command) reports eight unifiers (we only include the bindings for M, X and Y):

```
variant unify
  {[nil, -(pk(a, X)), +(pk(b, n(a, r2))) | -(X * n(a, r2))] &
   [nil, +(pk(a, n(b, r1))), -(pk(b, Y)), +(Y * n(b, r1)) | nil ] {(X * n(a, r2)) inI}}
  =?
  {SS & [L1,+(M) | L2] {M inI}} .
```

```
Unifier #1                      Unifier #4                        Unifier #7
M --> %1 * n(a, r2) * n(b, r1)  M --> #1 * n(a, r2)               M --> n(b, r1)
X --> %1 * n(b, r1)             X --> #1                          X --> n(a, r2) * n(b, r1)
Y --> %1 * n(a, r2)             Y --> #1 * n(a, r2) * n(b, r1)    Y --> 0


Unifier #2                      Unifier #5                        Unifier #8
M --> n(a, r2) * n(b, r1)       M --> 0                           M --> n(a, r2)
X --> n(b, r1)                  X --> n(a, r2)                    X --> 0
Y --> n(a, r2)                  Y --> n(b, r1)                    Y --> n(a, r2) * n(b, r1)


Unifier #3                      Unifier #6
M --> #1 * n(b, r1)             M --> %1
X --> #1 * n(a, r2) * n(b, r1)  X --> %1 * n(a, r2)
Y --> #1                        Y --> %1 * n(b, r1)
```

The canonical narrowing steps associated to unifiers 5, 6, and 7 would be discarded by the syntactic checks of Maude-NPA [21], since it cannot be possible that Alice receives her nonce before generating it.

Note that if we have a state with one extra strand containing an exclusive-or symbol, all its variants will also be generated by variant-based unification. Therefore, it is hard to argue why the canonical narrowing of Definition 7 works better in practice than the contextual narrowing of Definition 4. We provide some experimental results in Sect. 7.

Note that variant unification with irreducibility constraints has already been implemented in Maude 2.7.1, even though it is not yet documented in its manual. Let us consider the previous variant unification command with an irreducibility condition for the lefthand side.

```
variant unify
  {[nil, -(pk(a, X)), +(pk(b, n(a, r2)))] | -(X * n(a, r2))] &
   [nil, +(pk(a, n(b, r1)))], -(pk(b, Y)), +(Y * n(b, r1)) | nil ] {(X * n(a, r2)) inI}}
  =?
  {SS & [L1,+(M) | L2] {M inI}}
  such that X * n(a, r2) irreducible .

Unifier #1                    Unifier #2                    Unifier #3
X --> %1 * n(b, r1)           X --> n(b, r1)                X --> #1
Y --> %1 * n(a, r2)           Y --> n(a, r2)                Y --> #1 * n(a, r2) * n(b, r1)
M --> %1 * n(a, r2) * n(b, r1)  M --> n(a, r2) * n(b, r1)    M --> #1 * n(a, r2)
```

7   Experiments

We have performed several experiments[2] to compare the narrowing relation of Definition 2, the contextual constrained narrowing of Definition 4, and the canonical constrained narrowing of Definition 7. We use a rewrite theory representing the protocol of Example 1, without any intruder capability, and only two of the rewrite rules of Maude-NPA: (1) and (3). Note that no variant is generated for the lefthand side of these two transition rules. In this way we have a *finite* narrowing-based search space and focus on the impact on generating variants before each narrowing step. We have also considered, as initial term with variables, the attack pattern of Example 5 and ask whether it is possible to reach in a backwards manner the same term with variables but with all the vertical bars at the beginning (leftmost position). Also, the narrowing relation of Definition 2 is implemented in Full Maude version 27g[3] whereas the contextual narrowing of Definition 4 and the canonical narrowing of Definition 7 are implemented in an extended version of Full Maude version 27g; available for download with the experiments. The experiments have been performed using an Intel Core2 Quad CPU Q9300 (2.5 GHz) with 6 Gigabytes of RAM running Maude v2.7.1 and considering the average of ten executions.

In Table 1, we compare the three narrowing relations with the protocol of Example 1 and the attack pattern of Example 5. In Table 2, we compare again the

---

[2] Available at http://personales.upv.es/sanesro/canonical-narrowing.
[3] Available at https://github.com/maude-team/full-maude/.

Table 1. Experiments with different narrowing relations using exclusive-or.

Number of states	1 step	2 steps	3 steps	4 steps	5 steps	6 steps	Total	Time
Standard Narrowing	88	62	50	3	2	1	206	52141 ms
Contextual Narrowing	84	72	124	59	2	1	342	91685 ms
Canonical Narrowing	88	38	24	3	2	1	156	3702 ms

Table 2. Experiments with different narrowing relations using an Abelian Group.

Number of states	1 step	2 steps	Time
Standard Narrowing	6828	-	>24 h
Contextual Narrowing	-	-	>24 h
Canonical Narrowing	6828	680	~30 min

Table 3. Experiments with different narrowing relations using the vending example with an Abelian Group.

Number of states	1 step	2 steps	Time
Standard Narrowing	33	1598	~2 h
Contextual Narrowing	33	1598	~30 min
Canonical Narrowing	33	1598	~10 min

three narrowing relations with the protocol of Example 1 and the attack pattern of Example 5 but we replace the exclusive-or theory by an Abelian Group. In this case, the number of states is considerably higher than the exclusive-or theory and show only two steps of narrowing, without reaching the target term. In Table 3, we compare again the three narrowing relations with the AG-VENDING example of [14] that represents a typical narrowing-based reachability example using an Abelian Group. Similarly, the number of states is considerably higher but the solution is found in two steps for both standard and canonical narrowing whereas contextual is unable to find it. Canonical constrained narrowing is more efficient both in the total number of states and in execution time than the two other narrowing relations. Note that some of these states will be discarded by a protocol analysis tool such as Maude-NPA but we are not interested here in these additional syntactic optimizations. The impact of several syntactic optimizations of the Maude-NPA tool was presented in [16] and would be applicable to both the contextual constrained narrowing of Definition 4 and the canonical constrained narrowing of Definition 7.

8   Conclusions

This work has proposed *canonical constrained narrowing*, a new symbolic reachability analysis technique applicable to topmost rewrite theories of the form

$\mathcal{R} = (\Sigma, E \cup B, R)$ where the equations $E \cup B$ have the finite variant property. Our experiments suggest that canonical constrained narrowing is more efficient than both standard narrowing and the previously studied contextual constrained narrowing. These results are relevant not only for Maude-NPA, but also for symbolically analyzing many other concurrent systems specified by means of rewrite theories $\mathcal{R}$ of this form.

The natural next step is to *combine* the good properties of canonical constrained narrowing with those of various other narrowing based symbolic reachability analysis techniques. The key general idea for such combinations is that *irreducibility constraints* are a relevant and important notion of constraint that could and should be combined with other relevant constraint notions for greater overall efficiency and greater expresiveness. For example, Maude NPA supports constrained narrowing modulo *disequality constraints* [22]. Likewise, in [35] a very general notion of *constrained narrowing*, where sets of states are symbolically described by constrained pattern of the form $t \mid \varphi$, where t is a term with logical variables and φ is a quantifier-free Σ-formula is presented. All these combinations should make narrowing-based symbolic reachability analysis more efficient and expressive for general concurrent systems expressible as rewrite theories, and, in particular, for future versions of Maude-NPA.

References

1. 30th IEEE Computer Security Foundations Symposium, CSF 2017, Santa Barbara, CA, USA, 21–25 August 2017. IEEE Computer Society (2017)
2. Armando, A., et al.: The AVISPA tool for the automated validation of internet security protocols and applications. In: Etessami, K., Rajamani, S.K. (eds.) CAV 2005. LNCS, vol. 3576, pp. 281–285. Springer, Heidelberg (2005). https://doi.org/10.1007/11513988_27
3. Ateniese, G., Steiner, M., Tsudik, G.: Authenticated group key agreement and friends. In: ACM Conference on Computer and Communications Security, pp. 17–26 (1998)
4. Basin, D., Cremers, C., Meadows, C.: Model checking security protocols. Handbook of Model Checking, pp. 727–762. Springer, Cham (2018). https://doi.org/10.1007/978-3-319-10575-8_22
5. Basin, D.A., Dreier, J., Hirschi, L., Radomirovic, S., Sasse, R., Stettler, V.: A formal analysis of 5G authentication. In: Lie, D., Mannan, M., Backes, M., Wang, X. (eds.) Proceedings of the 2018 ACM SIGSAC Conference on Computer and Communications Security, CCS 2018, Toronto, ON, Canada, 15–19 October 2018, pp. 1383–1396. ACM (2018)
6. Blanchet, B.: Automatic verification of security protocols in the symbolic model: the verifier ProVerif. In: Aldini, A., Lopez, J., Martinelli, F. (eds.) FOSAD 2012–2013. LNCS, vol. 8604, pp. 54–87. Springer, Cham (2014). https://doi.org/10.1007/978-3-319-10082-1_3
7. Bull, J.: The authentication protocol. APM Report (1997)
8. Clavel, M., et al.: All About Maude - A High-Performance Logical Framework. LNCS, vol. 4350. Springer, Heidelberg (2007). https://doi.org/10.1007/978-3-540-71999-1

9. Clavel, M., et al.: Maude Manual (Version 2.7.1). SRI International - University of Illinois at Urbana-Champaign, July 2016

10. Comon-Lundh, H., Delaune, S.: The finite variant property: how to get rid of some algebraic properties. In: Giesl, J. (ed.) RTA 2005. LNCS, vol. 3467, pp. 294–307. Springer, Heidelberg (2005). https://doi.org/10.1007/978-3-540-32033-3_22

11. Cremers, C.J.F.: The scyther tool: verification, falsification, and analysis of security protocols. In: Gupta, A., Malik, S. (eds.) CAV 2008. LNCS, vol. 5123, pp. 414–418. Springer, Heidelberg (2008). https://doi.org/10.1007/978-3-540-70545-1_38

12. Delaune, S., Hirschi, L.: A survey of symbolic methods for establishing equivalence-based properties in cryptographic protocols. J. Log. Algebr. Meth. Program. **87**, 127–144 (2017)

13. Dreier, J., Hirschi, L., Radomirovic, S., Sasse, R.: Automated unbounded verification of stateful cryptographic protocols with exclusive OR. In: 31st IEEE Computer Security Foundations Symposium, CSF 2018, Oxford, United Kingdom, 9–12 July 2018, pp. 359–373. IEEE Computer Society (2018)

14. Durán, F., Eker, S., Escobar, S., Martí-Oliet, N., Meseguer, J., Talcott, C.: Built-in variant generation and unification, and their applications in Maude 2.7. In: Olivetti, N., Tiwari, A. (eds.) IJCAR 2016. LNCS (LNAI), vol. 9706, pp. 183–192. Springer, Cham (2016). https://doi.org/10.1007/978-3-319-40229-1_13

15. Durán, F., Eker, S., Escobar, S., Martí-Oliet, N., Meseguer, J., Talcott, C.L.: Associative unification and symbolic reasoning modulo associativity in Maude. In: Rusu [39], pp. 98–114 (2018)

16. Erbatur, S., et al.: Effective symbolic protocol analysis via equational irreducibility conditions. In: Foresti, S., Yung, M., Martinelli, F. (eds.) ESORICS 2012. LNCS, vol. 7459, pp. 73–90. Springer, Heidelberg (2012). https://doi.org/10.1007/978-3-642-33167-1_5

17. Erbatur, S., et al.: Asymmetric unification: a new unification paradigm for cryptographic protocol analysis. In: Bonacina, M.P. (ed.) CADE 2013. LNCS (LNAI), vol. 7898, pp. 231–248. Springer, Heidelberg (2013). https://doi.org/10.1007/978-3-642-38574-2_16

18. Escobar, S., Meadows, C., Meseguer, J.: Maude-NPA (Version 3.1.1), April 2018. http://maude.cs.uiuc.edu/tools/Maude-NPA

19. Escobar, S., Meadows, C., Meseguer, J., Santiago, S.: Sequential protocol composition in Maude-NPA. In: Gritzalis, D., Preneel, B., Theoharidou, M. (eds.) ESORICS 2010. LNCS, vol. 6345, pp. 303–318. Springer, Heidelberg (2010). https://doi.org/10.1007/978-3-642-15497-3_19

20. Escobar, S., Meadows, C., Meseguer, J., Santiago, S.: A rewriting-based forwards semantics for Maude-NPA. In: Proceedings of the 2014 Symposium and Bootcamp on the Science of Security, HotSoS 2014. ACM (2014)

21. Escobar, S., Meadows, C., Meseguer, J., Santiago, S.: State space reduction in the Maude-NRL protocol analyzer. Inf. Comput. **238**, 157–186 (2014)

22. Escobar, S., Meadows, C., Meseguer, J., Santiago, S.: Symbolic protocol analysis with disequality constraints modulo equational theories. In: Programming Languages with Applications to Biology and Security, pp. 238–261 (2015)

23. Escobar, S., Sasse, R., Meseguer, J.: Folding variant narrowing and optimal variant termination. J. Algebraic Log. Program. **81**, 898–928 (2012)

24. Fabrega, F.J.T., Herzog, J., Guttman, J.: Strand spaces: what makes a security protocol correct? J. Comput. Secur. **7**, 191–230 (1999)

25. González-Burgueño, A., Aparicio-Sánchez, D., Escobar, S., Meadows, C.A., Meseguer, J., Formal verification of the YubiKey and YubiHSM APIs in Maude-NPA. In: Barthe, G., Sutcliffe, G., Veanes, M. (eds.) LPAR-22, 22nd International Conference on Logic for Programming, Artificial Intelligence and Reasoning, Awassa, Ethiopia, 16–21 November 2018, EPiC Series in Computing, vol. 57, pp. 400–417. EasyChair (2018)
26. González-Burgueño, A., Santiago, S., Escobar, S., Meadows, C., Meseguer, J.: Analysis of the IBM CCA security API protocols in Maude-NPA. In: Chen, L., Mitchell, C. (eds.) SSR 2014. LNCS, vol. 8893, pp. 111–130. Springer, Cham (2014). https://doi.org/10.1007/978-3-319-14054-4_8
27. González-Burgueño, A., Santiago, S., Escobar, S., Meadows, C., Meseguer, J.: Analysis of the PKCS#11 API using the Maude-NPA tool. In: Chen, L., Matsuo, S. (eds.) SSR 2015. LNCS, vol. 9497, pp. 86–106. Springer, Cham (2015). https://doi.org/10.1007/978-3-319-27152-1_5
28. Jouannaud, J.-P., Kirchner, H.: Completion of a set of rules modulo a set of equations. SIAM J. Comput. 15(4), 1155–1194 (1986)
29. Lowe, G.: Breaking and fixing the Needham-Schroeder public-key protocol using FDR. In: Margaria, T., Steffen, B. (eds.) TACAS 1996. LNCS, vol. 1055, pp. 147–166. Springer, Heidelberg (1996). https://doi.org/10.1007/3-540-61042-1_43
30. Meadows, C.: The NRL protocol analyzer: an overview. J. Log. Program. 26(2), 113–131 (1996)
31. Meier, S., Schmidt, B., Cremers, C., Basin, D.: The TAMARIN prover for the symbolic analysis of security protocols. In: Sharygina, N., Veith, H. (eds.) CAV 2013. LNCS, vol. 8044, pp. 696–701. Springer, Heidelberg (2013). https://doi.org/10.1007/978-3-642-39799-8_48
32. Meseguer, J.: Conditional rewriting logic as a united model of concurrency. Theor. Comput. Sci. 96(1), 73–155 (1992)
33. Meseguer, J.: Membership algebra as a logical framework for equational specification. In: Presicce, F.P. (ed.) WADT 1997. LNCS, vol. 1376, pp. 18–61. Springer, Heidelberg (1998). https://doi.org/10.1007/3-540-64299-4_26
34. Meseguer, J.: Generalized rewrite theories and coherence completion. In: Rusu [39], pp. 164–183 (2018)
35. Meseguer, J.: Generalized rewrite theories, coherence completion and symbolic methods. Technical report, Computer Science Department, University of Illinois, December 2018
36. Meseguer, J.: Variant-based satisfiability in initial algebras. Sci. Comput. Program. 154, 3–41 (2018)
37. Meseguer, J., Thati, P.: Symbolic reachability analysis using narrowing and its application to verification of cryptographic protocols. High.-Order Symb. Comput. 20(1–2), 123–160 (2007)
38. Pereira, O., Quisquater, J.-J.: On the impossibility of building secure cliques-type authenticated group key agreement protocols. J. Comput. Secur. 14(2), 197–246 (2006)
39. Rusu, V. (ed.): WRLA 2018. LNCS, vol. 11152. Springer, Cham (2018). https://doi.org/10.1007/978-3-319-99840-4
40. Ryan, P.Y.A., Schneider, S.A.: An attack on a recursive authentication protocol. A cautionary tale. Inf. Process. Lett. 65(1), 7–10 (1998)
41. Santiago, S., Escobar, S., Meadows, C., Meseguer, J.: A formal definition of protocol indistinguishability and its verification using Maude-NPA. In: Mauw, S., Jensen, C.D. (eds.) STM 2014. LNCS, vol. 8743, pp. 162–177. Springer, Cham (2014). https://doi.org/10.1007/978-3-319-11851-2_11

42. Sasse, R., Escobar, S., Meadows, C., Meseguer, J.: Protocol analysis modulo combination of theories: a case study in Maude-NPA. In: Cuellar, J., Lopez, J., Barthe, G., Pretschner, A. (eds.) STM 2010. LNCS, vol. 6710, pp. 163–178. Springer, Heidelberg (2011). https://doi.org/10.1007/978-3-642-22444-7_11

43. TeReSe (ed.): Term Rewriting Systems. Cambridge University Press, Cambridge (2003)

44. Viry, P.: Equational rules for rewriting logic. Theor. Comput. Sci. **285**(2), 487–517 (2002)

45. Yang, F., Escobar, S., Meadows, C., Meseguer, J., Narendran, P.: Theories of homomorphic encryption, unification, and the finite variant property. In: Proceedings of PPDP 2014, pp. 123–134. ACM (2014)

46. Yang, F., Escobar, S., Meadows, C., Meseguer, J.: Modular verification of sequential composition for private channels in Maude-NPA. In: Katsikas, S.K., Alcaraz, C. (eds.) STM 2018. LNCS, vol. 11091, pp. 20–36. Springer, Cham (2018). https://doi.org/10.1007/978-3-030-01141-3_2

47. Yang, F., Escobar, S., Meadows, C.A., Meseguer, J., Santiago, S.: Strand spaces with choice via a process algebra semantics. In: Cheney, J., Vidal, G. (eds.) Proceedings of the 18th International Symposium on Principles and Practice of Declarative Programming, Edinburgh, United Kingdom, 5–7 September 2016, pp. 76–89. ACM (2016)

Finding Intruder Knowledge
with Cap-Matching

Erin Hanna[1], Christopher Lynch[2(✉)], David Jaz Myers[3],
and Corey Richardson[4]

[1] Department of Mathematics, Eastern University, St. Davids, USA
[2] Department of Computer Science, Clarkson University, Potsdam, USA
`clynch@clarkson.edu`
[3] Department of Mathematics, Johns Hopkins University, Baltimore, USA
[4] O(1) Labs, San Francisco, USA

Abstract. Given two terms s and t, a substitution σ matches s onto t if $s\sigma = t$. We extend the matching problem to handle **Cap**-terms, which are constructed of function symbols from the signature and a **Cap** operator which represents an unbounded number of applications of function symbols from the signature to a set of **Cap**-terms. A **Cap**-term represents an infinite number of terms. A **Cap**-substitution maps variables to **Cap**-terms and represents an infinite number of term substitutions. **Cap** matching is the problem of, given a term s and a **Cap**-term T, find a set of **Cap**-substitutions which represents the set of substitutions that matches s onto all the terms t represented by T. We give a sound, complete and terminating algorithm for **Cap**-matching, which has been implemented in Maude. We show how the **Cap**-matching problem can be used to find all the messages learnable by an active intruder in a cryptographic protocol, where the **Cap** operator represents all the possible functions that can be performed by the intruder.

1 Introduction

Matching is a key operation in such areas as automated theorem proving [11] and cryptographic protocol analysis [8]. It is the problem of finding an instantiation to make one term equal to another term. More specifically, given terms s and t, the *matching problem* is to find a substitution σ applied to the variables in s to make $s\sigma$ identical to t [3]. We can call s a *pattern*, and call t the *object*, and we want to find a way for the object to fit the pattern.

In this paper we extend the matching problem to another problem that we call **Cap**-matching. In **Cap**-matching the object is not a single object, but a representation of which infinitely many objects can be constructed. In other words, the object in the matching problem is now a pattern itself. The difference is that in the pattern s given on the left hand side of the matching problem, the

---

This work was done with support from NSF grant DMS-1262737 during the summer of 2015.

J. D. Guttman et al. (Eds.): Meadows Festschrift, LNCS 11565, pp. 39–53, 2019.
https://doi.org/10.1007/978-3-030-19052-1_5

pattern is instantiated by adding symbols at the leaves of the tree representation of the pattern. Now the right hand side t becomes a pattern where terms can be built by adding symbols in the interior or root of the tree.

We define **Cap** *terms* in this paper. A **Cap** term represents a set of ground terms, as opposed to one single term. **Cap** terms are built up as usual from symbols in the signature of the language. We also allow **Cap** terms to contain a union symbol, indicating the union of the set of terms that are represented. For example, if a and b are constant symbols then a represents the set $\{a\}$, and $a \cup b$ represents the set $\{a, b\}$. In addition to the union operator, we also allow a **Cap** operator, which is parameterized by a set of symbols from the language. The set of terms represented by a **Cap** term is the set of terms that can be constructed by adding those symbols on top of its arguments. For example, the **Cap** term $\mathbf{Cap}_{\{f\}}(a \cup b)$, where f is a binary symbol, represents the infinite set of terms: $\{a, b, f(a, a), f(a, b), f(b, a), f(b, b), f(a, f(a, a)), f(a, f(a, b))\}$, etc.

Cap terms were first introduced in [2] to study a passive intruder in cryptographic protocol analysis. In that paper, a **Cap** could only appear once at the top of a term. In other words, it did not allow terms of the form of $g(\mathbf{Cap}(a \cup b))$ or $f(\mathbf{Cap}(a), \mathbf{Cap}(b))$. The problem studied there was of a similar structure, but they studied the word problem instead of the matching problem. In other words, in our definition given at the beginning, s had to be a ground term. In that paper, they allowed equivalence modulo equational theories. There was also work on **Cap** terms in [1], which extended the work to unification problems. There, unification over a homomorphic theory was studied. But the intent in that paper was only to decide unification problems, not provide a representation of the set of all solutions.

The main result of this paper is that we have extended the terms to allow **Caps** anywhere in the term. Also, instead of just solving a decision problem, we want to find a representation of all the (usually infinite) set of solutions of a **Cap** matching problem.

To be precise, given standard term s, possibly containing variables, and **Cap** term T, we give a set of inference rules to return a *Cap substitution*, which is a representation of a (usually infinite) set of solutions to the **Cap** matching problem. We prove that our method is sound, complete and terminating.

Cap terms can be seen as a simple tree automata [4]. In fact, [10] considers a tree automata formalism, which can be shown to contain **Cap** terms, and gives some decision results for them.

Our motivation is to apply our results to cryptographic protocol analysis. Given a Horn Clause description of a protocol, we consider an active intruder who is trying to attack that protocol, and an unbounded number of sessions of the protocol. We show how to apply **Cap** matching to generate a set of all the messages that an intruder could learn. Of course, this procedure might not halt, because this problem is undecidable. But when it does halt, we have a representative of the infinite amount of knowledge that the intruder could learn. More work needs to be done to see how this works in practice, particularly to understand the termination behavior.

Cryptographic protocol analysis techniques are guaranteed to return a single attack on the protocol when they halt, but they do not always return all attacks. Our result gives a representative of all attacks. There other results which give a represenation of all attacks, such as [5] and [6], which use constraint solving techniques for a bounded number of sessions, which do not lose solutions. Their technique returns a set of constraints which is satisfied by all solutions.

We have focused our work on cryptographic protocol analysis, because the **Caps** naturally represent abilities of the intruder to construct messages. Note that matching is all that is necessary to determine what the intruder can learn, so we don't need to perform full unification. However, even though we focus on cryptographic protocol analysis, we believe these techniques can also be useful in SMT [7] in software verification, where **Cap** terms can be used to represent an infinite model.

The inference rules given in this paper are an extension of standard inference rules for unification or matching [3]. We look at the top symbol of the left and right hand side of the matching problem when deciding which inference rule to apply. When the top symbol is a function symbol then usual inference rules apply, but we need to introduce additional rules to handle the case when the right hand side symbol is a **Cap** symbol. We also need to handle the case when a single variable x maps to two different values. Inference rules, such as Variable Elimination will not work with **Cap** terms, since solutions will be lost. So we use an intersection operator. Therefore, we must extend the notion of **Cap** term to allow the intersection operator. But then we provide a set of inference rules that remove the intersection operator, so the final solution is expressed only in terms of **Cap** terms without intersection.

The paper is structured as follows. We give our notation in Sect. 2, especially the notation of **Caps**. In Sect. 3 we show how to apply this to cryptographic protocol analysis. In Sect. 4 we present the inference rules, plus a set of rewrite rules to remove intersections. In Sect. 5 we prove soundness, completeness and termination of the inference system. In Sect. 6 we conclude the paper and discuss future work and related work.

2   Definitions

In this section, we introduce the basic definitions. We will work over a fixed signature Σ, which is a set of function symbols with fixed arities. We will denote by Σ_n the set of n-ary functions, and will refer to Σ_0 as the set of constants. We will assume that Σ is finite.

Terms over Σ with variables from the set V are defined inductively to be

1. a constant $a \in \Sigma_0$, or a variable $x \in V$, or
2. $f(s_1, \ldots, s_n)$ where $f \in \Sigma_n$ and the s_i are all terms.

We will always assume a finite set of variables V which will contain only those variables used in the problems at hand. The set of terms over Σ in variables from

V is denoted $\mathcal{T}(\Sigma, V)$. If there are no variables in play, so that V is empty, then we abbreviate $\mathcal{T}(\Sigma, \emptyset)$ as $\mathcal{T}(\Sigma)$. The terms in this set are called *ground terms*.

A *substitution* σ is a function $\sigma : V \to \mathcal{T}(\Sigma, W)$ from variables to terms. If $V = \{x_1, \ldots, x_n\}$ and $x_i \sigma = t_i$, then we will write σ as $[x_1 \mapsto t_1, \ldots, x_n \mapsto t_n]$. We will identify σ with its homomorphic extension to $\mathcal{T}(\Sigma, V)$.

We introduce **Cap**-terms as a means of representing infinite sets of terms that can be inductively generated over subsets of the signature Σ.

Definition 1. *A **Cap**-term over a signature Σ is*

1. *a constant $a \in \Sigma_0$, or*
2. *$f(T_1, \ldots, T_n)$ for a function symbol $f \in \Sigma_n$, where the T_i are **Cap**-terms, or*
3. *$T_1 \cup T_2$, where T_1 and T_2 are **Cap**-terms, or*
4. *$\mathbf{Cap}_\Gamma(T)$ for a non-empty subset of function symbols $\Gamma \subseteq \Sigma$, where T is a **Cap**-term.*

*We denote the set of **Cap**-terms over a signature Σ by $\mathcal{T}_{Cap}(\Sigma)$.*

For example, $f(a, \mathbf{Cap}_\Sigma(b \cup c))$, and $g(\mathbf{Cap}_{\{h(\cdot)\}}(a))$ are **Cap**-terms over the signature $\Sigma = \{a, b, c, g(\cdot), h(\cdot), f(\cdot, \cdot)\}$. We think of a **Cap**-terms as representing sets of terms of a given shape. The above **Cap**-terms are thought of as representing "any term of the form $f(a, t)$, where t is any term only having constants b and c" and "any term of the form $g(h^n(a))$" respectively. This idea is made formal by the following definition.

Definition 2. *The interpretation $[\![T]\!]$ of a **Cap**-term T is defined inductively as follows:*

1. *$[\![a]\!] := \{a\}$ for constant $a \in \Sigma_0$,*
2. *$[\![f(T_1, \ldots, T_n)]\!] := \{f(s_1, \ldots, s_n) \mid s_i \in [\![T_i]\!]\}$ for function symbol $f \in \Sigma_n$,*
3. *$[\![T_1 \cup T_2]\!] := [\![T_1]\!] \cup [\![T_2]\!]$,*
4. *$[\![\mathbf{Cap}_\Gamma(T)]\!]$ is the smallest set S such that*
   (a) *$[\![T]\!] \subseteq S$, and*
   (b) *If $s_1, \ldots, s_n$ are in S and f is an n-ary function symbol in Γ, then $f(s_1, \ldots, s_n)$ is in S.*

A **Cap**-*substitution* is a function $\alpha : V \to \mathcal{T}_{\mathbf{Cap}}(\Sigma)$. As with usual substitutions, we identify α with its homomorphic extension to $\mathcal{T}(\Sigma, V)$.

Definition 3. *The interpretation $[\![\alpha]\!]$ of a **Cap**-substitution $\alpha = [x_1 \mapsto T_1, \ldots, x_n \mapsto T_n]$ is the set of all substitutions sending x_i to elements of $[\![T_i]\!]$,*

$$[\![\alpha]\!] := \{[x_1 \mapsto t_1, \ldots, x_n \mapsto t_n] \mid t_i \in [\![T_i]\!]\}$$

Now we are ready to define **Cap**-matching problems and their solutions. A *constraint* is of the form $s \overset{?}{\in} T$ where s is a term and T is a **Cap**-term. A *Cap-matching problem* is a set of constraints, usually written as $\varphi_1, \cdots, \varphi_n$, where each φ_i is a constraint. We say that a substitution τ is a *term-solution* of the **Cap**-matching problem $s_1 \in T_1, \ldots, s_n \in T_n$ when $s_i \tau \in [\![T_i]\!]$ for all i. We say that a **Cap**-substitution α is a **Cap**-*solution* of a **Cap**-matching problem Γ when every $\sigma \in [\![\alpha]\!]$ is a term-solution of Γ. When the context is clear, we will just call τ and α solutions.

We will also consider constrained terms.

Definition 4. *Let t be a term and φ be a **Cap** matching problem. Then $t \mid \varphi$ represents the set of all $t\sigma$ such that that there is a solution α of φ with σ an element of $[\![\alpha]\!]$.*

A set $\{\alpha_1, \ldots, \alpha_n\}$ of **Cap**-solutions for a **Cap**-matching problem Γ is called a *complete set of solutions* of Γ if every term solution σ is in some $[\![\alpha_i]\!]$. We will seek complete sets of solutions for **Cap**-matching problems.

For example, the problem $g(x) \stackrel{?}{\in} g(\mathbf{Cap}_{\{h(\cdot)\}}(a))$ is solved by the **Cap**-substitution $\alpha = [x \mapsto \mathbf{Cap}_{\{h(\cdot)\}}(a)]$ because every $\tau \in [\![\alpha]\!]$ is of the form $[x \mapsto h^n(a)]$ and $g(x)\tau = g(h^n(x)) \in [\![g(\mathbf{Cap}_{\{h(\cdot)\}}(a))]\!]$ always. Indeed, $\{\alpha\}$ is a complete set of solutions for this problem.

3   Application to Cryptographic Protocol Analysis

In this section we discuss how **Cap**-matching would be applied to cryptographic protocol analysis, since that is the main motivation of our work. We present this at a high level to motivate the rest of the paper, which gives inference rules for solving **Cap**-matching, and shows those inference rules correct. This section is independent of those sections.

In cryptographic protocol analysis, we analyze the properties of a protocol in the presence of a malicious intruder. In the Dolev-Yao model, the intruder is an omnipresent, omnipotent entity that can view all messages sent on the network. Intruders come in two varieties, *passive* and *active*. Passive intruders do not send messages or otherwise participate in the protocol. Active intruders do send messages and have the ability to modify messages other participants send.

Cryptographic protocol analysis either considers the bounded case or the unbounded case. In the bounded case, a protocol is only run a specific number of times. In the unbounded case, there is no bound on the number of times a protocol can be run. We deal with the unbounded case. In the unbounded case it is undecidable to decide if an intruder can learn a secret.

Cryptographic protocols can be modeled as Horn clauses in first-order logic, where messages are represented by terms. This gives an over-approximation of the execution of the protocol. Protocol rules correspond to definite clauses, or formulas of the form $P_1, \ldots, P_n \to C$, where $P_1, \cdots, P_n$ and C are terms. This can be understood in the context of a protocol as a participant responding to the combination of messages P_1 through P_n with C. Some or all of these messages could have been sent by an active intruder. Initial knowledge can be modeled as facts, which are terms. A secret learned by an intruder is represented as a goal clause, representing a term or set of terms to be learned. Variables represent pieces of a message where a participant in the protocol will accept anything, such as a new nonce or an encrypted message which the participant cannot decrypt.

These clauses represent the protocol, and they are sufficient for a passive intruder. However, we are interested in modelling an active intruder. With an active intruder, additional clauses are needed to represent how an intruder can construct and destruct data. We give examples of constructors and destructors involving the pairing (concatenation) operator $p(m_1, m_2)$, where m_1 and m_2 are the messages to be concatenated, and the symmetric encryption operator $e(m, k)$, where m is a message and k is a secret key. Constructors for these operators are the following:

$$m_1, m_2 \rightarrow p(m_1, m_2)$$

$$m, k \rightarrow e(m, k)$$

This indicates that the intruder can always concatenate two known messages together. In addition the intruder can encrypt a message with a key if he knows the message and key.

Destructors for these operators are the following:

$$p(m_1, m_2) \rightarrow m_1$$

$$p(m_1, m_2) \rightarrow m_2$$

$$e(m, k), k \rightarrow m$$

This indicates that an intruder can take a concatenated message apart, and the intruder can decrypt an encrypted message if he knows the key that was used to encrypt it.

A cryptographic protocol analysis method that searches backwards from a secret to the initial knowledge will never halt if the secret is not derivable, because of the destructors. A method that searches forward from the initial knowledge to a secret will never halt if the secret is not derivable, because of the constructors.

Instead of just determining whether an intruder can learn a particular secret, we want to represent all of the knowledge that an intruder can learn. For that reason, we need to use forward search. That means we can leave the destructors as Horn clauses. However, we must deal with constructors in a different way. So we do not consider the constructors as Horn clauses, and we instead incorporate them into a matching procedure. That is the reason for developing **Cap**-matching.

Normally, forward search proceeds by starting with the initial facts and repeatedly matching known facts against the left side of a Horn clause to create new known facts from the right side of that Horn clause. The fixed point of this process gives all the knowledge known by the intruder. Because of the constructors, this process will never halt.

In our method, each initial fact F is represented by the constrained term $F \mid \varphi$, where F is term and φ is a **Cap**-matching problem. We rename all the known constrained facts, so they do not share any variables with the other facts, and then we gather all the known facts $F_1 \mid \varphi_1, \ldots, F_m \mid \varphi_m$ together as a **Cap**-term $T = \mathbf{Cap}(F_1 \cup \cdots \cup F_m)$. and a **Cap**-matching problem $\varphi = \varphi_1, \cdots, \varphi_n$. Then, given a Horn Clause $P_1, \ldots, P_n \to C$, we form the **Cap**-matching problem $P_1 \stackrel{?}{\in} T, \ldots, P_n \stackrel{?}{\in} T, \varphi$. We run a **Cap**-matching algorithm on this problem. If this is solvable, the algorithm will return us a set of **Cap**-substitutions $\alpha_1, \ldots, \alpha_k$. This will give us k new constrained facts $C \mid \alpha_1, \ldots, C \mid \alpha_k$. These facts are added to our known facts, and this process is repeated until a fixed point is reached.

Using constraints makes this a little more complicated than just applying the **Cap** substitutions. If, for each rule $P_1, \ldots, P_n \to C$, the right hand side C does not have repeated variables, then it would be sound to apply the **Cap** substitution. But if C has repeated variables, then we must save the solutions as constraints to preserve soundness. The reason for this is that suppose that C was of the form $P(x, x)$ and some α_i was the **Cap**-substitution $[x \mapsto Cap(a \cup b]$. Then $P(x, x)\alpha_i$ would be $P(Cap(a \cup b), Cap(a \cup b))$. An instance of this is $P(a, b)$, but that is not an instance of $P(x, x)$.

4 Solving Cap-Matching Problems

Here we will present a deduction system which will find a (non-empty) complete set of solutions to a **Cap**-matching problem when one exists, and will fail if not. We proceed in two phases: Matching and Reduction. In the Matching phase, we find all solutions. In the Reduction phase, we handle conflicts. The Matching phase is given by a series of deduction rules, while the Reduction phase is given by a series of rewrite rules. We begin with Matching (Fig. 1).

As usual, to apply an inference rule, we don't-care nondeterministically select a constraint in the **Cap**-matching problem that is an instantiation of the top of an inference rule. We replace that constraint by the appropriate instantiation of the bottom of that inference rule.

We begin with a **Cap**-matching problem $\{s_1 \stackrel{?}{\in} T_1, \ldots, s_n \stackrel{?}{\in} T_n\}$, and saturate it under the inference rules. The **Clash** and **Decomp** rules are applied deterministically, because no other rule is applicable when they apply. The **Cap**-**Decomp** and **Split** rules are applied don't-know nondeterminstically.

The Clash rule fails if we have $s \stackrel{?}{\in} T$, where s and T contain different root symbols, and then the entire branch fails. The Decomp rule decomposes $s \stackrel{?}{\in} T$ if they have the same root symbol. These are standard rules for matching problems which are unchanged for **Cap**-matching. The **Cap**-Decomp rule is new. This deals with something of the form $s \stackrel{?}{\in} T$ where T has a **Cap** symbol at the root. In this case s must either match one of the elements in the union that **Cap** is applied to, or else the top symbol of s is a symbol that is introduced on the right hand side by **Cap**. Note that this breaks the problem into two branches. The Split rule handles the case where the right hand side has a union on the top, and it also breaks the problem into two branches.

$$\frac{f(s_1,\ldots,s_n) \overset{?}{\in} g(T_1,\ldots,T_m)}{\textbf{Fail} \quad (\text{if } f \neq g)} \text{ Clash}$$

$$\frac{f(s_1,\ldots,s_n) \overset{?}{\in} f(T_1,\ldots,T_n)}{s_1 \overset{?}{\in} T_1,\ldots,s_n \overset{?}{\in} T_n} \text{ Decomp}$$

$$\frac{f(s_1,\ldots,s_n) \overset{?}{\in} \textbf{Cap}_\Gamma(T)}{s_1 \overset{?}{\in} \textbf{Cap}_\Gamma(T),\ldots,s_n \overset{?}{\in} \textbf{Cap}_\Gamma(T) \quad (\text{if } f \in \Gamma)} \text{ Cap-Decomp 1}$$

$$\frac{f(s_1,\ldots,s_n) \overset{?}{\in} \textbf{Cap}_\Gamma(T)}{f(s_1,\ldots,s_n) \overset{?}{\in} T} \text{ Cap-Decomp 2}$$

$$\frac{f(s_1,\ldots,s_n) \overset{?}{\in} S \cup T}{f(s_1,\ldots,s_n) \overset{?}{\in} S} \text{ Split 1}$$

$$\frac{f(s_1,\ldots,s_n) \overset{?}{\in} S \cup T}{f(s_1,\ldots,s_n) \overset{?}{\in} T} \text{ Split 2}$$

Fig. 1. Matching phase rules

The algorithm terminates either by failing, or by reaching a point where each branch contains only problems of the form $x \overset{?}{\in} T$. Denote by $F = \{B_1^f,\ldots,B_n^f\}$ the set of final branches. We would like each final branch B_i^f to represent a **Cap**-solution to the original set of problems. If no variables were repeated in the original problem, then each final branch is of the form $\{x_1 \overset{?}{\in} T_1,\ldots,x_n \overset{?}{\in} T_n\}$, so that it represents the **Cap**-substitution $[x_1 \mapsto T_1,\ldots,x_n \mapsto T_n]$ as we wanted. But if the variables appear more than once, we may have $x \overset{?}{\in} S$ and $x \overset{?}{\in} T$ in the same branch. For a **Cap**-substitution α to solve this, we must have that $x\tau \in [\![S]\!] \cap [\![T]\!]$ for all $\tau \in [\![\alpha]\!]$. So α must map x to a **Cap**-term U such that $[\![U]\!] = [\![S]\!] \cap [\![T]\!]$. The goal of the Reduction phase is to find such a U.

At this point a standard matching procedure could easily solve the problem by checking if S and T are the same. It is more complicated in **Cap**-matching. S and T do not have to be the same. They just have to have some common instances. We need to find the common instances. But we must do it in such a way that x is mapped to the common instances.

We begin by applying the following rule to the final branches as much as possible. This obviously halts, because each step reduces the number of constraints.

$$\frac{x \stackrel{?}{\in} T, x \stackrel{?}{\in} S, \Gamma}{x \stackrel{?}{\in} S \cap T, \Gamma} \text{ Merge}$$

The intersection symbol $\cap$ is not part of the definition of a **Cap**-term. So we have to push the $\cap$ symbol inside the term and finally remove it in order to first determine if there is a solution to this intersection, and then to represent this solution as a **Cap**-term.

So we use the rewriting system given in the Reduction Phase Rules figure to remove each $\cap$ to find a **Cap**-term which represents this intersection. The $\cup$ and $\cap$ symbols in the Reduction Phase rules are viewed modulo AC.

After reduction, each variable will either map to a **Cap**-term containing no $\cap$ symbols and no $\emptyset$ symbols, or it will map to $\emptyset$. On a given branch, after reduction, if at least one variable maps to the empty set, then there is no solution, and this branch fails. If all variables map to a **Cap**-term, then there is guaranteed to be a solution. A solution can easily be found by examining the resulting **Cap**-terms. In fact, it is easy to enumerate all solutions. We believe another benefit of this notation is that it is easy for a human to understand the notation and to recognize interesting solutions.

5   Proofs

In this section, we prove that both the Matching and Reduction phases are terminating, sound, and complete. The Matching phase algorithm consists in applying the four rules above to a **Cap**-matching problem non-deterministically. The algorithm terminates when every matching problem in the set is in solved form $x \stackrel{?}{\in} T$. No rule may be applied to a problem of this form, since the left hand side of every matching problem has a function symbol from Σ on top. We quickly show that the Matching phase algorithm terminates (Fig. 2).

Proposition 1. *The Matching phase algorithm terminates.*

Proof. We provide a lexicographic ordering of terms and show that each rule decreases under this order. The order is (l, r), where l is the number of function symbols and **Caps** on the left of the $\stackrel{?}{\in}$, and r similarly on the right. Observe that each branch of each rule decreases under this order.

Now we can show that the Matching phase algorithm only produces solutions (is sound), and produces all solutions (is complete).

Proposition 2. *The Matching phase algorithm is sound and complete.*

$$f(S_1,\ldots,S_n) \cap f(T_1,\ldots,T_n) \rightarrow f(S_1 \cap T_1,\ldots,S_n \cap T_n) \tag{1}$$

$$f(S_1,\ldots,S_n) \cap \mathbf{Cap}_\Gamma(T) \rightarrow f(S_1,\ldots,S_n) \cap T \qquad \text{if } f \notin \Gamma \tag{2}$$

$$f(S_1,\ldots,S_n) \cap \mathbf{Cap}_\Gamma(T) \rightarrow f(S_1 \cap \mathbf{Cap}_\Gamma(T),\ldots,S_n \cap \mathbf{Cap}_\Gamma(T)) \cup (f(S_1,\ldots,S_n) \cap T) \qquad \text{if } f \in \Gamma \tag{3}$$

$$\mathbf{Cap}_\Gamma(S) \cap \mathbf{Cap}_\Delta(T) \rightarrow \mathbf{Cap}_{\Gamma \cap \Delta}((S \cap \mathbf{Cap}_\Delta(T)) \cup (\mathbf{Cap}_\Gamma(S) \cap T)) \tag{4}$$

$$S \cap (T_1 \cup T_2) \rightarrow (S \cap T_1) \cup (S \cap T_2) \tag{5}$$

$$\mathbf{Cap}_\emptyset(T) \rightarrow T \tag{6}$$

$$f(S_1,\ldots,S_n) \cap g(T_1,\ldots,T_m) \rightarrow \emptyset \qquad \text{if } f \neq g \tag{7}$$

$$\mathbf{Cap}_\Gamma(\emptyset) \rightarrow \emptyset \tag{8}$$

$$f(S_1,\ldots,\emptyset,\ldots,S_n) \rightarrow \emptyset \tag{9}$$

$$T \cap \emptyset \rightarrow \emptyset \tag{10}$$

$$T \cup \emptyset \rightarrow T \tag{11}$$

Fig. 2. Reduction phase rules

Proof. We begin by proving soundness. We will show that if α is a **Cap**-substitution which solves the bottom of a rule, then it solves the top. The only solution of a terminal branch $\{x_1 \stackrel{?}{\in} T_1, \ldots, x_n \stackrel{?}{\in} T_n\}$ is $[x_1 \mapsto T_1, \ldots, x_n \mapsto T_n]$, so we will show that this solves the original set of problems by passing it up through every application of a rule.

Since α solves a problem whenever every $\tau \in [\![\alpha]\!]$ solves it, we will work with term substitutions directly.

Decomp: Suppose that τ solves the bottom of the **Decomp** rule. That is, suppose that $s_i\tau \in [\![T_i]\!]$ for all i. Then $f(s_1\tau,\ldots,s_n\tau) \in [\![f(T_1,\ldots,T_n)]\!]$, so that τ solves the top of the **Decomp** rule.

Cap-Decomp: We have two cases to consider. First suppose that $s_i\tau \in [\![\mathbf{Cap}_\Gamma(T)]\!]$ for all i. Then for any $f \in \Gamma$, $f(s_1\tau,\ldots,s_n\tau) = f(s_1,\ldots,s_n)\tau \in [\![\mathbf{Cap}_\Gamma(T)]\!]$ by the definition of $[\![\mathbf{Cap}_\Gamma(T)]\!]$. So τ solves the top.

Now suppose that $f(s_1,\ldots,s_n)\tau \in [\![T]\!]$. Then since $[\![T]\!] \subseteq [\![\mathbf{Cap}_\Gamma(T)]\!]$ by definition, τ solves the top.

Split: If $s\tau \in [\![S]\!]$, then $s\tau \in [\![S]\!] \cup [\![T]\!] = [\![S \cup T]\!]$, and similarly if $s\tau \in [\![T]\!]$.

Now we turn to completeness. A **Cap**-matching problem may take the following forms:

$$x \overset{?}{\in} T \tag{1}$$

$$f(s_1, \ldots, s_n) \overset{?}{\in} g(T_1, \ldots, T_n) \tag{2}$$

$$f(s_1, \ldots, s_n) \overset{?}{\in} f(T_1, \ldots, T_n) \tag{3}$$

$$f(s_1, \ldots, s_n) \overset{?}{\in} \mathbf{Cap}_\Gamma(T) \tag{4}$$

$$f(s_1, \ldots, s_n) \overset{?}{\in} S \cup T \tag{5}$$

Possibilities (2)–(5) appear on the top of rules. We will show that if τ is a solution of any of these, then it is solution of the bottom of the respective rule. Since the algorithm terminates, any solution to any of these forms will also be a solution to a terminal branch of the algorithm, and will therefore have been produced by the algorithm.

1. This problem is in solved form.
2. There can be no solution to this problem since any term in the interpretation of the right hand side must have a g on top, but the left has an f on top. We may apply the **Clash** rule and rightly fail.
3. In this case, we may use the **Decomp** rule. If τ is a solution so that $f(s_1\tau, \ldots, s_n\tau) \in [\![f(T_1, \ldots, T_n)]\!]$, then $s_i\tau \in [\![T_i]\!]$ for all i so that τ is a solution of the bottom.
4. In this case, we may use the **Cap-Decomp** rule 1 or 2. Suppose that τ is a solution so that $f(s_1, \ldots, s_n)\tau \in [\![\mathbf{Cap}_\Gamma(T)]\!]$. This could happen in two ways: either $f(s_1\tau, \ldots, s_n\tau)$ is in $[\![\mathbf{Cap}_\Gamma(T)]\!]$ because the $s_i\tau$ are in $[\![\mathbf{Cap}_\Gamma(T)]\!]$ and we capped them with $f \in \Gamma$, or $f(s_1, \ldots, s_n)\tau$ is in $[\![T]\!]$ directly. These are precisely the bottom of the **Cap-Decomp** rule 1 or 2.
5. In this case, we may use the **Split** rule 1 or 2. Suppose that τ is a solution so that $f(s_1, \ldots, s_i)\tau \in [\![S \cup T]\!]$. By the definition of set union, either $f(s_1, \ldots, s_i)\tau \in [\![S]\!]$ or $f(s_1, \ldots, s_i)\tau \in [\![U]\!]$. The **Split** rules explore both possibilities.

We have now shown that the solutions which solve a set of **Cap**-matching problems are precisely those which solve the terminal branches of the Matching phase algorithm applied to that set. But, these terminal branches may contain repeated variables, e.g. $x \in S$ and $x \in T$. The Reduction phase finds a **Cap**-term U which represents the intersection $[\![S]\!] \cap [\![T]\!]$.

We begin by showing that the rewriting system given above is terminating.

Proposition 3. *The Reduction phase rewriting system is terminating.*

Proof. We provide a lexicographic path ordering. The precedence is $\cap \succ \mathbf{Cap} \succ \cup \succ \Sigma \succ \emptyset$, where all Σ-terms have equal precedence. We now show that the left hand side of every rule dominates the right.

– In rules (1), (3)–(6), the top symbol on the left precedes the top of the right. Therefore, we must compare the left to the subterms of the right. In (1), we see that $f(S_1, \ldots, S_n) \cap f(T_1, \ldots, T_n) > S_i \cap T_i$ since S_i is a subterm of $f(S_1, \ldots, S_n)$, and similarly for T_i. In (3), consider the left argument of the right hand side. Since $\cap \succ \Sigma$, we need to show that the whole of the right dominates each $S_i \cap \mathbf{Cap}_\Gamma(T)$, which follows since S_i is a subterm of $f(S_1, \ldots, S_n)$. The right argument of the right hand side is dominated because T is a subterm of $\mathbf{Cap}_\Gamma(T)$. Rule (4) follows because S is a subterm of $\mathbf{Cap}_\Gamma(S)$ and similarly for T. Rule (5) follows because T_1 and T_2 are subterms of $T_1 \cup T_2$, and rule (6) because the right is a subterm of the left.
– Rules (7)–(11) follow because all other symbols have precedence over $\emptyset$. Rule (2) follows since T is a subterm of $\mathbf{Cap}_\Gamma(T)$.

Since many **Cap**-terms can have the same intersection, we do not consider the possible uniqueness of normal forms produced by this rewriting system. Every such normal form, however, contains no $\cap$ symbols.

Proposition 4. *The normal form of a **Cap**-term S under the reduction system contains no $\cap$ symbols.*

Proof. We proceed by induction over the path ordering described above. The base case is if S contains no $\cap$ symbols, and is trivial as no rewrite rule adds $\cap$ symbols unless one was already present. Suppose that each term dominated by a term S will be rewritten to have no $\cap$ symbols. Recall that, in particular, S dominates each of its proper subterms. If S does not have a $\cap$ symbol on top, then we may rewrite its subterms separately so that they have no $\cap$ symbols by hypothesis so that S may be rewritten to remove all $\cap$ symbols. Suppose instead that $S = T_1 \cap T_2$. Clearly, the left hand sides of rules (1)–(5), (7) and (10) exhaust the possible forms $T_1 \cap T_2$ may take, modulo reordering. Then, applying each rule, we arrive at a term dominated by S which, by hypothesis, may be rewritten to remove all $\cap$ symbols.

Proposition 5. *The normal form of a **Cap**-term S under the reduction system is either $\emptyset$ or contains no $\emptyset$ symbols.*

Proof. If a constraint contains $\emptyset$ in any context, except for by itself, then some rule removes it.

Furthermore, the rewrites of the Reduction phase do not change interpretation. To prove this, we first prove a tiny lemma.

Lemma 1. *If $f(s_1, \ldots, s_n) \in [\![\mathbf{Cap}_\Gamma(T)]\!]$ and $f \notin \Gamma$, then $f(s_1, \ldots, s_n) \in [\![T]\!]$.*

Proof. We could not have found $f(s_1, \ldots, s_n) \in [\![\mathbf{Cap}_\Gamma(T)]\!]$ by capping the s_i with f, since f is not in Γ. Therefore, $f(s_1, \ldots, s_n)$ must have been in $[\![T]\!]$ to begin with.

Now we can show that if U is a normal form of the Reduction phase applied to $S \cap T$, then $[\![U]\!] = [\![S]\!] \cap [\![T]\!]$ as desired.

Proposition 6. *The Reduction phase rewrite system does not modify solution sets.*

Proof. We show that, for each rule, that the interpretation of the left and right hand sides are equal. For these purposes, we extend the definition of interpretation to include $[\![S \cap T]\!] = [\![S]\!] \cap [\![T]\!]$ and $[\![\emptyset]\!] = \emptyset$.

1. If $t \in [\![f(S_1, \ldots, S_n)]\!] \cap [\![f(T_1, \ldots, T_n)]\!]$, then t has the form $f(s_1, \ldots, s_n)$ and $f(t_1, \ldots, t_n)$ for $s_i \in S_i$ and $t_i \in T_i$. Therefore, the s_i must also be in T_i and likewise the t_i must be in the S_i, so that $t \in [\![f(S_1 \cap T_1, \ldots, S_n \cap T_n)]\!]$. The converse is routine.
2. If $t \in [\![f(S_1, \ldots, S_n)]\!] \cap [\![\mathbf{Cap}_\Gamma(T)]\!]$, and $f \notin \Gamma$, then t has an f on top, but this f could not have been placed by the $\mathbf{Cap}_\Gamma$. Therefore, t must be in $[\![T]\!]$. Since $[\![T]\!] \subseteq [\![\mathbf{Cap}_\Gamma(T)]\!]$, the converse holds as well.
3. If $t \in [\![f(S_1, \ldots, S_n)]\!] \cap [\![\mathbf{Cap}_\Gamma(T)]\!]$, and $f \in \Gamma$, then $t = f(s_1, \ldots, s_n)$ and either this f was not placed by the $\mathbf{Cap}_\Gamma$, or it was. If it was not placed, then the reasoning from above holds. If it was placed, then $s_i \in [\![\mathbf{Cap}_\Gamma(T)]\!]$ for all i, so that $t \in [\![f(S_1 \cap \mathbf{Cap}_\Gamma(T), \ldots, S_n \cap \mathbf{Cap}_\Gamma(T))]\!]$. The converse is routine.
4. We will prove this inclusion by induction,

$$[\![\mathbf{Cap}_\Gamma(S) \cap \mathbf{Cap}_\Delta(T)]\!] \subseteq [\![\mathbf{Cap}_{\Gamma \cap \Delta}((S \cap \mathbf{Cap}_\Delta(T)) \cup (T \cap \mathbf{Cap}_\Gamma(S)))]\!].$$

Denote the left and right hand sides of this inequality by **LHS** and **RHS** respectively. Suppose that $t \in$ **LHS**. If t is a constant symbol a, then by the above lemma, t is in $[\![S]\!]$ and $[\![T]\!]$, whence it is in the right hand side. Now suppose that $t = f(s_1, \ldots, s_n) \in$ **RHS** and that if $s_i \in$ **RHS**, then $s_i \in$ **LHS** for induction. We have three (not necessarily disjoint) cases:
   (a) Suppose that $f \notin \Gamma$. Then $t \in [\![S]\!]$, so that it is in $[\![S]\!] \cap [\![\mathbf{Cap}_\Delta(T)]\!] \subseteq$ **RHS**.
   (b) Similarly, suppose that $f \notin \Delta$. Then $t \in [\![T]\!]$, so that it is in $[\![T]\!] \cap [\![\mathbf{Cap}_\Gamma(S)]\!] \subseteq$ **RHS**.
   (c) Finally, suppose that $f \in \Gamma \cap \Delta$. Now, t may be in $[\![S]\!]$ or $[\![T]\!]$, in which case we use the arguments above. But if it is in neither, then it must have been reached by capping $s_1, \ldots, s_n$ with f. So s_i must have been in $[\![\mathbf{Cap}_\Gamma(S) \cap \mathbf{Cap}_\Delta(T)]\!]$, whence by induction they are in **LHS**. Then we may cap them with f on the left hand side, so that $f(s_1, \ldots, s_n) = t \in$ **LHS**.
   Now, going the other direction, we want to show that **RHS** $\subseteq$ **LHS**. Since $[\![S \cap \mathbf{Cap}_\Delta(T)]\!]$ and $[\![T \cap \mathbf{Cap}_\Gamma(S)]\!]$ are contained in **LHS**, capping them with any symbol from $\Gamma \cap \Delta$ remains in the **LHS**.
5. The rest are routine.

Taken all together, we have shown that the solutions τ of a given set of **Cap**-matching problems $\{s_1 \overset{?}{\in} T_1, \ldots, s_n \overset{?}{\in} T_n\}$ are precisely the solutions of the final branches $\{x_1 \overset{?}{\in} T_1, \ldots, x_n \overset{?}{\in} T_n\}$ of the Matching phase and the same branches with all duplicate variables removed by the reduction phase, $\{x_1 \overset{?}{\in} U_1, \ldots, x_n \overset{?}{\in} U_n\}$. The solutions to these last sets are precisely $[x_1 \mapsto U_1, \ldots, x_n \mapsto U_n]$. Therefore, the Matching and Reduction phases together give us all and only solutions to the original matching problems.

6 Conclusion

We have defined **Cap**-terms, which are an extension of standard terms. Terms are built from symbols in the signature as usual, but now they are allowed to contain **Cap** symbols, which represent an unbounded number of applications of function symbols to its arguments. A **Cap**-term represents infinitely many standard terms.

We have defined a new kind of matching called **Cap**-matching. A **Cap**-matching problem is of the form $s_1 \overset{?}{\in} T_1 \cdots, s_n \overset{?}{\in} T_n$, where the s_i are standard terms and the T_i are **Cap**-terms. The solution to a **Cap**-matching problem is a **Cap**-substitution, which potentially represents infinitely many standard substitutions.

The procedure has three phases. The first phase is a matching phase, which may result in a variable being mapped to more than one **Cap**-term. The second makes variables map to only one **Cap**-term by adding intersection symbols. The third phase rewrites the solutions to remove the intersection symbols. If the first phase fails then there is no solution. If it succeeds to then all branches give a potential **Cap**-solution. In any solution, if the third phase results in some variable mapped to $\emptyset$ then that branch fails. Any branch that does not fail in that way gives a **Cap**-term representing a possibly infinite set of solutions. Every **Cap**-term represents at least one solution. The solutions are easy to enumerate, and we believe this format allows humans to easily find interesting solutions.

Our definitions of **Cap**-matching are motivated by cryptographic protocol analysis. Usual techniques in this area determine if an intruder can learn a secret. On the other hand, our methods create a representation of a possibly infinite set of all terms that an intruder can learn. If this is an infinite set, such a process would not halt if **Cap**-matching were not used.

There are several directions of future work that we plan to pursue. In an implementation of **Cap**-matching in cryptographic protocol analysis, redundancy checking is crucial. In other words, when a new fact is created, it must be checked whether this fact is subsumed by a previous fact. Without this check, the procedure will rarely halt. In order to check if newly generated **Cap**-terms contain any new information, it is crucial to check if one **Cap**-term is contained in another one. We have already investigate ways of checking this by creating an algorithm to verify if one **Cap**-term is a subset of another one.

Equational theories are used to model properties of cryptographic algorithms. So another line of research we have already started pursuing is to perform **Cap**-matching modulo an equational theory. This is difficult, but it would be useful for applications.

We think that cryptographic protocol analysis is not the only area where **Cap**-matching is useful. It could also be used in program verification. SMT procedures sometimes need decision procedures modulo a theory of Horn clauses. **Cap**-matching could be used to create decision procedures that halt. It would also give a representation of an infinite model, whereas SMT solvers currently deal with finite models.

We have considered Horn clauses in this paper. However there is no reason this method cannot be extended to **Cap**-resolution with general clauses. We have begun research in this area.

References

1. Anantharaman, S., Lin, H., Lynch, C., Narendran, P., Rusinowitch M.: Cap unification: application to protocol security modulo homomorphic encryption. In: Proceedings of the 5th ACM Symposium on Information, Computer and Communications Security, ASIACCS 2010, Beijing, China, 13–16 April 2010, pp. 192–203 (2010)
2. Anantharaman, S., Narendran, P., Rusinowitch, M.: Intruders with caps. In: Baader, F. (ed.) RTA 2007. LNCS, vol. 4533, pp. 20–35. Springer, Heidelberg (2007). https://doi.org/10.1007/978-3-540-73449-9_4
3. Baader, F., Snyder, W.: Unification theory. Handbook of Automated Reasoning, vol. 1, pp. 445–532. Elsevier, Amsterdam (2001)
4. Comon, H., et al. Tree automata techniques and applications (2007). http://www.grappa.univ-lille3.fr/tata. Accessed 12 Oct 2007
5. Comon-Lundh, H., Cortier, V., Zalinescu, E.: Deciding security properties for cryptographic protocols. Application to key cycles. ACM Trans. Comput. Log. **11**(2), 9 (2010)
6. Comon-Lundh, H., Delaune, S., Millen, J.: Constraint solving techniques and enriching the model with equational theories. Formal Models and Techniques for Analyzing Security Protocols, vol. 5, pp. 35–61. IOS Press, Amsterdam (2010)
7. Ganzinger, H., Hagen, G., Nieuwenhuis, R., Oliveras, A., Tinelli, C.: DPLL(T): fast decision procedures. In: Alur, R., Peled, D.A. (eds.) CAV 2004. LNCS, vol. 3114, pp. 175–188. Springer, Heidelberg (2004). https://doi.org/10.1007/978-3-540-27813-9_14
8. Meadows, C.: The NRL protocol analysis tool: a position paper. In: Proceedings of 4th IEEE Computer Security Foundations Workshop - CSFW 1991, Franconia, NH, USA, 18–20 June 1991, p. 227 (1991)
9. Narendran, P., Marshall, A.M., Mahapatra, B.: On the complexity of the tidenarnborg algorithm for unification modulo one-sided distributivity. In: Proceedings 24th International Workshop on Unification, UNIF 2010, Edinburgh, UK, 14th July 2010, pp. 54–63 (2010)
10. Reuß, A., Seidl, H.: Bottom-up tree automata with term constraints. In: Fermüller, C.G., Voronkov, A. (eds.) LPAR 2010. LNCS, vol. 6397, pp. 581–593. Springer, Heidelberg (2010). https://doi.org/10.1007/978-3-642-16242-8_41
11. Robinson, J.A.: A machine-oriented logic based on the resolution principle. J. ACM (JACM) **12**(1), 23–41 (1965)

Robust Declassification by Incremental Typing

Matteo Busi[1], Pierpaolo Degano[1]([✉]), and Letterio Galletta[2]

[1] Dipartimento di Informatica, Università di Pisa, Pisa, Italy
{matteo.busi,degano}@di.unipi.it
[2] IMT School for Advanced Studies, Lucca, Italy
letterio.galletta@imtlucca.it

Abstract. Security of software systems has to be preserved while they
grow and change incrementally. The problem is to make the analysis
of their security properties adhere to such a development. In particular
we concentrate here on static type systems. Given a non-incremental
type system, the algorithm we propose permits using it incrementally,
so avoiding to develop new incremental versions of it. As a proof-of-
concept we show how our technique permits an incremental checking of
non-interference with robust declassification, starting from the classical
type system by Myers, Sabelfeld and Zdancewic.

1 Introduction

Program analysis concerns determining properties of programs that hold at run-
time without actually executing them but only examining their code, namely
statically. In this approach, type systems are widely used. Traditionally, they
assign to each program phrase (e.g., statements or expressions) a type describing
the set of possible values that the phrase can evaluate to at run-time. Through
static type systems many errors are detected at compile time, typically those
arising when an operation is not applied to arguments on which it is defined. In
addition, this kind of analysis fosters programmers to adopt good programming
practices, making the code more robust and modular.

Actually, type systems have the advantage of being easily integrated inside
the development process, because they typically operate during the compilation.
In addition, their flexibility supports the analysis of various semantics properties,
besides detecting operation/operands mismatches. Some early examples of these
properties concern exceptions [10], region inference [7] and communications in
concurrent programs [6].

Type systems have also been extensively used for checking and enforcing
security properties of software and of protocols [11]. For example, in [1,2] types

The first two authors have been partially supported by U. Pisa project PRA_2018_66
DECLware: Declarative methodologies for designing and deploying applications. The
last author is supported by IMT project *PAI VeriOSS*.

© Springer Nature Switzerland AG 2019
J. D. Guttman et al. (Eds.): Meadows Festschrift, LNCS 11565, pp. 54–69, 2019.
https://doi.org/10.1007/978-3-030-19052-1_6

are used to guarantee secrecy in the security protocols specified using the SPI-Calculus, a dialect of the π-calculus. In particular, if a protocol type checks, then it does not leak secret data. Other applications of type systems to security are those for checking access control, so preventing unauthorized use of possibly sensible information [3,9]. We are interested here in information flow and non-interference in imperative programs (see e.g., [13–15]). When a program type checks, it is ensured that no public output depends on private input.

Besides our interest in security and in static analysis, another pragmatic consideration has motivated this report. Nowadays software systems grow incrementally, evolve rapidly, change often and thus require continuous monitoring [5]. In this new scenario software is developed by changing existing components and modules and by adding new ones compositionally. Thus a shared code base is typically altered by many programmers submitting small code modifications (*diffs*). Also the analysis and verification algorithms should only work on the *diffs*, rather than on the entire codebase, to be effective in this new setting [8]. Developing new type systems that work in such an incremental way is quite a hard task (see a discussion on this topic in [4]). Even harder seems to be when non-interference is of interest, and therefore we instead propose a way to *incrementally* use *existing* type systems.

Actually, we adopt and slightly extend here the technique we proposed in [4], and we then put it at work on the type system for non-interference with robust declassification by Myers, Sabelfeld and Zdancewic [12]. Our technique is essentially based on caching and memoization: summaries of the analysis results for the program components are stored, and only the *diffs* are typed (possibly with a small surrounding context), re-using the cached summaries. A relevant point of our proposal is that it consists of an algorithmic schema *independent* of any specific language and type system, be it designed for type checking or for type inference. Actually, the rules that drive the incremental usage of the given type systems are automatically inferred by our schema, with little or no human intervention. Some mild assumptions are of course in order to guarantee that the results of the original type system and of the "incremental" one do coincide. The tightest caveat requires the original type system to be syntax-directed and to provide an algorithmic definition of the relationships between types, e.g. subtyping. With these provisos, given an *existing* typing algorithm, the schema is mechanically instantiated providing us with one that *incrementally* and *efficiently* type checks a changing code base, without re-doing work already done, but only analysing the *diffs*.

Plan of the Paper. We intuitively present our technique through a simple example in Sect. 2, while Sect. 3 formalises the steps needed to build, given a non-incremental type system, an equivalent incremental one. The type system of [12] is briefly recalled in Subsect. 4.1 and made incremental in Subsect. 4.2. Section 5 concludes.

2 A Working Example

To informally introduce our algorithmic schema we illustrate through an example how to incrementally use the type checking algorithm for *non-interference* with *robust declassification* [12]. Recall that a program enjoys robust declassification if "in a system that is separated into untrusted and trusted components, the untrusted components [are] not able to affect information release". More details are in Sect. 4.

Below, we consider the implementation of very simple login procedure, made by successive refinement steps, three actually. We show that possible leaks are found by only re-typing the code that changed from a step to another.

Suppose we have a large program that includes the following snippet of code, checking if the user provided the correct password for login (where pwd is a secret with high-integrity):

$$p \triangleq pwd := \mathtt{secret\_input}(); \; [\bullet];$$
$$\mathtt{if} \; \mathtt{check}(pwd) \; \mathtt{then} \; \mathtt{use}(pwd) \; \mathtt{else} \; \mathtt{skip}$$

Furthermore, assume that neither sub-routine **check** nor **use** leak information, and that [$\bullet$] represents the code that a possible attacker can inject at that point. As it is the program satisfies robust declassification, as witnessed by the full, *non-incremental* derivation of Fig. 1. However, since it might be useful for a user to know whether the login attempt was successful or not, one might want to refine the snippet above as follows (here, *res* is private and has high integrity and *out* is a public, low-integrity variable that is then printed on the console):

$$p' \triangleq pwd := \mathtt{secret\_input}(); \; [\bullet];$$
$$res := \mathtt{check}(pwd); \; out := res;$$
$$\mathtt{if} \; res \; \mathtt{then} \; \mathtt{use}(pwd) \; \mathtt{else} \; \mathtt{skip}$$

However, this refinement leaks the value of the private variable *res*. In the following, we show that the leak can be detected by only type checking the *diffs*, i.e., the new assignments to *res* and to *out*, the **if-then-else** and the code depending on them. To achieve that, we introduce a cache to store the typing information of p between two re-checkings so as to re-use as much as possible the already computed information.

Consider the abstract syntax tree of p and annotate its nodes with types. First, we build a *cache C* associating each statement of p along with its type and the typing environment needed to obtain it. Then we *incrementally* use this information to decide which existing results in the cache can be re-used and which are to be recomputed for type checking the refined program. More precisely, we follow these steps.

Defining the Shape of Caches. The cache is a set of triples that associate with each statement (i) a pair consisting of the typing environment needed to close

$$\frac{L \in \mathcal{L}_C}{(\Gamma, LL) \vdash_\mathcal{R} [\bullet]: OK}$$

$$\frac{\dfrac{(\Gamma, LL) \vdash_\mathcal{R} \text{check}(pwd): HH \quad (\Gamma, HH) \vdash_\mathcal{R} \text{use}(pwd): OK \quad (\Gamma, HH) \vdash_\mathcal{R} \text{skip}: OK}{(\Gamma, LL) \vdash_\mathcal{R} \text{if check}(pwd) \text{ then use}(pwd) \text{ else skip}: OK}}{(\Gamma, LL) \vdash_\mathcal{R} [\bullet]; \text{ if check}(pwd) \text{ then use}(pwd) \text{ else skip}: OK}$$

(a) The derivation tree **A** used in the derivation tree below.

$$\frac{\dfrac{(\Gamma, LL) \vdash_\mathcal{R} \text{secret\_input}(): HH \quad HH \sqcup LL \sqsubseteq HH}{(\Gamma, LL) \vdash_\mathcal{R} pwd := \text{secret\_input}(): OK} \quad \mathbf{A}}{(\Gamma, LL) \vdash_\mathcal{R} p: OK}$$

(b) The derivation tree.

Fig. 1. The full, non-incremental derivation for type checking p, with $\Gamma \triangleq \{pwd \mapsto HH\}$. With a little abuse, we assume $(\Gamma, pc) \vdash_\mathcal{R}$ check$(pwd): HH$; $(\Gamma, pc) \vdash_\mathcal{R}$ use$(pwd): OK$; and $(\Gamma, pc) \vdash_\mathcal{R}$ secret_input$(): HH$.

its free variables and the (type of the) program counter pc, and (ii) the type of the statement in hand (just OK in this case).

The information stored for expressions is similar except that the type is an element ℓ of the security lattice. For example, the following cache line records that in the environment where both pwd and `secret_input()` are secret and have high integrity (denoted by HH), and with a program counter public and of low integrity (LL) the first assignment is type correct:

$$(pwd := \texttt{secret\_input}(), (\{pwd \mapsto HH\}, LL), OK)$$

Building Caches. We visit the given annotated abstract syntax tree of p in a depth-first order and we cache the relevant triples for it and for its (sub-)trees. Consider again the first assignment for which the cache records the triple above, among others. All the entries for p are in Table 1.

Table 1. Tabular representation of the cache C for the program p.

Expression(s)	Environment	Type
p, $pwd := \texttt{secret\_input}()$, if $\texttt{check}(pwd)$ then $\texttt{use}(pwd)$ else $\texttt{skip}$	$(\{pwd \mapsto HH\}, LL)$	OK
$[\bullet]$	$(\{\}, LL)$	OK
$\texttt{use}(pwd)$	$(\{pwd \mapsto HH\}, HH)$	OK
$\texttt{skip}$	$(\{\}, HH)$	OK
pwd, $\texttt{check}(pwd)$	$(\{pwd \mapsto HH\}, LL)$	HH
$\texttt{secret\_input}()$	$(\{\}, LL)$	HH

Incremental Typing. We consider the typing algorithm of [12], called here $\mathcal{R}$ (see Fig. 3) as the input to our schema for building the algorithm $\mathcal{IR}$ that works in an incremental manner (see Fig. 5).

A judgement of the resulting type checker $\mathcal{IR}$ inputs a pair made of a typing environment Γ and a program counter pc, a cache C and a statement or an expression (we use below the letter t for both). Then it incrementally computes the type $R \in \{OK\} \cup \mathcal{L}$ (see Sect. 4) and C', which differs from C in possibly updated cache entries for the sub-terms of t:

$$(\Gamma, pc), C \vdash_{\mathcal{IR}} t : R \triangleright C'$$

The incremental algorithm is expressed as a set of inductively defined rules. Most of these simply mimic the structure of the rules defining $\mathcal{R}$. Consider the assignment that requires two rules. The first rule says that we can reuse the information available if the statement is cached, and in addition if the environments Γ and Γ' associate the same type with the free variables of c and the security level of the two program counters agree (this compatibility check is done by the predicate $compat_{env}((\Gamma, pc), (\Gamma', pc'), c)$ of Definition 2):

$$\frac{C(v := a) = \langle (\Gamma', pc'), OK \rangle \qquad compat_{env}((\Gamma, pc), (\Gamma', pc'), v := a)}{(\Gamma, pc), C \vdash_{\mathcal{IR}} v := a : OK \triangleright C}$$

The second rule is for when nothing is cached (the side condition *miss* holds), or the typing environments are not compatible. In this case, the new cache C' is obtained from C by inserting in it the triples for x, for the expression a and for the assignment itself through $\mathcal{IR}$.

$$\frac{(\Gamma, pc), C \vdash_{\mathcal{IR}} a : \ell \triangleright C'' \qquad \ell \sqcup pc \sqsubseteq \Gamma(v)}{(\Gamma, pc), C \vdash_{\mathcal{IR}} v := a : OK \triangleright C'} \quad miss(C, v := a, (\Gamma, pc))$$

where $C' = C \cup C'' \cup \{(v := a, (\Gamma_{| FV(v:=a)}, pc), OK)\}$

Back to our example, to discover the leak it suffices to type

$$res := \mathsf{check}(pwd); \; out := res$$

Indeed the cache already provides us with the type of *pwd* and no re-typing is needed for all the other statements. Actually *out := res* is not *OK* (the aborted deduction is in Fig. 2), and the obvious fix is replacing it with *out := declassify(res, LL)*, which instead is *OK*.

3   The Incremental Framework

This section briefly overviews the four steps needed in order to use an existing typing algorithm incrementally, recalling Sect. 3 of [4]. In addition, we also devise some conditions under which the schema can be instantiated and used with little effort by its users.

Remarkably, our algorithmic schema is independent of both the specific type system and the programming language (for that we use below $t \in Term$ to denote an expression or a statement). We only assume to have variables $x, y, \ldots \in Var$, types $\tau, \tau', \ldots \in Type$, typing environments $\Gamma \colon Var \rightarrow Type \in Env$; and in addition that the original typing algorithm $\mathcal{A}$ is syntax-directed and defined through inference rules. We also assume that $\mathcal{A}$ is invoked by writing $\mathcal{H} \vdash_{\mathcal{A}} t \colon R$, where $\mathcal{H}$ is a typing context, including a typing environment Γ and the additional information (e.g. the program counter used in the example of Sect. 2) that is needed to deduce the result $R \in Res$ (not necessarily a type only).

As a preliminary step, we rewrite the rules of $\mathcal{A}$ according to the following format. It is convenient to order the subterms of t, by stipulating $i \leq j$ provided that t_j requires the result of t_i to be typed $(i, j \leq n_t)$. For brevity, in the rest of this section we will simply let $\mathcal{H} = \Gamma$.

$$\frac{\forall i \in \mathbb{I}_t \, . \, tr_{t_i}^t(\Gamma, \{R_j\}_{j<i \, \wedge \, j \in \mathbb{I}_t}) \vdash_{\mathcal{A}} t_i : R_i \qquad checkJoin_t(\Gamma, \{R_i\}_{i \in \mathbb{I}_t}, \mathsf{out} \, R)}{\Gamma \vdash_{\mathcal{A}} t : R}$$

$$\frac{(\Gamma, LL), C \vdash_{IR} res: HH \triangleright C' \quad C'' = \{\dots\} \quad HH \not\sqsubseteq LL}{(\Gamma, LL), C \vdash_{IR} res: HH \triangleright C''}$$

$$(\Gamma, LL), C \vdash_{IR} out := res: ? \triangleright ?$$

$$\frac{\dots \qquad (\Gamma, LL) \vdash_{IR} \text{if } res \text{ then use}(pwd) \text{ else skip}: OK \triangleright C'''}{(\Gamma, LL) \vdash_{IR} out := res; \text{if } res \text{ then use}(pwd) \text{ else skip}: ? \triangleright ?} \quad \textbf{A}$$

(a) The derivation tree **A** used in part (b) below.

$$\frac{C(\text{check}(pwd)) = \langle\langle\{pwd \mapsto HH\}, LL, HH\rangle}{(\Gamma, LL), C \vdash_{IR} \text{check}(pwd): HH \triangleright C} \quad HH \sqsubseteq HH \quad C' = C \cup \{res := \text{check}(pwd), (\Gamma|_{FV(res:=\text{check}(pwd))}, LL, OK)\}$$

$$(\Gamma, LL) \vdash_{IR} res := \text{check}(pwd): OK \triangleright C'$$

$$(\Gamma, LL) \vdash_{IR} res := \text{check}(pwd); out := res; \text{if } res \text{ then use}(pwd) \text{ else skip}: ? \triangleright ?$$

(b) The derivation tree **B** used in part (c) below.

$$\frac{C(pwd := \texttt{secret\_input}()) = \langle\langle\{pwd \mapsto HH\}, LL, OK\rangle}{(\Gamma, LL), C \vdash_{IR} pwd := \texttt{secret\_input}(): OK \triangleright C}$$

$$\frac{C([\bullet]) = \langle\langle\{\}, LL, OK\rangle}{(\Gamma, LL), C \vdash_{IR} [\bullet]: OK \triangleright C} \quad \textbf{B}$$

$$(\Gamma, LL), C \vdash_{IR} [\bullet]; res := \text{check}(pwd); out := res; \text{if } res \text{ then use}(pwd) \text{ else skip}: ? \triangleright ?$$

$$(\Gamma, LL), C \vdash_{IR} p': ? \triangleright ?$$

(c) The derivation tree.

Fig. 2. The incremental, aborted derivation for type checking p', under the environment $\Gamma \triangleq \{pwd \mapsto HH, res \mapsto HH, out \mapsto LL\}$. Results found in cache are highlighted in green, failures in orange. (Color figure online)

where $\mathbb{I}_t \subseteq \{1,\ldots,n_t\}$. The function $tr^t_{t_i}$ maps Γ and a set of typing results into the typing environment needed by t_i. The (conjunction of) predicate(s) $checkJoin_t$ checks that the subterms have compatible results R_i and combines them in the overall result R. (Both tr and $checkJoin$ are easily defined when typing rules in the usual format are rendered in the format above).

For example the standard typing rule for variables:

$$\frac{x \in dom(\Gamma) \qquad \tau = \Gamma(x)}{\Gamma \vdash_{\mathcal{A}} x : \tau}$$

is rendered in our format as follows (note that $\mathbb{I}_x = \emptyset$ just as the function tr)

$$\frac{checkJoin_x(\Gamma, \emptyset, \mathsf{out}\,\tau)}{\Gamma \vdash_{\mathcal{A}} x : \tau} \quad \text{where } checkJoin_x(\Gamma, \emptyset, \mathsf{out}\,\tau) \triangleq x \in dom(\Gamma) \wedge \tau = \Gamma(x)$$

As a further example consider the rule for the expression $\mathsf{let}\ x = e_2\ \mathsf{in}\ e_3$ below

$$\frac{\Gamma \vdash_{\mathcal{A}} e_2 : \tau_2 \qquad \Gamma[x \mapsto \tau_2] \vdash_{\mathcal{A}} e_3 : \tau_3}{\Gamma \vdash_{\mathcal{A}} \mathsf{let}\ x = e_2\ \mathsf{in}\ e_3 : \tau_3}$$

that becomes as follows (we abuse the set notation, e.g. omitting $\emptyset$ or $\{$ and $\}$).

$$\frac{tr^{\mathsf{let}\ x = e_2\ \mathsf{in}\ e_3}_{e_2}(\Gamma, \emptyset) \vdash_{\mathcal{A}} e_2 : \tau_2}{tr^{\mathsf{let}\ x = e_2\ \mathsf{in}\ e_3}_{e_3}(\Gamma, \tau_2) \vdash_{\mathcal{A}} e_3 : \tau_3 \qquad checkJoin_{\mathsf{let}\ x = e_2\ \mathsf{in}\ e_3}(\Gamma, \tau_2, \tau_3, \mathsf{out}\,\tau)}{\Gamma \vdash_{\mathcal{A}} \mathsf{let}\ x = e_2\ \mathsf{in}\ e_3 : \tau}$$

Note that the definition of function tr is immediate; that we need the type of e_2 for typing e_3; and that the second parameter of $tr^{\mathsf{let}\ x = e_2\ \mathsf{in}\ e_3}_{e_2}$ is empty, because we only need the enviroment to type e_2.

$$tr^{\mathsf{let}\ x = e_2\ \mathsf{in}\ e_3}_{e_2}(\Gamma, \emptyset) \triangleq \Gamma \qquad\qquad tr^{\mathsf{let}\ x = e_2\ \mathsf{in}\ e_3}_{e_3}(\Gamma, \tau) \triangleq \Gamma[x \mapsto \tau] \qquad (1)$$

Also the following definition is immediate

$$checkJoin_{\mathsf{let}\ x = e_2\ \mathsf{in}\ e_3}(\Gamma, \tau_2, \tau_3, \mathsf{out}\,\tau) \triangleq (\tau = \tau_3)$$

The predicate $checkJoin$ can be mechanically inferred also when the type system has relations between types richer than the equality used above, e.g. sub-typing or cohercion. As a precondition, the considered relations should be algorithmically expressible, within the inference rules of the original type system.

To enhance readability, we will hereto highlight the occurrences of $\boxed{tr^t_{t'}}$ (red in the pdf) and $\overline{checkJoin_t}$ (blue in the pdf).

Defining the Shape of Caches. The shape of the cache is crucial for re-using incrementally portions of the available typing results. The set of caches C is defined as:

$$Cache = \wp(Terms \times Env \times Res)$$

Intuitively, a cache associates the input data t and Γ with the result R. We write $C(t) = \langle \Gamma, R \rangle$ if the cache has an entry for t, and $C(t) = \bot$ otherwise.

Building Caches. Given a term, we assume that the nodes of its abstract syntax tree (called *annotated abstract syntax tree* or *aAST*) are annotated with the result of the typing for the subterm they represent, written $t : R$. Let $\mathbb{I}_t$, $\{t_i\}_{i\in\mathbb{I}_t}$, and $tr^t_{t_i}$ be as above, and let $\Gamma_{\mid FV(t)}$ be the restriction of Γ to the free variables of t. Then the following procedure visits the aAST in a depth-first manner and builds the cache.

$$buildCache\ (t : R)\ \Gamma = \{(t, \Gamma_{\mid FV(t)}, R)\} \cup$$
$$\bigcup_{i\in\mathbb{I}_t} \left(buildCache\ (t_i : R_i) \left[tr^t_{t_i}(\Gamma, \{R_j\}_{j<i\,\wedge\,j\in\mathbb{I}_t}) \right] \right)$$

The following immediate theorem ensures that each entry of a cache returned by *buildCache* represents correct typing information.

Theorem 1 (Cache correctness). *For all* t, R, Γ

$$(t, \Gamma, R) \in (buildCache\ (t : R)\ \Gamma) \iff \Gamma \vdash_{\mathcal{A}} t : R$$

Incremental Typing. The third step consists of instantiating the rule templates that make typing incremental. We remark that no change to the original algorithm $\mathcal{A}$ is needed: it is used as a *grey-box*—what matters is just the shape of the original judgements, the rules and some domain-specific knowledge. The judgements for the incremental typing algorithm $\mathcal{IA}$ have the form:

$$\Gamma, C \vdash_{\mathcal{IA}} t : R \triangleright C'$$

We have three different rule templates defining the incremental typing algorithm. The first template is for the case when there is a cache hit:

$$\frac{C(t) = \langle \Gamma', R \rangle \qquad compat_{env}(\Gamma, \Gamma', t)}{\Gamma, C \vdash_{\mathcal{IA}} t : R \triangleright C}$$

where $compat_{env}(\Gamma, \Gamma', t)$ is a predicate testing the compatibility of typing environments for the term t and means that Γ' includes the information represented by Γ for t and that they are compatible (see the example in Sect. 2). The definition of this predicate is immediate if it involves relations over types that are algorithmically computed. Otherwise $compat_{env}$ must be defined for *each* algorithm $\mathcal{A}$ and, as discussed below, it must meet a mild requirement to make the algorithm $\mathcal{IA}$ coherent with $\mathcal{A}$.

The second rule template is for when there is a cache miss and the term in hand has no subterms:

$$\frac{\Gamma \vdash_{\mathcal{A}} t : R \qquad C' = C \cup \{(t, \Gamma_{\mid FV(t)}, R)\}}{\Gamma, C \vdash_{\mathcal{IA}} t : R \triangleright C'} \; miss(C, t, \Gamma)$$

where $\Gamma \vdash_{\mathcal{A}} t : R$ is the invocation to $\mathcal{A}$, and the predicate *miss* is defined as

$$miss(C, t, \Gamma) \triangleq \nexists \Gamma', R.\ (C(t) = \langle \Gamma', R \rangle \wedge compat_{env}(\Gamma, \Gamma', t))$$

Intuitively, this predicate means that either there is no association for t in C, or if an association (t, Γ', R) exists the typing environment Γ' is not compatible with the current Γ.

Finally, the last template applies when there is a cache miss, but the term t is inductively defined starting from its subterms. In this case the rule invokes the incremental algorithm on the subterms, by composing the results available in the cache (if any):

$$\frac{\forall i \in \mathbb{I}_t \, . \, \boxed{tr_t^{t_i}(\Gamma, \{R_j\}_{j<i \wedge j \in \mathbb{I}_t})}, C \vdash_{\mathcal{IA}} t_i : R_i \rhd C^i}{\Gamma, C \vdash_{\mathcal{IA}} t : R \rhd C'} \quad \underset{\begin{subarray}{c} \overline{checkJoin_t(\Gamma, \{R_i\}_{i \in \mathbb{I}_t}, \text{out } R)} \end{subarray}}{} \quad C' = \{(t, \Gamma_{\upharpoonright FV(t)}, R)\} \cup \bigcup_{i \in \mathbb{I}_t} C^i \quad miss(C, t, \Gamma)$$

Typing Coherence. The resulting algorithm $\mathcal{IA}$ preserves the correctness of the original one $\mathcal{A}$, provided that the rule templates above, and especially the predicate $compat_{env}$ are carefully instantiated.

The following definition characterises when two environments are compatible, and it helps in proving that our incremental typing correctly implements the given non-incremental one. Remarkably, when the relations among types are defined algorithmically, the involved predicates $compat_{env}$ can be mechanically obtained and satisfy the requirement above. Anyway, a common part of these predicates is that the compared typing environments Γ and Γ' should bind all the free variables occurring in the considered term t. Formally:

$$dom(\Gamma) \supseteq FV(t) \wedge dom(\Gamma') \supseteq FV(t).$$

Definition 1 (Typing environment compatibility). *A predicate* $compat_{env}$ *expresses compatibility* iff

$$\forall \Gamma, \Gamma', t \, . \, compat_{env}(\Gamma, \Gamma', t) \wedge \Gamma' \vdash_{\mathcal{A}} t : R \implies \Gamma \vdash_{\mathcal{A}} t : R$$

Note that the notion of compatibility guarantees that Γ and Γ' share all the information needed to correctly type the term t. This is the basic condition to ensure that the incremental typing algorithm is concordant with the original one. In particular, the following theorem suffices to establish the correctness of the incremental algorithm $\mathcal{IA}$, provided that the original algorithm $\mathcal{A}$ is such. In its statement, the cache is universally quantified because $\mathcal{IA}$ re-uses $\mathcal{A}$ to re-build the needed cache as soon as a cache miss occurs.

Theorem 2 (Typing coherence). *If* $compat_{env}$ *expresses compatibility, then for all terms* t, *caches* C, *typing environments* Γ, *and typing algorithm* $\mathcal{A}$

$$\Gamma \vdash_{\mathcal{A}} t : R \iff \Gamma, C \vdash_{\mathcal{IA}} t : R \rhd C'.$$

4   Incrementally Checking for Robust Declassification

Here, we make our algorithmic schemata at work on the type system for non-interference with robust declassification [12]. First, we briefly survey the original version and then we make it incremental.

4.1   Recalling the Type System for Robust Declassification

Assume a security lattice $\mathcal{L}$, whose ordering specifies the relationship between different security levels $\ell \in \mathcal{L}$. The ordering encodes constraints on how data at a given security level can be used. To reason about both confidentiality and integrity, $\mathcal{L}$ is a product $\mathcal{L}_C \times \mathcal{L}_I$ of confidentiality and integrity lattices. Let x and y be in $\mathcal{L}_C$, we write $x \sqsubseteq_C y$ when data at level x is no more confidential than data at level y. Similarly, we write $x \sqsubseteq_I y$ for some $x, y \in \mathcal{L}_I$ when data at level x is not less trustworthy than data at level y. Thus, the elements of $\ell \in \mathcal{L}$ are pairs $\ell = (\ell_C, \ell_I)$, and hereafter we denote with $C(\cdot)$ and $I(\cdot)$ the confidentiality and the integrity part, respectively. The ordering $\sqsubseteq$ of $\mathcal{L}$ is built by using $\sqsubseteq_I$ and the dual of $\sqsubseteq_C$, i.e., for all $\ell, \ell' \in \mathcal{L}$, $\ell \sqsubseteq \ell'$ if and only if $C(\ell) \sqsubseteq_C C(\ell')$ and $I(\ell') \sqsubseteq_I I(\ell)$. The underlying idea for preventing information leaks is to constrain more the usage of high-confidentiality data than low-confidentiality data. Conversely, using low-integrity data is to be more constrained than high-integrity data to prevent information corruption.

Consider a simple imperative language consisting of expressions and commands. Let $val \in Val = \{\,\text{false}, \text{true}, 0, 1, \dots\,\}$ denote a value; let v range over variables Var; let op represent arithmetic and boolean operators; and let $\ell \in \mathcal{L}$ range over the security levels of a lattice $\mathcal{L}$. The syntax of the language is defined by the following grammar:

$$e \ ::\ = val \mid v \mid e \text{ op } e' \mid \text{declassify}(e, \ell)$$
$$c \ ::\ = \text{skip} \mid v := e \mid c_1; c_2 \mid \text{if } e \text{ then } c_1 \text{ else } c_2 \mid \text{while } e \text{ do } c$$

The language constructs are standard except for the expression $\text{declassify}(\text{e}, \ell)$ that declassifies the security level of the expression e to the level $\ell \in \mathcal{L}$.

The semantics is standard and can be defined using a small-step transition relation between configurations (see [12] for details). The result of evaluating $\text{declassify}(\text{e}, \ell)$ is the same as that of e, but it allows controlling the security level of the computed value. Intuitively, the resulting security level is the join of ℓ and of the security levels associated with the free variables of e.

A security policy is specified by using a *security environment* $\Gamma \colon Var \to \mathcal{L}$, that assigns each program variable with a security level. Intuitively, the policy permits an information flow from variable x to variable y only if $\Gamma(x) \sqsubseteq \Gamma(y)$. Hereafter, we assume as given the security environment.

Assume that an attacker can read and write some data manipulated by the program. The power of an attacker to observe and modify a state of the system can be described by an element of the security lattice. A passive attacker of level ℓ_A may read data with a security level of at most $C(\ell_A)$; whereas, an active attacker can also manipulate data with a security level of at least $I(\ell_A)$ (recall the definition of $\sqsubseteq_I$ above). In [12] a low-integrity piece of code is represented by a hole • that occurs in a program c in the point $c[\bullet]$. An attacker of level ℓ_A can inject in those points possibly malicious code fragments a, but it cannot insert any declassify. Actually, defining $\bot_C$ as the least element of $\mathcal{L}_C$, makes a to type check when the program counter is $(\bot_C, I(\ell_A))$. A passive attacker fills all holes with the low-integrity code from the original program; whereas, an active attacker fills the holes in a way that changes the original program behaviour. Intuitively, a program satisfies robust declassification when for all program fragments a, a', the attacker's observations about the execution of $c[a']$ does not reveal any secrets apart from what the attacker already knows from observations about $c[a]$.

The type system is defined through two typing relations, one for expressions and one for commands. Hereafter, we denote with pc the value of the program counter as usual. The typing relation for expressions is:

$$(\Gamma, pc) \vdash_{\mathcal{R}} e : \ell$$

meaning that under the environment Γ and in the program counter pc, the expression e has the security level $\ell \in \mathcal{L}$. Although the program counter pc is immaterial for expressions (we denote it with the don't care symbol $\_$), we introduce it to make typing rules of commands and expression homogeneous.

Similarly, the typing relation for commands is:

$$(\Gamma, pc) \vdash_{\mathcal{R}} c : OK$$

with the intuitive meaning that under Γ and in the program counter pc, the command c enjoys robust declassification ($OK \notin \mathcal{L}$).

$$(\mathcal{R}\text{-}\textsc{Val})\over{(\Gamma, \_) \vdash_{\mathcal{R}} val : \ell}$$

$$(\mathcal{R}\text{-}\textsc{Var})\quad \Gamma(v) = \ell \over (\Gamma, \_) \vdash_{\mathcal{R}} v : \ell$$

$$(\mathcal{R}\text{-}\textsc{Op})\over{\boxed{(\Gamma, \_)} \vdash_{\mathcal{R}} e : \ell \qquad \boxed{(\Gamma, \_)} \vdash_{\mathcal{R}} e' : \ell' \qquad op : \ell_{op} \times \ell_{op} \rightarrow \ell_{op} \wedge \ell \sqsubseteq \ell_{op} \wedge \ell' \sqsubseteq \ell_{op} \over (\Gamma, \_) \vdash_{\mathcal{R}} e\ op\ e' : \ell_{op}}$$

$$(\mathcal{R}\text{-}\textsc{Skip})\over{(\Gamma, pc) \vdash_{\mathcal{R}} \mathbf{skip} : OK}$$

$$(\mathcal{R}\text{-}\textsc{Assign})\quad \boxed{(\Gamma, pc)} \vdash_{\mathcal{R}} e : \ell \qquad \ell \sqcup pc \sqsubseteq \Gamma(v) \over (\Gamma, pc) \vdash_{\mathcal{R}} v := e : OK$$

$$(\mathcal{R}\text{-}\textsc{Seq})\quad \boxed{(\Gamma, pc)} \vdash_{\mathcal{R}} c_1 : OK \qquad \boxed{(\Gamma, pc)} \vdash_{\mathcal{R}} c_2 : OK \over (\Gamma, pc) \vdash_{\mathcal{R}} c_1; c_2 : OK$$

$$(\mathcal{R}\text{-}\textsc{If})\quad \boxed{(\Gamma, pc)} \vdash_{\mathcal{R}} e : \ell \qquad \boxed{(\Gamma, \ell \sqcup pc)} \vdash_{\mathcal{R}} c_1 : OK \qquad \boxed{(\Gamma, \ell \sqcup pc)} \vdash_{\mathcal{R}} c_2 : OK \over (\Gamma, pc) \vdash_{\mathcal{R}} \mathbf{if}\ e\ \mathbf{then}\ c_1\ \mathbf{else}\ c_2 : OK$$

$$(\mathcal{R}\text{-}\textsc{While})\quad \boxed{(\Gamma, pc)} \vdash_{\mathcal{R}} e : \ell \qquad \boxed{(\Gamma, \ell \sqcup pc)} \vdash_{\mathcal{R}} c : OK \over (\Gamma, pc), C \vdash_{\mathcal{R}} \mathbf{while}\ e\ \mathbf{do}\ c : OK$$

$$(\mathcal{R}\text{-}\textsc{Declassify})\quad \boxed{(\Gamma, pc)} \vdash_{\mathcal{R}} e : \ell' \qquad \ell \sqcup pc \sqsubseteq \Gamma(v) \wedge I(\ell) = I(\ell') \wedge pc, \ell' \in H_I \over (\Gamma, pc), C \vdash_{\mathcal{R}} v := \mathbf{declassify}(e, \ell) : OK$$

$$(\mathcal{R}\text{-}\textsc{Inject})\quad pc \in L_C \over (\Gamma, pc) \vdash_{\mathcal{R}} \bullet : OK$$

Fig. 3. The standard type system $\mathcal{R}$. (Color figure online)

The typing rules are displayed in Fig. 3, where in the pdf we highlight in red and in blue the parts that will originate the meta-functions *tr* and *checkJoin*, respectively. They are quite standard and we do not comment on them. The only exception is the rule $\mathcal{R}$-DECLASSIFY that only allows high-integrity data to be declassified when the declassification occurs in a high-integrity program point. Actually, the type system in Fig. 3 differs from the original one in [12] because the sub-typing relation has been incorporated in the rules, so making it completely syntax-directed.

4.2   Robust Declassification, Incrementally

In this subsection we put our schema at work illustrating the four steps for defining the typing relation $\vdash_{\mathcal{IR}}$, through which one can incrementally use the typing algorithm $\mathcal{R}$ to check non-interference with robust declassification.

Defining the Shape of Caches. The first easy step consists of devising the shape of the caches, each line of which is constituted by term of the language, a pair built from the typing environment and the program counter, and a type:

$$Cache \subseteq (Expr \cup Cmd) \times (Env \times \mathcal{L}) \times (\mathcal{L} \cup \{OK\})$$

Building Caches. The second step instantiates the *buildCache* template to fit the language at hand. The straightforward instantiation is in Fig. 4, where for brevity we have used the results of *tr* rather than the relevant invocations.

$buildCache\ (val : \ell)\ (\Gamma, pc) \triangleq \{(val, (\emptyset, pc), \ell)\} \qquad val \in \mathbb{N} \cup \{true, false\}$

$buildCache\ (v : \ell)\ (\Gamma, pc) \triangleq \{(v, ([v \mapsto \ell], pc), \ell)\}$

$buildCache\ (e\ op\ e' : \ell_{op})\ (\Gamma, pc) \triangleq \{(e\ op\ e', (\Gamma_{\restriction FV(e\ op\ e')}, pc), \ell_{op})\}$
$\qquad \cup (buildCache\ (e : \ell)\ \boxed{(\Gamma, pc)}) \cup (buildCache\ (e' : \ell')\ \boxed{(\Gamma, pc)})$

$buildCache\ (\mathtt{declassify}(e, \ell') : \ell)\ (\Gamma, pc) \triangleq \{(\mathtt{declassify}(e, \ell'), (\Gamma_{\restriction \mathtt{declassify}(e, \ell')}, pc), \ell)\}$

$buildCache\ (\mathtt{skip} : OK)\ (\Gamma, pc) \triangleq \{(\mathtt{skip}, (\emptyset, pc), OK)\}$

$buildCache\ (v := e : OK)\ (\Gamma, pc) \triangleq \{(v := e, (\Gamma_{\restriction FV(v:=e)}, pc), OK)\}$
$\qquad \cup (buildCache\ (v : \ell_v)\ \boxed{(\Gamma, pc)}) \cup (buildCache\ (e : \tau_e)\ \boxed{(\Gamma, pc)})$

$buildCache\ (\mathtt{if}\ e\ \mathtt{then}\ c_1\ \mathtt{else}\ c_2 : OK)\ (\Gamma, pc) \triangleq$
$\qquad \{(\mathtt{if}\ e\ \mathtt{then}\ c_1\ \mathtt{else}\ c_2, (\Gamma_{\restriction FV(\mathtt{if}\ e\ \mathtt{then}\ c_1\ \mathtt{else}\ c_2)}, pc), OK)\}$
$\qquad \cup (buildCache\ (e : \ell_e)\ \boxed{(\Gamma, pc)}) \cup (buildCache\ (c_1 : OK)\ \boxed{(\Gamma, pc)})$
$\qquad \cup (buildCache\ (c_2 : OK)\ \boxed{(\Gamma, pc)})$

$buildCache\ (\mathtt{while}\ e\ \mathtt{do}\ c : OK)\ (\Gamma, pc) \triangleq \{(\mathtt{while}\ e\ \mathtt{do}\ c, (\Gamma_{\restriction FV(\mathtt{while}\ e\ \mathtt{do}\ c)}, pc), OK)\}$
$\qquad \cup (buildCache\ (e : \ell_e)\ \boxed{(\Gamma, pc)}) \cup (buildCache\ (c : \ell_c)\ \boxed{(\Gamma, pc)})$

$buildCache\ (c_1; c_2 : OK)\ (\Gamma, pc) \triangleq \{(c_1; c_2, (\Gamma_{\restriction FV(c_1; c_2)}, pc), OK)\}$
$\qquad \cup (buildCache\ (c_1 : OK)\ \boxed{(\Gamma, pc)}) \cup (buildCache\ (c_2 : OK)\ \boxed{(\Gamma, pc)})$

$buildCache\ (\bullet : OK)\ (\Gamma, pc) \triangleq \{(\bullet, (\emptyset, pc), OK)\}$

Fig. 4. Instantiation of the template *buildCache* for the imperative language equipped to the robust declassification type checking from [12].

$(\mathcal{IR}\text{-}\textsc{Hit})$

$$\frac{C(t) = \langle(\Gamma', c'), R\rangle \qquad compat_{env}((\Gamma, c), (\Gamma', c'), t)}{(\Gamma, c), C \vdash_{\mathcal{IR}} t \colon R \triangleright C}$$

$(\mathcal{IR}\text{-}\textsc{Val-Miss})$

$$\frac{(\Gamma, \_) \vdash_{\mathcal{R}} val \colon \ell \qquad C' = C \cup \{(val, (\emptyset, \_), \ell)\}}{(\Gamma, \_), C \vdash_{\mathcal{IR}} val \colon \ell \triangleright C'} \; miss(C, val, (\Gamma, \_))$$

$(\mathcal{IR}\text{-}\textsc{Var-Miss})$

$$\frac{(\Gamma, \_) \vdash_{\mathcal{R}} v \colon \ell \qquad C' = C \cup \{(v, (\{v \mapsto \ell\}, \_), \ell)\}}{(\Gamma, \_), C \vdash_{\mathcal{IR}} v \colon \ell \triangleright C'} \; miss(C, v, (\Gamma, \_))$$

$(\mathcal{IR}\text{-}\textsc{Op-Miss})$

$$\frac{\boxed{(\Gamma, \_)}, C \vdash_{\mathcal{IR}} e \colon \ell \triangleright C''}{\boxed{(\Gamma, \_)}, C \vdash_{\mathcal{IR}} e' \colon \ell' \triangleright C''' \quad op \colon \ell_{op} \times \ell_{op} \to \ell_{op} \wedge \ell \sqsubseteq \ell_{op} \wedge \ell' \sqsubseteq \ell_{op}} \atop {C' = C \cup C'' \cup C''' \cup \{(e\;op\;e', (\Gamma_{|FV(e\;op\;e')}, \_), \ell_{op})\} \over (\Gamma, \_), C \vdash_{\mathcal{IR}} e\;op\;e' \colon \ell_{op} \triangleright C'} \; miss(C, e\;op\;e', (\Gamma, \_))$$

$(\mathcal{IR}\text{-}\textsc{Skip-Miss})$

$$\frac{(\Gamma, pc) \vdash_{\mathcal{R}} \mathbf{skip} \colon OK \qquad C' = C \cup \{(\mathbf{skip}, (\emptyset, pc), OK)\}}{(\Gamma, pc), C \vdash_{\mathcal{IR}} \mathbf{skip} \colon OK \triangleright C'} \; miss(C, \mathbf{skip}, (\Gamma, pc))$$

$(\mathcal{IR}\text{-}\textsc{Assign-Miss})$

$$\frac{\boxed{(\Gamma, pc)}, C \vdash_{\mathcal{IR}} e \colon \ell \triangleright C''}{\ell \sqcup pc \sqsubseteq \Gamma(v) \qquad C' = C \cup C'' \cup \{(v := e, (\Gamma_{|v:=e}, pc), OK)\}} \atop {(\Gamma, pc), C \vdash_{\mathcal{IR}} v := e \colon OK \triangleright C'} \; miss(C, v := e, (\Gamma, pc))$$

$(\mathcal{IR}\text{-}\textsc{Seq-Miss})$

$$\frac{\boxed{(\Gamma, pc)}, C \vdash_{\mathcal{IR}} c_1 \colon OK \triangleright C'' \qquad \boxed{(\Gamma, pc)}, C \vdash_{\mathcal{IR}} c_2 \colon OK \triangleright C'''}{C' = C \cup C'' \cup C''' \cup \{(c_1; c_2, (\Gamma_{|c_1; c_2}, pc), OK)\}} \atop {(\Gamma, pc), C \vdash_{\mathcal{IR}} c_1; c_2 \colon OK \triangleright C'} \; miss(C, c_1; c_2, (\Gamma, pc))$$

$(\mathcal{IR}\text{-}\textsc{If-Miss})$ $\qquad\qquad\qquad\qquad\qquad miss(C, \mathbf{if}\;e\;\mathbf{then}\;c_1\;\mathbf{else}\;c_2, (\Gamma, pc))$

$$\frac{\boxed{(\Gamma, pc)}, C \vdash_{\mathcal{IR}} e \colon \ell \triangleright C''}{\boxed{(\Gamma, \ell \sqcup pc)}, C \vdash_{\mathcal{IR}} c_1 \colon OK \triangleright C''' \qquad \boxed{(\Gamma, \ell \sqcup pc)}, C \vdash_{\mathcal{IR}} c_2 \colon OK \triangleright C^{iv}} \atop {C' = C \cup C'' \cup C''' \cup C^{iv} \cup \{(\mathbf{if}\;e\;\mathbf{then}\;c_1\;\mathbf{else}\;c_2, (\Gamma_{|\mathbf{if}\;e\;\mathbf{then}\;c_1\;\mathbf{else}\;c_2}, pc), OK)\} \over (\Gamma, pc), C \vdash_{\mathcal{IR}} \mathbf{if}\;e\;\mathbf{then}\;c_1\;\mathbf{else}\;c_2 \colon OK \triangleright C'}$$

$(\mathcal{IR}\text{-}\textsc{While-Miss})$

$$\frac{\boxed{(\Gamma, pc)}, C \vdash_{\mathcal{IR}} e \colon \ell \triangleright C'' \qquad \boxed{(\Gamma, \ell \sqcup pc)}, C \vdash_{\mathcal{IR}} c \colon OK \triangleright C'''}{C' = C \cup C'' \cup C''' \cup \{(\mathbf{while}\;e\;\mathbf{do}\;c, (\Gamma_{|\mathbf{while}\;e\;\mathbf{do}\;c}, pc), OK)\}} \atop {(\Gamma, pc), C \vdash_{\mathcal{IR}} \mathbf{while}\;e\;\mathbf{do}\;c \colon OK \triangleright C'} \; miss(C, \mathbf{while}\;e\;\mathbf{do}\;c, (\Gamma, pc))$$

$(\mathcal{IR}\text{-}\textsc{Declassify-Miss})$ $\qquad\qquad\qquad miss(C, v := \mathbf{declassify}(e, \ell), (\Gamma, pc))$

$$\frac{\boxed{(\Gamma, pc)}, C \vdash_{\mathcal{IR}} e \colon \ell' \triangleright C'' \qquad \ell \sqcup pc \sqsubseteq \Gamma(v) \wedge I(\ell) = I(\ell') \wedge pc, \ell' \in H_I}{C' = C \cup C'' \cup \{(v := \mathbf{declassify}(e, \ell), (\Gamma_{|v:=\mathbf{declassify}(e, \ell)}, pc), OK)\}} \atop {(\Gamma, pc), C \vdash_{\mathcal{IR}} v := \mathbf{declassify}(e, \ell) \colon OK \triangleright C'}$$

$(\mathcal{IR}\text{-}\textsc{Inject-Miss})$

$$\frac{(\Gamma, pc) \vdash_{\mathcal{R}} \bullet \colon OK \qquad C' = C \cup \{(\bullet, (\emptyset, pc), OK)\}}{(\Gamma, pc), C \vdash_{\mathcal{IR}} \bullet \colon OK \triangleright C'} \; miss(C, \bullet, (\Gamma, pc))$$

Fig. 5. The set of rules for using $\mathcal{R}$ incrementally.

Incremental Typing. The third step of the process consists in instantiating the rule templates of Sect. 3. The full set of rules of the incremental type system $\mathcal{IR}$ is in Fig. 5, the judgements of which have the general form:

$$(\Gamma, pc), C \vdash_{\mathcal{IR}} t \colon R \rhd C'$$

where Γ is the typing environment; pc is the security level of the program counter (or $\_$); t is either an expression or a command in the language; R is in $\mathcal{L} \cup \{OK\}$; C and C' are the initial and updated cache, respectively.

Typing Coherence. Since the type system of [12] has been put in a fully algorithmic style, the predicate *compat$_{env}$* uses equality as the relation for deciding when two types are compatible, and can be inferred easily. Its definition follows:

Definition 2. *Given a term t, two typing environments Γ, Γ' and two security levels pc, pc', let*

$$compat_{env}((\Gamma, pc), (\Gamma', pc'), t) \triangleq$$
$$dom(\Gamma) \supseteq FV(t) \wedge dom(\Gamma') \supseteq FV(t) \wedge \forall y \in FV(t).\ \Gamma(y) = \Gamma'(y) \wedge pc \sqsubseteq pc'$$

Consequently, we can instantiate Theorem 2 to guarantee that the results of the original type system $\mathcal{R}$ and of its incremental version $\mathcal{IR}$ coincide:

Corollary 1. *For any term t, cache C, typing environment Γ, and $c \in \mathcal{L} \cup \{\_\}$*

$$(\Gamma, c), C \vdash_{\mathcal{IR}} t \colon R \rhd C' \Leftrightarrow (\Gamma, c) \vdash_{\mathcal{R}} t \colon R.$$

5 Conclusions

We have presented and generalised the algorithmic schema of [4] that permits to incrementally use a non-incremental type system, provided its definition is syntax-directed. Our schema consists of four steps, and works on systems that both check and infer types. Its users are only required to possibly re-write the original inference rules so as to make them fully algorithmic, e.g. for dealing with specific relations among types, like sub-typing or cohercion. The schema guarantees then that the obtained incremental version is coherent with the original type system. Mild conditions and a little hand tuning also guarantee such a correctness if the relations among types are not defined algorithmically. To show the flexibility and the potentialities of the proposed shema, we have here applied it to the type system for checking non-interference with robust declassification by Myers, Sabelfeld and Zdancewic [12]. Different languages are considered in [4], and their type systems are used incrementally. The same paper also reports some experiments about the performance of a preliminary implementation, available at https://github.com/mcaos/incremental-mincaml, and contains the proofs of our results.

References

1. Abadi, M.: Secrecy by typing in security protocols. In: Abadi, M., Ito, T. (eds.) TACS 1997. LNCS, vol. 1281, pp. 611–638. Springer, Heidelberg (1997). https://doi.org/10.1007/BFb0014571
2. Abadi, M.: Secrecy by typing in security protocols. J. ACM **46**(5), 749–786 (1999)
3. Bartoletti, M., Degano, P., Ferrari, G.L., Zunino, R.: Local policies for resource usage analysis. ACM Trans. Program. Lang. Syst. **31**(6), 23:1–23:43 (2009)
4. Busi, M., Degano, P., Galletta, L.: Using standard typing algorithms incrementally. In: 11th NASA Formal Methods, Proceedings. To appear in LNCS. Springer (2019). https://arxiv.org/abs/1808.00225
5. Calcagno, C., et al.: Moving fast with software verification. In: Havelund, K., Holzmann, G., Joshi, R. (eds.) NFM 2015. LNCS, vol. 9058, pp. 3–11. Springer, Cham (2015). https://doi.org/10.1007/978-3-319-17524-9_1
6. Flanagan, C., Abadi, M.: Types for safe locking. In: Swierstra, S.D. (ed.) ESOP 1999. LNCS, vol. 1576, pp. 91–108. Springer, Heidelberg (1999). https://doi.org/10.1007/3-540-49099-X_7
7. Grossman, D., Morrisett, G., Jim, T., Hicks, M., Wang, Y., Cheney, J.: Region-based memory management in cyclone. SIGPLAN Not. **37**(5), 282–293 (2002). https://doi.org/10.1145/543552.512563
8. Harman, M., O'Hearn, P.: From start-ups to scale-ups: opportunities and open problems for static and dynamic program analysis. In: IEEE International Working Conference on Source Code Analysis and Manipulation (2018)
9. Higuchi, T., Ohori, A.: A static type system for JVM access control. ACM Trans. Program. Lang. Syst. **29**(1), 4 (2007)
10. Leroy, X., Pessaux, F.: Type-based analysis of uncaught exceptions. ACM Trans. Program. Lang. Syst. **22**(2), 340–377 (2000)
11. Meadows, C.A.: Formal methods for cryptographic protocol analysis: emerging issues and trends. IEEE J. Sel. Areas Commun. **21**(1), 44–54 (2003)
12. Myers, A.C., Sabelfeld, A., Zdancewic, S.: Enforcing robust declassification and qualified robustness. J. Comput. Secur. **14**(2), 157–196 (2006)
13. Sabelfeld, A., Myers, A.C.: Language-based information-flow security. IEEE J. Sel. Areas Commun. **21**(1), 5–19 (2003). https://doi.org/10.1109/JSAC.2002.806121
14. Smith, G.: Principles of secure information flow analysis. In: Christodorescu, M., Jha, S., Maughan, D., Song, D., Wang, C. (eds.) Malware Detection, pp. 291–307. Springer, Boston (2007). https://doi.org/10.1007/978-0-387-44599-1_13
15. Volpano, D.M., Irvine, C.E., Smith, G.: A sound type system for secure flow analysis. J. Comput. Secur. **4**(2/3), 167–188 (1996)

JRIF: Reactive Information Flow Control for Java

Elisavet Kozyri[1]([✉]), Owen Arden[2], Andrew C. Myers[1], and Fred B. Schneider[1]

[1] Cornell University, Ithaca, USA
{ekozyri,andru,fbs}@cs.cornell.edu
[2] University of California, Santa Cruz, USA
owen@soe.ucsc.edu

Abstract. A *reactive information flow* (RIF) automaton for a value v specifies (i) restrictions on uses for v and (ii) the RIF automaton for any value that might be derived from v. RIF automata thus specify how transforming a value alters restrictions for the result. As labels, RIF automata are both expressive and intuitive vehicles for describing allowed information flows. JRIF is a dialect of Java that uses RIF automata for specifying information flow control policies. The implementation of JRIF involved replacing the information flow type system of the Jif language by a RIF-based type system. JRIF demonstrates (i) the practicality and utility of RIF automata, and (ii) the ease with which an existing information flow control system can be modified to support the expressive power of RIF automata.

Keywords: Information flow control · Reclassification · Automata

1 Introduction

Many language-based enforcement mechanisms (e.g., [4,22,29]) work by enriching traditional type systems with information flow labels; the labels specify restrictions on confidentiality and sometimes integrity, too. Restrictions that programmers wish to impose on how the outputs of an operation may be used are likely to differ from any restrictions that were imposed on inputs to that operation. Consider, for example, a program that tallies votes for an election. Each vote would be considered confidential to a single voter, whereas the majority value is made public. So fewer restrictions are imposed on the output than on the inputs. As another example, consider a conference management application. The list of reviewers and the list of papers is likely public, but the identity of each paper's reviewers should be kept confidential. In this case, more restrictions are imposed on the output of an operation that matches papers to reviewers than the restrictions imposed on its input.

Supported in part by AFOSR grants F9550-06-0019 and FA9550-11-1-0137, National Science Foundation grants 0430161, 0964409, and CCF-0424422 (TRUST), ONR grants N00014-01-1-0968 and N00014-09-1-0652, and grants from Microsoft.

J. D. Guttman et al. (Eds.): Meadows Festschrift, LNCS 11565, pp. 70–88, 2019.
https://doi.org/10.1007/978-3-030-19052-1_7

Previous work in language-based enforcement for information flow control allows restrictions on outputs to be different from the restrictions on inputs. Explicit expressions for declassification (for confidentiality) and endorsement (for integrity) [21,22], as well as capability-based mechanisms for downgrading security policies [18,27,33] are unsatisfying, though, because output restrictions are not connected to input restrictions or to the operation performed on that input. Rather, with these mechanisms, restrictions can be replaced in arbitrary ways. For example, an explicit declassification expression [21,22] allows the label on an expression to be replaced with a new label in much the same way that a type-cast operation changes an expression from having one type to having another. Other approaches deduce output restrictions based on input restrictions and run-time events (e.g., [4,5,7]) instead of considering the operations applied in computing these inputs. Some techniques do consider operations applied during computation (e.g., [13,20,25,26,31]), but only to specify transformation of secret information into public information.

This paper introduces information flow labels that specify arbitrary changes between classes of restrictions, with changes explicitly connected to the operations that transform the labeled data. *Reactive Information Flow* automata (RIF automata) [16] are automata whose states define restrictions and whose transitions are triggered by operations on a labeled value. Thus, RIF automata specify how restrictions are transformed in step with transformations to the data they protect; the connection between information transformations and changes to restrictions is, consequently, explicit.

In this paper, we explore the practicality and utility of RIF automata. We developed JRIF, a new dialect of Java for supporting reactive information flow control, to study the practicality of RIF automata for statically enforcing information flow policies. JRIF is derived from the Jif [21,22] compiler and run time, and the modifications to Jif were straightforward. Jif's labels, which are based on the Decentralized Label Model [23], were replaced by RIF automata, and Jif's restrictiveness relation on labels was modified accordingly. Our experience in building JRIF gives confidence that other languages for information flow control could be extended similarly. To illustrate the utility of RIF automata, we programmed two JRIF applications that leverage the expressive power of RIF automata: a Battleship game and a shared calendar application. A public release of the source code for the JRIF compiler and run time, along with the example applications are available at the JRIF web page [17].

We proceed as follows. Section 2 defines RIF automata. In Sect. 3, we present JRIF. Section 4 illustrates the practicality of JRIF by describing two applications. The implementation of JRIF is outlined in Sect. 5. Section 6 compares JRIF to related work, including other language-based models for controlling declassification and endorsement, and Sect. 7 concludes.

2   RIF Automata

A RIF automaton specifies restrictions on a value and how those restrictions change according to the history of operations involved in deriving that value.

- For confidentiality, the restrictions identify principals allowed to read the value.
- For integrity, the restrictions identify principals that should be trusted for the value to be trusted.

So, in both cases, restrictions are given as sets of principals.

Operations of interest to a programmer are associated with identifiers. We call these identifiers *reclassifiers*. So sequences of reclassifiers are abstract descriptions for the series of operations that were applied to values as program execution proceeds. A sequence of reclassifiers thus provides a basis for determining how the confidentiality or integrity of the output of series of operations differs from that of its inputs.

A RIF automaton is a finite-state automaton whose states map to sets of principals and whose transitions are associated with reclassifiers. Formally, a RIF automaton λ is defined to be a 5-tuple $\langle Q, \Sigma, \delta, q_0, Prins \rangle$, where:

- Q is a finite set of automaton states,
- Σ is a finite set of reclassifiers,
- δ is a total, deterministic transition function $Q \times \Sigma \to Q$,
- q_0 is the initial automaton state $q_0 \in Q$, and
- *Prins* is a function from states to sets of principals.

RIF automata compactly represent certain mappings from sequences of reclassifiers to sets of principals. In theory, the number of states in a RIF automaton could be large; in practice, relatively small RIF automata suffice for representing many policies of practical interest. By requiring transition function δ to be total, any sequence of reclassifiers induces a sequence of transitions.[1] A RIF automaton for confidentiality is called a *c-automaton*; for integrity, an *i-automaton*.

Changes to the confidentiality or integrity restrictions associated with a value have straightforward descriptions using RIF automata.

- For confidentiality, a reclassifier *triggers* a *declassification* when it causes a transition whose ending state is mapped to a superset of the principals mapped by its starting state. A reclassifier triggers a *classification* when it causes a transition whose ending state is mapped to a subset of the principals mapped by its starting state.
- For integrity, transitioning to a superset of principals triggers a *deprecation* (since a superset must now be trusted) whereas transitioning to a subset triggers an *endorsement* (because only a subset must be trusted).

We use the term *reclassification* to describe all relationships between starting and ending states.

Two simple examples illustrate how RIF automata express interesting information flow policies. Focusing on confidentiality, consider a system to support

---

[1] Reclassifiers that do not trigger a transition between states (i.e., self-transitions) need not be specified explicitly, thereby permitting compact representation of δ, as we illustrate in Sect. 3.

paper reviewing. For each submitted paper, three referees provide integer review scores. The system logs each referee's name with her review score for each given paper. This logging operation is identified by reclassifier *log*. The system accepts the paper if three reviews have been provided and the average review score is higher than some threshold. This comparison operation is identified by reclassifier *avg*.

A sensible confidentiality policy for each review score would be that (i) each review score can be read by the paper's authors and the referee, (ii) the pair matching a referee to her review score (i.e., the result of *log*) may be read by the referee but not by the author (review scores are thus anonymous), (iii) the paper's final accept/reject result (i.e., the result of *avg*) can be read by everyone.[2] Notice that values covered by (i)–(iii) all derive at least partially from review scores. Figure 1 illustrates the corresponding *c*-automaton for review scores. Here, r denotes the referee, a a specific author, and P represents public, a set containing every principal. Reclassifier *avg* triggers a declassification, as specified by (i) and (iii), and reclassifier *log* triggers a classification, as specified by (i) and (ii). The asterisk "*" matches all reclassifiers and "¬(*avg*, *log*)" matches all reclassifiers except for *avg* and *log*. Finally, gray indicates the initial state of the RIF automaton.

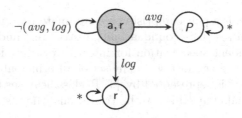

Fig. 1. A *c*-automaton for a review score. Submitted review scores can be read by author a and referee r. The result of logging (*log*) each referee's score can be read only by that referee, and the final accept/reject result (*avg*) can be read by every principal.

A second example sketches RIF automata that enforce integrity policies for a document management system.[3] Given is an *original* document *doc* with high integrity. Empty set ∅ models high integrity (i.e., no principal must be trusted for the documents to be trusted). Operation *ext(doc, rules)* derives a new document from document *doc* according to instructions (in *rules*) describing what text to excerpt. Because creative excerpting (e.g., omitting the text that gives conditions under which some agreement is made) can be used to generate a document that has different meaning from the original, *derived* documents have low integrity. We use set P to model low integrity (i.e., all principals must be trusted for

---

[2] This example thus addresses only a subset of information flow policies that a conference system needs to satisfy [15].
[3] This example is inspired by TruDocs [32].

the derived documents to be trusted). The *i*-automaton in Fig. 2 illustrates the desired integrity label for *doc*. Here, reclassifier *ext* triggers the deprecation.

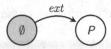

Fig. 2. An *i*-automaton of the document *doc*. When the excerpt operation (annotated with *ext*) is applied, the result is deprecated.

3   JRIF

JRIF (Java with Reactive Information Flow) extends Java's types to incorporate RIF automata. Programmers can tag fields, variables, and method signatures with RIF automata, and the JRIF compiler checks whether a program satisfies these RIF automata.

3.1   Syntax of JRIF

In JRIF, a *JRIF label* is a pair comprising a *c*-automaton λ_c and an *i*-automaton λ_i. The *c*-automaton specifies confidentiality restrictions and the *i*-automaton provides the independent specification for integrity restrictions. The JRIF syntax[4] of a JRIF label is given in Fig. 3. The set of all principals is represented by {_}, and the empty set is represented by {}. Reclassifications that are not given explicitly in a JRIF label are taken to be transitions whose starting and ending states are identical.

Figure 4 illustrates how the *i*-automaton in Fig. 2 is coded using JRIF syntax. The initial state s is distinguished by an asterisk * and maps to empty set {} of principals. State t maps to the set {_} of all principals. Reclassifier ext triggers a transition from s to t.

JRIF has the ordinary expressions of Java (e.g., constants, variables, etc.). In addition, an ordinary expression $\mathcal{E}$ can be annotated with a reclassifier f by writing

$$\texttt{reclassify}(\mathcal{E}, \texttt{f}).$$

An annotated expression can appear wherever an ordinary Java expression can (e.g., in right-hand side expressions of assignments or in guard expressions of conditional commands). Expressions not explicitly annotated trigger no transition on JRIF labels.

A simple method for PIN (personal identification number) checking written in JRIF is shown in Fig. 5. Here, method check takes as arguments an integer input in and an integer PIN; it checks if these two arguments are equal. The arguments

---

[4] For clarity, the syntax presented in this section simplifies the syntax actually used in our JRIF implementation.

$$\begin{aligned}
\lambda &::= \{\lambda_c; \lambda_i\} \\
\lambda_c &::= c\,[ListOfTerms] \\
\lambda_i &::= i\,[ListOfTerms] \\
ListOfTerms &::= T \mid T, ListOfTerms \\
T &::= State \mid InitialState \mid Transition \\
State &::= ID : \{ListOfPrincipals\} \\
InitialState &::= ID* : \{ListOfPrincipals\} \\
Transition &::= ID : ID \to ID
\end{aligned}$$

Fig. 3. Syntax for JRIF labels, where *ID* represents an alphanumeric string.

$$i[\,s*:\{\},\ t:\{\_\},\ ext:s{\to}t\,]$$

Fig. 4. Syntactic representation of an *i*-automaton

are tagged with different *c*-automata.[5] Input `in` is, for simplicity, considered public (all principals can read it). `PIN` can initially be read only by principal `p` (the principal that picked this `PIN`), but the result of applying the equality check (annotated with reclassifier C) on `PIN` is public. Method **check** returns the boolean value that results from this equality check, which is considered public. JRIF's compiler decides whether this method is safe, based on typing rules we discuss next.

Label Checking. Label checking in JRIF is performed by a procedure that decides whether the restrictions imposed by one JRIF label are not weaker than the restrictions imposed by another JRIF label. This is a *restrictiveness relation* between JRIF labels, and it is analogous to the subtyping relation in ordinary type systems. Whenever a value will be stored into a variable, the JRIF label that tags this variable must be at least as restrictive as the JRIF label on the value because, otherwise, the restrictions imposed by the value's JRIF label might be violated (e.g., more principals may read values than those allowed by that JRIF label) as execution proceeds.

```
boolean{c[q0*:{_}]} check (int{c[q0*:{_}]} in,
    int{c[q1*:{p},q2:{_},C:q1→q2]} PIN)
{   boolean{c[q0*:{_}]} res=false;
    if (reclassify(in==PIN,C))
        res=true;
    return res; }
```

Fig. 5. PIN check

---

[5] We focus only on confidentiality for this example.

We formalize the restrictiveness relation first for RIF automata and then for JRIF labels. Let $\mathcal{R}$ map each RIF automaton to the set of principals mapped by its initial state[6], and let $\mathcal{T}$ map a RIF automaton and a sequence F of reclassifiers to the RIF automaton obtained by taking the corresponding sequence of transitions.[7]

For c-automata, define λ'_c to be at least as restrictive as λ_c, denoted $\lambda_c \sqsubseteq_c \lambda'_c$, if for each possible sequence F of reclassifiers, principals allowed to read the resulting value according to λ'_c are also allowed by λ_c. Specifically, the set of principals in the state reached by taking F transitions on λ'_c is a subset of the principals in the corresponding state of λ_c. Relation $\sqsubseteq_c$ is formally defined as follows:

$$\lambda_c \sqsubseteq_c \lambda'_c \triangleq (\forall F\colon \mathcal{R}(\mathcal{T}(\lambda_c, F)) \supseteq \mathcal{R}(\mathcal{T}(\lambda'_c, F))). \tag{1}$$

For i-automata, λ'_i is at least as restrictive as λ_i, denoted $\lambda_i \sqsubseteq_i \lambda'_i$, if for all possible sequences of reclassifiers, principals that must be trusted according to λ'_i include those that must be trusted according to λ_i. So, relation $\sqsubseteq_i$ is defined as follows:

$$\lambda_i \sqsubseteq_i \lambda'_i \triangleq (\forall F\colon \mathcal{R}(\mathcal{T}(\lambda_i, F)) \subseteq \mathcal{R}(\mathcal{T}(\lambda'_i, F))). \tag{2}$$

We extend these restrictiveness relations to JRIF labels by comparing RIF automata pointwise:

$$\{\lambda_c; \lambda_i\} \sqsubseteq \{\lambda'_c; \lambda'_i\} \triangleq (\lambda_c \sqsubseteq_c \lambda'_c) \wedge (\lambda_i \sqsubseteq_i \lambda'_i).$$

The least restrictive JRIF label is denoted with $\{\}$; it allows all principals to read values, and it requires no principal to be trusted. JRIF label $\{\lambda_c\}$ imposes restrictions on confidentiality (according to λ_c), but it imposes no restriction on integrity (no principal is required to be trusted). Similarly, JRIF label $\{\lambda_i\}$ imposes restrictions on integrity, but it imposes no restriction on confidentiality.

JRIF labels inferred by the JRIF compiler for an expression are at least as restrictive as the JRIF labels of all variables in this expression. In particular, the c-automaton of an expression allows principals to read derived values only if these principals are allowed to do so by all c-automata of variables comprising that expression. JRIF constructs such a c-automaton by taking the product of all c-automata of the referenced variables, assigning the intersection of the allowed principals at each state. For integrity, the i-automaton of an expression requires principals to be trusted whenever these principals are required to be trusted by some i-automata of variables in that expression. Again, JRIF constructs such

---

[6] $\mathcal{R}(\langle Q, \Sigma, \delta, q_0, Prins \rangle) \triangleq Prins(q_0)$.

[7] $\mathcal{T}(\langle Q, \Sigma, \delta, q_0, Prins \rangle, F) \triangleq \langle Q, \Sigma, \delta, \delta^*(q_0, F), Prins \rangle$. Here δ^* is the transitive closure of δ: $\delta^*(q_0, F'\mathsf{f}) \triangleq \delta(\delta^*(q_0, F'), \mathsf{f})$ and $\delta^*(q_0, \epsilon) \triangleq q_0$, where ϵ denotes the empty sequence.

an i-automaton by taking the product of all i-automata of the used variables, assigning the union of the required principals at each state.[8]

The JRIF label of an annotated expression `reclassify`$(\mathcal{E},\mathsf{f})$ is the JRIF label of expression $\mathcal{E}$ after performing an f transition. Specifically, if $\lambda = \{\lambda_c; \lambda_i\}$ is the JRIF label of $\mathcal{E}$, then $\mathcal{T}(\lambda,\mathsf{f}) \triangleq \{\mathcal{T}(\lambda_c,\mathsf{f}); \mathcal{T}(\lambda_i,\mathsf{f})\}$ is the JRIF label of `reclassify`$(\mathcal{E},\mathsf{f})$. This rather simple rule is what gives JRIF labels their expressive power.

Information flows can be explicit or implicit [8,34]. An *explicit flow* occurs when information flows from one variable to another due to an assignment

$$\mathsf{x} = \texttt{reclassify}(\mathcal{E},\mathsf{f}). \tag{3}$$

An *implicit flow* occurs when assignment takes place because of a conditional branch, as in the `if`-statement

$$\texttt{if (reclassify}(\mathcal{E},\mathsf{f}))\ \{\mathsf{x} = 1\}\ \texttt{else}\ \{\mathsf{x} = 2\}. \tag{4}$$

Knowing the value of x after statement (4) completes reveals whether $\mathcal{E}$ evaluates to *true* or *false*.

JRIF, like other static information flow languages, controls implicit flows using a *program counter* (pc) label to represent the confidentiality and integrity of the control flow. Assignment (3) is secure if the JRIF label of x is at least as restrictive as both the pc label and the JRIF label of `reclassify`$(\mathcal{E},\mathsf{f})$. When control flow branches, as in (4), the pc label is increased to being at least as restrictive as the current pc label and the JRIF label of `reclassify`$(\mathcal{E},\mathsf{f})$. This increase ensures that assignments in either branch are constrained to variables with JRIF labels at least as restrictive as the JRIF label of `reclassify`$(\mathcal{E},\mathsf{f})$.

JRIF employs label checking rules for all basic Java features, including method overloading, class inheritance, and exceptions.[9] The formal description for all rules employed by JRIF is out of scope for this paper. However, the ideas that underlie these rules are based on the rules just explained for explicit and implicit flows.

We illustrate label checking by returning to method `check` from Fig. 5. This method compiles successfully in JRIF, because:

- the c-automaton of `res` is at least as restrictive as the c-automata of `in` and `PIN`, after their taking a C transition, and

---

[8] The product of two c-automata $\lambda_c = \langle Q, \Sigma, \delta, q_0, Prins\rangle$ and $\lambda'_c = \langle Q', \Sigma', \delta', q'_0, Prins'\rangle$ is defined to be $\lambda_c \sqcup_c \lambda'_c \triangleq \langle Q \times Q', \Sigma \cup \Sigma', \delta_\times, \langle q_0, q'_0\rangle, Prins_\times\rangle$ where $\delta_\times$ and $Prins_\times$ are defined for $\langle q, q'\rangle \in Q \times Q'$ as: $\delta_\times(\langle q, q'\rangle, \mathsf{f}) \triangleq \langle \delta(q,\mathsf{f}), \delta'(q',\mathsf{f})\rangle$, and $Prins_\times(\langle q, q'\rangle) \triangleq Prins(q) \cap Prins'(q')$. The definition for the product of two i-automata is the same with the only difference being the definition of $Prins_\times$, where instead of intersection we take the union of sets. RIF automata form a lattice.

[9] Label checking rules for Java features already exist in Jif. Their core component is a call to a decision algorithm for the restrictiveness relation. So, we were able to support JRIF labels simply by substituting Jif's decision algorithm with JRIF's decision algorithm for JRIF label restrictiveness.

– the c-automaton of the return value is at least as restrictive as the c-automaton of res.

More JRIF examples can be found on the JRIF web page [17].

Dynamic Labels. Sometimes an information flow label only becomes known at run time. To accommodate this, JRIF adopts Jif's *dynamic labels*. So JRIF dynamic labels may be instantiated as run-time values, stored in variables, and compared dynamically.

Since the actual JRIF label that a dynamic label denotes is not known at compile time, the JRIF label checker requires the programmer to provide code that checks for unsafe flows at run time. For example, consider

$$y = \texttt{reclassify}(x \bmod 4, f) \tag{5}$$

where x has been declared to have a dynamic label L1, and y a dynamic label L2. This assignment statement is secure only when $\mathcal{T}(\texttt{L1}, \texttt{f}) \sqsubseteq \texttt{L2}$ holds. In JRIF, programmers can write T(L1,f) to represent a dynamic label whose value is $\mathcal{T}(\texttt{L1}, \texttt{f})$. So, to ensure that $\mathcal{T}(\texttt{L1}, \texttt{f}) \sqsubseteq \texttt{L2}$ holds when (5) executes, the JRIF programmer must insert a conditional test to guard (5):

$$\texttt{if } (\texttt{T(L1,f)} \sqsubseteq \texttt{L2}) \; y = \texttt{reclassify}(x \bmod 4, f) \tag{6}$$

– At compile time, constraint $\texttt{T(L1,f)} \sqsubseteq \texttt{L2}$ informs the type system about the necessary relationship between L1 and L2, because the type system may assume $\texttt{T(L1,f)} \sqsubseteq \texttt{L2}$ holds when the "then" clause starts executing.
– At run time, the system constructs the JRIF label that results from an f transition on L1 and checks whether L2 is at least as restrictive.

This example also illustrates an interesting property of JRIF labels: the same reclassifier may have different effects on different labels. For some instantiations of L1, transitioning according to f may satisfy relation $\texttt{T(L1,f)} \sqsubseteq \texttt{L2}$, and for other instantiations of L1, that transition may not satisfy this relation.

Programming with RIF Versus Classic Labels. We use the term *classic label* to refer to an information flow label that specifies the same restrictions on all values derived from the value with which this label is associated (e.g., [8]).[10] For example, if a user's PIN is associated with a classic label specifying that only this user is allowed to read PIN, then even the result of a PIN check involving PIN is allowed to be read only by that user, instead of by everyone. Classic labels often impose more restrictions than needed.

Information flow control systems employing classic labels (e.g., [21,22]) are forced to use explicit declassification (for confidentiality) and endorsement (for integrity) commands to attach appropriate labels to derived values (i.e., labels

---

[10] Classic labels can be simulated by one-state RIF automata.

that impose weaker restrictions). Reclassifications in JRIF have a concise description in terms of an identifier (i.e., the reclassifier); declassifications and endorsements for classic labels are more verbose, since they glue a target label (i.e., the label that will be attached to the output) and, sometimes, must include the source label (i.e., the label attached to the input) as well.

JRIF labels are more verbose than classic labels, but there is a pay-off—changes to confidentiality and integrity specified in JRIF labels are not expressible by classic labels. Systems using classic labels need additional program code to emulate JRIF labels. This additional code is not automatically checkable for security, and thus, the programmer bears the full responsibility to implement the intended policy correctly.

Compared to languages using classic labels, JRIF better separates program logic from information flow policies. This makes JRIF programs easier to write and easier to maintain. Suppose, for example, that a programmer decides that some input value—a game player's name—should not be declassified when formerly it was.

– In JRIF, this change to the program involves modifying the JRIF label declaration on any field storing the player's name. The c-automaton of the label would be inspected and edited so that it contains no transitions to automaton states that map to additional principals.
– To accommodate this change in languages that use classic labels, the programmer must not only find and remove all declassification commands that involve the name field explicitly, but she also must remove all declassification commands that involve any expressions to which the game player's name flows. Getting these deletions right is error prone, since the programmer must reason about the flow of information in the code—something the type system was supposed to do.

4   Example Applications Using JRIF

4.1   Battleship

The Battleship game is a good example, because both confidentiality and integrity are important to prevent cheating. Over the course of the game, confidential information is declassified. Ship coordinates are initially fixed and secret, but revealed when opponents guess their adversary's ship coordinates correctly. Also, players must be restricted from changing the position of their ships after initial placements.

A simple c-automaton suffices to specify the confidentiality policy for the ship-coordinates of each player. Values derived from ship-coordinates selected by player p_1 should be read only by p_1, because opponent player p_2 is not allowed to learn the position of p_1's ships. The result of whether a ship of p_1 has been hit by the opponent player p_2 may be read by everyone, including p_2. A c-automaton that expresses this policy appears in Fig. 6a, where Q is the reclassifier for the

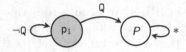

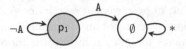

(a) A *c*-automaton for ship-coordinates.

(b) An *i*-automaton for ship-coordinates.

Fig. 6. RIF automata for ship-coordinates

```
boolean{c[q0*:{_}];i[q1*:{}]} processQuery
(Coordinate[{i[q1*:{}]}]{i[q1*:{}]} query)
{
  Board[{c[q0*:{P},q1:{_},Q:q0→q1];i[q1*:{}]}] brd = this.board;
  List[{i[q1*:{}]}] oppQueries = this.opponentQueries;
  oppQueries.add(query);
  boolean result = brd.testPosition(query);
  return reclassify(result,Q);
}
```

Fig. 7. Method `processQuery` from JRIF implementation. It checks the success of opponent's hit.

operation that checks whether an opponent's attack succeeded, and P is the set of all principals.

The integrity policy of ship-coordinates can be expressed using an *i*-automaton. Once p_1 selects the coordinates of her ships, they are as trusted as p_1. After ship-coordinates are chosen, they should not be changed during the game. So, before the game starts, there is a game operation whose reclassifier raises the integrity of all ship-coordinates, thereby ensuring that neither player can make changes. An *i*-automaton that expresses this policy is presented in Fig. 6b, where A is the reclassifier annotating the operation that accepts the initial coordinates.

We borrowed Jif's implementation of Battleship [21] to show that Jif programs are easily ported to JRIF. To obtain that JRIF port, we replaced Jif labels with JRIF labels, and we replaced various Jif declassification or endorsement commands with JRIF reclassifications. Methods in the Jif implementation that involved only label parameters and dynamic labels could be used without any modification in the JRIF implementation. Figure 7 contains a method of the Battleship implementation in JRIF. This method demonstrates the use of the *c*-automaton in Fig. 6a and the application of reclassifier Q. The full JRIF source for the Battleship implementation is found on JRIF's web page [17], along with the original Jif source (for comparison).

4.2 A Shared Calendar

To explore the expressive power of JRIF labels, we developed a shared calendar application from scratch.[11] The application allows users to create and share events in calendars. Each event consists of fields: time, date, duration, and description. Declassification, classification, endorsement, and deprecation all are employed in this application. Also, users may choose dynamic JRIF labels to associate with values.

Operations supported by our shared calendar include:

- Create a personal event or a shared event.
- Invite a user to participate in a shared event.
- Accept an invitation to participate in a shared event.
  Reclassifier: *Accept*
- Cancel a shared event.
  Reclassifier: *Cancel*
- Check and announce a conflict between personal events (not shared or canceled events) and an invitation for a new shared event.
  Reclassifier: *CheckConflict*
- Publish an event date and time (but not the event description).
  Reclassifier: *PubSlot*
- Hide an event date and time. Reclassifier: *HideSlot*

The reclassifiers that annotate these operations change the confidentiality and integrity of events. Once an event is accepted (*Accept* is applied), the resulting shared event is given the highest integrity, since all of the attendees endorse it. Having the highest integrity implies that no attendee is able to modify this shared event, thereafter. If an event is cancelled (*Cancel* is applied), then this event is given the lowest integrity, as are all values that subsequently may be derived from it by applying supported operations. With lowest integrity, cancelled events and all values derived from them can be distinguished. If *CheckConflict* is applied to a personal event and an invitation for a new shared event, then the result gets the lowest confidentiality and the highest integrity. This is because the result is readable and trusted by all principals that learn about the conflict. If *PubSlot* is applied to an event, then the event's date and time can flow to all principals, until a *HideSlot* is subsequently applied to that event.

Figure 8 illustrates c-automata for events created by a principal p_1. The c-automaton in Fig. 8a permits a full declassification triggered by reclassifier *CheckConflict*; the c-automaton in Fig. 8b does not. Both c-automata specify a declassification under *PubSlot*, and a classification under *HideSlot*. Figure 9 gives corresponding i-automata for the events of p_1. The i-automaton in Fig. 9a permits a full endorsement triggered by reclassifier *CheckConflict*; the i-automaton in Fig. 9b does not. Both i-automata specify an endorsement under *Accept*, and a deprecation under *Cancel*. Notice that *CheckConflict* triggers transitions in both a c-automaton and an i-automaton, contrary to, say, *PubSlot*.

---

[11] Source code for this shared calendar implementation in JRIF can be found on JRIF's web page [17].

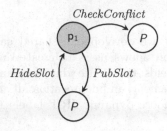

(a) A *c*-automaton that permits declassification for conflict checking.

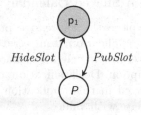

(b) A *c*-automaton that does not permit declassification for conflict-checking.

Fig. 8. RIF automata for event confidentiality. Self-loops are omitted for clarity.

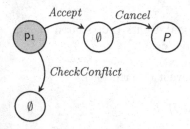

(a) An *i*-automaton that permits endorsement for conflict checking.

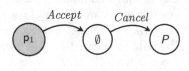

(b) An *i*-automaton that does not permit endorsement for conflict-checking.

Fig. 9. RIF automata for event integrity. Self-loops are omitted; for instance, the result of applying *CheckConflict* to a canceled event has low integrity.

Dynamic labels are used extensively in the shared calendar application. Figure 10 excerpts from the conflict-checking method. Here, the label of the event is checked dynamically to see whether it permits the result from the conflict check to be declassified and endorsed before performing the corresponding operation. In Fig. 10, `lEvt` is the dynamic label of the requested shared event `e`, `lCal` is the dynamic label of events in the calendar `cal`, against which the conflict will be checked, and method `hasConflict` returns `true` if a conflict is detected. If `lEvt` and `lCal` after having taken a C transition impose no restrictions to the resulting value, and if `hasConflict` is `true`, then a conflict will be announced.

Different users may tag events with different dynamic labels. For example, a user might pick the *c*-automaton in Fig. 8a for some events but pick the *c*-automaton in Fig. 8b for others. Events can have different *i*-automata, too. An unshared event has one of the *i*-automata in Fig. 9, but an accepted event can be treated with higher integrity and thus be tagged with the *i*-automaton denoted by taking the *Accept* transition. In addition, the time slot of some events could be

```
if (T(lEvt,C) ⊑ {c[q0*:{_}];i[q1*:{}]}
   && T(lCal,C) ⊑ {c[q0*:{_}];i[q1*:{}]}){
   if (reclassify(cal.hasConflict(e,lEvt,lCal),C)
      result = true;        // A conflict will be announced
   else
      result = false;       // No conflict will be announced
}
```

Fig. 10. Checking if the conflict is allowed to be declassified and endorsed, where C corresponds to reclassifier *CheckConflict*.

either hidden or public. To accommodate these heterogeneously labeled events, we store events in a data structure that makes it easier to aggregate events with different labels. The data structure has two fields: an event and a label. Before processing an event, its label is checked to prevent unspecified flows. Such data structures are common in Jif programs, and they are studied formally in [36].

5 Building the JRIF Compiler

We built a JRIF compiler by modifying the existing Jif compiler in relatively straightforward ways.[12] Extending compilers for other information flow languages ought to be similar. This should not be so surprising: JRIF labels expose the same interface to a type system as native information flow labels.

Our strategy for building JRIF involved three steps:

1. Add syntax for JRIF labels and for annotating expressions with reclassifiers.
2. Add typing rules for annotated expressions (according to Sect. 3.1).
3. Modify the type checker to handle this more expressive class of labels:
   (a) implement the restrictiveness relation on JRIF labels,
   (b) add an axiom stipulating that this relation is monotone with respect to transition function $\mathcal{T}$.

Item (3b) is essential for supporting our richer language of label comparisons. For example, if relation $l2 \sqsubseteq l1$ holds for two dynamic JRIF labels, then the type checker must be able to deduce that $\mathcal{T}(l2, f) \sqsubseteq \mathcal{T}(l1, f)$ holds for every f.

We decided to build JRIF by extending the Jif compiler because Jif is a widely studied language for information flow control and the Jif compiler is readily available. JRIF adds 6k lines of code to Jif (which contains 230k LOC). Out of the 494 Java classes comprising Jif, we modified only 31 and added 48 new classes for JRIF. Of these new classes, 37 are extensions of Jif classes—primarily abstract syntax tree nodes for labels, confidentiality and integrity policies, and code generation classes. Thus, most of the effort in building JRIF focused on extending Jif's functionality rather than on building new infrastructure. Moreover, extending Jif enabled us to harness Jif features, such as dynamic labels,

---

[12] The source code for JRIF can be found on JRIF's web page [17].

label parameters, and label inference, which reduce the annotation burden on the programmer.

Some features of Jif are orthogonal to enforcing JRIF labels, and JRIF ignores them, for the time being. For instance, Jif uses authority and policy ownership to constrain how labels may be downgraded. Since JRIF labels are concerned with what operation is applied to what value, authority and ownership are ignored for the enforcement of JRIF labels.

What the JRIF Compiler Enforces
Label checking in information flow control systems usually enforces noninterference [11] or some variation. For confidentiality, noninterference stipulates that changes to values that principal p cannot read initially should not cause changes to values that p can read during program execution. Equivalently, if the initial states of two program executions agree on values that principal p can read, then these executions should agree on computed values that p can read. For integrity, noninterference requires values that initially depend on trusting p do not cause changes to values whose trust does not depend on p. Moreover, these conditions must hold for each principal p.

Reclassifications complicate a definition of permissible information flow by changing what values are of concern during an execution. For example, if a reclassifier causes a transition that permits p to read the result of an operation on secret variables, then classic noninterference would be violated. Instead, *piesewise noninterference* (PWNI) [16] can handle arbitrary reclassifications caused by applied operations. PWNI allows flows through specified declassifications, but also it prevents classified information from being leaked. We have proven that RIF automata enforce PWNI for a simple imperative language [16], giving us confidence in the formal guarantees enforced by the JRIF type system. Many models (e.g., [1,2,7,19,30]) have been proposed for expressing and enforcing policies that permit changing the restrictions imposed on values, but PWNI is the first to handle arbitrary reclassifications caused by applied operations.

6   Related Work

Expressive structures, like automata, have previously been used to represent information flow specifications. Program dependence graphs [12,14], which represent data and flow dependencies between values, specify allowable declassifications. And Rocha et al. [25,26] employ *policy graphs* to specify sequences of functions that cause declassifications. However, this work does not handle arbitrary reclassifications; it only handles declassifications.

Several programming language approaches that control declassification (e.g., [13]) employ some notion of *trusted processes* or *code* [3]. Early versions of Jif used *selective downgrading* [24] to refine this idea by allowing different principals to trust different pieces of code. These systems enforce a form of *intransitive* flow policy [28], since direct flows that do not involve the declassifying operation are prohibited.

In capability-based systems, such as Flume [18], HiStar [35], Asbestos [9], Aeolus [6], Laminar [27], and LIO [33], declassifications are allowed to be performed by procedures possessing specific capabilities. Implementing fine-grained information flow policies in these systems would require a large number of different kinds of capabilities, possibly reaching the number of objects that should be protected in a system.

Chong and Myers [7] introduce information flow specifications that use conditions on program state as a basis for deciding when a value may be reclassified. Paragon [4] and SHAI [10] can also support policies that specify reclassifications based on program state predicates. These policies cannot always be translated into RIF automata, because the former specify reclassification based on a richer set of conditions. RIF automata could be compiled to such policies. The translation requires extending the JRIF program state: each JRIF variable is implemented using a value and the sequences of operations involved in deriving this value. It is a cumbersome translation, and we believe that it will generally be difficult to express a RIF automaton as a policy that specifies reclassifications based on program state predicates.

Li and Zdancewic [19] formalize downgrading (i.e., declassification and endorsement) policies by using simply-typed lambda terms. Here, information flow labels are sets of lambda terms (i.e. functions); when one of these lambda terms is applied to the corresponding value, the result is downgraded. RIF automata with no cycles can be modified to express such information flow labels, by associating reclassifiers with particular sets of lambda terms, by mapping the last reachable states to a low label (e.g. all sets of principals for confidentiality, empty set for integrity), and by mapping all other states to a high label (e.g. empty set for confidentiality, all sets of principals for integrity).

Sabelfeld et al. [31] introduce a four-dimension categorization (what, where, who, when) of declassification. In JRIF, a reclassifier that causes a declassification indicates "what" will be declassified and "where" in the program.

7   Conclusion

JRIF is an extension of Java for supporting Reactive Information Flow Control based on RIF automata. RIF automata specify restrictions on the values they are associated with, along with the RIF automaton to associate with derived values. The JRIF compiler was implemented by extending the Jif compiler and run time, thereby demonstrating that RIF automata are easily incorporated into languages that already support information flow types.

JRIF's type system is more expressive than classic information flow type systems. For instance, JRIF allows programmers to specify rich policies based on the sequence of operations used to derive a value. Existing programming languages allow such policies to be emulated in the state and control flow of a program, but doing so invariably makes code more complex and provides few security guarantees.

We illustrated JRIF programs with an implementation of Battleship and a shared calendar application. Our implementation of Battleship demonstrates that applications developed with Jif may be ported easily to JRIF; the shared calendar demonstrates the separation between policies and program logic that JRIF enables.

References

1. Askarov, A., Sabelfeld, A.: Gradual release: unifying declassification, encryption and key release policies. In: IEEE Symposium on Security and Privacy, pp. 207–221 (2007). https://doi.org/10.1109/SP.2007.22
2. Banerjee, A., Naumann, D., Rosenberg, S.: Expressive declassification policies and modular static enforcement. In: IEEE Symposium on Security and Privacy, pp. 339–353 (2008). https://doi.org/10.1109/SP.2008.20
3. Bell, E.D., LaPadula, J.L.: Secure computer systems: mathematical foundations (1973)
4. Broberg, N., van Delft, B., Sands, D.: Paragon for practical programming with information-flow control. In: Shan, C. (ed.) APLAS 2013. LNCS, vol. 8301, pp. 217–232. Springer, Cham (2013). https://doi.org/10.1007/978-3-319-03542-0_16
5. Broberg, N., Sands, D.: Flow locks: towards a core calculus for dynamic flow policies. In: Sestoft, P. (ed.) ESOP 2006. LNCS, vol. 3924, pp. 180–196. Springer, Heidelberg (2006). https://doi.org/10.1007/11693024_13
6. Cheng, W., et al.: Abstractions for usable information flow control in Aeolus. In: Proceedings of the 2012 USENIX Conference on Annual Technical Conference, USENIX ATC 2012, p. 12. USENIX Association, Berkeley (2012). http://dl.acm.org/citation.cfm?id=2342821.2342833
7. Chong, S., Myers, A.: End-to-end enforcement of erasure and declassification. In: 2008 IEEE 21st Computer Security Foundations Symposium, CSF 2008, pp. 98–111 (2008). https://doi.org/10.1109/CSF.2008.12
8. Denning, D.E.R.: Secure information flow in computer systems. Ph.D. thesis, West Lafayette, IN, USA (1975)
9. Efstathopoulos, P., et al.: Labels and event processes in the Asbestos operating system. In: Proceedings of the Twentieth ACM Symposium on Operating Systems Principles, SOSP 2005, pp. 17–30. ACM, New York (2005). https://doi.org/10.1145/1095810.1095813
10. Elnikety, E., Garg, D., Druschel, P.: SHAI: enforcing data-specific policies with near-zero runtime overhead. Technical report, Max Planck Institute for Software Systems, Saarland Informatics Campus, Germany, January 2018
11. Goguen, J.A., Meseguer, J.: Security policies and security models. In: IEEE Symposium on Security and Privacy, pp. 11–20 (1982)
12. Hammer, C., Snelting, G.: Flow-sensitive, context-sensitive, and object-sensitive information flow control based on program dependence graphs. Int. J. Inf. Secur. 8(6), 399–422 (2009). https://doi.org/10.1007/s10207-009-0086-1
13. Hicks, B., King, D., McDaniel, P., Hicks, M.: Trusted declassification: high-level policy for a security-typed language. In: Proceedings of the 2006 Workshop on Programming Languages and Analysis for Security, PLAS 2006, pp. 65–74. ACM, New York (2006). https://doi.org/10.1145/1134744.1134757
14. Johnson, A., Waye, L., Moore, S., Chong, S.: Exploring and enforcing security guarantees via program dependence graphs. In: Proceedings of the 36th ACM SIGPLAN Conference on Programming Language Design and Implementation, PLDI 2015, pp. 291–302. ACM, New York (2015). https://doi.org/10.1145/2737924.2737957

15. Kanav, S., Lammich, P., Popescu, A.: A conference management system with verified document confidentiality. In: Biere, A., Bloem, R. (eds.) CAV 2014. LNCS, vol. 8559, pp. 167–183. Springer, Cham (2014). https://doi.org/10.1007/978-3-319-08867-9_11

16. Kozyri, E.: Enhancing expressiveness of information flow labels: reclassification and permissiveness. Ph.D. thesis, Ithaca, NY, USA (2018)

17. Kozyri, E., Arden, O., Myers, A.C., Schneider, F.B.: JRIF: Java with Reactive Information Flow, February 2016. Software release http://www.cs.cornell.edu/jrif/

18. Krohn, M., et al.: Information flow control for standard OS abstractions. In: Proceedings of Twenty-First ACM SIGOPS Symposium on Operating Systems Principles, SOSP 2007, pp. 321–334. ACM, New York (2007). https://doi.org/10.1145/1294261.1294293

19. Li, P., Zdancewic, S.: Downgrading policies and relaxed noninterference. In: Proceedings of the 32nd ACM SIGPLAN-SIGACT Symposium on Principles of Programming Languages, POPL 2005, pp. 158–170. ACM, New York (2005). https://doi.org/10.1145/1040305.1040319

20. Li, P., Zdancewic, S.: Practical information-flow control in web-based information systems. In: Proceedings of the 18th IEEE Workshop on Computer Security Foundations, CSFW 2005, pp. 2–15. IEEE Computer Society, Washington, DC (2005). https://doi.org/10.1109/CSFW.2005.23

21. Myers, A.C., Zheng, L., Zdancewic, S., Chong, S., Nystrom, N.: JIF 3.0: Java Information Flow. Software release http://www.cs.cornell.edu/jif, July 2006

22. Myers, A.C.: JFlow: Practical mostly-static information flow control. In: Proceedings of the 26th ACM SIGPLAN-SIGACT Symposium on Principles of Programming Languages, POPL 1999, pp. 228–241. ACM, New York (1999). https://doi.org/10.1145/292540.292561

23. Myers, A.C., Liskov, B.: A decentralized model for information flow control. In: Proceedings of the Sixteenth ACM Symposium on Operating Systems Principles, SOSP 1997, pp. 129–142. ACM, New York (1997). https://doi.org/10.1145/268998.266669

24. Pottier, F., Conchon, S.: Information flow inference for free. In: Proceedings of the Fifth ACM SIGPLAN International Conference on Functional Programming, ICFP 2000, pp. 46–57. ACM, New York (2000). https://doi.org/10.1145/351240.351245

25. Rocha, B., Bandhakavi, S., den Hartog, J., Winsborough, W., Etalle, S.: Towards static flow-based declassification for legacy and untrusted programs. In: IEEE Symposium on Security and Privacy, pp. 93–108 (2010). https://doi.org/10.1109/SP.2010.14

26. Rocha, B., Conti, M., Etalle, S., Crispo, B.: Hybrid static-runtime information flow and declassification enforcement. IEEE Trans. Inf. Forensics Secur. 8(8), 1294–1305 (2013). https://doi.org/10.1109/TIFS.2013.2267798

27. Roy, I., Porter, D.E., Bond, M.D., McKinley, K.S., Witchel, E.: Laminar: practical fine-grained decentralized information flow control. In: Proceedings of the 30th ACM SIGPLAN Conference on Programming Language Design and Implementation, PLDI 2009, pp. 63–74. ACM, New York (2009). https://doi.org/10.1145/1542476.1542484

28. Rushby, J.: Noninterference, transitivity and channel-control security policies. Technical report (1992)

29. Sabelfeld, A., Myers, A.: Language-based information-flow security. IEEE J. Sel. Areas Commun. 21(1), 5–19 (2003). https://doi.org/10.1109/JSAC.2002.806121

30. Sabelfeld, A., Myers, A.C.: A model for delimited information release. In: Futatsugi, K., Mizoguchi, F., Yonezaki, N. (eds.) ISSS 2003. LNCS, vol. 3233, pp. 174–191. Springer, Heidelberg (2004). https://doi.org/10.1007/978-3-540-37621-7_9

31. Sabelfeld, A., Sands, D.: Declassification: dimensions and principles. J. Comput. Secur. **17**(5), 517–548 (2009). http://dl.acm.org/citation.cfm?id=1662658.1662659

32. Schneider, F.B., Walsh, K., Sirer, E.G.: Nexus Authorization Logic (NAL): design rationale and applications. ACM Trans. Inf. Syst. Secur. **14**(1), 8:1–8:28 (2011). https://doi.org/10.1145/1952982.1952990

33. Stefan, D., Russo, A., Mitchell, J.C., Mazières, D.: Flexible dynamic information flow control in Haskell. In: Proceedings of the 4th ACM Symposium on Haskell, Haskell 2011, pp. 95–106. ACM, New York (2011). https://doi.org/10.1145/2034675.2034688

34. Volpano, D., Irvine, C., Smith, G.: A sound type system for secure flow analysis. J. Comput. Secur. **4**(2–3), 167–187 (1996). http://dl.acm.org/citation.cfm?id=353629.353648

35. Zeldovich, N., Boyd-Wickizer, S., Kohler, E., Mazières, D.: Making information flow explicit in HiStar. In: Proceedings of the 7th USENIX Symposium on Operating Systems Design and Implementation-Volume 7, OSDI 2006, p. 19. USENIX Association, Berkeley (2006). http://dl.acm.org/citation.cfm?id=1267308.1267327

36. Zheng, L., Myers, A.C.: Dynamic security labels and static information flow control. Int. J. Inf. Secur. **6**(2), 67–84 (2007). https://doi.org/10.1007/s10207-007-0019-9

Symbolic Timed Trace Equivalence

Vivek Nigam[1,2], Carolyn Talcott[3](✉), and Abraão Aires Urquiza[1]

[1] Federal University of Paraíba, João Pessoa, Brazil
abraauc@gmail.com
[2] fortiss GmbH, Munich, Germany
nigam@fortiss.org
[3] SRI International, Menlo Park, USA
clt@csl.sri.com

Abstract. Intruders can infer properties of a system by measuring the time it takes for the system to respond to some request of a given protocol, that is, by exploiting time side channels. These properties may help intruders distinguish whether a system is a honeypot or concrete system helping them avoid defense mechanisms, or track a user among others violating his privacy. Observational and trace equivalence are technical machineries used for verifying whether two systems are distinguishable. Automating the check for trace equivalence suffers the state-space explosion problem. Symbolic verification is used to mitigate this problem allowing for the verification of relatively large systems. This paper introduces a novel definition of timed trace equivalence based on symbolic time constraints. Protocol verification problems can then be reduced to problems solvable by off-the-shelf SMT solvers. We implemented such machinery in Maude and carry out a number of experiments demonstrating the feasibility of our approach.

Catherine Meadows has been a constant inspiration to us and to our work. We are honoured to be associated with Cathy as a collegue and a friend.

1 Introduction

This paper is dedicated to Catherine Meadows. Protocol security verification has emerged in the past decades as an exciting research field in which Meadows has had a key role. Meadows has been influential in the development of mathematical theories, formal languages, and tools for protocol analysis. Her technical expertise combined with deep insights into security issues has enabled her to successfully apply both formal and informal logical analysis to diverse aspects of computer security. Of particular importance is Meadow's work formalizing and analyzing protocols and standards widely used in practice, leading to new insights into and improvements of the specifications and implementations. Examples include: the Internet Key Exchange protocol [32]; the RSA Laboratories Public Key Standards PKCS#11, a widely used application API to crypto

© Springer Nature Switzerland AG 2019
J. D. Guttman et al. (Eds.): Meadows Festschrift, LNCS 11565, pp. 89–111, 2019.
https://doi.org/10.1007/978-3-030-19052-1_8

libraries [23]; and fully automatic analysis of YubiKey and the YubiHSM hardware security module [22]. Meadows' careful formalizations and insights into attack models has been particularly inspiring in our work, especially analysis of Distance Bounding Protocols with application to complexity reduction and collusion analysis [34]; Denial of Service [33]; and most related to this paper is recent work resulting in a formal definition of protocol indistinguishability and a method to check using Maude NPA [40].

Much of Meadows' recent work has been undertaken using the Maude NPA tool [19] which is implemented in the Maude rewriting logic system. Maude NPA builds on ideas developed for NPA [31], an earlier tool developed by Meadows, and supports reasoning about cryptographic algorithms subject to equational theories. Meadows has been instrumental in guiding the extensions of Maude to support unification and narrowing in the presence of a rich collection of crypto primitives.

One important aspect that has been foreseen by Meadows in previous papers, but not yet fully formalized/investigated are attacks using *time side channels*. Time side channels can be exploited by intruders in order to infer properties of systems, helping them avoid defense mechanisms, and track users, violating their privacy. For example [26], honeypots are normally used for attracting intruders in order to defend real systems from their attacks. However, as honeypots run on virtual machines whereas normal client systems usually do not, it takes longer for a honeypot to respond to some protocol requests. This information can be used by the attacker to determine which servers are real and which are honeypots. For another example [11], passports using RFID mechanisms have been shown to be vulnerable to privacy attacks. An intruder can track a particular's passport by replaying messages of previous sessions and measuring response times.

The formal verification of whether an intruder can infer such properties is different from usual reachability based properties, such as secrecy, authentication and other correspondence properties. In the verification of reachability properties, one searches for a trace that exhibits the flaw, *e.g.*, the intruder learning a secret. In attacks such as the ones described above, one searches instead for behaviors that can distinguish two systems, *e.g.*, a behavior that can be observed when interacting with one system, but that cannot be observed when interacting with the other system. That is, to check whether the systems are *observationally distinguishable*. This requires reasoning over sets of traces.

Various notions of *trace equivalence*[1] have been proposed in the programming languages community as well as in concurrent systems [2,7,25,35] using, for example, logical relations and bisimulation. Trace equivalence has also been proposed for protocol verification notably the work of Cortier and Delaune [14]. A number of properties, *e.g.*, unlinkability and anonymity [3], have been reduced to the problem of trace equivalence. As protocol verification involves infinite domains, the use of symbolic methods has been essential for the success of such approaches.

The contribution of this paper is three-fold:

---

[1] And more generally, observational equivalence.

- **Symbolic Timed Trace Equivalence:** We propose a novel definition of timed equivalence over timed protocol instances [38]. Timing information, *e.g.*, duration of computation, is treated symbolically and can be specified in the form of time constraints relating multiple time symbols, *e.g.*, $tt_1 \geq tt_2 + 10$;

- **SMT Solvers for Proving Timed Trace Equivalence:** SMT solvers are used in two different ways. We specify the operational semantics of timed protocols using Rewriting Modulo SMT [39], reducing considerably the search space needed to enumerate these traces.

  The second application of SMT-Solvers is on the proof of timed trace equivalence, namely, to check whether the timing of observations can be matched. This check involves the checking for the satisfiability of $\exists \forall$ formulas [18].

  The use of general SMT solvers means that our implementations can immediately profit from improvements made to these solvers. Also, as SMT solvers have large communities using them, we have some confidence on the soundness of the implementations.

- **Implementation:** Relying on the Maude [12] support for Rewriting Modulo SMT using the SMT-solvers CVC4 [4] or Yices [18], we implemented in Maude the machinery necessary for enumerating symbolic traces. However, as checking for the satisfiability of $\exists \forall$ formulas [18] is not supported by Maude, we integrate our Maude machinery with the SMT solver Yices [18]. We carry out some proof-of-concept experiments demonstrating the feasibility of our approach.

This paper only considers the case of bounded protocol sessions. The case of unbounded protocol sessions is left to future work.

Section 2 describes some motivating examples of how an intruder can use time side channels for his benefit. We introduce the basic symbolic language and the timed protocol language in Sect. 3. Section 4 gives the operation semantics of the timed protocol language. Section 5 introduces symbolic timed trace equivalence describing how to prove this property. Section 6 describes our implementation architecture and the experiments carried out. Finally, in Sect. 7, we conclude by commenting on related and future work. Finally, missing proofs and additional material can be found in the accompanying technical report [37].

2 Examples

We discuss some motivating examples illustrating how intruders can exploit time side channels of protocols.

Red Pill. Our first example is taken from [26]. The attack is based on the concept of *red pills*. As honeypots trying to lure attackers normally run on virtual machines, determining if a system is running on a virtual machines or not gives an attacker one means to avoid honeypots [26]. The system running in a virtual machine or a concrete machine follows exactly the same protocol.

When an application connects to the malicious server, the server first sends a *baseline* request followed by a *differential* request. The time to respond to the baseline request is the same whether running in a virtual machine or not and is used for calibration. The time to respond to the differential request is longer when executed in a virtual machine. When not taking time into account, the set of traces for this exchange is the same whether the application is running on a virtual machine or not. However, if we also consider the time to respond to the two requests, the timed traces of applications running on virtual machines can be distinguished from those of applications running on native hardware.

Passport RFID. Our second example comes from work of Chothia and Smirnov [11] investigating the security of *e-passports*. These passports contain an RFID tag that, when powered, broadcasts information intended for passport readers. Chothia and Smirnov identified a flaw in one of the passport protocols that makes it possible to trace the movements of a particular passport, without having to break the passport's cryptographic key. In particular, if the attacker records one session between the passport and a legitimate reader, one of the recorded messages can be replayed to distinguish that passport from other passports. Assuming that the target carried their passport on them, an attacker could place a device in a doorway that would detect when the target entered or left a building. In the protocol, the passport receives an encryption and a mac verifying the integrity of the encryption. The protocol first checks the mac, and reports an error if the check fails. If the mac check succeeds, it checks the encryption. This will fail if the encryption isn't fresh. When the recorded encryption, mac pair is replayed to the recorded passport, the mac check will succeed but the encryption check will fail, while the mac check will fail when carried out by any other passport as it requires a key unique to the passport. The time to failure is significantly longer for the targeted passport than for others, since only the mac check is needed and it is faster.

Anonymous Protocol. Abadi and Fournet [1] proposed an anonymous group protocol where members of a group can communicate with each other without revealing that they belong to the same group. A member of a group broadcasts a message, m, encrypted with the shared group key. Whenever a member of a group receives this message, it is able to decrypt the message and then check whether the sender indeed belongs to the group and if the message is directed to him. In this case, the receiver broadcasts an encrypted response m'.

Whenever a player that is not member of the group receives the message m, it does not simply drop the message, but sends a decoy message with the same shape as if he belongs to the group, *i.e.*, in the same shape as m'. In this way, other participants and outsiders cannot determine whether two players belong to the same group or not.

However, as argued in [13], by measuring the time when a response is issued, an intruder can determine whether two players belong to the same group. This is because decrypting and generating a response take longer than just sending a decoy message.

3   Timed Protocols

We use a basic message term language which contains the usual cryptographic operators such as encryption, nonces, and tuples, augmented with time constraints. Trace and observational equivalence involving terms richer than the ones we use has been subject of a number of works. Here we introduce enough to write our examples. As the specification of timing aspects of protocols are orthogonal to the term language, extensions to the term language, such as constructs for hash, MAC, fresh keys, etc., can be made without affecting our main results.

The term language is defined by the following grammar. We assume given countable sets for text constants, $\mathcal{T}$, player names, $\mathcal{P}$, nonces, $\mathcal{N}$, symmetric keys, $\mathcal{K}$, symbols, Syms, and variables, $\mathcal{V}$, where $\mathcal{T}, \mathcal{P}, \mathcal{N}, \mathcal{K}$, Syms and $\mathcal{V}$ are disjoint. Below v_p represents a variable of sort player.

Basic Constants:
$$c := \quad t \in \mathcal{T} \qquad \text{Text Constants}$$
$$\mid p \in \mathcal{P} \qquad \text{Player Names}$$
$$\mid n \in \mathcal{N} \qquad \text{Nonces}$$

Keys:
$$k := \quad \text{symk} \in \mathcal{K} \qquad \text{Symmetric keys}$$
$$\mid \text{pk}(p) \mid \text{pk}(v_p) \quad \text{Public key of a player}$$
$$\mid \text{sk}(p) \mid \text{sk}(v_p) \quad \text{Secret key of a player}$$

Symbols:
$$\text{sym} := \mid \text{sym} \in \text{Syms} \text{ Symbol}$$

Terms:
$$m := c \qquad \text{Basic constants}$$
$$\mid k \qquad \text{Keys}$$
$$\mid v \in \mathcal{V} \qquad \text{Variables}$$
$$\mid \text{sym} \in \text{Syms} \qquad \text{Symbols}$$
$$\mid e(m, k) \qquad \text{Encrypted term}$$
$$\mid \langle m_1, \ldots, m_n \rangle \qquad \text{Tuples}$$

A term is *ground* if it does not contain any occurrence of variables and symbols. A term is *symbolic* if it does not contain any occurrence of variables, but it may contain occurrences of symbols. $\text{ms}, \text{ms}_1, \text{ms}_2, \ldots$ will range over symbolic terms.

Time. Assume a time signature, Ξ, containing a set of numbers, $r_1, r_2, \ldots$, a set of time variables, $tt_1, tt_2, \ldots$, including the special variable cur, and a set of pre-defined function symbols, including, $+, -, \times, /, \text{floor}, \text{ceiling}$.

Time Expressions are constructed inductively from numbers and variables by applying function symbols to time expressions. For example $\text{ceiling}((2 + tt + \text{cur})/10)$ is a Time Expression. The symbols $tr_1, tr_2, \ldots$ range over Time Expressions. The time variable cur is a keyword in our protocol specification language denoting the current global time. We do not constrain the set of numbers and function symbols in Ξ, but, in practice, we allow only the signatures supported by the SMT solver used. We assume that time expressions are disjoint from message terms.

Definition 1 (Symbolic Time Constraints). *Let Ξ be a time signature. The set of symbolic time constraints is constructed using time expressions as follows: Let tr_1, tr_2 be time expressions, then*

$$tr_1 = tr_2, \quad tr_1 \geq tr_2 \quad tr_1 > tr_2, \quad tr_1 < tr_2, \text{ and } tr_1 \leq tr_2$$

are symbolic time constraints.

For example, $\mathsf{cur} + 10 < \mathsf{floor}(\mathsf{tt} - 5)$ is a time constraint. $\mathsf{tc}, \mathsf{tc}_1, \mathsf{tc}_2, \ldots$ will range over time constraints.

Intuitively, given a set of time constraints $\mathcal{TC}$, each of its models with concrete instantiations for the time variables corresponds to a particular scenario. This means that one single set of time constraints denotes a possibly infinite number of concrete scenarios. For example, the set of constraints $\{\mathsf{tt}_1 \leq 2, \mathsf{tt}_2 \geq 1 + \mathsf{tt}_1\}$ has an infinite number of models, *e.g.*, $[\mathsf{tt}_1 \mapsto 1.9, \mathsf{tt}_2 \mapsto 3.1415]$.

Finally, SMT-solvers, such as CVC4 [4] and Yices [18], can check for the satisfiability of a set of time constraints.

3.1   Timed Protocol Language

The language used to specify a timed cryptographic protocol, introduced in our previous work [38], has the standard constructions, such as the creation of fresh values, sending and receiving messages, and "if then else" constructors, each annotated with time constraints.

Definition 2 (Timed Protocols). *A timed protocol consists of a set of timed protocol roles. The set of Timed Protocols Roles, $\mathsf{pl} \in \mathcal{TL}$, is generated by the following grammar:*

nil	*Empty Protocol*
$\mid (\mathsf{new}\ \mathsf{v}\ \#\ \mathsf{tc}), \mathsf{pl}$	*Fresh Constant*
$\mid (+\mathsf{m}\ \#\ \mathsf{tc}), \mathsf{pl}$	*Timed Message Send*
$\mid (-\mathsf{m}\ \#\ \mathsf{tc}), \mathsf{pl}$	*Timed Message Receive*
$\mid (\mathsf{if}\ (\mathsf{m}_1 := \mathsf{m}_2)\ \#\ \mathsf{tc}\ \mathsf{then}\ \mathsf{pl}_1\ \mathsf{else}\ \mathsf{pl}_2)$	*Timed Conditional*

Intuitively, new generates a fresh value binding it to the variable v, $(+\mathsf{m}\ \#\ \mathsf{tc})$ denotes sending the term m and $(-\mathsf{m}\ \#\ \mathsf{tc})$ denotes receiving a term matching m. For the term $(\mathsf{if}\ \mathsf{m}_1 := \mathsf{m}_2\ \#\ \mathsf{tc}\ \mathsf{then}\ \mathsf{pl}_1\ \mathsf{else}\ \mathsf{pl}_2)$, we assume that m_1 is ground when it is evaluated. Then if m_1 can be matched with m_2, that is, instantiate the variables in m_2 so that the resulting term is m_1, then the protocol proceeds to execute pl_1 and otherwise to execute pl_2. Moreover, the variables in m_2 are instantiated with the witnessing matching substitution in pl_1. We also assume that pl_2 does not contain variables in ms_2. This is because the binding of these variables to concrete terms only happens when the condition is true. Finally, a command is only applicable if the associated constraint tc is satisfiable.

We elide the associated time constraint whenever tc is a tautology, *i.e.*, it is always true. If we restrict the time constraints to be tautologies (say $1 = 1$), the timed protocol language can be considered as one of the usual security protocol specification languages. The following two examples illustrate this by specifying the traditional Needham-Schroeder protocol (suppressing trivially true time constraints).

Example 1. The Needham-Schroeder [36] protocol is specified as follows where X, Y, Z are variables:

$Alice(Z) := (\text{new } N_a), (+e(\langle N_a, alice\rangle, \text{pk}(Z))), (-e(\langle N_a, Y\rangle, \text{pk}(alice)\})), (+e(Y, \text{pk}(Z)))$
$Bob := (-e(\langle X, Z\rangle, \text{pk}(bob))), (\text{new } N_b), (+e(\langle X, N_b\rangle, \text{pk}(Z)\})), (-e(N_b, \text{pk}(bob)))$

The "if then else" constructs and pattern matching allows to specify protocols with branching, as illustrated by the following example:

Example 2. Consider the following protocol role which is a modification of Alice's role in the Needham-Schroeder's protocol (Example 1):

$Alice(Z) := (\text{new } N_a), (+e(\langle N_a, alice\rangle, \text{pk}(Z))), (-v),$
$\quad\quad\quad \text{if } v := e(\langle N_a, Y\rangle, \text{pk}(alice)\}) \text{ then } (+e(Y, \text{pk}(Z))) \text{ else } (+error)$

Here, Alice checks whether the received message v has the expected shape before proceeding. If it does not have this shape, then she sends an error message.

Time constraints can be used to specify timing aspects of security protocols. The following example illustrates how time constraints can specify the timing of a ping-pong message. It can be used to check the latency of a communication channel with a party. Similar constructs can be used to specify Distance-Bounding protocols [8].

Example 3. The following role specifies a ping-pong protocol where the response is only accepted within 4 time units:

$$(\text{new } v), (+v \# \text{tt} = \text{cur}), (-v \# \text{cur} \leq \text{tt} + 4)$$

It creates a fresh constant and sends it to the prover, remembering the current global time by assigning it to the time variable tt. It only concludes if the response is received within 4 time units.

The next example illustrates how time constraints can be used to specify protocol decisions based on timing aspects.

Example 4. The following role modifies the ping-pong protocol:

$(\text{new } v), (+v \# \text{tt} = \text{cur}), (-v_2 \# \text{tt}' = \text{cur}),$
$\quad (\text{if } (v := v_2 \# \text{tt} + 4 \geq \text{tt}')) \text{ then } (+ok \# \text{cur} < \text{tt}' + 2) \text{ else } (+ko \# \text{cur} < \text{tt}' + 2)$

It sends a nonce and receives a response. The protocol checks the response matches the nonce and whether it is received within 4 time units. If so, it responds *ok* and *ko* otherwise. Moreover, the response is sent within 2 time units after receiving the response.

Finally, as illustrated by the examples below, described in Sect. 2, time constraints can also be used to specify the duration of operations, such as checking whether some message is of a given form. In practice, the duration of these operations can be measured empirically to obtain a finer analysis of the protocol as done in [11].

Example 5 (Passport). Consider the following protocol role, taken from our previous work [38], which is the role of the passport used for identification.

$(\text{new } v), (+v), (-\langle v_{enc}, v_{mac} \rangle \;\#\; tt_0 = cur)$
$\text{if } (v_{mac} := e(v_{enc}, k_M)) \;\#\; tt_1 = tt_0 + r_{mac} \text{ then}$
$\quad \text{if } (v_{enc} := e(v, k_E)) \;\#\; tt_2 = tt_1 + r_{enc}) \text{ then } (+done \;\#\; cur = tt_2) \text{ else } (+error \;\#\; cur = tt_2)$
$\text{else } (+error \;\#\; cur = tt_1)$

This role creates a fresh value v and sends it. Then it is expecting a pair of two messages v_{mac} and v_{enc}, which is received at tt_0. It then checks whether the first component v_{mac} is of the form $e(v_{enc}, k_M)$, *i.e.*, it is the correct MAC. This operation takes r_{mac} time units. The time variable tt_1 is equal to the time $tt_0 + r_{mac}$, *i.e.*, the time when the message was received plus the MAC check duration. If the MAC is not correct, an *error* message is sent at time tt_1. Otherwise, if the first component, v_{mac}, is as expected, the role checks whether the second component, v_{enc}, is an encryption of the form $e(v, k_E)$, which takes (a longer) time r_{enc}. If so it sends the *done* message, otherwise the *error* message, both at time tt_2 which is $tt_1 + r_{enc}$.

Notice that instead of using concrete values r_{mac} and r_{enc} for the time of verifying the MAC and the encrypted terms, respectively, we could have specified intervals for these operations. For example, the time constraints $tt_0 + r_{mac-} \leq tt_1 \leq tt_0 + r_{mac+}$ express that it takes a time between r_{mac-} and r_{mac+} to check the whether the MAC term is correctly formed.

Example 6 (Red Pill Example). We abstract the part of sending the baseline message, *e.g.*, the messages that establish the connection to the server, and the part that sends the differential messages. We assume that it takes dBase to complete the exchange of the baseline messages.

$$(-(\text{baseline\_req}) \;\#\; tt_0 = cur), (+(\text{baseline\_done}) \;\#\; cur = tt_0 + \mathsf{dBase}),$$
$$(-(\text{diff\_req}) \;\#\; tt_1 = cur), (+(\text{diff\_done}) \;\#\; cur = tt_1 + \mathsf{dAppl})$$

Then the part of the protocol that depends on the application starts. We abstract this part using the messages diff_req and diff_done. If the application is running over a virtual machine, then dAppl takes dVirtual time units; otherwise dAppl takes dReal time units, where dVirtual > dReal.

The intruder can distinguish whether an application is running over a virtual machine or not by measuring the time it takes to complete the exchange of diff_req and diff_done messages.

Example 7 (Anonymous Protocol). We specify (a simplified version of) the anonymous group protocol proposed by Abadi and Fournet for private authentication [1]. Whenever a broadcasted message is received by an agent, it checks whether it has been encrypted using his public key KB. If so, the agent learns the group key k_A and responds with a message encrypted with the group key. Otherwise, the agent sends a decoy message encrypted with a fresh key k_ν, only known to the agent.

$-(\mathsf{v})$, if $\mathsf{v} := \langle \mathsf{hello}, \mathsf{e}(\{\mathsf{hello}, \mathsf{v}_n, \mathsf{k}_A\}, \mathsf{k}_G) \rangle$ $\#$ $\mathsf{tt}_1 = \mathsf{cur} + \mathsf{dEnc}$ then
if $(\mathsf{k}_G := KB \ \# \ \mathsf{tt}_2 = \mathsf{tt}_1 + \mathsf{dChk})$ then $+(\langle \mathsf{ack}, \mathsf{e}(\mathsf{rsp}, \mathsf{k}_A) \rangle)$ $\#$ $\mathsf{cur} = \mathsf{tt}_1 + \mathsf{dCrt}$
    else $(\mathsf{new} \ \mathsf{k}_\nu), +(\langle \mathsf{ack}, \mathsf{e}(\mathsf{decoy}, \mathsf{k}_\nu) \rangle)$ $\#$ $\mathsf{cur} = \mathsf{tt}_1$
else $(\mathsf{new} \ \mathsf{k}_\nu), +(\langle \mathsf{ack}, \mathsf{e}(\mathsf{decoy}, \mathsf{k}_\nu) \rangle)$ $\#$ $\mathsf{cur} = \mathsf{tt}_1$

Here $\mathsf{dEnc}, \mathsf{dChk}$ and dCrt are numbers specifying the time needed for, respectively, decrypting the received message, checking whether the key is the group key, and creating and sending the response message.

4   Operational Semantics for Timed Protocols

This section formalizes the operational semantics for configurations with a fixed number of timed protocol role instances. The operational semantics uses symbolic terms, where instead of instantiating variables with concrete terms, one uses symbolic terms, where each symbol represents a possibly infinite set of ground terms that satisfies suitable constraints. This simple idea has enabled the verification of security protocols, which have infinite search space on ground terms, but finite state space using symbolic terms [5,10,14].

In Subsect. 4.1, we introduce the types of symbolic term constraints necessary for our examples. Methods needed for operations involving symbolic terms and solving constraints can be found in, for example, [14,37]. The specific methods and algorithms used in our Maude implementation are detailed in [37].[2]

4.1   Symbolic Term Constraints

We will use two types of (capture avoiding) substitutions. *Variable substitutions* written $\mathsf{sb}, \mathsf{sb}_1, \mathsf{sb}_2, \ldots$ which are maps from variables to symbolic terms. $\mathsf{sb} = [\mathsf{v}_1 \mapsto \mathsf{ms}_1, \mathsf{v}_2 \mapsto \mathsf{ms}_2, \ldots, \mathsf{v}_n \mapsto \mathsf{ms}_n]$. *Symbol substitutions* written $\mathsf{ssb}, \mathsf{ssb}_1, \mathsf{ssb}_2, \ldots$ mapping symbols to symbolic terms $\mathsf{ssb} = [\mathsf{sym}_1 \mapsto \mathsf{ms}_1, \ldots, \mathsf{sym}_n \mapsto \mathsf{ms}_n]$.

The operational semantics uses two forms of constraints: derivability constraints and equality constraints.

Definition 3. *A derivability constraint has the form* $\mathsf{dc}(\mathsf{sym}, S)$, *where S is a set of symbolic terms and* sym *a symbol. This constraint denotes that* sym *can be any (symbolic) term derived from S.*[3]

For example, the derivability constraint

$$\mathsf{dc}(\mathsf{sym}, \{alice, \mathsf{n}_1, \mathsf{e}(\mathsf{sym}_2, \mathsf{sk}(alice)), \mathsf{pk}(bob)\})$$

specifies that sym may be instantiated by, *e.g.*, the terms $\langle alice, \mathsf{e}(\mathsf{sym}_2, \mathsf{sk}(alice)) \rangle$, $\langle alice, \mathsf{n}_1 \rangle$, $\mathsf{e}(alice, \mathsf{pk}(bob))$, $\mathsf{e}(\langle alice, bob \rangle, \mathsf{pk}(bob))$ and so on.

---

[2] The accompanying implementation can be found at https://github.com/SRI-CSL/VCPublic/obseq.git.

[3] S always includes guessables–names, text, fresh nonces, ... Guessables are left implicit in our examples.

Notice that any $dc(sym, \mathcal{S})$ denotes a infinite number of symbolic terms due to the tupling closure. We will abuse notation and use $ms \in dc(sym, \mathcal{S})$ to denote that the symbolic term ms is in the set of terms that can be derived from $\mathcal{S}$. Moreover, we assume that for any given set of derivability constraints $\mathcal{DC}$, there is at most one derivability constraint for any given sym.

We will need to determine whether a symbolic term ms' can represent another symbolic term ms, written $ms \in \mathcal{DC}(ms')$. Roughly, this means that ms can be obtained by repeated substitution of a symbol, sym in ms' by one of its instantiations according to $dc(sym, \mathcal{S}) \in \mathcal{DC}$. For example, assume that $\mathcal{DC}$ contains $dc(sym_1, \{t_1\}), dc(sym_2, \{t_2\})$, then $\langle t_1, t_2 \rangle \in \mathcal{DC}(\langle sym_1, sym_2 \rangle)$. The technical report [37] describe an algorithm to decide $ms \in \mathcal{DC}(ms')$[4].

Definition 4. *A symbol substitution* ssb *satisfies a set of derivability constraints* $\mathcal{DC}$, *written,* $ssb \models \mathcal{DC}$, *if for each* $sym \mapsto ms \in ssb$, $ms \in \mathcal{DC}(sym)$.

The following definition specifies the second type of symbolic term constraints called comparison constraints.

Definition 5. *A* comparison constraint *is either an* equality constraint $eq(ms_1, ms_2)$ *or an* inequality constraint $neq(ms_1, ms_2)$, *where* ms_1, ms_2 *are symbolic terms.*

A set $\mathcal{EQ}$ of comparison constraints is interpreted as a conjunction of constraints. We write $\mathcal{DC} \models \mathcal{EQ}$ to denote that $\mathcal{EQ}$ is satisfiable with respect to derivability constraints $\mathcal{DC}$. The set of equality constraints impacts the ground terms a symbolic term represents. For example, given $dc(sym_1, \{t_1\}), dc(sym_2, \{t_2\}) \in \mathcal{DC}$ and $\mathcal{EQ} = \{eq(sym_1, sym_2)\}$, the symbolic term $\langle sym_1, sym_2 \rangle$ may represent $\langle t_1, t_2 \rangle$ when considering only $\mathcal{DC}$, but not when considering both $\mathcal{DC}$ and $\mathcal{EQ}$, as it falsifies the constraint that sym_1 and sym_2 are equal, witnessed by the matching substitution $\theta = \{sym_1 \mapsto t_1, sym_2 \mapsto t_2\}$. We write $ms \in \mathcal{DC}(ms')\,|_{\mathcal{EQ}}$ to denote when the symbolic term ms' can represent the symbolic term ms assuming the constraints $\mathcal{DC}$ and $\mathcal{EQ}$. Algorithms to decide $\mathcal{DC} \models \mathcal{EQ}$ and $ms \in \mathcal{DC}(ms')\,|_{\mathcal{EQ}}$ are given in [37].

4.2 Symbolic Constraint Solving

For protocol verification, we assume a traditional Dolev-Yao intruder [15], *i.e.*, he can construct messages from his knowledge by tupling and encrypting messages. However, he can only decrypt a message for which he possesses the inverse key.

Definition 6. *An intruder knowledge* $\mathcal{IK}$ *is a set of symbolic terms.*

---

[4] Strictly, $\mathcal{DC}$ needs to satisfy some conditions in order for this membership relation to be well-defined. For example, the symbol dependency graph of $\mathcal{DC}$ shall be acyclic. We assume that this relation is undefined whenever this is not the case.

Suppose an honest player is ready to receive a message matching a term m, possibly containing variables. Rather than considering all possible ground instances of m that the intruder could send, we consider a finite representation of this set, namely symbolic messages where the possible values of the symbols are constrained by derivability constraints. To compute this representation the intruder replaces variables with symbolic terms, possibly containing fresh symbols, and then constrains the symbols so that the allowed instances are exactly the terms matching m that the intruder can derive from (allowed instantiations of) his current knowledge $I\mathcal{K}$.

For example, consider the term $m = e(\langle v_1, sym, v_1, v_2 \rangle, k)$ (which is expected as input by an honest player). Here v_1 and v_2 are variables and sym is constrained by derivability constraints $\mathcal{DC}$. We create two fresh symbols sym_1 and sym_2 for, respectively, the variables v_1 and v_2. Letting $sb = [v_1 \mapsto sym_1, v_2 \mapsto sym_2]$, we obtain $ms = sb[m] = e(\langle sym_1, sym, sym_1, sym_2 \rangle, k)$.

It remains to constrain the symbols so that ms represents the ground terms matching instances of m (given $\mathcal{DC}$) that the intruder can generate given $I\mathcal{K}$.

The function sgen. We implemented a function called sgen that enumerates representations of the required instances of ms. Each representation has the form $\{ssb_i, \mathcal{DC}_i\}$ where ssb_i represents symbols that have been constrained to a single value and $\mathcal{DC}_i$ constrains the remaining symbols. In particular, sgen(m, $I\mathcal{K}$, $\mathcal{DC}$) takes as input a term m, which is expected by the honest participant, the intruder knowledge $I\mathcal{K}$ and the derivability constraints $\mathcal{DC}$ for the existing symbols. sgen(m, $I\mathcal{K}$, $\mathcal{DC}$) then generates as output a pair:

$$\{sb, \{ssb_1, \mathcal{DC}_1\} \ldots \{ssb_k, \mathcal{DC}_k\}\}$$

where sb maps the variables of m to fresh symbols, and each $\{ssb_i, \mathcal{DC}_i\}$ is a solution to the problem above for $ms = sb[m]$. If $k = 0$, then there are no solutions, that is, the intruder is not able to generate a term which matches m. We describe sgen informally and illustrate it with some examples. The full specification and proof can be found in [37]. A similar algorithm is also used by [14].

Intuitively, the function sgen constructs a solution by either matching m with a term in his knowledge $I\mathcal{K}$ or deriving m from terms in $I\mathcal{K}$. The following example illustrates the different cases involved:

Example 8. Consider the following cases for deriving the term $m = e(\langle v, sym \rangle, k)$.

- Case 1 (matching with a term in $I\mathcal{K}$): Assume:

$$I\mathcal{K} = \{e(\langle n_a, sym_1 \rangle, k)\} \qquad \mathcal{DC} = dc(sym, \{n_a, n_c\})\ dc(sym_1, \mathcal{S})$$

Then the solution of sgen is:

$$\{sb, \{[sym_v \mapsto n_a, sym \mapsto sym_1], dc(sym_1, \{n_a, n_c\} \cap \mathcal{S})\}\}$$

where $sb = [v \mapsto sym_v]$ and sym_v is a fresh symbol. Notice that since sym_v is mapped to a particular term (n_a), no derivability constraint for it is generated. Additionally, notice that sym is constrained to be the same as sym_1. This causes the removal of the derivability constraint $dc(sym, \mathcal{S})$;

- Case 2 (constructing terms from $I\mathcal{K}$): Assume that $k \in I\mathcal{K}$ and $I\mathcal{K}$ has no encryption terms. Then the solution of sgen is:

$$\{[v \mapsto sym_v], \{[], \mathcal{DC} \cup \{dc(sym_v, I\mathcal{K})\}\}\}$$

which corresponds to generating the term $e(\{sym_v, sym\}, k)$. Moreover, sym_v can be any term derivable from the intruder's knowledge.

- Case 3 (No Solution): Assume that $I\mathcal{K} = \{e(\langle n_a, n_b\rangle, k)\}$ and $\mathcal{DC} = dc(sym, \{n_a, n_c\})$. Since sym cannot be instantiated to n_b, the intruder cannot use the term $e(\langle n_a, n_b\rangle, k)$.

4.3   Operational Semantics

The operational semantics of timed protocols is given by rules that rewrite configurations defined below:

Definition 7. *A symbolic configuration has the form $\langle \mathcal{P}, I\mathcal{K}, \mathcal{DC}, \mathcal{EQ}, \mathcal{TC}\rangle@tG$, where*

- *$\mathcal{P}$ is a finite set of player roles of the form $[n \mid pl \mid keys]$ composed of an identifier, n, a protocol role pl, and a set keys, keys, known to the player;*
- *$I\mathcal{K}$ is the intruder knowledge;*
- *$\mathcal{DC}$ is a set of derivability constraints;*
- *$\mathcal{EQ}$ is a set of comparison constraints;*
- *$\mathcal{TC}$ is a set of time constraints;*
- *tG is a time symbol representing global time.*

The operational semantics of timed protocols is defined in Fig. 1. The **New** rule replaces the (bound) variable v by a fresh nonce n^v. The **Send** rule sends a message ms which is then added to the intruder knowledge. The **Receive** rule expects a term of the form m. The function $sgen(m, I\mathcal{K}, \mathcal{DC})$ returns the variable substitution sb and a set of solutions $\{ssb, \mathcal{DC}_1\}$ css. Each solution intuitively generates a different trace. We apply sb in the remaining of the program pl and apply the symbol substitution ssb to all symbols in the resulting configuration. This rule also has a proviso that the message ms $=$ ssb[sb[m]] is encrypted with keys that can be decrypted by the honest participant. This is specified by the function *isReceivable*. Finally, it also adds to the set of keys of the honest participant keys, the keys he can learn from the message ms.

The rule **If-true** checks whether the terms ms_1 and ms_2 can be matched given the constraints $\mathcal{DC}$. This is done by the function sgenB which uses sgen. It first matches the structure of the terms in the matching problem $ms_1 = ms_2$, where symbols are considered as variables. If they cannot be matched, then the empty solution set is returned. Otherwise, there is a witnessing match $sym_1 \mapsto ms_1, \ldots, sym_n \mapsto ms_n$. It then calls sgen on the terms $\langle sym_1, \ldots, sym_n\rangle$ and $\langle ms_1, \ldots, ms_n\rangle$ returning its output. The rule **If-true** then adds the equality constraint to the set of comparison constraints.

Finally, the rule **If-false** adds the corresponding inequality constraint stating that ms_1 and ms_2 are not equal.

Example 9. Consider the Needham-Schroeder protocol in Example 1. Assume that the intruder initially only knows his secret key (and the guessables), $I\mathcal{K}_0 = \{sk(eve)\}$ and there are no symbols $\mathcal{DC} = \emptyset$. An execution of Alice's protocol role is as follows. Alice creates a fresh constant N_a and sends the message $e(\langle N_a, alice\rangle, pk(eve))$. At this point, the intruder knowledge is:

$$I\mathcal{K}_1 = I\mathcal{K}_0 \cup \{N_a\}$$

He now can send a message to *Bob*, namely $e(\langle sym_1, sym_2\rangle, pk(bob))$ where sym_1, sym_2 are fresh and constrained $\mathcal{DC}_1 = \{dc(sym_1, I\mathcal{K}_1), dc(sym_2, I\mathcal{K}_1)\}$. At this point, Bob creates a fresh value N_b and sends the message $e(\langle sym_1, N_b\rangle, pk(sym_2)\})$. The intruder learns this message:

$$I\mathcal{K}_2 = I\mathcal{K}_1 \cup \{e(\langle sym_1, N_b\rangle, pk(sym_2)\})\}$$

Now, the intruder can fool alice by sending her a message of the form $e(\langle N_a, Y\rangle, pk(alice)\})$. We create a fresh symbol sym_3 for Y obtaining $e(\langle N_a, sym_3\rangle, pk(alice)\})$ and attempt to generate this message from $I\mathcal{K}_2$ using sgen. Indeed we can generate this message using $e(\langle sym_1, N_b\rangle, pk(sym_2)\}) \in I\mathcal{K}_2$. This generates the ssb $= [sym_1 \mapsto N_a, sym_2 \mapsto alice, sym_3 \mapsto N_b]$. This substitution is consistent with $\mathcal{DC}_1$. The protocol finishes by the intruder simply forwarding the message sent by alice to bob. Bob then thinks he is communicating with alice, but he is not.

Each rule has two general provisos. The first is that the resulting set of comparison constraints should be consistent.

The second, more interesting, condition is on the time symbols. Whenever a rule is applied, time constraints $\mathcal{TC}_1$ are added to the configuration's constraint set. These time constraints are obtained by replacing cur in tc with tG_1 together with the constraint $tG_1 \geq tG_0$ specifying that time can only advance. The rule is fired only if the resulting set of time constraints $(\mathcal{TC} \cup \mathcal{TC}_1)$ is consistent, which is done by calling an SMT solver. This way of specifying systems is called Rewriting Modulo SMT [39].

Definition 8. *Let $\mathcal{R}$ be the set of rules in Fig. 1. A timed trace is a labeled sequence of transitions written $C_1 \xrightarrow{l_1} C_2 \xrightarrow{l_2} \cdots \xrightarrow{l_{n-1}} C_n$ such that for all $1 \leq i \leq n - 1$, $C_i \longrightarrow C_{i+1}$ is an instance of a rule in $\mathcal{R}$ and l_i is $+ms@tG_1$ if it is an instance of Send rule sending term ms at time tG_1, $-ms@tG_1$ if it is an instance of Receive rule receiving term ms at time tG_1, and $\emptyset$ otherwise.*

The use of rewriting modulo SMT considerably reduces the search space. Timed protocols are infinite state systems, as time symbols can be instantiated by any (positive) real number. With the use of rewriting modulo SMT we simply have to accumulate constraints. Only traces with satisfiable sets of time

New: $\langle[n \mid (\text{new v \# tc}), \text{pl} \mid \text{keys}] \, \mathcal{P}, \mathcal{IK}, \mathcal{DC}, \mathcal{EQ}, \mathcal{TC}\rangle@\text{tG}_0$
$\qquad \longrightarrow \langle[n \mid \text{sb[pl]} \mid \text{keys}] \, \mathcal{P}, \mathcal{IK}, \mathcal{DC}, \mathcal{EQ}, \mathcal{TC}_1\rangle@\text{tG}_1$
where n^v is a fresh nonce and $\text{sb} = [v \mapsto n^v]$

Send: $\langle[n \mid (\text{+ms \# tc}), \text{pl} \mid \text{keys}] \, \mathcal{P}, \mathcal{IK}, \mathcal{DC}, \mathcal{EQ}, \mathcal{TC}\rangle@\text{tG}_0$
$\qquad \longrightarrow \langle[n \mid \text{pl} \mid \text{keys}] \, \mathcal{P}, \mathcal{IK} \cup \{\text{ms}\}, \mathcal{DC}, \mathcal{EQ}, \mathcal{TC}_1\rangle@\text{tG}_1$

Receive: $\langle[n \mid (\text{-m \# tc}), \text{pl} \mid \text{keys}] \, \mathcal{P}, \mathcal{IK}, \mathcal{DC}, \mathcal{EQ}, \mathcal{TC}\rangle@\text{tG}_0$
$\qquad \longrightarrow \text{ssb}[\langle[n \mid \text{sb[pl]} \mid \text{addKeys(ms, keys)}] \, \mathcal{P}, \mathcal{IK}, \mathcal{DC}_1, \mathcal{EQ}, \mathcal{TC}_1\rangle]@\text{tG}_1$
where $\{\text{sb}, \{\text{ssb}, \mathcal{DC}_1\} \text{ css}\} := \text{sgen}(m, \mathcal{IK}, \mathcal{DC})$ and $\text{ms} = \text{ssb[sb[m]]}$ and $isReceivable(\text{ms, keys})$

If-true: $\langle[n \mid (\text{if } (\text{ms}_1 := \text{ms}_2 \, \# \, \text{tc}) \text{ then pl}_1 \text{ else pl}_2) \mid \text{keys}] \, \mathcal{P}, \mathcal{IK}, \mathcal{DC}, \mathcal{EQ}, \mathcal{TC}\rangle@\text{tG}_0$
$\qquad \longrightarrow \text{ssb}[\langle[n \mid \text{sb[pl}_1\text{]} \mid \text{keys} \, \mathcal{P}, \mathcal{IK}, \mathcal{DC}_1, \mathcal{EQ} \cup \{\text{eq(sb[ms}_1\text{], sb[ms}_2\text{])}\}, \mathcal{TC}_1\rangle]@\text{tG}_1$
where $\{\text{sb}, \{\text{ssb}, \mathcal{DC}_1\} \text{ css}\} := \text{sgenB}(\text{ms}_1 = \text{ms}_2, \mathcal{IK}, \mathcal{DC})$

If-false: $\langle[n \mid (\text{if } \text{ms}_1 := \text{ms}_2 \, \# \, \text{tc} \text{ then pl}_1 \text{ else pl}_2) \mid \text{keys}] \, \mathcal{P}, \mathcal{IK}, \mathcal{DC}, \mathcal{EQ}\rangle$
$\qquad \longrightarrow \langle[n \mid \text{pl}_2 \mid \text{keys}] \, \mathcal{P}, \mathcal{IK}, \mathcal{DC} \cup \mathcal{DC}', \mathcal{EQ} \cup \{\text{neq(ms}_1, \text{ms}_2)\}\rangle$

Fig. 1. Operational semantics for basic protocols. In each rule tc_1 is the time constraint obtained by replacing cur in tc by the global time tG_1; and $\mathcal{TC}_1 = \mathcal{TC} \cup \{\text{tG}_1 \geq \text{tG}_0, \text{tc}_1\}$. The function *isReceivable* checks whether the message ssb[sb[m]] can be decrypted with the keys he has in keys. Every rule has the proviso that to be applicable, the set of comparison constraints and the set of time constraints should be satisfiable.

constraints are allowed. Indeed, as we describe in Sect. 6, the number of traces is not only finite (as stated in the following Proposition), but very low (less than 40 traces).

Proposition 1. *The set of traces starting from any configuration C_0 is finite.*

Proposition 2. *Let $\tau = C_1 \xrightarrow{l_1} C_2 \xrightarrow{l_2} \cdots \xrightarrow{l_{n-1}} C_n$ be a trace. For any configuration $C_i = \langle \mathcal{P}_i, \mathcal{IK}_i, \mathcal{DC}_i, \mathcal{EQ}_i, \mathcal{TC}_i \rangle@\text{tG}_i$, such that $1 \leq i \leq n$, the following holds:*

- *For any $i \leq j \leq n$, $\mathcal{DC}_n(\mathcal{IK}_i)|_{\mathcal{EQ}_n} \subseteq \mathcal{DC}_n(\mathcal{IK}_j)|_{\mathcal{EQ}_n}$, that is, the intruder knowledge can only increase;*
- *Let sym_k be a symbol new in some C_k, $k < i$ and let sym_i be a symbol new in C_i. If $\text{dc}(\text{sym}_k, S_k), \text{dc}(\text{sym}_i, S_i) \in \mathcal{DC}_i$, then $S_k \subseteq S_i$. That is, symbols that are introduced by later transitions can be instantiated by more terms than symbols introduced at earlier transitions.*

Timed Intruders: In fact, our implementation generalizes the machinery in this section by considering multiple timed intruders [28,38]. As described in [28], the standard Dolev-Yao may not be suitable for the verification of Cyber-Physical Security Protocols where the physical properties of the environment are important. Differently from the Dolev-Yao intruder, a timed intruder needs to wait for the message to arrive before he can learn it. [38] proved an upper-bound on the number of timed intruders. Our tool implements this strategy. However, for the examples considered here, a single Dolev-Yao intruder is enough.

5 Timed Trace Equivalence

Our goal now is to determine when two configurations:

$$C_I = \langle \mathcal{P}_I, \mathcal{IK}_I, \mathcal{DC}_I, \mathcal{EQ}_I, \mathcal{TC}_I \rangle @\mathsf{tG} \text{ and } C'_I = \langle \mathcal{P}'_I, \mathcal{IK}'_I, \mathcal{DC}'_I, \mathcal{EQ}'_I, \mathcal{TC}'_I \rangle @\mathsf{tG}'$$

cannot be distinguished by the Dolev-Yao intruder. That is, for any trace starting from C_I there is *an equivalent trace* starting from C'_I. Intuitively, the intruder participates in the same interactions (sends and receives) with the same timing. The following definition specifies observables which collect the necessary information from a trace:

Definition 9. *Let* $\tau = C_1 \xrightarrow{l_1} C_2 \xrightarrow{l_2} \cdots \xrightarrow{l_{n-1}} C_n = \langle \mathcal{P}_n, \mathcal{IK}_n, \mathcal{DC}_n, \mathcal{EQ}_n, \mathcal{TC}_n \rangle @\mathsf{tG}_n$ *be a timed trace. Its observable is the tuple* $\langle \mathsf{tt}_I, \mathcal{L}_\tau, \mathcal{IK}_n, \mathcal{DC}_n, \mathcal{EQ}_n, \mathcal{TC}_n \rangle$, *where* tt_I *is the global time at configuration* C_1, $\mathcal{L}_\tau$ *is the sequence of non-empty labels in* τ. *Let* C *be a configuration. Let* $\mathcal{T}(C)$ *be the set of all traces with initial configuration* C. *The observables of* C *is* $O(C) = \{O_\tau \mid \tau \in \mathcal{T}(C)\}$, *that is, the set of all observables of traces starting from* C.

Two configurations are trace equivalent if their observables are equivalent.

Definition 10. *A configuration* C *approximates a configuration* C', *written* $C \preceq C'$ *if for any* $O \in O(C)$ *there exists an equivalent observable* $O' \in O(C')$, *that is,* $O \sim O'$ *(Definition 11). The configurations are observationally equivalent, written* $C \sim C'$, *if and only if* $C \preceq C'$ *and* $C' \preceq C$.

Definition 11. *Consider the observables* $O = \langle \mathsf{tt}_I, \mathcal{L}, \mathcal{IK}, \mathcal{DC}, \mathcal{EQ}, \mathcal{TC} \rangle @\mathsf{tG}$ *and* $O' = \langle \mathsf{tt}'_I, \mathcal{L}', \mathcal{IK}', \mathcal{DC}', \mathcal{EQ}', \mathcal{TC}' \rangle @\mathsf{tG}'$, *such that*

$$\mathcal{L} = \langle (\pm_1 \mathsf{ms}_1 @\mathsf{tG}_1) \ldots (\pm_p \mathsf{ms}_p @\mathsf{tG}_p) \rangle \text{ and } \mathcal{L}' = \langle (\pm'_1 \mathsf{ms}'_1 @\mathsf{tG}'_1) \ldots (\pm'_n \mathsf{ms}'_n @\mathsf{tG}'_n) \rangle$$

The observation O *is equivalent to* O', *written* $O \sim O'$ *if the following conditions are all true:*

1. $p = n = N$, *that is, they have the same length* N;
2. $\pm_i = \pm'_i$, *for all* $1 \leq i \leq N$, *that is, have the same label type;*
3. *The messages observed are equivalent, that is,* $\langle \mathsf{ms}_1, \ldots, \mathsf{ms}_N \rangle \sim_{O,O'} \langle \mathsf{ms}'_1, \ldots, \mathsf{ms}'_N \rangle$;
4. *Assume* $\widetilde{\mathsf{tt}}$ *and* $\widetilde{\mathsf{tt}'}$ *are the set of time symbols in* $\mathcal{TC}$ *and* $\mathcal{TC}'$, *respectively. These sets of time symbols are assumed disjoint without loss of generality. The following formulas are tautologies:*

$$\forall \widetilde{\mathsf{tt}}. \left[\mathcal{TC} \Rightarrow \exists \widetilde{\mathsf{tt}'}. \left[\mathcal{TC}' \wedge \mathsf{tG}_1 = \mathsf{tG}'_1 \wedge \cdots \wedge \mathsf{tG}_N = \mathsf{tG}'_N \right] \right]$$

$$\forall \widetilde{\mathsf{tt}'}. \left[\mathcal{TC}' \Rightarrow \exists \widetilde{\mathsf{tt}}. \left[\mathcal{TC} \wedge \mathsf{tG}_1 = \mathsf{tG}'_1 \wedge \cdots \wedge \mathsf{tG}_N = \mathsf{tG}'_N \right] \right]$$

The first two conditions are clear. If two observables differ on the number of observations or they differ on their types, then they can be distinguished. The third condition specifies that the terms observed shall be equivalent. Here, we do not specify its definition, as any definition which considers the Dolev-Yao intruder capabilities in the literature could be, in principle, used. Our technical report describes one such possible definition. Notice, however, that the knowledge of the intruder at the end of the traces shall be used, as he may have learned keys allowing him to distinguish more terms.

The fourth condition involves the timing aspects of the protocols. Intuitively, two observables are equivalent, that is, not distinguishable by the intruder, whenever the timings of when messages are observed are identical. Take the first clause below:

$$\forall \widetilde{\mathsf{tt}}. \left[\mathcal{TC} \Rightarrow \exists \widetilde{\mathsf{tt}'}. \left[\mathcal{TC}' \wedge \mathsf{tG}_1 = \mathsf{tG}_1' \wedge \cdots \wedge \mathsf{tG}_N = \mathsf{tG}_N' \right] \right]$$

It specifies that for all instances of $\widetilde{\mathsf{tt}}$ that satisfy the constraints $\mathcal{TC}$ in O, it is possible to find instances of $\widetilde{\mathsf{tt}'}$ that satisfy the constraints $\mathcal{TC}'$ in O', that is, are valid instances, and moreover, the times of the observed messages are identical.

Example. Consider the passport protocol role, $\mathcal{P}$, described in Example 5. Moreover, consider the following two initial configurations:

$$C_I = \langle [0 \mid \mathcal{P} \mid \{\mathsf{k}_M, \mathsf{k}_E\}], \{\mathsf{c}_{enc}, \mathsf{c}_{mac}\}, \emptyset, \emptyset, \mathsf{tG} = 0 \rangle @\mathsf{tG}$$
$$C_I' = \langle [0 \mid \mathcal{P} \mid \{\mathsf{k}_M, \mathsf{k}_E\}], \emptyset, \emptyset, \emptyset, \mathsf{tG}' = 0 \rangle @\mathsf{tG}'$$

where in C_I the intruder has already eavesdropped a communication between the passport and the identification machine, learning the constants, $\mathsf{c}_{enc} = \mathsf{e}(\mathsf{n}_{old}, \mathsf{k}_E)$ and $\mathsf{c}_{mac} = \mathsf{e}(\mathsf{c}_{enc}, \mathsf{k}_M)$. Notice that these messages contain a nonce generated during the first encounter of the intruder with the passport.

This means that there is a trace starting from C_I where after the passport generating a nonce, n_{new}, and sending it, the intruder responds with the pair $\{\mathsf{c}_{enc}, \mathsf{c}_{mac}\}$. At this point, the passport checks that c_{mac} is encrypted with the correct key k_M, but then it checks that c_{enc} has the wrong nonce, returning the *error* message. Thus, the observable corresponding to this trace has the following form:

$\mathcal{L} = \langle (+\mathsf{n}_{new}@\mathsf{tG}_1), (-\langle\mathsf{sym}_1, \mathsf{sym}_2\rangle)@\mathsf{tG}_2), (+error@\mathsf{tG}_6) \rangle$,
$\mathcal{IK} = \{\mathsf{c}_{enc}, \mathsf{c}_{mac}, \mathsf{n}_{new}\}, \quad \mathcal{DC} = \{\mathsf{dc}(\mathsf{sym}_1, \mathcal{IK}), \mathsf{dc}(\mathsf{sym}_2, \mathcal{IK})\}$,
$\mathcal{EQ} = \{\mathsf{eq}(\mathsf{sym}_2, \mathsf{e}(\mathsf{sym}_1, \mathsf{k}_M)), \mathsf{neq}(\mathsf{sym}_1, \mathsf{e}(\mathsf{n}_{new}, \mathsf{k}_E))\}$
$\mathcal{TC} = \{\mathsf{tG}_0 = 0, \mathsf{tt}_0 = \mathsf{tG}_2, \mathsf{tt}_1 = \mathsf{tt}_0 + r_{mac}, \mathsf{tt}_2 = \mathsf{tt}_1 + r_{enc}, \mathsf{tG}_6 = \mathsf{tt}_2\} \cup \{\mathsf{tG}_{i+1} \geq \mathsf{tG}_i \mid 0 \leq i \leq 5\}$

From the time constraints $\mathcal{TC}$, we deduce that $\mathsf{tG}_6 = r_{mac} + r_{enc} + \mathsf{tG}_2$.

On the other hand, there is only one trace from C_I', which yields the observable:

$\mathcal{L}' = \langle (+\mathsf{n}_{new}@\mathsf{tG}_1'), (-\langle\mathsf{sym}_1, \mathsf{sym}_2\rangle)@\mathsf{tG}_2'), (+error@\mathsf{tG}_3') \rangle$,
$\mathcal{IK}' = \{\mathsf{n}_{new}\}, \quad \mathcal{DC} = \{\mathsf{dc}(\mathsf{sym}_1', \mathcal{IK}'), \mathsf{dc}(\mathsf{sym}_2', \mathcal{IK}')\}$,
$\mathcal{EQ}' = \{\mathsf{neq}(\mathsf{sym}_2', \mathsf{e}(\mathsf{sym}_1, \mathsf{k}_M))\}$
$\mathcal{TC}' = \{\mathsf{tG}_0' = 0, \mathsf{tt}_0' = \mathsf{tG}_2', \mathsf{tt}_1' = \mathsf{tt}_0' + r_{mac}, \mathsf{tG}_3' = \mathsf{tt}_1'\} \cup \{\mathsf{tG}_{i+1}' \geq \mathsf{tG}_i' \mid 0 \leq i \leq 2\}$

From the time constraints $\mathcal{TC}'$, we can infer that $tG_3' = tG_2' + r_{mac}$.

Clearly, the condition on the time variables for observational equivalence cannot be satisfied, as $tG_2 = tG_2'$ and $tG_6 = tG_3'$ cannot be both satisfied.

The condition Definition 11.4 assumes a powerful intruder that can distinguish observables associated with different times, even with infinitesimal differences. This may result in false positives, as our definition would flag attacks that in practice are not possible to carry out. We can, however, relax the condition Definition 11.4· and consider observables equivalent even if the time of observables are different within some range. We replace the condition Definition 11.4 by the following:

$$\forall \widetilde{tt}. \left[\mathcal{TC} \Rightarrow \exists \widetilde{tt'}. \left[\mathcal{TC}' \wedge |tG_1 - tG_1'| \le \epsilon \wedge \cdots \wedge |tG_N = tG_N'| \le \epsilon \right] \right]$$

$$\forall \widetilde{tt'}. \left[\mathcal{TC}' \Rightarrow \exists \widetilde{tt}. \left[\mathcal{TC} \wedge |tG_1 - tG_1'| \le \epsilon \wedge \cdots \wedge |tG_N - tG_N'| \le \epsilon \right] \right]$$

The greater the value of ϵ, the weaker is the capability of the intruder to measure the timing of observables. For example, if ϵ is the time for encrypting terms, the correspondingly weak intruder could not carry out the passport attack.

5.1   Automating the Check of Time Approximation

For Condition 11.4, we reduce the formulas to formulas for which existing solvers can be used [18], namely formulas of the form $\exists \forall$:

$$\forall \widetilde{tt}. \left[\mathcal{TC} \Rightarrow \exists \widetilde{tt'}. \left[\mathcal{TC}' \wedge tG_1 = tG_1' \wedge \cdots \wedge tG_N = tG_N' \right] \right] \text{ is a tautology}$$

$$\Leftrightarrow \neg \forall \widetilde{tt}. \left[\mathcal{TC} \Rightarrow \exists \widetilde{tt'}. \left[\mathcal{TC}' \wedge tG_1 = tG_1' \wedge \cdots \wedge tG_N = tG_N' \right] \right] \text{ is unsat}$$

$$\Leftrightarrow \exists \widetilde{tt}. \left[\mathcal{TC} \wedge \forall \widetilde{tt'}. \left[\mathcal{TC}' \Rightarrow \neg \left[tG_1 = tG_1' \wedge \cdots \wedge tG_N = tG_N' \right] \right] \right] \text{ is unsat}$$

6   Experimental Results

We implemented a tool that checks for timed observational equivalence. Its architecture is depicted in Fig. 2. It is constructed using Maude [12] and the Yices SMT solver [17], coordinated by the IOP framework [30]. In particular, we use Yices for solving $\exists \forall$ formulas where all time variables have type Real (which is decidable [18]).

- **Maude:** We implemented in Maude all the machinery necessary for specifying timed protocols as well as checking the term equivalence of observables. Since Alpha version 111 Maude provides a builtin function to call an SMT solver to check satisfiability of constraints supported by the SMT API.[5] This allows the implementation of Rewriting Modulo SMT by using conditional rewrite rules that are only allowed to rewrite if the resulting constraint set is

---

[5] Initially this was implemented using CVC4 [4]. Since Alpha 114 there is also the option to use Yices2.

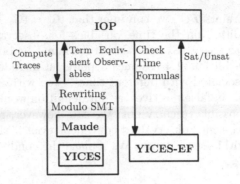

Fig. 2. Timed observational equivalence solver architecture.

satisfiable. Our rewrite rules include as a condition a call to the SMT solver to check satisfiability of the time constraints whenever firing the rule would add to the constraints.

– **YICES-EF:** Since the SMT standard interface does not provide an API for checking $\exists\forall$ formulas needed for proving time equivalence, we integrated our Maude machinery with YICES-EF, a wrapper for Yices2 that translates $\exists\forall$ formulas into the Yices2 language and calls Yices to check the satisfiability of such formulas.

Communication between Maude and YICES-EF is implemented using the IOP message passing framework [30]. Given two initial configuration C and C' to be checked for their timed trace equivalence, the user uses IOP to send a command to the Maude+Yices tool to enumerate all observables for C and C', then compute for each observable O of C the set of term-equivalent observables $\{O'_1, \ldots, O'_n\}$ of C' and vice-versa. If Maude finds some observable of C that does not have at least one match, that is, $n = 0$, C and C' are not equivalent. (Similarly for matching some C'.) Otherwise, for each O, O' match Maude asks YICES-EF to check the timing equivalence condition. If for each O there is at least one O' such that the timing equivalence condition is satisfied (YICES-EF returns Sat), then C approximates C'. In the same way, Maude also checks whether C' approximates C. If both directions succeed then the two configurations are timed trace equivalent. If either direction fails then they are not equivalent. To make the above request to YICES-EF, Maude builds (a representation of) the formula described in Sect. 5.1 for checking for the timing equivalence of O with O'_i, which is transformed by YICES-EF to Yices2 input format.

Experimental Results. We carried out the following experiments:

– **Red Pill Example:** Consider the timed protocol role specified in Example 6. We checked whether it is possible for an intruder to distinguish whether an application is running over a virtual machine or not. That is, we checked whether an initial configuration with a player running an application over a

Table 1. Experimental Results. Each experiment involves proving the timed observational equivalence of two configurations. It contains number of observables (traces) for each configuration and the total number of states in the whole search tree required to traverse to enumerate all observables.

Scenario	Result	Observables	States
Red-Pill	Not Equiv	19/19	74/74
Passport	Not Equiv	36/27	138/112
Passport-Corrected	Equiv	36/27	138/112
Anonymous	Not Equiv	2/3	7/9

virtual machine is timed equivalent to the initial configuration with a player running the same application over a non-virtual machine.

- **Passport Example:** Consider the timed protocol role specified in Example 5. We checked whether the intruder can distinguish the following two configurations both with two protocol sessions: the first where both protocol sessions are carried out with the same passport and the second where the protocol sessions are carried out with different passports.
- **Corrected Passport Example:** We additionally considered a modification of the Passport example where the timed protocol is corrected in the sense that it sends both error messages at the same time.
- **Anonymous Protocol:** Consider the timed protocol specified in Example 7. We checked whether it is possible for an intruder to distinguish whether two players belong to the same group or not. That is, we checked whether the initial configuration with a player that receives a message from a member of the same group is timed equivalent to the initial configuration with a player that receives a message from a player of a different group.

Table 1 summarizes the results of our experiments. Our tool was able to (correctly) identify the cases when the given configurations are timed observational equivalent. More impressive, however, is the number of states and observables it needed to traverse for doing so. In all experiments the number of states in the whole search tree was less than 140 states and the number of observables were less than 40. This is a very small number when compared to usual applications in Maude (which can handle thousands of states even when using Rewriting Modulo SMT [38]). This demonstrates the advantage of representing timing symbolically. As expected the number of observables for the passport example were greater as its configurations had two protocol sessions, while in the remaining experiments configurations have only one protocol session. Finally, since the number of observables was small, the number of calls to Yices was small and therefore, verification for all experiments took less than a few seconds.

7   Related and Future Work

In this paper we introduce a novel definition of timed trace equivalence for security protocols using symbolic time constraints. We demonstrate how symbolic time equivalence can be proved automatically with the use of Rewriting Modulo SMT and existing SMT-solvers assuming a bounded number of protocol sessions. The combination of such constraints with Rewriting Modulo SMT greatly reduces the number of states required to enumerate all traces. We implemented the machinery for proving the timed observational equivalence and showed experimentally with some proof-of-concept examples that our technique is practical.

For future work, we will be integrating the machinery developed here with the Maude's generic unification capability [16] which can be used for the analysis of security protocols that use a wide range of crypto algebras and weaker notions of encryption. This will take advantage of the independence of the symbolic message constraints and the time constraints.

In our current approach, we verify scenarios with a bounded number of protocol sessions. We are investigating how to adapt techniques, such as Narrowing used in Maude-NPA [19], to support time constraints.

We are also investigating notions of timed observational equivalence and their relation to the timed trace equivalence proposed here. It seems possible to define timed observational equivalence by using the intruder upper bound result in our previous work [38] with the notion of trace equivalence towards the definition of a notion of timed observational equivalence, *i.e.*, with quantificaion over intruder contexts, that can be solved using SMT-solvers.

Furthermore, we plan to investigate how to use SMT solvers in order to answer questions such as, what is the weakest intruder that can carry out an attack. In particular, given the more relaxed notion of time equivalence described at the end of Sect. 5, we can consider ϵ as a variable to be maximized by an SMT optimizer.

Related Work: The literature on symbolic verification is vast [5,9,14,19,21]. However, most of this work uses symbolic reasoning for proving either reachability properties or properties not involving timing aspects.

One exception is the work of [14]. Indeed, for the observational equivalence involving terms, we have been heavily inspired by [14], but there are some differences. The main difference is that our timed protocols includes both message and time symbols. We also implemented our machinery for term equivalence in Maude and use SMT-solvers for search (Rewriting Modulo SMT) and proving the timing equivalence.

Cheval and Cortier [10] propose a definition of timed equivalence reducing it to other notions of equivalence taking into account the length of messages. We take a different approach by using timed constraints and SMT-Solvers. This allows us to relate time symbols using inequalities, *e.g.*, $tt_1 \geq tt_2 + 10$, which can be solved by off-the-shelf SMT solvers. Moreover, time constraints can also specify timing aspects not directly related to the length of messages, such as, the properties used in Distance Bounding protocols. Finally, as we illustrate one can also define coarser definitions of time equivalence, involving intruders with weaker time measuring mechanisms, potentially leading to less false positives.

Gazeau *et al.* [21] demonstrate how to automate the proof of observational equivalence of protocols that may contain branching and xor. While we allow for branching, we do not yet consider theories involving xor. However, we do consider timing aspects, which is not considered in [21]. Thus these works are complementary. As described above, we expect in the future to support xor (and other equational theories) by using the built-in Maude matching and unification functionality [16].

Finally, there have been other frameworks for the verification of timing properties of systems [6,20,24,27,29]. A main difference is that the properties verified were reachability properties and not equivalence notions involving timing aspects.

Acknowledgments. We thank the anonymous reviewer for careful reading and helpful suggestions for improvement. Nigam was partially supported by NRL grant N0017317-1-G002 and by CNPq grant 303909/2018-8. Talcott was partly supported by ONR grant N00014-15-1-2202 and NRL grant N0017317-1-G002.

References

1. Abadi, M., Fournet, C.: Private authentication. Theor. Comput. Sci. **322**(3), 427–476 (2004)
2. Agha, G., Mason, I.A., Smith, S.F., Talcott, C.L.: A foundation for actor computation. J. Funct. Program. **7**, 1–72 (1997)
3. Arapinis, M., Chothia, T., Ritter, E., Ryan, M.: Analysing unlinkability and anonymity using the applied pi calculus. In: Proceedings of the 23rd IEEE Computer Security Foundations Symposium, CSF 2010, Edinburgh, United Kingdom, 17–19 July 2010, pp. 107–121 (2010)
4. Barrett, C., et al.: CVC4. In: Gopalakrishnan, G., Qadeer, S. (eds.) CAV 2011. LNCS, vol. 6806, pp. 171–177. Springer, Heidelberg (2011). https://doi.org/10.1007/978-3-642-22110-1_14
5. Basin, D., Sebastian Mödersheim, L.V.: OFMC: a symbolic model checker for security protocols. Int. J. Inf. Secur. (2004). https://doi.org/10.1007/s10207-004-0055-7
6. Bella, G., Paulson, L.C.: Kerberos version IV: inductive analysis of the secrecy goals. In: Quisquater, J.-J., Deswarte, Y., Meadows, C., Gollmann, D. (eds.) ESORICS 1998. LNCS, vol. 1485, pp. 361–375. Springer, Heidelberg (1998). https://doi.org/10.1007/BFb0055875
7. Benton, N., Hofmann, M., Nigam, V.: Effect-dependent transformations for concurrent programs. In: Proceedings of the 18th International Symposium on Principles and Practice of Declarative Programming, 5–7 September 2016, Edinburgh, United Kingdom, pp. 188–201 (2016)
8. Brands, S., Chaum, D.: Distance-bounding protocols (extended abstract). In: EUROCRYPT, pp. 344–359 (1993)
9. Cervesato, I., Durgin, N.A., Lincoln, P., Mitchell, J.C., Scedrov, A.: A meta-notation for protocol analysis. In: CSFW, pp. 55–69 (1999)

10. Cheval, V., Cortier, V.: Timing attacks in security protocols: symbolic framework and proof techniques. In: Focardi, R., Myers, A. (eds.) POST 2015. LNCS, vol. 9036, pp. 280–299. Springer, Heidelberg (2015). https://doi.org/10.1007/978-3-662-46666-7_15

11. Chothia, T., Smirnov, V.: A traceability attack against e-passports. In: Sion, R. (ed.) FC 2010. LNCS, vol. 6052, pp. 20–34. Springer, Heidelberg (2010). https://doi.org/10.1007/978-3-642-14577-3_5

12. Clavel, M., et al.: All About Maude - A High-Performance Logical Framework. LNCS, vol. 4350. Springer, Heidelberg (2007). https://doi.org/10.1007/978-3-540-71999-1

13. Corin, R., Etalle, S., Hartel, P.H., Mader, A.: Timed model checking of security protocols. In: Proceedings of the 2004 ACM Workshop on Formal Methods in Security Engineering, FMSE 2004, New York, NY, USA, pp. 23–32. ACM (2004)

14. Cortier, V., Delaune, S.: A method for proving observational equivalence. In: Proceedings of the 22nd IEEE Computer Security Foundations Symposium, CSF 2009, Port Jefferson, New York, USA, 8–10 July 2009, pp. 266–276 (2009)

15. Dolev, D., Yao, A.: On the security of public key protocols. IEEE Trans. Inf. Theory 29(2), 198–208 (1983)

16. Durán, F., Eker, S., Escobar, S., Martí-Oliet, N., Meseguer, J., Talcott, C.: Built-in variant generation and unification, and their applications in Maude 2.7. In: Olivetti, N., Tiwari, A. (eds.) IJCAR 2016. LNCS (LNAI), vol. 9706, pp. 183–192. Springer, Cham (2016). https://doi.org/10.1007/978-3-319-40229-1_13

17. Biere, A., Bloem, R. (eds.): CAV 2014. LNCS, vol. 8559. Springer, Cham (2014). https://doi.org/10.1007/978-3-319-08867-9

18. Dutertre, B.: Solving exists/forall problems with yices. In: SMT (2015)

19. Escobar, S., Meadows, C., Meseguer, J.: Maude-NPA: cryptographic protocol analysis modulo equational properties. In: Aldini, A., Barthe, G., Gorrieri, R. (eds.) FOSAD 2007-2009. LNCS, vol. 5705, pp. 1–50. Springer, Heidelberg (2009). https://doi.org/10.1007/978-3-642-03829-7_1

20. Evans, N., Schneider, S.: Analysing time dependent security properties in CSP using PVS. In: Cuppens, F., Deswarte, Y., Gollmann, D., Waidner, M. (eds.) ESORICS 2000. LNCS, vol. 1895, pp. 222–237. Springer, Heidelberg (2000). https://doi.org/10.1007/10722599_14

21. Gazeau, I., Kremer, S.: Automated analysis of equivalence properties for security protocols using else branches. In: Foley, S.N., Gollmann, D., Snekkenes, E. (eds.) ESORICS 2017. LNCS, vol. 10493, pp. 1–20. Springer, Cham (2017). https://doi.org/10.1007/978-3-319-66399-9_1

22. González-Burgueño, A., Aparicio-Sánchez, D., Escobar, S., Meadows, C.A., Meseguer, J.: Formal verification of the YubiKey and YubiHSM APIs in Maude-NPA. In: 22nd International Conference on Logic for Programming, Artificial Intelligence and Reasoning, pp. 400–417 (2018)

23. González-Burgueño, A., Santiago, S., Escobar, S., Meadows, C.A., Meseguer, J.: Analysis of the PKCS#11 API using the Maude-NPA tool. In: Proceedings of the Security Standardisation Research - Second International Conference, SSR 2015, Tokyo, Japan, 15–16 December 2015, pp. 86–106 (2015)

24. Gorrieri, R., Locatelli, E., Martinelli, F.: A simple language for real-time cryptographic protocol analysis. In: Degano, P. (ed.) ESOP 2003. LNCS, vol. 2618, pp. 114–128. Springer, Heidelberg (2003). https://doi.org/10.1007/3-540-36575-3_9

25. Gunter, C.A.: Semantics of Programming Languages - Structures and Techniques. Foundations of Computing. MIT Press, Cambridge (1993)

26. Ho, G., Boneh, D., Ballard, L., Provos, N.: Tick tock: building browser red pills from timing side channels. In: Bratus, S., Lindner, F.F.X. (eds.) 8th USENIX Workshop on Offensive Technologies, WOOT 2014 (2014)
27. Jakubowska, G., Penczek, W.: Modelling and checking timed authentication of security protocols. Fundam. Inf. **79**(3–4), 363–378 (2007)
28. Kanovich, M.I., Kirigin, T.B., Nigam, V., Scedrov, A., Talcott, C.L.: Towards timed models for cyber-physical security protocols (2014). Available in Nigam's homepage
29. Kanovich, M.I., Kirigin, T.B., Nigam, V., Scedrov, A., Talcott, C.L., Perovic, R.: A rewriting framework for activities subject to regulations. In: 23rd International Conference on Rewriting Techniques and Applications (RTA 2012), Nagoya, Japan, 28 May–2 June 2012, pp. 305–322 (2012)
30. Mason, I.A., Talcott, C.L.: IOP: The interoperability platform & IMaude: an interactive extension of Maude. In: Fifth International Workshop on Rewriting Logic and Its Applications (WRLA 2004). Electronic Notes in Theoretical Computer Science. Elsevier (2004)
31. Meadows, C.: The NRL protocol analyzer: an overview. J. Logic Program. **26**(2), 113–131 (1996)
32. Meadows, C.A.: Analysis of the internet key exchange protocol using the NRL protocol analyzer. In: 1999 IEEE Symposium on Security and Privacy, pp. 216–231 (1999)
33. Meadows, C.A.: A cost-based framework for analysis of denial of service networks. J. Comput. Secur. **9**(1/2), 143–164 (2001)
34. Meadows, C.A., Poovendran, R., Pavlovic, D., Chang, L., Syverson, P.F.: Distance bounding protocols: authentication logic analysis and collusion attacks. In: Secure Localization and Time Synchronization for Wireless Sensor and Ad Hoc Networks, pp. 279–298 (2007)
35. Milner, R.: Communicating and Mobile Systems - The Pi-Calculus. Cambridge University Press, Cambridge (1999)
36. Needham, R.M., Schroeder, M.D.: Using encryption for authentication in large networks of computers. Commun. ACM **21**(12), 993–999 (1978). https://doi.org/10.1145/359657.359659
37. Nigam, V., Talcott, C., Urquiza, A.A.: Symbolic timed observational equivalence (2018). https://arxiv.org/abs/1801.04066
38. Nigam, V., Talcott, C., Aires Urquiza, A.: Towards the automated verification of cyber-physical security protocols: bounding the number of timed intruders. In: Askoxylakis, I., Ioannidis, S., Katsikas, S., Meadows, C. (eds.) ESORICS 2016. LNCS, vol. 9879, pp. 450–470. Springer, Cham (2016). https://doi.org/10.1007/978-3-319-45741-3_23
39. Rocha, C.: Symbolic reachability analysis for rewrite theories. Ph.D. thesis, University of Illinois at Urbana-Champagne (2012)
40. Santiago, S., Escobar, S., Meadows, C., Meseguer, J.: A formal definition of protocol indistinguishability and its verification using Maude-NPA. In: Mauw, S., Jensen, C.D. (eds.) STM 2014. LNCS, vol. 8743, pp. 162–177. Springer, Cham (2014). https://doi.org/10.1007/978-3-319-11851-2_11

Symbolic Analysis of Identity-Based Protocols

David Basin[1], Lucca Hirschi[2], and Ralf Sasse[1(✉)]

[1] Department of Computer Science, ETH Zurich, Zurich, Switzerland
`{basin,ralf.sasse}@inf.ethz.ch`
[2] Inria & LORIA, Nancy, France
`lucca.hirschi@inria.fr`

Dedicated to Catherine Meadows on her 65th Birthday.

Abstract. We show how the TAMARIN tool can be used to model and reason about security protocols using identity-based cryptography, including identity-based encryption and signatures. Although such protocols involve rather different primitives than conventional public-key cryptography, we illustrate how suitable abstractions and TAMARIN's support for equational theories can be used to model and analyze realistic industry protocols, either finding flaws or gaining confidence in their security with respect to different classes of adversaries.

Technically, we propose two models of identity-based cryptography. First, we formalize an abstract model, based on simple equations, in which verification of realistic protocols is feasible. Second, we formalize a more precise model, leveraging TAMARIN's support for bilinear pairing and exclusive-or. This model is much closer to practical realizations of identity-based cryptography, but deduction is substantially more complex. Along the way, we point out the limits of precise modeling and highlight challenges in providing support for equational reasoning. We also evaluate our models on an industrial protocol where we find and fix flaws.

1 Introduction

Context and Problem Statement. Networked information systems are deeply embedded in modern society. Communication, finance, energy distribution, transport, and even our social lives all critically depend on their correct and secure operation. In such domains, the use of cryptographic protocols is essential, but such protocols require predistributed secrets and this in turn necessitates key distribution and management. In general, security does not come for free: you need pre-established secrets to create new secrets, needed to protect communication.

For application domains where not all parties know each other and may not have pre-established relationships, a starting point is to use cryptographic

This work was done while the second author was also at ETH Zurich.

J. D. Guttman et al. (Eds.): Meadows Festschrift, LNCS 11565, pp. 112–134, 2019.
https://doi.org/10.1007/978-3-030-19052-1_9

protocols based on asymmetric cryptography to bootstrap security associations. This requires the use of public keys, which are authentically distributed using a public key infrastructure (PKI). This approach underpins the modern web. Website owners generate private/public key pairs and Certificate Authorities (CAs) sign certificates stating that the public key belongs to the entity controlling the website. The certificates are then used by web clients in security protocols like TLS to authenticate servers and setup the additional keys used to secure client-server communication. Although theoretically pleasing, this approach is prone to problems in practice, as amply documented in the literature.

An intriguing alternative is *identity-based cryptography* [25], where each participant is assigned a public key based on her public identity. The corresponding private key is generated by an entity running a *private key generator* (PKG). Identity-based cryptography therefore has a different setup, with different primitives and different assumptions than traditional public-key cryptography. For example, the PKG (not the participant) computes the private keys, which enables private key escrow, and the PKG must therefore be trusted not to reveal these keys.

Formal methods, in particular those based on a symbolic model of cryptography, have been shown to be effective for reasoning about cryptographic protocols built from standard primitives like symmetric and asymmetric encryption and the PKI setup explained before. Our focus in this paper is to explore their use in the context of identity-based cryptography. We present a case study on formalizing and analyzing identity-based cryptographic primitives and protocols based on them. Our emphasis is on how, with the right modeling language and deduction support, one can easily formalize such primitives and explore associated protocols. In this way, one can quickly identify design issues, clarify trust assumptions, and produce security proofs.

Contribution. We present the first symbolic models of identity-based cryptography. We present an abstract model that captures the basic functionality of identity-based signatures and encryption. This model is parametric and can be used for signatures, encryption, and their combination. Afterwards, we present a second, more precise, model based on a symbolic model of bilinear pairings (BP). Pairings are often used to realize identity-based cryptography and thus this model captures more of the cryptographic details found in implementations, which can be potentially exploited by an adversary.

We exemplify the use of both models with a simple protocol, and show the limitations of the precise model in terms of efficient deduction. Afterwards, we use the abstract model for a case study analyzing different versions of an industry-proposed protocol for identity-based Authentication and Key Agreement (AKA). The protocol combines key agreement based on bilinear pairing supporting key escrow, and identity-based signatures. Using TAMARIN, we find numerous weaknesses. After fixing these weaknesses, we prove the security of the resulting protocol in our abstract model.

Related Work. We will discuss identity-based cryptography in detail in Sect. 2. Here we focus on symbolic analysis and provide some historical background.

The use of tools for the symbolic analysis of security protocols has a long history starting with Millen's Interrogator [22], the Longley–Rigby search tool [18], and Meadow's NRL Protocol Analyzer (NRLPA) [19]. These tools were based on a *symbolic model* of cryptography going back to the seminal work of Dolev and Yao [13], which represents cryptographic operations within a term algebra that is amenable to efficient mechanized proof. The early tools constituted proto-model checkers. Indeed the NRLPA offered many features of a modern model checker, including an automated means of proving that exhaustive search of a finite state space implied exhaustive search of the infinite state space, and later, a temporal logic language, NPATRL [26], for describing protocol security properties. A good overview of symbolic security protocol analysis is available in an article in the Handbook of Model Checking by Basin, Cremers, and Meadows [5].

The current generation of tools includes the spiritual successor to the NRLPA tool, Maude-NPA [16], which follows the same basic ideas but is built on backwards narrowing within Maude [11]. Our tool of choice is TAMARIN [20, 23], which uses a combination of constraint solving, as introduced by Millen and Shmatikov [21], as well as backwards search as in Maude-NPA. We will provide further details in Sect. 3, in particular for TAMARIN.

Outline. We introduce identity-based cryptography in Sect. 2. Afterwards we provide background on security protocol analysis in the symbolic model in Sect. 3. We present our symbolic model for identity-based cryptography in Sect. 4 and our case study in Sect. 5. We draw conclusions in Sect. 6.

2   Identity-Based Cryptography

Identity-based cryptography was proposed by Shamir [25] in the early 1980s. Realizations of an identity-based signature scheme quickly followed [17], whereas a realization of an encryption scheme took longer and was first proposed by Boneh and Franklin [9] in 2001. The basic idea, found in all realizations, has a feature that makes the use of identity-based cryptography less attractive than public-key cryptography in many settings: intrinsic key escrow.[1] In identity-based cryptography, the private key generation center stores a master secret that it uses to create the private keys for all participants. This is deeply embedded into identity-based cryptography although there have been proposals to split the master secret, using secret sharing schemes, so that there are multiple private key generators instead of one. However no such trust-reduction mechanisms have found wide-spread use. The public key of any participant can be generated using the public master key and the participant's name. Thus, only the public master key needs to be authentically distributed, not individual public keys.

We shall first describe abstract signature and encryption schemes, and then present some realizations. Our account here closely follows [2].

---

[1] There are settings where key escrow may be desirable or even required, for example due to legal reasons. In such cases, identity-based cryptography fits perfectly.

2.1 Signature Scheme

An Identity-based Signature (IBS) scheme relies on a trusted party, called the *private key generator* (PKG), for generating users' private signature keys. Users are identified by their id, which can be their name, an email address, or other uniquely identifying information. The PKG is also in charge of assigning private keys, which are bound to the identities id of the appropriate users, while the master public key can be freely distributed. The PKG must therefore adopt appropriate authentication methods to verify that a user can claim a given identity id.

In terms of functionality, an IBS scheme should offer the following functions:

- Setup() $\mapsto$ $\mathsf{sk}_M, \mathsf{pk}_M$: The PKG creates its master private and public keys sk_M and pk_M, where pk_M can be made public to all users.
- KeyRequest(id) $\mapsto$ $\mathsf{sk}_{\mathsf{id}}$: A user with the identity id requests a private signature key from the PKG. Upon authenticating the user, the PKG creates a signing key $\mathsf{sk}_{\mathsf{id}}$ associated to id and sends it to the user.
- SignatureGeneration($\mathsf{sk}_{\mathsf{id}}, m$) $\mapsto$ $\sigma_{m,\mathsf{id}}$: A user with the signing key $\mathsf{sk}_{\mathsf{id}}$ produces a signature $\sigma_{m,\mathsf{id}}$ for the message m.
- SignatureVerification($\sigma, m, \mathsf{id}, \mathsf{pk}_M$) $\mapsto$ yes/no: Anyone possessing a signature σ supposedly signed by a user with the identity id for the message m can verify the signature using id (and pk_M).

Note that users can verify signatures without prior knowledge of any user-specific verification keys; only the master public key pk_M and the supposed signer's id are required.

Example 1 (Running example). We shall use a simple, signed, challenge response protocol as a running example throughout the paper. We illustrate how an IBS scheme can be used to implement such a protocol in Fig. 1. In this protocol, Alice challenges Bob with a random nonce c and a signature on (Alice, Bob, c), and then expects to receive from Bob a valid signature on the nonce c.

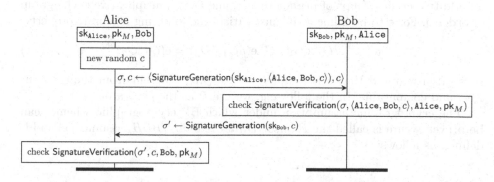

Fig. 1. Protocol flow of our running example.

2.2   Encryption Scheme

Just like IBS schemes, Identity-based Encryption (IBE) schemes rely on a PKG for generating private decryption keys. IBE schemes offer the following functions:

- Setup() $\mapsto$ $\mathsf{sk}_M, \mathsf{pk}_M$: The PKG creates its master private and public keys sk_M and pk_M, where pk_M can be made public to all users.
- KeyRequest(id) $\mapsto$ $\mathsf{sk}_{\mathsf{id}}$: A user with identity id requests a private decryption key from the PKG. Upon authenticating the user, the PKG creates a decryption key $\mathsf{sk}_{\mathsf{id}}$ associated to id and sends it to the user.
- Encryption(id, m, pk_M) $\mapsto$ $\{m\}_{\mathsf{id}}$: Anyone possessing id (and pk_M) produces a ciphertext $\{m\}_{\mathsf{id}}$ that can be decrypted only with $\mathsf{sk}_{\mathsf{id}}$.
- Decryption($\{m\}_{\mathsf{id}}, \mathsf{sk}_{\mathsf{id}}$) $\mapsto$ m: A user with the decryption key $\mathsf{sk}_{\mathsf{id}}$ decrypts a ciphertext $\{m\}_{\mathsf{id}}$ that has been encrypted with identity id (and pk_M).

Note that users can encrypt messages for other users without prior knowledge of any encryption keys; only pk_M and id are required. The intention is that decryption can only be performed by the user whose identity is id, as she is the only one to receive the associated private key. In contrast, conventional PKIs require users to request, and authentically receive, public keys of the intended recipients before encryption.

Example 2 (Continuing Example 1). One can use an IBE scheme to implement a challenge response mechanism as follows: Alice sends a random nonce encrypted with Bob's public key and then expects to receive the nonce c in plaintext.

2.3   Realization Using Bilinear Pairing

Many recent IBE and IBS schemes are implemented using bilinear pairing [2]. We briefly recall bilinear pairing and explain its use in two identity-based schemes.

Bilinear Pairing. Let $\mathsf{e} : G \times G \mapsto G'$ be a symmetric bilinear mapping for G, an additive cyclic group[2] of prime order q, and G' a multiplicative cyclic group of order q. For e to be bilinear, it must satisfy the following algebraic property:

$$\forall a, b \in \mathbb{F}_{\mathsf{q}}^*. \forall Q_1, Q_2 \in G. \ \mathsf{e}(aQ_1, bQ_2) = \mathsf{e}(Q_1, Q_2)^{ab}. \tag{1}$$

It is often required that e is non-degenerate (*i.e.*, different from the constant $\mathbb{1}_{G'}$) and computable. In the following, we use P as the generator.

The cryptographic assumption under which BP cryptographic schemes can be proven secure is called the *Bilinear Diffie-Hellman (BDH)* assumption and is defined as follows:

---

[2] In general, bilinear pairings can take values in two different groups, provided that they are of the same order. For simplicity and because our formal model will eventually require it, we only present bilinear pairing taking values in the same group.

BDH: Given $(G, \mathsf{q}, \mathsf{e}, P, aP, bP, cP)$ where G, q, and e are as specified above and where $P \in G$ and a, b, c are chosen at random from $\mathbb{F}_\mathsf{q}^*$, it is infeasible to compute $\mathsf{e}(P, P)^{abc}$.

Note that the BDH assumption is relevant for computational proofs, which manipulate bitstrings, probabilities, and probabilistic-polynomial time computations. Working in such a *computational model* typically necessitates manual proofs. In contrast we work in the *symbolic model* using a term representation and that is amenable to automated proofs. The guarantees one gets from the computational model are generally considered more fine-grained. However, given that they require time-consuming manual proof construction, computational proofs do not in practice cover entire protocols with all their modes and options. Compare, for example, the computational proofs for TLS 1.3 (e.g., [14]), which cover single modes only, to the symbolic proofs using TAMARIN that cover the interaction of all modes and the protocol's entire internal state machine [12].

Since we work in the symbolic model, we are only interested in capturing algebraic properties of cryptographic primitives; *i.e.*, Eq. 1 for bilinear pairing. As we later see, this equation can be directly modelled in TAMARIN.

BP-Based IBE Scheme by Boneh and Franklin [9]. Let the following be given: a plaintext length $l \in \mathbb{N}$, a set of identities identities, and two hash functions $h_1 :$ identities $\mapsto G^*$ and $h_2 : G' \mapsto \{0,1\}^l$. Using the pairing function e, the IBE functionalities are then implemented as follows:

- Setup() $\mapsto$ sk$_M$, pk$_M$: The PKG picks s at random in $\mathbb{F}_\mathsf{q}^*$ and computes sk$_M :=$ s and pk$_M := sP$, where P is a generator in G.
- KeyRequest(id) $\mapsto$ sk$_{id}$: Upon reception of id, the PKG creates a private decryption key sk$_{id} :=$ sk$_M Q_{id}$, where $Q_{id} := h_1(\text{id})$.
- Encryption(id, pk$_M$, m) $\mapsto \{m\}_{id}$: To encrypt a message $m \in \{0,1\}^l$ using id and pk$_M$, a user picks r at random from $\mathbb{F}_\mathsf{q}^*$, computes $U = rP$ and $V = h_2(\mathsf{e}(Q_{id}, \text{pk}_M)^r) \oplus m$, where $\oplus$ denotes the eXclusive-OR (XOR) operator. The ciphertext is $\{m\}_{id} := (U, V)$.
- Decryption($\{m\}_{id}$, sk$_{id}$) $\mapsto m$: A user possessing sk$_{id} =$ sk$_M Q_{id}$ can decrypt $\{m\}_{id} := (U, V)$ by computing $V \oplus h_2(\mathsf{e}(\text{sk}_{id}, U)) = (h_2(\mathsf{e}(Q_{id}, \text{sk}_M P)^r) \oplus m) \oplus h_2(\mathsf{e}(\text{sk}_M Q_{id}, rP)) = m$.

We show in Sect. 4.2 how this scheme can be modelled in TAMARIN.

BP-Based IBS Scheme by Choon and Cheon [10]. This IBS scheme uses the hash function h_1 described above and an additional hash function $h_3 : \{0,1\}^* \times G \mapsto \mathbb{F}_\mathsf{q}^*$. The IBS functionalities are then implemented as follows, also using e:

- Setup() $\mapsto$ sk$_M$, pk$_M$: The PKG picks s at random in $\mathbb{F}_\mathsf{q}^*$ and computes sk$_M :=$ s and pk$_M := sP$, where P is a generator in G.
- KeyRequest(id) $\mapsto$ sk$_{id}$: Upon reception of id, the PKG creates a private signing key sk$_{id} :=$ sk$_M Q_{id}$, where $Q_{id} := h_1(\text{id})$.

- SignatureGeneration($\mathsf{sk_{id}}, m$) $\mapsto \sigma_{m,\mathsf{id}}$: A user with the signing key $\mathsf{sk_{id}}$ can sign a message $m \in \{0,1\}^*$ by picking an $r \in \mathbb{F}_q^*$ at random and computing: $U = rQ_{\mathsf{id}}$, $V = (r + h_3(m,U))\mathsf{sk_{id}}$, and, $\sigma_{m,\mathsf{id}} = (U,V)$, where $+$ is addition in $\mathbb{F}_q^*$.
- SignatureVerification($\sigma_{m,\mathsf{id}}, m, \mathsf{id}, \mathsf{pk}_M$) $\mapsto$ yes/no: Anyone having the signature $\sigma_{m,\mathsf{id}} := (U,V)$ supposedly signed by the user with the identity id can verify the signature using pk_M and id by checking whether $\mathsf{e}(P,V) =^?$ $\mathsf{e}(\mathsf{pk}_M, U + h_3(m,U) \cdot Q_{\mathsf{id}})$. Indeed if $\sigma_{m,\mathsf{id}}$ is a genuine signature, then:

$$\begin{aligned}
\mathsf{e}(P,V) &= \mathsf{e}(P, (r + h_3(m,U))\mathsf{sk_{id}}) \\
&= \mathsf{e}(P, \mathsf{sk}_M \cdot (r + h_3(m,U)) \cdot Q_{\mathsf{id}}) \\
&= \mathsf{e}(\mathsf{pk}_M, r \cdot Q_{\mathsf{id}} + h_3(m,U) \cdot Q_{\mathsf{id}}) \\
&= \mathsf{e}(\mathsf{pk}_M, U + h_3(m,U) \cdot Q_{\mathsf{id}}).
\end{aligned}$$

We shall see in Sect. 4.2 that the algebraic properties involved in this scheme are too complex to automate reasoning about using state-of-the art verification tools. This is the main reason why we also explore in Sect. 4.1 a less precise abstraction of IBS schemes that we can more efficiently reason about.

We summarize next the symbolic model of protocol analysis in Sect. 3, before applying it to identity-based cryptography in Sect. 4.

3   Symbolic Analysis of Protocols

In this section, we briefly introduce the symbolic model for security protocols and the tool TAMARIN which automates reasoning in this model. We also describe how security properties are modeled using TAMARIN.

3.1   The TAMARIN Prover

TAMARIN is a state-of-the-art protocol verification tool that automates reasoning in the *symbolic model* of cryptographic protocols. TAMARIN supports stateful protocols specified using a large collection of equationally defined operators, including bilinear pairing. It has previously been applied to numerous real-world protocols with complex state machines, numerous messages, and complex security properties such as TLS 1.3 [12] and 5G-AKA [6].

In the symbolic model, messages are described as terms. For example, $enc(m,k)$ represents the message m encrypted using the key k. The algebraic properties of the cryptographic functions are then specified using equations over terms. For example, the equation $dec(enc(m,k),k) = m$ specifies the expected property of symmetric encryption: decryption with the encryption key k yields the plaintext m. As is common in the symbolic model, cryptographic messages do not satisfy other properties than those specified by explicit algebraic properties. This reflects the so-called *black box cryptography assumption*: one cannot exploit potential weaknesses in the cryptographic primitives themselves. TAMARIN also supports further algebraic properties, including hashing, XOR, Diffie-Hellman, and bilinear pairing.

In TAMARIN, a protocol is described using multiset rewrite rules. These rules manipulate multisets of *facts*, with *terms* as arguments, which model the system's state.

Example 3. The following rules describe a simple protocol that sends a MACed message. The first rule creates a new long-term shared key k (the fact !Ltk is *persistent*: it can be used as a premise multiple times). The second rule describes the agent A who sends a fresh message m together with its MAC with the shared key k to B. Finally, the third rule describes B, who is expecting as input a message and a corresponding MAC with k. Note that the third rule can only be triggered if the input matches the premise, *i.e.*, if the input message is correctly MACed with k.

$$Create\_Ltk : [\mathsf{Fr}(k)] \dashv [\ ] \mapsto [!\mathsf{Ltk}(k)],$$
$$Send\_A : [!\mathsf{Ltk}(k), \mathsf{Fr}(m)] \dashv \mathsf{Sent}(m) \mapsto [\mathsf{Out}(\langle m, mac(m, k)\rangle)],$$
$$Receive\_B : [!\mathsf{Ltk}(k), \mathsf{In}(\langle m, mac(m, k)\rangle)] \dashv \mathsf{Received}(m) \mapsto [\ ]$$

These rules (written $[l] \dashv [\ a\ ] \mapsto [r]$ with a the actions) yield a labeled transition system describing the possible protocol executions (see [1, 23] for details on TAMARIN's syntax and semantics), where the traces are sequences of the action labels. TAMARIN combines the rules formalizing the protocol with rules formalizing a Dolev-Yao [13] style adversary. This adversary controls the entire network and can thereby intercept, delete, modify, delay, inject, and build new messages. However, the adversary is limited by the cryptography: he cannot forge signatures or decrypt messages without knowing the key due to the black box cryptography assumption. He can nevertheless apply any function, e.g., hashing, XOR, encryption, pairing, etc., to messages he knows and thus compute new messages.

3.2 Formalizing Security Properties in TAMARIN

In TAMARIN, security properties are specified in two ways. First, trace properties, such as secrecy or variants of authentication, are specified using formulas in a first-order logic with timepoints. Second, equivalence properties, e.g., for unlinkability, can be given as *diff-terms* [7]; these are not considered in this paper.

Example 4. Consider the multiset rewrite rules given in Example 3. The following property specifies a form of non-injective agreement on the message m, *i.e.*, that any message received by B was previously sent by A:

$$\forall i, m.Received(m)@i \Rightarrow (\exists j.Sent(m)@j \wedge j < i).$$

For each specified property, TAMARIN checks that the property holds for all possible protocol executions and all possible adversary behaviors. To achieve this, TAMARIN explores all possible executions in a backward manner, searching for reachable attack states, which are counterexamples to the security properties.

In fully automatic mode, TAMARIN either returns a proof that the property holds, or a counterexample representing an attack if the property is violated. It may also fail to terminate, which is unsurprising given that the underlying problem is undecidable. TAMARIN can also be used in an interactive mode where the user can guide the proof search. Moreover, the user can supply heuristics called *oracles* to guide the proof search in a sound way.

4   Modeling Identity-Based Cryptography

We now show how identity-based cryptography can be modeled symbolically and how protocols that use the associated cryptographic primitives can be analyzed.

We first present an abstract model in Sect. 4.1 that captures, at a high-level, the intended algebraic properties of identity-based schemes as described in Sects. 2.1 and 2.2. Although abstract, this model suffices to identify nontrivial logical attacks, as illustrated by our case study in Sect. 5.

In practice, many identity-based schemes are based on bilinear pairings and thus have additional algebraic properties (see Sect. 2.3) that can be exploited by the adversary. We therefore provide a second, more concrete model in Sect. 4.2, inspired by the state-of-the-art, bilinear pairing-based, identity-based schemes described in Sect. 2.3. Unsurprisingly, protocols formalized in this second model are harder to reason about. As we shall see, we reach TAMARIN's limits, which suggests that our abstract model is a good compromise.

Note that for each of our two identity-based cryptography models, we provide a TAMARIN model [8] that illustrates its use on our running example (Example 1 for IBS and Example 2 for IBE).

4.1   Abstract Model of Identity-Based Schemes

We now present a parametric model of Identity-Based Schemes, formalized in TAMARIN. Most of this model is parametric in the type of scheme (IBE or IBS). We first describe our model of IBS and afterwards explain the main differences with our model of IBE.

Modeling IBS Schemes. Our abstract model of the *private key generator*'s (PKG) capabilities consists of a user-defined equational theory together with setup and initialization rules that generate the identity-based signing private master key and sets up users with their private keys.

The equational theory of Sign-PKG with its signature and equation is depicted in Fig. 2. Here, `idsign` models identity-based signing, `idverify` models signature verification, and `IBMasterPubK` is the operator deriving the master public key from the master private key. The signature also includes the function `IBPriv` used by the PKG to provision a user with a private key (as this provisioning requires the private master key) and the function `IBPub` that derives public keys from identities. The single equation guarantees that a properly created signature can be successfully validated by anyone holding the signer's name and

```
functions: IBPriv/2, IBPub/2, IBMasterPubK/1,                    1
           idsign/2, idverify/3, true/0                          2
equations: idverify(idsign(m,IBPriv(A, IBMasterPrivK)),          3
              m,                                                  4
              IBPub(A, IBMasterPubK(IBMasterPrivK))) = true      5
```

Fig. 2. Function symbols and equation declaration for IBS. Undeclared identifiers represent variables.

the PKG's public signature verification key, while no other signature is accepted for this message m by this participant A.

In Fig. 3, we depict the two rules that comprise our theory. The setup rule create_IB_PrivateKeyGenerator generates the signing master key and the associated public key, which is constructed by applying IBMasterPubK to the secret. The public key is published by sending it out on the network while the private key is, of course, stored by the PKG. The rule create_IB_identity models the setup of a new participant with identity $A[3] (KeyRequest($A)), initialized with (i) the master public key Master_pk that will be used to compute signature verification keys, and (ii) the user's private signing key, which is provided by the PKG. The user's private key is derived from the signing master key and the user's identity, IBPriv($A, IBMasterPrivK).

```
// Create the trusted entity holding the id-based master private key    1
rule create_IB_PrivateKeyGenerator:    // Setup()                       2
 [ Fr(~IBMasterPrivK) ]                                                 3
-->                                                                     4
 [ !IB_MasterPrivateKey('PKG', ~IBMasterPrivK)                         5
 , Out(<'PKG', IBMasterPubK(~IBMasterPrivK)>) ] //adversary gets pkM   6
// Setup rules for identities                                          7
rule create_IB_identity:                 // KeyRequest($A)             8
  let Master_pk = IBMasterPubK(IBMasterPrivK)                         9
      User_sk = IBPriv($A, IBMasterPrivK) in                          10
 [ !IB_MasterPrivateKey('PKG', IBMasterPrivK)                         11
 , Fr(~id) ]                                                          12
--[ CreateId($A, <Master_pk, User_sk>), User() ]->                   13
 [ !IB_Identity(~id, $A, Master_pk, User_sk) ]                       14
```

Fig. 3. Modeling PKG. Variables prefixed with ~ are fresh.

Finally, we model the adversary's compromise capabilities in Fig. 4. We model a strong adversary who can completely compromise the system by revealing the PKG's master private key (rule Reveal_IB_MasterPrivateKey) as well as compromising individual agents by revealing their private signing key (rule

---

[3] $A denotes a variable that can be instantiated by any public constant.

```
// Reveals the id-based master private key of the PKG       1
rule Reveal_IB_MasterPrivateKey:                            2
  [ !IB_MasterPrivateKey(PKG, IBMasterPrivK) ]              3
--[ Reveal('PKG',PKG) ]->                                   4
  [ Out(IBMasterPrivK) ]                                    5
// Reveals the id-based private key of an agent A           6
rule Reveal_IB_privkey:                                     7
  [ !IB_Identity(~id, A, Master_pk, User_sk) ]              8
--[ Reveal('USER',A) ]->                                    9
  [ Out(User_sk) ]                                         10
```

Fig. 4. Adversary compromise rules.

Reveal_IB_privkey). Security properties would then typically be conditioned by the absence of specific compromises.

We build on this representation of identity-based signatures to model different versions of a protocol that combines bilinear pairing-based authentication and key agreement, with key escrow and identity-based signatures (see Sect. 5). We also develop a complete TAMARIN model for Example 1 (see [8]) including this representation of IBS; we depict the rule corresponding to Alice's first action in Fig. 5.

```
rule Alice_send:                                               1
let m = <'Alice', 'Bob', ~c>                                   2
    mOut = <idsign(m, User_sk),~c> in   // SignatureGeneration(...)  3
  [ !IB_Identity(~id, 'Alice', Master_pk, User_sk)             4
  , Fr(~) ]                                                    5
--[ Running('Alice', 'Bob', <'Initiator', 'Responder', ~c>) ]->  6
  [ Out(mOut)                                                  7
  , St_Alice_0(~id, Master_pk, User_sk, ~c) ]                  8
```

Fig. 5. Example usage of our abstract IBS model for our running example.

Modeling IBE Schemes. Our IBS representation can be simply modified to model IBE schemes by making minor changes to the function symbols and equations as shown in Fig. 6.

The rules for modeling the PKG and the reveals are identical. A complete TAMARIN model of Example 2 is given in [8].

4.2   More Precise Modeling of Bilinear Pairing-Based ID-Based Schemes

By leveraging TAMARIN's built-in theory for bilinear pairing, it is possible to model concrete IBE or IBS schemes much more precisely than in Sect. 4.1. Our

```
functions: IBPriv/2, IBPub/2, GetIBMasterPublicKey/1,               1
           idenc/2, iddec/2                                          2
equations: iddec(idenc(plaintext,                                   3
                    IBPub(A,                                        4
                        GetIBMasterPublicKey(IBMasterPrivateKey))), 5
                IBPriv(A, IBMasterPrivateKey)) = plaintext          6
```

Fig. 6. Function symbols and equation declaration for IBE.

next theory features four function symbols: $\mathtt{pmult}, \mathtt{em}, \hat{} \,$, and, $*$. The function symbol $\mathtt{pmult}$ is of arity 2 and models the multiplication of a group element (*e.g.*, $P \in G$) by a scalar (*e.g.*, $s \in \mathbb{F}_q^*$), $\mathtt{em}$ models the bilinear pairing e and is modulo AC, $\hat{}\,$ models the exponentiation of group elements (*e.g.*, $g \in G'$) by a scalar, and $*$ of arity 2 models the multiplication between scalars.

The function symbols $\hat{}\,$ and $*$ are subject to the equations of the built-in Diffie-Hellman theory, while $\mathtt{pmult}$ and $\mathtt{em}$ are subject to the equational theory for bilinear pairing, also built-in [24], which is summarized as:

```
pmult(x,(pmult(y,p)) = pmult(x*y,p)
pmult(1,p)           = p
em(p,q)              = em(q,p)
em(pmult(x,p),q)     = pmult(x,em(q,p)).
```

Modeling IBE Scheme Using Bilinear Pairing. One can leverage the built-in theories for bilinear pairing and XOR, recently added to TAMARIN [15], which can be combined, to model the Boneh and Franklin IBE scheme.

Using this more precise representation, we have developed a full model of Example 2 (see [8]). Our model introduces two function symbols h_1 and h_2 for modeling the two independent hash functions. The setup rules are now a bit different as the master private key and the user's private keys are computed with $\mathtt{pmult}$, as depicted in Fig. 7. We also show in Fig. 8 an example of a protocol rule using encryption, which corresponds to Alice's first output in our example.

Our model of Example 2 loads in ca. 1 hour of (pre-computation) CPU time. However, due to the heavy branching required to explore all possible variants, proofs or counterexamples cannot be automatically computed in reasonable time. However, when simplifying the protocol by removing Bob's response (hence with only one encryption and decryption), the pre-computation and the proof of secrecy of the plaintext could be computed in minutes, with both BP and XOR.

We thus conclude that, thanks to recent advances in the scope of the equational theories that TAMARIN handles, TAMARIN supports such a precise model of IBE schemes. However, the real limitation is now the efficiency of the proof search, which is negatively impacted by the numerous variants introduced by the combination of the built-in theories for bilinear pairing and XOR. Therefore, we do not use this precise model for our case study in Sect. 5.

```
// Create the trusted entity holding the master private key      1
rule create_IB_PrivateKeyGenerator:      // Setup()               2
  let Master_pk = pmult(~IBMasterPrivateKey, 'P') in // pkM        3
  [ Fr(~IBMasterPrivateKey) ]                                     4
--[ Once('PKG') ]->                                               5
  [ !IB_MasterPrivateKey('PKG', ~IBMasterPrivateKey)              6
  , Out(<'PKG', Master_pk>) ]           // adversary gets pkM     7
// Setup rules for identities                                    8
rule create_IB_identity:                  // KeyRequest($A)       9
  let Master_pk = pmult(~IBMasterPrivateKey, 'P')                10
      Qid = h1($A)                                               11
      User_sk = pmult(~IBMasterPrivateKey, Qid) in  // 'skM.Qid' 12
  [ !IB_MasterPrivateKey('PKG', ~IBMasterPrivateKey)             13
  , Fr(~id) ]                                                    14
--[ CreateId($A, <Master_pk, User_sk>) ]->                       15
  [ !IB_Identity(~id, $A, Master_pk, User_sk) ]                  16
```

Fig. 7. PKG model for our precise IBE scheme.

```
rule Alice_send:                                                  1
let plaintext = <'Alice', 'Bob', ~c>                              2
    Qbob = h1('Bob')                                              3
    U = pmult(~r, 'P')                                            4
    V = h2(em(Qbob, Master_pk)^(~r)) XOR plaintext               5
    mOut = <U,V> in      // Encryption(...)                       6
  [ !IB_Identity(~id, 'Alice', Master_pk, User_sk)               7
  , Fr(~c)                                                        8
  , Fr(~r) ]                                                      9
-->                                                              10
  [ Out(mOut)                                                    11
  , St_Alice_0(~id, Master_pk, User_sk, ~c) ]                    12
```

Fig. 8. Example usage of our precise IBE model for Example 2.

Modeling IBS Scheme Using Bilinear Pairing.

The Cha and Cheon IBS scheme described in Sect. 2.3 relies on $\mathbb{F}_q^*$ being a field, and *a fortiori*, a ring with an associative and commutative $+$, where $\cdot$ distributes over $+$. Unfortunately, TAMARIN, and all other symbolic tools, are currently unable to deal with such equational theories.

At first sight, the random scalar r in $V = (r + h_3(m, U))\mathsf{sk_{id}}$ seems to be only useful for randomizing the signature $\sigma = \langle rQ_{\mathsf{id}}, V \rangle$. Therefore, we modeled a simplified scheme that does not rely on $+$ over $\mathbb{F}_q^*$ for which $\sigma = \langle Q_{\mathsf{id}}, h_3(m, U))\mathsf{sk_{id}} \rangle$ and SignatureVerification() is modified straightforwardly. Interestingly, when using this model, TAMARIN automatically finds an attack on a supposedly secure protocol (namely, our fixed variant of the case study we describe in Sect. 5). After inspection, we found that this attack actually reveals a flaw in our simplified scheme where we omit r. Indeed, an adversary obtaining a signature $\sigma = \langle Q_{\mathsf{id}}, h_3(m, U)\mathsf{sk}_{\mathsf{id}} \rangle =: \langle U, V \rangle$ over a message m can forge a new signature over any other message m' as follows: $\sigma' := \langle U, h_3(m', U) \cdot (h_3(m, U))^{-1} \cdot V \rangle = \langle Q_{\mathsf{id}}, h_3(m', U)\mathsf{sk}_{\mathsf{id}} \rangle$. We have not found another simplification of the original scheme that would still be secure in the symbolic model.

All IBS realizations in the literature rely on the same kind of problematic equational theories. Hence, to the best of our knowledge, it is currently out of the scope of existing verification tools to reason about such a BP-based model of IBS schemes. This limitation could be tackled by developing new built-in theories with dedicated automated reasoning algorithms. We leave this task for future work.

5   Case Study

As a case study, we formalize and analyze an identity-based *Authentication and Key Agreement* (AKA) protocol, provided by an industry partner. The key agreement is based on identity-based signing and on bilinear pairing (see [1,24]) for key derivation, which also supports key escrow. We refer to this protocol as *BP-IBS* and depict it in Fig. 9.

BP-IBS is a 2-party AKA protocol that relies on a trusted PKG. It aims to achieve the following properties:

1. *mutual authentication* and *agreement* on the session key;
2. *session key escrow*: the master secret held by the PKG can be combined with a session transcript to compute the associated session key;
3. *weak forward secrecy*: session keys remain secret even after the long-term keys of one of the two involved agents are revealed; and
4. *strong forward secrecy*: session keys remain secret even after the long-term keys of both involved agents are revealed.

Note that the properties of weak and strong forward secrecy are necessarily violated once one of the authentication properties is violated. Note too that strong forward secrecy implies weak forward secrecy, which itself implies secrecy.

5.1   Specification

Starting from the informal presentation provided by our industrial partner, we developed a more formal specification, which we describe in this section.

Setting. BP-IBS relies on two infrastructures that can be provided by one or two separate PKGs. For generality, we describe the protocol where these two infrastructures are provided by two distinct PKGs, called respectively Sign-PKG and Auth-PKG.

– *Sign-PKG.* A *PKI infrastructure* that provides identity-based signatures. It provides, for any user of identity ID_i, a signing key sk_i. Any other user can

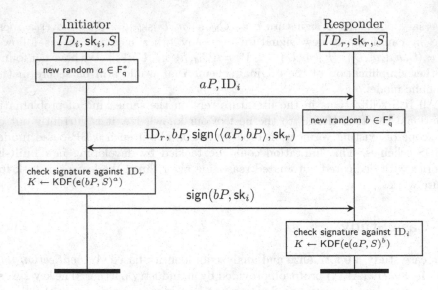

Fig. 9. Alice & Bob specification of BP-IBS.

verify that a message has been signed by a user ID_i using the master public key of Sign-PKG and ID_i. We model this PKG using our abstract model from Sect. 4.1.

- *Auth-PKG.* A *key escrow* setup that is used in the protocol to allow the corresponding PKG to learn session keys, *i.e.,session escrow*. This PKG initially generates a master private key $s \in \mathsf{F}_q^*$ and publicly discloses to its users the corresponding master public escrow share $S = sP$. We model this PKG using our precise model based on bilinear pairing (see Sect. 4.2) without including user encryption and decryption. Indeed, we do not need this PKG to provide users with id-based encryption keys.

Note that we could have modeled a single PKG providing both requirements. Our presentation, however, supports a more fine-grained analysis, *e.g.*, in terms of compromise scenarios.

BP-IBS. The protocol flow is depicted in Fig. 9. When a condition fails to hold, the corresponding agent aborts the protocol. Here, KDF models a key derivation function, abstracting away any implementation choices. The protocol shown is a 2-party authenticated key exchange protocol that uses identity-based signatures to authenticate key shares and allows session key escrow. Note that the session key established by the initiator and the responder satisfies:

$$K = \mathsf{KDF}(e(bP, S)^a) = \mathsf{KDF}(e(aP, S)^b) = \mathsf{KDF}(e(P, P)^{abs}) = \mathsf{KDF}(e(aP, bP)^s).$$

The last term in this equality chain shows that the protocol provides Auth-PKG with the ability to escrow all sessions.

5.2 Modeling BP-IBS

Figure 10 shows the setup of the key generation center, with key escrow functionality. In the rule `create_IB_AUTH_PrivateKeyGenerator`, the PKG's private key is generated randomly as `~IBMasterPrivK`. The associated public key, `pmult(~IBMasterPrivK, 'P')`, is constructed by multiplying the generator `'P'` with the secret. It is output to the adversary and stored and made available to all agents in `!IB_MasterPublicEscrowShare(...)`.

```
// Create the trusted entity holding the master private key for        1
    authentication escrow
rule create_IB_AUTH_PrivateKeyGenerator:                               2
  let pk_master_secret = pmult(~IBMasterPrivK, 'P') in                  3
  [ Fr(~IBMasterPrivK) ]                                                4
--[ Once('AUTH') ]->                                                    5
  [ !IB_MasterPrivateKey('AUTH', ~IBMasterPrivK)                        6
  , !IB_MasterPublicEscrowShare(pk_master_secret)                       7
  , Out(<'AUTH', pk_master_secret>) ] // adversary gets pkM             8
```

Fig. 10. Modeling the PKG for Authentication Escrow.

To initialize an agent for a run, we combine the look-up of both its private signing key and the key escrow share. The private signing key look-up works as described in the previous section, using the fact `!IB_Identity(...)`. Access to the key escrow share x is available in the argument of the `!IB_MasterPublicEscrowShare(x)` fact. Using the key escrow share, as designated by the protocol, allows the key escrow holder subsequent access to all agreed-upon keys between all users, without being involved in the key exchange.

Modeling the Core Protocol. Based on the aforementioned infrastructures, the core protocol of BP-IBS can be straightforwardly modeled in TAMARIN. We provide the full model in [8] (file `BP-IBS_0.spthy`).

Easing Reasoning with an Oracle. TAMARIN's default proof strategy is nonterminating, due to our model's complexity. We therefore implemented a dedicated oracle (see [1]). Oracles are lightweight tactics that can be used to guide proof search in TAMARIN. Our oracle is available at [8] (file `oracle_BP-IBS`).

5.3 Security Properties

We now describe the different security properties BP-IBS should meet, as stated earlier in Sect. 5, which we verify in TAMARIN.

Threat Model. We model a setting where the communication channel between the initiator and responder is assumed to be insecure. We formalize a standard network adversary (the *Dolev-Yao adversary*), which is an active adversary that can eavesdrop on and tamper with all exchanged messages

As is standard, we assume that the two PKGs, Sign-PKG and Auth-PKG, are honest. However, their long term secrets, including their master private keys, may be revealed to the adversary. Similarly, the long term secrets sk_i and sk_r may also be revealed. We therefore symbolically model capabilities analogous to those assumed in computational models where the adversary is equipped with "reveal queries" [3,4]; we establish our security properties in the presence of an adversary who can carry out such queries.

Authentication Properties. For each role (*i.e.*, initiator, responder), we analyze four types of authentication properties: aliveness, weak agreement, and non-injective agreement on the session key, and injective agreement on the session key. These authentication properties are only checked when there is no long-term signing key reveal (*i.e.*, $\mathsf{sk}_i, \mathsf{sk}_r$) and no reveal of the master private key of Sign-PKG[4].

Secrecy Properties. We first check *weak secrecy*: session keys remain secret when there is no reveal at all. *Weak Forward Secrecy* states a stronger property: the session key established by ID_i and ID_r remains secret even when either the key sk_i or the key sk_r is revealed *after* the session. *Strong Forward Secrecy* is even stronger: the session key established by ID_i and ID_r remains secret even when both keys sk_i or sk_r are revealed *after* the session.

Session Escrow. This property simply checks that there must be an execution where the adversary learns the session key between some ID_i and ID_r, when he knows the master private key of Auth-PKG but without further reveals. This represents that the escrow key holder is able to derive session keys as expected.

5.4   Analysis Results

We have automatically analyzed the aforementioned security properties using TAMARIN with our oracle; this analysis is supported by our model of BP-IBS, which is amenable to automation. Our analyses revealed several attacks in the original protocol. We have proposed protocol improvements that incorporate countermeasures, and have automatically verified that the improved protocols have the desired security properties. We summarize our results in Table 1.

We stress that all attacks were found automatically with TAMARIN, as well as the proofs of the correctness of our improved versions with countermeasures.

---

[4] We also checked that all authentication properties fail in the presence of signing key reveals but when the master private key of AUTH-PKG is not revealed. This result is as expected since one cannot then rely on signatures to authenticate agents.

Table 1. Analysis outcomes. "NI-Agr." stands for "Non-Injective-Agreement", "I-Agr." for "Injective-Agreement" and "FS" for forward secrecy. "(I/R)" means that we first describe the authentication property from the initiator's and then from the responder's point of view. When there is an attack, we indicate its type (see Sect. 5.4) with a subscript. Results labeled † were not directly obtained with TAMARIN, as the attack found on weak agreement for the respective protocol version immediately translates to an attack on secrecy.

Protocol	Aliveness (I/R)	Weak Agr. (I/R)	NI-Agr. (I/R)	I-Agr. (I/R)
BP-IBS (0)	$\boldsymbol{X}_1/\checkmark$	$\boldsymbol{X}_1/\boldsymbol{X}_1$	$\boldsymbol{X}_1/\boldsymbol{X}_1$	$\boldsymbol{X}_1/\boldsymbol{X}_1$
BP-IBS + check P (1)	$\boldsymbol{X}_2/\checkmark$	$\boldsymbol{X}_2/\boldsymbol{X}_2$	$\boldsymbol{X}_2/\boldsymbol{X}_2$	$\boldsymbol{X}_2/\boldsymbol{X}_2$
+ tags (2)	$\checkmark/\checkmark$	$\boldsymbol{X}_3/\boldsymbol{X}_3$	$\boldsymbol{X}_3/\boldsymbol{X}_3$	$\boldsymbol{X}_3/\boldsymbol{X}_3$
+ ID_r (3)	$\checkmark/\checkmark$	$\checkmark/\boldsymbol{X}_4$	$\checkmark/\boldsymbol{X}_4$	$\checkmark/\boldsymbol{X}_4$
+ ID_i (4)	$\checkmark/\checkmark$	$\checkmark/\checkmark$	$\checkmark/\checkmark$	$\checkmark/\checkmark$

Protocol	Weak Secrecy	Weak FS	Strong FS	Session Escrow
BP-IBS (0)	$\boldsymbol{X}_1$†	$\boldsymbol{X}_1$	$\boldsymbol{X}_1$	$\checkmark$
BP-IBS + check P (1)	$\boldsymbol{X}_2$†	$\boldsymbol{X}_2$	$\boldsymbol{X}_2$	$\checkmark$
+ tags (2)	$\checkmark$	$\boldsymbol{X}_3$	$\boldsymbol{X}_3$	$\checkmark$
+ ID_r (3)	$\checkmark$	$\boldsymbol{X}_4$	$\boldsymbol{X}_4$	$\checkmark$
+ ID_i (4)	$\checkmark$	$\checkmark$	$\checkmark$	$\checkmark$

Attack 1: Empty Shares. This attack violates weak agreement for the initiator as well as weak secrecy. We first discovered that, in the original protocol (modeled in the file `BP-IBS_0.spthy` from [8]), the initiator and responder do not check that the received shares are different from P, which is the generator. In combination with other authentication weaknesses that we describe next, the adversary can trick a responder to accept the share $aP = P$ as coming from an honest initiator. The adversary can then compute the session key without any further key reveal. From the regular participant's view, the session key is $K = \mathsf{KDF}(e(P, S)^b)$, and note that the other share uses $a = 1$, so $aP = P$. This key can be computed by the adversary since $K = \mathsf{KDF}(e(bP, S))$ and he knows the master public key S of Auth-PKG as well as the responder's share bP that is sent in the clear.

Suggested Countermeasure. We suggest that the initiator and responder should check that the received shares are different from P. We call the resulting protocol BP-IBS (1), which is modeled in `BP-IBS_1.spthy` in [8].

Attack 2: Reflection Attack. Other properties of the protocol BP-IBS (1) are still violated. We have found that a reflection attack violates aliveness for the initiator. This attack is caused by a possible confusion between the signed message sent by the responder and the signed message sent by the initiator. As a direct consequence, one can use the signature produced by an initiator that has received a dishonest share (essentially a type-flaw) to forge a message that is accepted by another initiator as coming from a legitimate responder. One can use this weakness to mount attacks against the aliveness property for the initiator (meaning the supposed partner of the initiator did not take part in the protocol) as well as secrecy of session keys and weak agreement properties for both sides. We show in Fig. 11 the attack flow violating aliveness for the initiator.

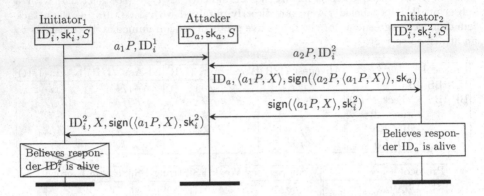

Fig. 11. Attack 2 on BP-IBS (1). Note that X can be chosen by the adversary.

Suggested Countermeasure. We suggest adding tags (i.e., R for the responder and I for the initiator) in the signed message expressing message origin. We call the resulting protocol BP-IBS (2), which is modeled in the file `BP-IBS_2.spthy` in [8]. We proved that this model ensures aliveness for the initiator and weak secrecy of session keys, hence our fix address the aforementioned attack.

Attacks 3 and 4: Lack of Identity-Binding. The protocol BP-IBS (2) does not provide weak agreement for either of the two roles. This is because neither role includes the other role's identity in the signed part of their messages. One of these attacks is shown in Fig. 12. There is a similar attack that violates weak agreement for the responder.

Suggested Countermeasure. We suggest adding the responder's (respectively initiator's) identity in the message signed by the initiator (respectively responder). We call BP-IBS (3) the protocol one obtains from BP-IBS (2) by adding the responder's identity and BP-IBS (4) the protocol where both identities are added. These protocols are respectively modeled in the files `BP-IBS_3.spthy` and `BP-IBS_4.spthy` in [8]. We depict BP-IBS (4) in Fig. 13.

5.5   Summary

Due to numerous problems, the original protocol does not meet its security requirements. Fortunately, the discovered attacks are easy to repair as shown by BP-IBS (4) in Fig. 13. We were able to prove automatically with TAMARIN that our model of the resulting protocol fulfills all its security requirements. We provide the full TAMARIN model of BP-IBS equipped with all our fixes as `BP-IBS_4.spthy` in [8]. Our industrial partner acknowledged the problems.

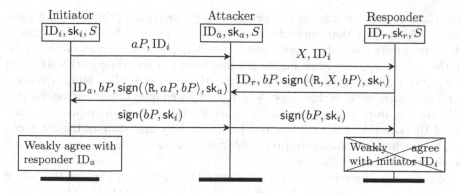

Fig. 12. Attack 3 on BP-IBS (2). The responder ID_r believes it has established a session with ID_i as initiator. But this view does not match with ID_i's view.

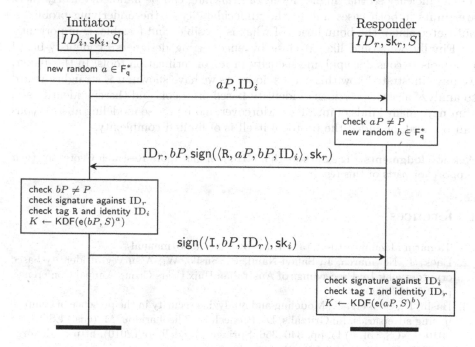

Fig. 13. Description of BP-IBS (4).

As expected, we have established that a compromise of AUTH-PKG breaks all secrecy properties of the session keys, and a compromise of SIGN-PKG violates all authentication properties.

6   Conclusion

Our case studies support the thesis that symbolic methods are very useful for improving the security of cryptographic protocols. A prerequisite, of course, is that the methods can handle the protocol's cryptographic primitives and complexity. We showed that current state-of-the-art tools can be used for a larger set of protocols than those previously considered and with reasonable effort. At the same time, our work highlights limitations of the state-of-the-art when faced with realistic protocols involving equational theories, like bilinear pairing in combination with exclusive-or, which lead to combinatorial explosions due to branching during proof search. Another limitation is with respect to equational theories that currently cannot be handled by any state-of-the-art tools, e.g., Diffie-Hellman exponentiation combined with addition in the exponent that distributes over multiplication.

We see two directions for future work. The first is to expand the set of equational theories that can be handled by tools like TAMARIN. This requires progress in unification theory. The second is for tool-builders to improve their tools' efficiency so that higher levels of branching can be handled. Clearly there are limits in both cases due to the undecidability of the underlying problems, but determining the boundaries of what is possible, and feasible, is important.

Finally, we would like to close by encouraging designers of identity-based protocols to consider applying security protocol verification tools. In this paper, we have illustrated how this can be done. As we have shown, it is straightforward to analyze abstract versions of identity-based protocols and thereby identify and eliminate many kinds of mistakes. Moreover, more precise modeling abstractions can be used, provided the protocol itself is of limited complexity.

Acknowledgments. The authors thank Huawei Singapore Research Center for their support for parts of this research.

References

1. Tamarin Manual. https://tamarin-prover.github.io/manual/
2. Baek, J., Newmarch, J., Safavi-Naini, R., Susilo, W.: A survey of identity-based cryptography. In: Proceedings of Australian Unix Users Group Annual Conference, pp. 95–102 (2004)
3. Basin, D., Cremers, C.: Modeling and analyzing security in the presence of compromising adversaries. In: Gritzalis, D., Preneel, B., Theoharidou, M. (eds.) ESORICS 2010. LNCS, vol. 6345, pp. 340–356. Springer, Heidelberg (2010). https://doi.org/10.1007/978-3-642-15497-3_21
4. Basin, D., Cremers, C.: Know your enemy: compromising adversaries in protocol analysis. ACM Trans. Inf. Syst. Secur. **17**(2), 7:1–7:31 (2014)
5. Basin, D., Cremers, C., Meadows, C.: Model checking security protocols. Handbook of Model Checking, pp. 727–762. Springer, Cham (2018). https://doi.org/10.1007/978-3-319-10575-8_22
6. Basin, D., Dreier, J., Hirschi, L., Radomirović, S., Sasse, R., Stettler, V.: A formal analysis of 5G authentication. In: Proceedings of the 2018 ACM SIGSAC Conference on Computer and Communications Security, CCS 2018, pp. 1383–1396. ACM, New York (2018)

7. Basin, D., Dreier, J., Sasse, R.: Automated symbolic proofs of observational equivalence. In: Ray, I., Li, N., Kruegel, C. (eds.) Proceedings of the 2015 ACM SIGSAC Conference on Computer and Communications Security, pp. 1144–1155. ACM (2015)
8. Basin, D., Hirschi, L., Sasse, R.: Case study Tamarin models (2019). https://github.com/tamarin-prover/tamarin-prover/tree/develop/examples/idbased. Accessed 05 Mar 2019
9. Boneh, D., Franklin, M.: Identity-based encryption from the weil pairing. In: Kilian, J. (ed.) CRYPTO 2001. LNCS, vol. 2139, pp. 213–229. Springer, Heidelberg (2001). https://doi.org/10.1007/3-540-44647-8_13
10. Choon, J.C., Hee Cheon, J.: An identity-based signature from gap Diffie-Hellman groups. In: Desmedt, Y.G. (ed.) PKC 2003. LNCS, vol. 2567, pp. 18–30. Springer, Heidelberg (2003). https://doi.org/10.1007/3-540-36288-6_2
11. Clavel, M., et al.: All About Maude-A High-Performance Logical Framework: How to Specify, Program and Verify Systems in Rewriting Logic, vol. 4350. Springer, Heidelberg (2007). https://doi.org/10.1007/978-3-540-71999-1
12. Cremers, C., Horvat, M., Hoyland, J., Scott, S., van der Merwe, T.: A comprehensive symbolic analysis of TLS 1.3. In: Proceedings of the 2017 ACM SIGSAC Conference on Computer and Communications Security, pp. 1773–1788. ACM (2017)
13. Dolev, D., Yao, A.C.: On the security of public key protocols. IEEE Trans. Inf. Theory **29**(2), 198–208 (1983)
14. Dowling, B., Fischlin, M., Günther, F., Stebila, D.: A cryptographic analysis of the TLS 1.3 handshake protocol candidates. In: Proceedings of the 22nd ACM SIGSAC Conference on Computer and Communications Security, pp. 1197–1210. ACM (2015)
15. Dreier, J., Hirschi, L., Radomirović, S., Sasse, R.: Automated unbounded verification of stateful cryptographic protocols with exclusive OR. In: 31st IEEE Computer Security Foundations Symposium, CSF 2018, Oxford, United Kingdom, 9–12 July 2018, pp. 359–373. IEEE Computer Society (2018)
16. Escobar, S., Meadows, C., Meseguer, J.: A rewriting-based inference system for the NRL protocol analyzer and its meta-logical properties. Theor. Comput. Sci. **367**(1–2), 162–202 (2006)
17. Fiat, A., Shamir, A.: How to prove yourself: practical solutions to identification and signature problems. In: Odlyzko, A.M. (ed.) CRYPTO 1986. LNCS, vol. 263, pp. 186–194. Springer, Heidelberg (1987). https://doi.org/10.1007/3-540-47721-7_12
18. Longley, D., Rigby, S.: An automatic search for security flaws in key management schemes. Comput. Secur. **11**(1), 75–89 (1992)
19. Meadows, C.: The NRL protocol analyzer: an overview. J. Log. Program. **26**(2), 113–131 (1996)
20. Meier, S., Schmidt, B., Cremers, C., Basin, D.: The TAMARIN prover for the symbolic analysis of security protocols. In: Sharygina, N., Veith, H. (eds.) CAV 2013. LNCS, vol. 8044, pp. 696–701. Springer, Heidelberg (2013). https://doi.org/10.1007/978-3-642-39799-8_48
21. Millen, J., Shmatikov, V.: Constraint solving for bounded-process cryptographic protocol analysis. In: Proceedings of the 8th ACM Conference on Computer and Communications Security, pp. 166–175. ACM (2001)
22. Millen, J.K., Clark, S.C., Freedman, S.B.: The interrogator: protocol security analysis. IEEE Trans. Softw. Eng. **13**(2), 274–288 (1987)
23. Schmidt, B., Meier, S., Cremers, C., Basin, D.: Automated analysis of Diffie-Hellman protocols and advanced security properties. In: Proceedings of the 25th IEEE Computer Security Foundations Symposium (CSF), pp. 78–94 (2012)

24. Schmidt, B., Sasse, R., Cremers, C., Basin, D.: Automated verification of group key agreement protocols. In: 2014 IEEE Symposium on Security and Privacy, SP 2014, Berkeley, CA, USA, 18–21 May 2014, pp. 179–194. IEEE Computer Society (2014)
25. Shamir, A.: Identity-based cryptosystems and signature schemes. In: Blakley, G.R., Chaum, D. (eds.) CRYPTO 1984. LNCS, vol. 196, pp. 47–53. Springer, Heidelberg (1985). https://doi.org/10.1007/3-540-39568-7_5
26. Syverson, P.F., Meadows, C.: A formal language for cryptographic protocol requirements. Des. Codes Crypt. **7**(1–2), 27–59 (1996)

Enrich-by-Need Protocol Analysis
for Diffie-Hellman

Moses D. Liskov, Joshua D. Guttman, John D. Ramsdell[✉], Paul D. Rowe,
and F. Javier Thayer

The MITRE Corporation, Bedford, USA
{mliskov,guttman,ramsdell,prowe}@mitre.org

Abstract. Enrich-by-need analysis characterizes all executions of a
security protocol that extend a given scenario. It computes a strongest
security goal the protocol achieves in that scenario. CPSA, a Cryptographic Protocol Shapes Analyzer, implements enrich-by-need analysis.

In this paper, we show how CPSA now analyzes protocols with Diffie-
Hellman key agreement (DH) in the enrich-by-need style. While this
required substantial changes both to the CPSA implementation and its
theory, the new version retains CPSA's efficient and informative behavior.
Moreover, the new functionality is justified by an algebraically natural
model of the groups and fields which DH manipulates.

The model entails two lemmas that describe the conditions under
which the adversary can deliver DH values to protocol participants.
These lemmas determined how CPSA handles the new cases. The lemmas may also be of use in other approaches.

This paper is dedicated to Cathy Meadows, with warmth and
gratitude.

1 Introduction

Diffie-Hellman key agreement (DH) [8], while widely used, has been challenging
for mechanized security protocol analysis. Some techniques, e.g. [7,12,15,22],
have produced informative results, but focus only on proving or disproving individual protocol security goals. A protocol and a specific protocol goal are given
as inputs. If the tool terminates, it either proves that this goal is achieved, or
else provides a counterexample. However, constructing the *right* security goals
for a protocol requires a high level of expertise.

By contrast, the *enrich-by-need* approach starts from a protocol and some
scenario of interest. For instance, if the initiator has had a local session, with a
peer whose long-term secret is uncompromised, what other local sessions have
occurred? What session parameters must they agree on? Must they have hap-
pened recently, or could they be stale?

Enrich-by-need protocol analysis identifies all essentially different smallest
executions compatible with the scenario of interest. While there are infinitely
many possible executions—since we put no bound on the number of local
sessions—often surprisingly few of them are really different. The Cryptographic
Protocol Shapes Analyzer (CPSA) [24], a symbolic protocol analysis tool based

© Springer Nature Switzerland AG 2019
J. D. Guttman et al. (Eds.): Meadows Festschrift, LNCS 11565, pp. 135–155, 2019.
https://doi.org/10.1007/978-3-030-19052-1_10

on strand spaces [13,18,27], efficiently enumerates these minimal, essentially different executions. We call the minimal, essentially different executions the protocol's *shapes* for the given scenario.

Knowing the shapes tells us a *strongest* relevant security goal, i.e. a formula that expresses authentication and confidentiality trace properties, and is at least as strong as any one the protocol achieves in that scenario [14,23]. Using these shapes, one can resolve specific protocol goals. The hypothesis of a proposed security goal tells us what scenario to consider, after which we can simply check the conclusion in each resulting shape (see [25] for a precise treatment).

Moreover, enrich-by-need has key advantages. Because it can also compute strongest goal formulas directly for different protocols, it allows comparing the strength of different protocols [25], for instance during standardization. Moreover, the shapes provide the designer with *visualizations* of exactly what the protocol may do in the presence of an adversary. Thus, they make protocol analysis more widely accessible, being informative even for those whose expertise is not mechanized protocol analysis.

In this paper, we show how we strengthened CPSA's enrich-by-need analysis to handle DH. We will not focus on the underlying theory, which is presented at length in a report [17]. Instead, we will focus here on how CPSA uses that theory. It is efficient, and has a flexible adversary model with corruptions.

Foundational issues needed to be resolved. Finding solutions to equations in the natural underlying theories is undecidable in general, so mechanized techniques must be carefully circumscribed. Moreover, these theories, which include fields, are different from many others in security protocol analysis. The field axioms are not (conditional) equations, meaning that they do not have a simplest (or "initial") model for the analysis to work within. Much work on mechanized protocol analysis, even for DH relies on equational theories and their initial models, e.g. [7,12,15,22]. However, an analysis method should have an explicit theory justifying it from standard mathematical structures such as fields. CPSA now has a transparent foundation in the algebraic properties of the fields that DH manipulates. This extends our earlier work [11,16].

Contributions. In this paper, we describe how we extended CPSA to analyze DH protocols. CPSA is currently restricted to the large class of protocols that do not use addition in the exponents, which we call *multiplicative* protocols. CPSA is also restricted to protocols that disclose randomly chosen exponents one-by-one. This allows modeling a wide range of possible types of corruption; however, it excludes a few protocols in which products of exponents are disclosed. A protocol *separates disclosures* if it satisfies our condition.

These restrictions justify two principles—Lemmas 1 and 2—that are valid for all executions of protocols that separate disclosures. The lemmas characterize how the adversary can obtain an exponent value such as xy or an exponentiated DH value such as g^{xy}, respectively. They tell CPSA what information to add to enrich a partial analysis to describe the possible executions in which the adversary obtains these values. Lemmas 1 and 2 are a distinctive contribution that may also prove useful to other analysis tools, helping to narrow their search.

To formulate and prove these lemmas, we had to clarify the algebraic structures we work with. The messages in our protocol executions contain mathematical objects such as elements of fields and cyclic groups. We regard the random choices of the compliant protocol participants as "transcendentals," i.e. primitive elements added to a base field that have no algebraic relationship to members of the base field.

CPSA yields results within a language of first order logic. The analysis delivers truths about all protocol executions; the executions are the *models* of the *theories* used in the analysis. This provides a familiar foundational setting. A long version [17] has a through discussion. Guttman [14] developed the underlying ideas, and Rowe et al. [25] applied them to "measure" the strength of protocols using the goal formulas the protocols achieve. That formal machinery is independent of whether the protocols use DH or not.

CPSA is very efficient. When executed on a rich set of variants of Internet Key Exchange (IKE) versions 1 and 2, our analysis required less than 30 s on a laptop. Section 7 tabulates results.

To Cathy, with Gratitude. As so often, Cathy Meadows explored this area long before us. Maude-NPA has delivered informative results about Diffie-Hellman protocols for a long time, and her work jointly with Dusko Pavlovic a dozen years ago identified core protocol characteristics of Diffie-Hellman in a compact and informative way. We were certainly aware of an echo of their *guard* notion in our Lemmas 1–2. Perhaps the analysis we give in Sect. 4 should be regarded as an explanation of why the *guard* idea is properly applicable here.

2 An Example Protocol: Unified Model

In many Diffie-Hellman protocols [8], the participants A, B exchange both:
- certified, long-term values g^a and g^b, and also
- one-time, ephemeral values g^x and g^y.

The peers compute session keys using *key computation functions* $\mathsf{KCF}^{(\cdot)}$, where in successful sessions, $\mathsf{KCF}^A(a, x, g^b, g^y) = \mathsf{KCF}^B(b, y, g^a, g^x)$. The ephemeral values ensure the two parties agree on a different key in each session. The long-term values are intended for authentication: Any party that obtains the session key must be one of the intended peers. Different functions $\mathsf{KCF}^{(\cdot)}$ yield different security properties. Protocol analysis tools for DH key exchanges must be able to use algebraic properties to identify these security consequences.

We consider here a simple DH Challenge-Response protocol DHCR in which nonces from each party form a challenge and response protected by a shared, derived DH key (see Fig. 1).

A and B's long-term DH exponents are values $\mathsf{ltx}(A), \mathsf{ltx}(B)$, which we will mainly write as a lower case a, b resp. We assume the principals are in bijection with distinct long-term $\mathsf{ltx}(\cdot)$ values.

The *initiator* and *responder* each receive two self-signed certificates, certifying the long term public values $g^{\mathsf{ltx}(\cdot)}$ of his peer and himself.

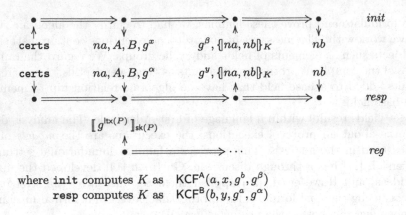

Fig. 1. Protocol DHCR: Initiator, responder, and ltx() self-certifying roles. The **certs** are $[\![\,g^{\mathsf{ltx}(A)}\,]\!]_{\mathsf{sk}(P)}$ and $[\![\,g^{\mathsf{ltx}(B)}\,]\!]_{\mathsf{sk}(P)}$ for each role.

Each will send an ephemeral public DH value g^x, g^y in cleartext, and also a nonce. Each will receive a value which may be the peer's ephemeral, or may instead be some value selected by an active adversary. Neither participant can determine the exponent for the ephemeral value he receives, but since the value is a group element, it must be some value of the form g^α or g^β.

Each participant computes a session key using his $\mathsf{KCF}^{(\cdot)}$. The responder uses the key to encrypt the nonce received together with his own nonce. The initiator uses the key to decrypt this package, and to retransmit the responder's nonce in plaintext as a confirmation.

The *registration* role allows any principal P to emit its long-term public group value $g^{\mathsf{ltx}(P)}$ under its own digital signature. In full-scale protocols, a certifying authority's signature would be used, but in this paper we omit the CA so as not to distract from the core DH issues.

We will assume that each instance of a role chooses its values for certain parameters freshly. For instance, each instance of the registration role makes a fresh choice of $\mathsf{ltx}(P)$. Each instance of the initiator role chooses x and na freshly, and each responder instance chooses y and nb freshly.

DHCR is parameterized by the key computations. The Unified Model [1] offers three key computations, with a hash function $\#(\cdot)$ standing for key derivation. The shared keys—when each participant receives the ephemeral value $g^\alpha = g^x$ or $g^\beta = g^y$ that the peer sent—are:

Plain UM: $\qquad\qquad\qquad \#(g^{ab}, g^{xy})$
Criss-cross UMX: $\qquad\quad\; \#(g^{ay}, g^{bx})$
Three-component UM3: $\quad \#(g^{ay}, g^{bx}, g^{xy})$

We discuss three security properties:

Authentication: If either the initiator or responder completes the protocol, and *both* principals' private long-term exponents are secret, then the intended peer must have participated in a matching conversation.

The key computations UM, UMX, and UM3 all enforce the authentication goal.

Impersonation resistance: If either the initiator or responder completes the protocol, and the intended peer's private long-term exponent is secret, then the intended peer must have participated in a matching conversation.

Here we do not assume that *ones own* private long-term exponent is secret. Can the adversary impersonate the intended peer if ones own key is compromised?

DHCR with the plain UM KCF is susceptible to an impersonation attack: An attacker who knows Alice's own long-term exponent can impersonate any partner to Alice. The adversary can calculate g^{ab} from a and g^b, and can calculate the g^{xy} value from g^x and a y it chooses itself.

On the other hand, the UMX and UM3 KCFs resist the impersonation attack.

Forward secrecy: If the intended peers complete a protocol session and then the private, long-term exponent of each party is exposed *subsequently*, then the adversary still cannot derive the session key.

This is sometimes called *weak* forward secrecy.

To express forward secrecy, we allow the registration role to continue and subsequently disclose the long term secret $\mathsf{ltx}(P)$ as in Fig. 2. If we assume in an analysis that $\mathsf{ltx}(P)$ is uncompromised, that implies that this role does not complete. The dummy second node allows specifying that the $\mathsf{ltx}(P)$ release node occurs after some other event, generally the completion of a normal session.

$$\bullet \Longrightarrow \bullet \Longrightarrow \bullet$$
$$\downarrow \qquad\quad \uparrow \qquad \downarrow$$
$$[\![g^{\mathsf{ltx}(P)}]\!]_{\mathsf{sk}(P)} \quad \mathsf{dummy} \quad \mathsf{ltx}(P)$$

Fig. 2. The full registration role

The UM KCF guarantees forward secrecy, but UMX does not. In UMX, if an adversary records g^x and g^y during the protocol and learns a and b later, it can compute the key by exponentiating g^x to the power b and g^y to the power a. UM3 restores forward secrecy, meeting all three of these goals.

2.1 Strand Terminology

A sequence of transmission and reception events as illustrated in Figs. 1 and 2 is a *strand*. Each send-event or receive-event on it is a *node*. We draw strands either horizontally as in Figs. 1 and 2 or vertically, as in diagrams generated by CPSA itself. We write $\mathsf{msg}(n)$ for the message sent or received by node n.

A *protocol* consists of a finite set of these strands, which we call the *roles* of the protocol. The roles contain variables, called the *parameters* of the roles, and by plugging in values for the parameters, we obtain a set of strands called the *instances* of the roles. We also call a strand a *regular strand* when it is an instance of a role, because it then complies with the rules. *Regular nodes* are the nodes that lie on regular strands. We speak of a *regular principal* associated with a secret if that secret is used only in accordance with the protocol, i.e. only in regular strands.

In an execution, events are (at least) partially ordered, and values sent on earlier transmissions are available to the adversary, who would like to provide the messages expected by the regular participants on later transmission nodes. The adversary can also generate primitive values on his own. We will make assumptions restricting which values the adversary does generate to express various scenarios and security goals.

3   How CPSA Works: UMX Initiator

Here we will illustrate the main steps that CPSA takes when analyzing DHCR. For this illustration, we will focus on the impersonation resistance of the UMX key computation, in the case where the initiator role runs, aiming to ensure that the responder has also taken at least the first three steps of a matching run. The last step of the responder is a reception, so the initiator can never infer that it has occurred. We choose this case because it is typical, yet quite compact.

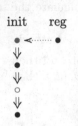

init   reg

Fig. 3. Initial scenario, skeleton 0: $\mathsf{ltx}(B)$ non-compromised and $A \neq B$ (Color figure online)

Starting Point. We start CPSA on the problem shown in Fig. 3, in which A, playing the initiator role, has made a full local run of the protocol, and received the long term public value of B from a genuine run of the registration role. These are shown as the vertical column on the left and the single transmission node at the top to its right. We will assume that B's private value $\mathsf{ltx}(B)$ is non-compromised and freshly generated, so that the public value $g^{\mathsf{ltx}(B)}$ originates only at this point. In particular, this run definitely does not progress to expose the secret as in the third node of Fig. 2. The fresh selection of $\mathsf{ltx}(B)$ must certainly precede the reception of $g^{\mathsf{ltx}(B)}$ at the beginning of the initiator's run. This is the meaning of the dashed arrow between them. We *do not* assume that A's long term secret $\mathsf{ltx}(A)$ is uncompromised, although we will assume that the ephemeral x value is freshly generated by the initiator run, and not available to the adversary. We assume $A \neq B$, which is the case of most interest.

Exploration Tree. Figure 4 shows the exploration tree that CPSA generates. Each item in the tree—we will call each item a *skeleton*—is a scenario describing some behavior of the regular protocol participants, as well as some assumptions. For instance, skeleton 0 contains the assumptions about $\mathsf{ltx}(B)$ and A's ephemeral value x mentioned before. The exploration tree contains one blue, bold face entry, skeleton 1 (shown in Fig. 5), as well as a subtree starting from 2 that is all red. The bold blue skeleton 1 is a *shape*, meaning it describes a simplest possible execution that satisfies the starting skeleton 0. The red skeletons are *dead skeletons*, meaning possibilities that the search has excluded; no executions can occur that satisfy these

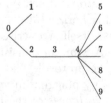

Fig. 4. CPSA exploration tree (Color figure online)

skeletons. Thus, skeleton 1 is the only shape, and CPSA has concluded that all executions that satisfy skeleton 0 in fact also satisfy skeleton 1.

In other examples, there may be several shapes identified by the analysis, or in fact zero shapes. The latter means that the initial scenario cannot occur in any execution. This may be the desired outcome, for instance when the initial scenario exhibits some disclosure that the protocol designer would like to ensure is prevented.

First Step. CPSA, starting with skeleton 0 in Fig. 3, identifies the third node of the initiator strand, which is shown in red, as unexplained. This is the initiator receiving the DH ephemeral public value g^y and the encryption $\{\!|na, nb|\!\}_K$, where K is the session key A computes using g^y and the other parameters. The node is red because the adversary cannot supply this message on his own, given the materials we already know that the regular, compliant principals have transmitted. Thus, CPSA is looking for additional information, including other transmissions of regular participants, that could explain it. Two possibilities are relevant here, and they lead to skeletons 1 and 2 (see Figs. 5 and 6).

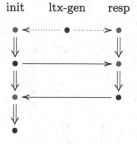

Fig. 5. Skeleton 1, the sole resulting shape. (Color figure online)

In skeleton 1, a regular protocol participant executing the responder role transmits the message $g^y, \{\!|na, nb|\!\}_K$. Given the values in this message—including those used to compute K using the UMX function—all of the parameters in the responder role are determined.

This is an encouraging result: The initiator has interacted with a run of the responder role. Moreover, the solid arrows indicate that the responder has received exactly what the initiator has transmitted, and *vice versa*. CPSA's accompanying text output confirms that the two strands agree on all of their parameters. Thus, they agree about their identities, the names A, B; the long-term exponents $\mathsf{ltx}(A), \mathsf{ltx}(B)$; the ephemeral values x, y, and the nonces na, nb. Thus, the initiator has authenticated the responder with an exactly matching run [5,20].

Skeleton 2 considers whether the key $K = \#(g^{ay}, g^{bx})$, computed by the initiator, might be compromised. K is the value received on the rightmost strand. The reception node is called a *listener node*, because it witnesses for the availability of K to the adversary. The "heard" value K is then retransmitted so that CPSA can register that this event must occur before the initiator's third node. This listener node is red because CPSA cannot yet explain

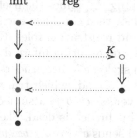

Fig. 6. Skeleton 2: Can the UMX encryption key K be exposed, on the rightmost strand? (Color figure online)

how K would become available. However, if additional information, such as more actions of the regular participants, would explain it, then the adversary could use K to encrypt na, nb and forge the value A receives. Thus, skeleton 2 identifies this listener node for further exploration.

Step 2. Proceeding from skeleton 2, CPSA performs a simplification on $K = \#(g^{ay}, g^{bx})$. The value y is available to the adversary, as is a, since we have not assumed them uncompromised. Thus, g^{ay} is available. The adversary will be able to compute K if he can obtain g^{bx}. Skeleton 3 (not shown) is similar to skeleton 2 but has a red node asking CPSA to explain how to obtain g^{bx}.

This requires a step which is distinctive to DH protocols. CPSA adds Skeleton 4 (Fig. 7), which has a new rightmost strand with a red node, receiving the pair $g^{bx/w}, w$. To resolve this, CPSA must meet two constraints. First, it must choose an exponent w that can be exposed and available to the adversary. Second, for this value of w, either $w = bx$ or else the "leftover" DH value $g^{bx/w}$ must be transmitted by a regular participant and extracted by the adversary.

One of our key lemmas, Lemma 2, justifies this step.

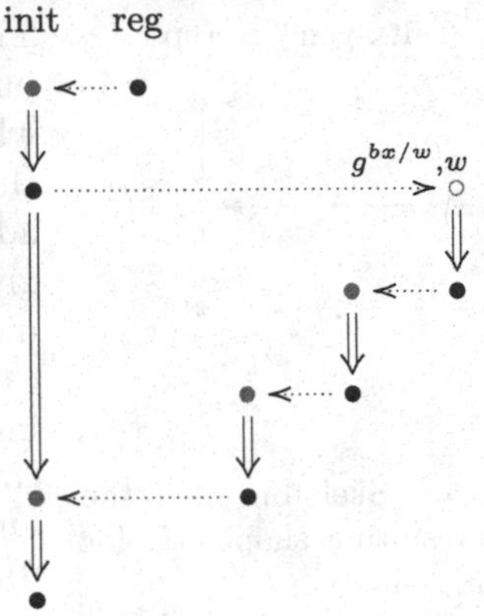

Step 3, Clean-Up. From skeleton 4, CPSA considers the remaining possibilities in this branch of its analysis. First, it immediately eliminates the possibility $w = bx$, since the protocol offers no way for the adversary to obtain b and x.

In fact, because b and x are random values, independently chosen by different principals, the adversary cannot obtain their product without obtaining the values themselves.

Fig. 7. Skeleton 4: Is $w = bx$? Or is there an exposed exponent w where $g^{bx/w}$ was sent by a regular participant? (Color figure online)

CPSA then considers each protocol role in turn, namely the initiator, responder, and registration roles. Can any role transmit a DH value of the form $g^{bx/w}$, where the resulting inferred value for w would be available to the adversary?

In skeleton 5, it considers the case in which the initiator strand is the original starting strand, which transmits g^x. Thus, $x = bx/w$, which is to say $w = b$. However, since b is assumed uncompromised, the adversary cannot obtain it, and this branch is dead. Skeleton 6 explores the case where a different initiator strand sends g^z, so $z = bx/w$, i.e. $w = bx/z$. However, this is unobtainable, since it too is compounded from independent, uncompromised values b, x, z.

Skeleton 7 considers the responder case, and skeletons 8 and 9 consider a registration strand which is either identical with the initial one (skeleton 8) or not (skeleton 9). They are eliminated for corresponding reasons.

Thus, the whole subtree below skeleton 2 (Fig. 6) is dead, i.e. there is no possible execution to which skeleton 2 leads.

The entire analysis takes about 0.2 s.

$\text{init}(z_1, 4) \wedge \text{init\_na}(z_1, na) \wedge \text{init\_nb}(z_1, nb) \wedge \text{init\_a}(z_1, a) \wedge \text{init\_b}(z_1, b)$
$\wedge \text{init\_ltxa}(z_1, ltxa) \wedge \text{init\_ltxb}(z_1, ltxb) \wedge \text{init\_x}(z_1, x) \wedge \text{init\_y}(z_1, y)$
$\wedge \text{reg}(z_2, 1) \wedge \text{reg\_self}(z_2, b) \wedge \text{reg\_l}(z_2, ltxb)$
$\wedge (z_2, 1) \prec (z_1, 1) \wedge \text{non}(ltxb)$
$\Longrightarrow$
$\exists z_3.$

$\quad \text{resp}(z_3, 3) \wedge \text{resp\_na}(z_3, na) \wedge \text{resp\_nb}(z_3, nb) \wedge \text{resp\_a}(z_3, a) \wedge \text{resp\_b}(z_3, b)$
$\quad \wedge \text{resp\_ltxa}(z_3, ltxa) \wedge \text{resp\_ltxb}(z_3, ltxb) \wedge \text{resp\_x}(z_3, x) \wedge \text{resp\_y}(z_3, y)$
$\quad \wedge (z_2, 1) \prec (z_3, 1) \wedge (z_1, 2) \prec (z_2, 2) \wedge (z_2, 3) \prec (z_3, 3)$
$\quad \wedge \text{uniq\_at}(na, (z_1, 2)) \wedge \text{uniq\_at}(nb, (z_2, 3))$

Fig. 8. Shape analysis sentence: UMX initiator impersonation

Result of the Analysis. Having eliminated everything below skeleton 2 (Fig. 6), the analysis has left only skeleton 1 (Fig. 5) as a shape. In that skeleton, the initiator has authenticated the responder with an exactly matching run. Thus, the analysis shows that an implication holds: For every execution, if it contains at least the structure shown in skeleton 0, then it has all of the structure shown in skeleton 1.

CPSA generates a *shape analysis sentence* that expresses this. Its antecedent describes the facts present in skeleton 0, and the conclusion describes the facts in skeleton 1. If there were multiple alternative shapes rather than just one, the conclusion would be a disjunction of the descriptions of the different possible outcomes. In the important special case in which the whole search tree is dead, so that the initial scenario—which may describe some undesired disclosure of values that should remain confidential—cannot occur, the conclusion is the disjunction of the empty set of formulas, i.e. the formula `false`.

Specifically, in our example analysis, the hypothesis is that there is an initiator strand and an registration strand, in which the registration strand generates $\text{ltx}(B)$ and moreover $\text{ltx}(B)$ is non-compromised. The conclusion is that there is also a responder strand with exactly matching parameters.

The formula generated by CPSA is shown, in a more humanly readable form, and without its leading universal quantifiers, in Fig. 8.

The variables z_1, z_2 range over strands; na, nb range over data; a, b range over names; and $ltxa, ltxb, x$ range over randomly chosen exponents. These are *transcendentals* of the exponent field. By contrast, y may be a field member that is not a simple random value, but e.g. a product of field values.

The strand z_1 is an instance of the *init* role, and it is of "full height," meaning that all four steps have occurred. The next eight atomic formulas fix each of the parameters of strand z_1, using the predicates init_na, init_nb, etc., to make assertions about the parameters in question, and the variables na, nb, etc. to refer to their values.

The second strand z_2 is an instance of the *reg* role, with one node, the transmission node. It stipulates that the self parameter refers to the same intended peer b, with the same long term exponent $ltxb$. It states a precedence relation between the first node on the two strands, and assumes that $ltxb$ is non-compromised, i.e. never transmitted as part of a payload, or by the adversary.

The conclusion asserts the existence of a strand z_3 which is an instance of the *resp* role, and has the matching parameter values. It also records the precedence ordering, as determined by CPSA, and some freshness properties $\mathsf{uniq\_at}(na, (z_1, 2)) \land \mathsf{uniq\_at}(nb, (z_2, 3))$ for the nonces, which follow from the definitions of the roles.

4 Modeling DH Values and Executions

The analysis of Sect. 3 depends on some modeling decisions. For one, encryption and digital signature are assumed to satisfy the Dolev-Yao properties [10]:

digital signatures can be produced only using the signing key;
encryptions can be produced only from the plaintext using the encryption key;
plaintext can be recovered from an encryption only using the decryption key;
keys cannot be recovered from signatures or encryptions.

Step 1 assumes that, for the adversary to produce the encryption $\{\!|na, nb|\!\}_K$, he can obtain the key K. A regular responder may produce the encryption, as in skeleton 1, in a session with the right parameters, since $K = \mathsf{KCF}^\mathsf{B}(b, \beta, g^a, g^x)$.

There are also important modeling properties of the DH values. First, the adversary can certainly carry out the four basic algebraic operations on exponents α and β to obtain $\alpha + \beta$, $\alpha \cdot \beta$, etc. Given a DH value g^α and an exponent β, the adversary can exponentiate, obtaining $(g^\alpha)^\beta = g^{\alpha\beta}$. Given two DH values g^α and g^β, they may be combined to yield $g^\alpha g^\beta = g^{\alpha+\beta}$.

Thus, the exponents form a *field*, i.e. a structure with commutative addition and multiplication operations and identity elements $\mathbf{0}, \mathbf{1}$, related by a distributive law. Addition has an inverse, as does multiplication, for non-$\mathbf{0}$ divisors.

The DH values form a *cyclic group*, generated from a generator g by repeated multiplication. Since, e.g., $ggg = g^3$, we can regard the cyclic group as built from g by using field elements as exponents. Although we have been writing the group operation multiplicatively, and combining a group element and a field element by exponentiation, the algebra is isomorphic if the group operation is written additively as $+$. Then the field elements are combined with group elements by a scalar multiplication αP. We will continue to write the group operation with the same multiplicative convention.

Each field $\mathcal{F}$ determines a cyclic group, with domain $\{g^\alpha : \alpha \in \mathcal{F}\}$. Its group operation maps g^α and g^β to $g^{\alpha+\beta}$. Its inverse maps g^α to $g^{-\alpha}$ since $g^\alpha g^{-\alpha} = g^\mathbf{0}$.

But: what fields $\mathcal{F}$ are relevant? In particular, we must decide how to represent random choices of the regular principals (or the adversary) as field elements. The criterion for this depends on our view of the adversary.

Adversary Model. A protocol designer designs a protocol with some scenarios of interest in mind, with authentication and confidentiality goals for each. The adversary's goal is to exhibit protocol executions that provide counterexamples to these goals of the designer. A counterexample is an execution, so the adversary must be able to supply every message received during the execution.

Executions involve cyclic group and field values, structures that are not freely generated, and our adversary works directly with polynomials, within the mathematical structures. Thus, our adversary performs group and field operations, which have the same effect regardless of how the structures are implemented as bitstrings. The adversary does not perform arbitrary efficient computations on bitstrings, unlike in the standard computational model.

This is similar to the generic group model [21,26]. This is an asymptotic computational model, in which the adversary is assumed to get negligible advantage from the bitstrings but can use group operations. Barthe et al. [3] show that an adversary which solves equations in a non-asymptotic model soundly approximates the generic group model. If the adversary's recipe for generating values for a recipient is a polynomial p_0, and the recipient expects the values produced by p_1, the adversary succeeds when the arguments satisfy $p_0 - p_1 = 0$. If the underlying fields are the prime order fields $\mathcal{F}_q$, then as q increases (or, better, as $\log q$ increases), the adversary wins with non-negligible probability only if p_0 and p_1 are identically equal (cf. also [19]). Otherwise, $p_0 - p_1$ has at most d zeros, where d is the (constant) maximum of their degrees.

Thus, the adversary uses polynomials as recipes, and wins when the polynomials evaluate to a result acceptable to the regular principals.

Fields and Extension Elements. The "variables" in these polynomials are *extension elements* that represent the random choices of the regular participants and the adversary. A set X of extension elements means a set of new values adjoined to a base field $\mathcal{F}$. They generate a new field $\mathcal{F}(X)$ in which the elements are polynomials in X, as well as quotients of polynomials. Extension elements come in two flavors. Some, called *algebraic extension elements*, like the square root of two, are introduced to supply a root for a polynomial, in this case $x^2 - 2$. Others, introduced without an associated polynomial, are called *transcendental extension elements*, because transcendentals such as π and e arise in this way. The random choices are effectively transcendental extension elements, because from the adversary's point of view, they are:

- disjoint from the underlying field: the adversary loses with overwhelming probability if he assumes a random choice equals a particular member.
- algebraically independent of each other: the adversary loses with overwhelming probability if he assumes the random choices will furnish a **0** for a polynomial p, other than the vacuous polynomial with all zero coefficients.

Fix an infinite set trsc as the transcendentals. We will work over a single base field $\mathbb{Q}$ of the rationals. $\mathbb{Q}$ is the right base field. If a set of polynomials has a solution in the finite field $\mathcal{F}_q$ for infinitely many choices of a prime q, then it also has solutions in $\mathbb{Q}$. Conversely, any solution in $\mathbb{Q}$ yields a solution in every $\mathcal{F}_q$.

Creation: $\mathbf{g}\uparrow$ $1\uparrow$ $a\uparrow$ for a: CREATE

Multiplicative: $\downarrow w_1 \Rightarrow \downarrow w_2 \Rightarrow w_1 \cdot w_2 \uparrow$ $\downarrow w_1 \Rightarrow \downarrow w_2 \Rightarrow w_1/w_2 \uparrow$
$\downarrow h \Rightarrow \downarrow w \Rightarrow \exp(h, w) \uparrow$

Additive: $\downarrow w_1 \Rightarrow \downarrow w_2 \Rightarrow (w_1 + w_2) \uparrow$ $\downarrow w_1 \Rightarrow \downarrow w_2 \Rightarrow (w_1 - w_2) \uparrow$
$\downarrow \exp(h, w_1) \Rightarrow \downarrow \exp(h, w_2) \Rightarrow \exp(h, w_1 + w_2) \uparrow$

Construction: $\downarrow m \Rightarrow \downarrow K \Rightarrow \{\!|m|\!\}_K \uparrow$ $\downarrow m_1 \Rightarrow \downarrow m_2 \Rightarrow (m_1, m_2) \uparrow$

Destruction: $\downarrow (m_1, m_2) \Rightarrow m_1 \uparrow$ $\downarrow (m_1, m_2) \Rightarrow m_2 \uparrow$
$\downarrow \{\!|m|\!\}_K \Rightarrow \downarrow K^{-1} \Rightarrow m \uparrow$

$\downarrow m$ and $m \uparrow$ mean reception and transmission of m, resp.
$+, -$ mean field addition and subtraction

Fig. 9. Adversary strands

Analysis in $\mathbb{Q}(\mathsf{trsc})$ is thus faithful for adversary strategies that work in $\mathcal{F}_q(\mathsf{trsc})$ for infinitely many q. Thus, for the remainder of this paper, we fix $\mathcal{F} = \mathbb{Q}(\mathsf{trsc})$ as the extension field. Fix the cyclic group $\mathcal{C}$ to be the cyclic group generated from $\mathbf{g}$ using as exponents the members of $\mathcal{F}$.

Viewing random choices as members of trsc justifies our reasoning in Sect. 3, Step 3, where we argued that the adversary could not obtain products of independent random choices of the regular principals. The distinct random choices cannot cancel out to leave a value the adversary can obtain.

Adversary Strands. The adversary constructs new values from available values via the strands in Fig. 9. In the *creation* strands, the sort CREATE is the union of sorts for atomic symmetric keys; asymmetric keys; texts; principal names; and transcendentals trsc. Group elements are not created; instead, one obtains a field element and exponentiates. The *multiplicative* and *additive* operations apply the field and group operations. The remaining strands are standard Dolev-Yao operations. The adversary concatenates or separates tuples; and applies encryption, decryption, or digital signature given the necessary keys, plaintext, or cipher text. Messages can be non-atomic symmetric keys. The adversary "routes" messages from one adversary strand to another for compound operations.

Corruption. We do not model corruption as an adversary action. Instead, we treat corruption as an action of a regular participant, who may disclose any parameter. The *registration* role shown in Fig. 2, which transmits the long term value $\mathsf{ltx}(P)$ in its last step, is an example. We can select which executions to query by stipulating that particular values are non-compromised: Then, the strand that chooses that value does not progress to the disclosure in the relevant executions. Any value not governed by an assumption may be compromised.

Although DHCR allows compromise of long term exponents, but not ephemerals, that is specific to the example. Protocols can be instrumented to allow compromise of any parameter. CPSA queries can exclude specific compromises [25].

Messages. Messages include the field $\mathcal{F}$ and its generated group $\mathcal{C}$, with additional sorts of atomic symmetric keys, asymmetric keys, texts, and names. We close the messages under free operations of tupling and cryptographic operations, e.g. symmetric and asymmetric encryption, digital signature, and hashing.

We do not distinguish notationally among symmetric encryption, asymmetric encryption, and digital signature. We say that $K = K^{-1}$ whenever K is an atomic symmetric key or a compound key, and $K \neq K^{-1}$ iff K is an asymmetric key. Then the adversary powers summarized in Fig. 9 are reasonable. We regard a hash $\#(m)$ as a symmetric encryption $\{\!|0|\!\}_m$, using the argument as key to encrypt a fixed, irrelevant value. We use the word *encryption* as shorthand for all of these cryptographic operations.

Our claims hold across a wide range of choices of operators for the tupling and cryptographic operators, as long as they freely generate their results.

Definition 1. *We say that m_0 is* visible *in iff $m_0 = m_1$, or recursively m_1 is a tuple (m_2, m_3) and m_0 is visible in either m_2 or m_3.*

We say that m_0 is carried *in m_1 iff $m_0 = m_1$, or recursively m_1 is either:*
a tuple $m_1 = (m_2, m_3)$ *and m_0 is carried in either m_2 or m_3; or*
an encryption $m_1 = \{\!|m_2|\!\}_K$ *and m_0 is carried in m_2.*

In defining *visible*, we do not look inside encryptions at all. In *carried*, we look inside the plaintext m_2, but not the key K.

Executions are Bundles. In our model, the executions of a protocol Π are *bundles*. A bundle is a set of strands that are either adversary strands or else instances of the roles of Π, or initial segments of them (see Sect. 2.1), and in which every reception is explained by an earlier matching transmission. We formalize bundles via *nodes*, i.e. the transmission and reception events along the strands.

A binary relation $\rightarrow$ on nodes is a *communication relation* iff $n_1 \rightarrow n_2$ implies that n_1 is a transmission node, n_2 is a reception node, and $\mathsf{msg}(n_1) = \mathsf{msg}(n_2)$.

Definition 2. *Let $\mathcal{B} = (\mathcal{N}, \rightarrow)$ be a set of nodes together with a communication relation on $\mathcal{N}$. $\mathcal{B}$ is a bundle iff:*
1. *$n_2 \in \mathcal{N}$ and $n_1 \Rightarrow n_2$ implies $n_1 \in \mathcal{N}$;*
2. *$n_2 \in \mathcal{N}$ and n_2 is a reception node implies there exists a unique $n_1 \in \mathcal{N}$ such that $n_1 \rightarrow n_2$; and*
3. *Letting $\Rightarrow_\mathcal{B}$ be the restriction of $\Rightarrow$ to $\mathcal{N} \times \mathcal{N}$, the reflexive-transitive closure $(\Rightarrow_\mathcal{B} \cup \rightarrow)^*$ is a well-founded partial order.*

We write $\mathsf{nodes}(\mathcal{B})$ for $\mathcal{N}$, and $\preceq_\mathcal{B}$ for $(\Rightarrow_\mathcal{B} \cup \rightarrow)^*$.

Clause 3 is an *induction principle* for bundles. Any non-empty set S of nodes will have nodes that are $\preceq_\mathcal{B}$-minimal among nodes in S; proofs often take cases on $\preceq_\mathcal{B}$-minimal nodes.

Definition 3. *Let $\mathcal{B}$ be a bundle, m a message, and $n \in \mathsf{nodes}(\mathcal{B})$. Then m* originates *at n iff m is carried in $\mathsf{msg}(n)$, n is a transmission node, and for all earlier $n_0 \Rightarrow^+ n$ on the same strand, m is not carried in $\mathsf{msg}(n_0)$.*

The message m originates uniquely in B iff there is exactly one n ∈ nodes(B) such that m originates at n. The message m is non-originating in B if there is no such n ∈ nodes(B).

We can now define two special classes of protocol that CPSA analyzes.

One is that when an instance of a role transmits a field element in carried position, then that field element should simply be a transcendental $x \in$ trsc. This covers two important reasons why protocols disclose field values. First, disclosing a random choice models a corruption step, as in the registration role, Fig. 2. Second, disclosing a random choice may be part of a decommit step that allows a third party to validate a previously committed value. In these cases, an independent random choice, i.e. some $x \in$ trsc, is the value to disclose. There are, by contrast, also protocols such as signature protocols in which polynomials such as $r - xe$ may be disclosed. We do not model these as protocols, but can certainly model systems that use these types of signature as a primitive cryptographic operation. We say that a protocol *separates disclosures* if it satisfies this property.

Second, many protocols—though again, not all—involve field multiplication and division, but not field addition or subtraction. The four operations together lead in general to an undecidable class of unification problems. Thus, we adopt a limitation that is common to many mechanized protocol analysis systems [7, 12,15,22], and focus on the protocols in which the regular participants do not add or subtract field values, or use the group operation (which is addition in exponents).

Recall that a protocol contains a set of roles, which are strands containing parameters (i.e. variables) and terms built from them. Some of these variables are of sort *transcendental*, and variables and compound terms may be of sort *field*. The sort *transcendental* is a subsort of field, and in our current implementation, all terms of the narrower sort *transcendental* are variables. Bundles, however, contain actual field members, i.e. polynomials in our extension field $\mathcal{F} = \mathbb{Q}(\text{trsc})$.

Definition 4. *Let Π be a protocol. Π separates disclosures iff, for all transmission nodes $n \in$ nodes(Π), and all v of sort field carried in msg(n), v is simply a parameter of sort transcendental.*

Π is multiplicative iff, for all transmission nodes $n \in$ nodes(Π), and all v of sort field occurring in msg(n), neither addition nor subtraction occurs in v.

A bundle $\mathcal{B}$ is purely monomial iff, for every node $n \in$ nodes$(\mathcal{B})$ and every $p \in \mathcal{F}$, if p occurs in msg(n), then p is a monomial.

The methods of our earlier paper [16] show that, when Π is a multiplicative protocol, and a security goal G for Π has a counterexample, then there is a purely monomial bundle $\mathcal{B}$ that is a counterexample for G.

CPSA focuses on protocols that are multiplicative and separate disclosures. Thus, we need consider only purely monomial bundles. For more detail on this section, see the long version [17].

5   Two Key Lemmas

We now state our two main results about how the adversary obtains field and group elements. The first holds even for protocols using the additive structure. When a field element is exposed to the adversary in a bundle, then every transcendental present in it has also been exposed:

Lemma 1. *Suppose Π separates disclosures, $\mathcal{B}$ is a Π-bundle, and $x \in$ trsc has non-0 degree in $p \in \mathcal{F}$. Let $n_p \in$ nodes$(\mathcal{B})$ be a node where p is visible in $\mathsf{msg}(n_p)$. There is a node $n_x \in$ nodes$(\mathcal{B})$ such that $n_x \preceq_{\mathcal{B}} n_p$, and x is visible in $\mathsf{msg}(n_x)$.*

The proof in the appendix illustrates a standard technique, namely proof using the induction principle on bundles (Definition 2, Clause 3), after which we take cases on the minimal node in a set S.

The second lemma says how an adversary obtains a group element g^μ, in purely monomial bundles. It says that μ is a product of two monomials. The first, ν, consists of compromised transcendentals. The rest, ξ, yields a group element g^ξ that some regular participant has sent in carried position.

Lemma 2. *Suppose Π separates disclosures; $\mathcal{B}$ is a purely monomial Π-bundle; $n_\mu \in$ nodes$(\mathcal{B})$; and $\mathsf{g}^\mu \in \mathcal{C}$ is carried in $\mathsf{msg}(n_\mu)$. Then there is a monomial $\nu \in \mathcal{F}$ s.t. ν is a product of transcendentals visible before n_μ, and either*

1. *$\nu = \mu$ or else*
2. *letting $\xi = \mu/\nu$, there is a regular transmission node $n_\xi \in$ nodes$(\mathcal{B})$ such that $n_\xi \preceq_{\mathcal{B}} n_\mu$ and g^ξ is carried in $\mathsf{msg}(n_\xi)$.*
   Moreover, either $\nu = 1$ or g^ξ was previously visible.

The proof is similar in form; in the main case, g^μ is constructed by an adversary exponentiation, and the new exponent factor is combined into ν.

6   The CPSA Algorithm

Overall Algorithm. CPSA manipulates descriptions of executions that we call *skeletons*. The initial scenario is a skeleton from which CPSA starts. At any step, CPSA has a set $\mathcal{S}$ of skeletons available. If $\mathcal{S}$ is empty, the run is complete.

Otherwise, CPSA selects a skeleton $\mathbb{A}$ from $\mathcal{S}$. If $\mathbb{A}$ is *realized*, meaning that it gives a full description of some execution, then CPSA records it as a result. Otherwise, there is some reception node n within $\mathbb{A}$ that is not explained. This n is the *target node*. That means that CPSA cannot show how the message received by n could be available, given the actions the adversary can perform on his own, or using messages received from earlier transmissions.

CPSA replaces $\mathbb{A}$ with a "cohort." This is a set $\mathbb{C}_1, \ldots, \mathbb{C}_k$ of extensions of $\mathbb{A}$. CPSA must not "lose" executions: For every execution satisfying $\mathbb{A}$, there should be at least one of the $\mathbb{C}_i$ which this execution satisfies. When $k = 0$ and there are no cohort members, CPSA has recognized that $\mathbb{A}$ is *dead*, i.e. it describes no executions. CPSA then repeats this process starting with $\mathcal{S} \setminus \{\mathbb{A}\} \cup \{\mathbb{C}_1, \ldots, \mathbb{C}_k\}$.

Regular transmission: A regular principal has transmitted a message in this execution which is not described in A. E.g. Skeleton 1 in step 1 of Section 3.

Encryption key available: An encrypted value is received. CPSA explores if the adversary can obtain the encryption key. E.g. Skeleton 2 in step 1.

Decryption key available: A value escaped from a previously transmitted encryption. CPSA explores if the adversary can obtain the decryption key.

Specialization: The execution satisfies additional equations, not included in A. CPSA explores if in this special case the adversary can obtain the target node message.

DH value computed: The adversary obtains a DH value g^α, by exponentiation $g^{\alpha/w}$ to power w, which must also be available. (Lemma 2.) Skeleton 4 in step 2.

Exponent value computed: The adversary obtains an exponent xw. There are then two subcases (Lemma 1.):

1. CPSA explores how x and w are obtained; or
2. w is instantiated as some v/x, and x cancels out. Thus, x is absent from the instance of xw.

Fig. 10. Kinds of cohort members.

Cohort Selection. CPSA generates its cohorts by adding one or more facts, or new equalities, to A, to generate each $\mathbb{C}_i$.

The facts to add is based on a taxonomy of the executions satisfying A. In each one of them, the reception on the target node n must somehow be explained. There are only a limited number of types of explanation, which are summarized in Fig. 10. The first three kinds are identical to the forms they take without Diffie-Hellman; they are essentially about encryption and freshness. The *Specialization* clause is implemented by a unification algorithm implemented as a combination of theories. It treats transcendentals as primitive values, leading to faster solutions. The last two clauses, justified by Lemmas 2 and 1 (resp.), are new. The last clause, which is infrequently used, is applied in forward secrecy results in which the exponents take center stage.

7   Results and Related Work

The CPSA implementation is highly efficient (Fig. 11), running on a mid-2015 MacBook Pro with a 4-core 2.2 GHz Intel Core i7 processor, running up to 8 parallel threads using the Haskell run-time system.

We analyzed DHCR with each key derivation option, confirming the claims of Sect. 2. Each CPSA run checked five scenarios, determining the initiator and responder's guarantees under two sets of assumptions, as well as a forward secrecy property. Each run examines 90 to 230 skeletons.

We ran CPSA on the Station-to-Station protocol [9], together with two weakenings of it. In one, we do not assume the peer necessarily chooses a fresh exponent. In the other, we omit the flip in the second signed unit, enabling a reflection attack. In each, we test authentication, key secrecy, and forward secrecy, finding attacks against the weakened versions, and examining 55–190 skeletons.

DHCR, STS: Example & Time

dhcr-um	4.06s	dhcr-umx	0.72s	dhcr-um3	0.47s
sts	0.36s	sts-weak	0.08s	sts-unflip	0.17s

IKEv1: Example & Time

IKEv1-pk2-a	1.06s	IKEv1-pk2-a2	1.02s
IKEv1-pk2-m	0.49s	IKEv1-pk2-m2	0.58s
IKEv1-pk-a1	1.27s	IKEv1-pk-a12	1.09s
IKEv1-pk-a2	1.00s	IKEv1-pk-a22	1.10s
IKEv1-pk-m	0.51s	IKEv1-pk-m2	0.49s
IKEv1-psk-a	0.43s	IKEv1-psk-m	0.68s
IKEv1-psk-m-perlman	0.69s	IKEv1-quick	0.66s
IKEv1-psk-quick-noid	0.65s	IKEv1-quick-nopfs	0.09s
IKEv1-sig-a1	0.15s	IKEv1-sig-a2	0.16s
IKEv1-sig-a-perlman	0.17s	IKEv1-sig-a-perlman2	0.19s
IKEv1-sig-m	0.21s	IKEv1-sig-m-perlman	0.19s

IKEv2: Example & Time

IKEv2-eap	1.35s	IKEv2-eap2	1.36s
IKEv2-mac	0.76s	IKEv2-mac2	0.97s
IKEv2-mac-to-sig	0.83s	IKEv2-mac-to-sig2	0.82s
IKEv2-sig	0.56s	IKEv2-sig2	0.54s
IKEv2-sig-to-mac	0.70s	IKEv2-sig-to-mac2	0.69s

Fig. 11. CPSA runtime: DHCR-UM*, Station-to-Station, Intern. Key Exch. v. 1 and 2.

We also ran a rich set of variants of Internet Key Exchange (IKE) versions 1 and 2. Scyther analyzed this same set of variants circa 2010 [7], requiring more substantial runtimes, although recent timings are similar to ours (cf. also [4]). This suggests that CPSA is broadly efficient, with or without DH. Performance data for Tamarin and Maude-NPA is less available. We analyzed each IKE variant for about five properties, yielding conclusions similar to those drawn using Scyther. We found no novel attacks, but did sharpen the previous analysis, because CPSA reflects the algebraic properties of Diffie-Hellman natively, while Scyther emulated some properties of Diffie-Hellman.

Related Work. Our primary novelty is enrich-by-need for DH. CPSA provides a visualization of all of the minimal, essentially different executions compatible with a starting scenario. CPSA also computes a strongest security goal for the scenario. Moreover, CPSA is founded in the fields and cyclic groups that DH manipulates, with a clear connection with the generic group model [3,21,26].

It is, however, hardly the first method for DH. Within AVISPA [2,29], CL-Atse treated DH within a bounded session model [28]. In the unbounded session model, Küsters and Truderung [15] allow using ProVerif for DH; essentially, they compute a priori a set of DH terms that will suffice for ProVerif, and equip those terms with the rewrites ProVerif needs. The method is efficient and clever. However, it lacks a direct connection with the underlying algebra, and is not intended to support enrich-by-need. Like ProVerif, Scyther was not designed for

DH's algebra; special-purpose roles were added to coerce messages to different forms, thereby simulating the commutative principle $g^{xy} = g^{yx}$ [6].

By contrast, multiplicative DH protocols are native to Maude-NPA [12] and Tamarin [22]. Indeed, both of these systems allow general rewrite systems, even with associative-commutative operators, which is not a CPSA goal. However, neither supports enrich-by-need. CPSA appears to provide a higher level of automation and efficiency than Maude-NPA. CPSA's treatment of the algebra of DH is also preferable, as Maude-NPA lacks a multiplicative inverse. Tamarin has a faithful theory for the multiplicative fragment, which—since it lacks 0—has an equational axiomatization. Although it offers great flexibility, performance information on Tamarin is hard to find.

Neither Maude-NPA nor Tamarin appears to have a sharp distinction between the primitive random choices—our "transcendentals"—and other exponents. Their variables are not similar to transcendentals, since they range over all exponents. Thus, random choices may appear or disappear in unification, so the distinction between the narrower sort of transcendentals and the larger sort of exponents sharpens our treatment of unification [17]. It also helped us to formulate the Lemmas 1–2.

The distinction between underlying transcendentals and exponents in general, and the two lemmas to which it leads, are reusable ideas that could well provide other systems with a strategy for more focused search.

A   Appendix: Proofs

Lemma 1. Suppose Π separates disclosures, $\mathcal{B}$ is a Π-bundle, and $x \in$ trsc has non-0 degree in $p \in \mathcal{F}$. Let $n_p \in$ nodes($\mathcal{B}$) be a node where p is visible in msg(n_p). There is a node $n_x \in$ nodes($\mathcal{B}$) such that $n_x \preceq_\mathcal{B} n_p$, and x is visible in msg(n_x).

Proof. Choose $\mathcal{B}$, and if there are any x, p, n_p that furnish a counterexample let $n_p \in$ nodes($\mathcal{B}$) be $\preceq_\mathcal{B}$-minimal among counterexamples for any x, p. Observe first that $x \neq p$, since if $x = p$ this is not a counterexample: let $n_x = n_p$.

Since p is carried in msg(n_p), there exists an $n_o \preceq_\mathcal{B} n_p$ such that p originates on n_o. By the definition of originates, n_o is a transmission node.

First, we show that n_o does not lie on an adversary strand, by taking cases on the adversary strands. The **creation** strands that emit values in FLD originate $\mathbf{1}$ and transcendentals y : trsc. But x is not present in $\mathbf{1}$, and if x is present in y, then x and y are identical, which we have excluded.

If n_o lies on a **multiplicative** or **additive** strand, then it takes incoming field values p_1, p_2. Since x has non-zero degree in p only if it has non-zero degree in at least one of the p_i, this contradicts the $\preceq_\mathcal{B}$-minimality of the counterexample.

Node n_o does not lie on an **construction** or **destruction** strand, which never originate field values. Thus, n_o does not lie on an adversary strand.

Finally, n_o does not lie on a regular strand of Π: Since Π separates disclosures, if n_o originates the field value p, then p is a transcendental. Thus, if x is present, $p = x$, which was excluded above. $\square$

Lemma 2. Suppose Π separates disclosures; $\mathcal{B}$ is a purely monomial Π-bundle; $n_\mu \in \mathsf{nodes}(\mathcal{B})$; and $\mathbf{g}^\mu \in \mathcal{C}$ is carried in $\mathsf{msg}(n_\mu)$. Then there is a monomial $\nu \in \mathcal{F}$ s.t. ν is a product of transcendentals visible before n_μ, and either

1. $\nu = \mu$ or else
2. letting $\xi = \mu/\nu$, there is a *regular* transmission node $n_\xi \in \mathsf{nodes}(\mathcal{B})$ such that $n_\xi \preceq_\mathcal{B} n_\mu$ and $\mathbf{g}^\xi$ is carried in $\mathsf{msg}(n_\xi)$.

Moreover, either $\nu = 1$ or $\mathbf{g}^\xi$ was previously visible.

Proof. Let $\mathcal{B}$ be a bundle, let $n_\mu \in \mathsf{nodes}(\mathcal{B})$, and assume inductively that the claim holds for all nodes $n \prec n_\mu$. If n_μ is a reception node, then the (earlier) paired transmission node satisfies the property by the IH. However, the same ν and n_ξ also satisfy the property for n_μ. If n_μ is a regular transmission, then the conclusion holds with $\nu = 1$, the empty product of transcendentals.

So suppose n_μ lies on an adversary strand. If n_μ transmits the group element $\mathbf{g}$, then let $\nu = \mu = 1$. The constructive strands for tupling or encryption provide no new group elements in carried position. Nor do the destructive strands for untupling or decryption.

Thus, the remaining possibility is that n_μ is the transmission on an exponentiation strand $-h \Rightarrow -w \Rightarrow +\mathbf{exp}(h, w)$ where $\mathbf{exp}(h, w) = y^\mu$. By the IH, for the node receiving $h \in \mathcal{C}$, the property is met. Thus, $h = \mathbf{g}^{\mu_0}$, where there exist ν_0, ξ_0 satisfying the conditions.

Hence, we may take $\nu = \nu_0 w$ and $\xi = \xi_0$. By Lemma 1, w is a product of previously visible transcendentals, so the requirements are met. $\square$

References

1. Ankney, R., Johnson, D., Matyas, M.: The Unified Model. Contribution to ANSI X9F1. Standards Projects (Financial Crypto Tools), ANSI X, 42 (1995)
2. Armando, A., et al.: The AVISPA tool for the automated validation of internet security protocols and applications. In: Etessami, K., Rajamani, S.K. (eds.) CAV 2005. LNCS, vol. 3576, pp. 281–285. Springer, Heidelberg (2005). https://doi.org/10.1007/11513988_27
3. Barthe, G., Fagerholm, E., Fiore, D., Mitchell, J.C., Scedrov, A., Schmidt, B.: Automated analysis of cryptographic assumptions in generic group models. In: Garay, J.A., Gennaro, R. (eds.) CRYPTO 2014. LNCS, vol. 8616, pp. 95–112. Springer, Heidelberg (2014). https://doi.org/10.1007/978-3-662-44371-2_6
4. Basin, D.A., Cremers, C., Meier, S.: Provably repairing the ISO/IEC 9798 standard for entity authentication. J. Comput. Secur. **21**(6), 817–846 (2013)
5. Bellare, M., Rogaway, P.: Entity authentication and key distribution. In: Stinson, D.R. (ed.) CRYPTO 1993. LNCS, vol. 773, pp. 232–249. Springer, Heidelberg (1994). https://doi.org/10.1007/3-540-48329-2_21
6. Cremers, C.: Key exchange in IPsec revisited: formal analysis of IKEv1 and IKEv2. In: Atluri, V., Diaz, C. (eds.) ESORICS 2011. LNCS, vol. 6879, pp. 315–334. Springer, Heidelberg (2011). https://doi.org/10.1007/978-3-642-23822-2_18
7. Cremers, C., Mauw, S.: Operational Semantics and Verification of Security Protocols. Springer, Heidelberg (2012). https://doi.org/10.1007/978-3-540-78636-8
8. Diffie, W., Hellman, M.: New directions in cryptography. IEEE Trans. Inf. Theory **22**(6), 644–654 (1976)

9. Diffie, W., van Oorschot, P.C., Wiener, M.J.: Authentication and authenticated key exchanges. Des. Codes Cryptogr. **2**(2), 107–125 (1992)
10. Dolev, D., Yao, A.: On the security of public-key protocols. IEEE Trans. Inf. Theory **29**, 198–208 (1983)
11. Dougherty, D.J., Guttman, J.D.: Decidability for lightweight Diffie-Hellman protocols. In: IEEE Symposium on Computer Security Foundations (2014)
12. Escobar, S., Meadows, C., Meseguer, J.: Maude-NPA: cryptographic protocol analysis modulo equational properties. In: Aldini, A., Barthe, G., Gorrieri, R. (eds.) FOSAD 2007-2009. LNCS, vol. 5705, pp. 1–50. Springer, Heidelberg (2009). https://doi.org/10.1007/978-3-642-03829-7_1
13. Guttman, J.D.: Shapes: surveying crypto protocol runs. In: Cortier, V., Kremer, S. (eds.) Formal Models and Techniques for Analyzing Security Protocols, Cryptology and Information Security Series. IOS Press (2011)
14. Guttman, J.D.: Establishing and preserving protocol security goals. J. Comput. Secur. **22**(2), 201–267 (2014)
15. Küsters, R., Truderung, T.: Using ProVerif to analyze protocols with Diffie-Hellman exponentiation. In: IEEE Computer Security Foundations Symposium, pp. 157–171. IEEE (2009)
16. Liskov, M., Javier Thayer, F.: Modeling Diffie-Hellman derivability for automated analysis. In: IEEE Computer Security Foundations, pp. 232–243 (2014)
17. Liskov, M.D., Guttman, J.D., Ramsdell, J.D., Rowe, P.D., Javier Thayer, F.: Enrich-by-need protocol analysis for Diffie-Hellman (extended version), April 2018. http://arxiv.org/abs/1804.05713
18. Liskov, M.D., Rowe, P.D., Javier Thayer, F.: Completeness of CPSA. Technical Report MTR110479, The MITRE Corporation, March 2011. http://www.mitre. org/publications/technical-papers/completeness-of-cpsa
19. Liskov, M.D., Javier Thayer, F.: Formal modeling of Diffie-Hellman derivability for exploratory automated analysis. Technical report, MITRE, June 2013. TR 13–0411
20. Lowe, G.: A hierarchy of authentication specifications. In: 10th Computer Security Foundations Workshop Proceedings, pp. 31–43. IEEE CS Press (1997)
21. Maurer, U.M.: Abstract models of computation in cryptography. In: Smart, N.P. (ed.) Cryptography and Coding 2005. LNCS, vol. 3796, pp. 1–12. Springer, Heidelberg (2005). https://doi.org/10.1007/11586821_1
22. Meier, S., Schmidt, B., Cremers, C., Basin, D.: The TAMARIN prover for the symbolic analysis of security protocols. In: Sharygina, N., Veith, H. (eds.) CAV 2013. LNCS, vol. 8044, pp. 696–701. Springer, Heidelberg (2013). https://doi.org/10.1007/978-3-642-39799-8_48
23. Ramsdell, J.D.: Deducing security goals from shape analysis sentences. The MITRE Corporation, April 2012. http://arxiv.org/abs/1204.0480
24. Ramsdell, J.D., Guttman, J.D.: CPSA: a cryptographic protocol shapes analyzer (2009). http://hackage.haskell.org/package/cpsa
25. Rowe, P.D., Guttman, J.D., Liskov, M.D.: Measuring protocol strength with security goals. Int. J. Inf. Secur. **15**(6), 575–596 (2016). https://doi.org/10.1007/s10207-016-0319-z. http://web.cs.wpi.edu/~guttman/pubs/ijis_measuring-security.pdf
26. Shoup, V.: Lower bounds for discrete logarithms and related problems. In: Fumy, W. (ed.) EUROCRYPT 1997. LNCS, vol. 1233, pp. 256–266. Springer, Heidelberg (1997). https://doi.org/10.1007/3-540-69053-0_18
27. Javier Thayer, F., Herzog, J.C., Guttman, J.D.: Strand spaces: proving security protocols correct. J. Comput. Secur. **7**(2/3), 191–230 (1999)

28. Turuani, M.: The CL-Atse protocol analyser. In: Pfenning, F. (ed.) RTA 2006. LNCS, vol. 4098, pp. 277–286. Springer, Heidelberg (2006). https://doi.org/10. 1007/11805618_21
29. Viganò, L.: Automated security protocol analysis with the AVISPA tool. Electron. Notes Theor. Comput. Sci. **155**, 61–86 (2006)

Key Agreement via Protocols

Andrew William Roscoe[1(✉)] and Lei Wang[1,2]

[1] University College Oxford Blockchain Research Centre, Oxford, UK
awroscoe@gmail.com
[2] Oxford-Hainan Blockchain Research Institute, Oxford, UK

Abstract. Inspired by the ideas of *no cloning* and *measurable degrading* that quantum key agreement protocols rely on, we devise novel key agreement protocols for the classical world. Our protocols are based on identical devices that are mass produced and distributed among parties participating in the protocol. We thus use protocols a little outside their normal range and seemingly achieve the impossible by relying on certain assumptions on the devices.

1 Introduction

Cathy Meadows is a truly seminal figure in the field of cryptographic protocols. She has contributed to the development and understanding of this subject, both directly through her own work and through the many people that she and her work [8–10] have inspired. More specifically, her work on the automation of the analysis of protocols has lead to a range of sophisticated and powerful tools for creating and analysing protocols, which used to a black art and certainly immensely risky. She was already well established in this field when, together with Gavin Lowe and Michael Goldsmith, Roscoe joined in 1994/5 [6,7,11,14]. Her friendship and advice have been a constant inspiration ever since.

Security protocols and cryptography are both powerful tools for attaining security goals. Initially, these two communities stayed rather separate. The protocol community relied on perhaps simplistic assumptions such as "perfect cryptography", and gradually expanded to encompass finitely presented algebraic weaknesses in cryptosystems such as Vernam and RSA. They seek a wide range of secure goals including sharing and authenticating keys privately in symmetric schemes, achieving transactions such as the transfer of value, voting for consensus, or achieving a linked and authenticated data stream. Cryptographers have sought lower level proofs about the cryptographic constructs themselves. While historically there were no sufficient links between the two groups, there have been better integration recently through a series of papers, e.g. [1,5].

In this paper we show that it is possible to replace expensive cryptosystems, which are built on complex mathematical operations and hence have certain limitation in practical applications because of heavy resource requirement and low performance, by security protocols, which only use standard symmetric ciphers and hash functions. Loosely speaking, we are moving a problem from the world

© Springer Nature Switzerland AG 2019
J. D. Guttman et al. (Eds.): Meadows Festschrift, LNCS 11565, pp. 156–166, 2019.
https://doi.org/10.1007/978-3-030-19052-1_11

of cryptography to the world of security protocols. More precisely, our goal is to find replacements for asymmetric constructs such as public key cryptosystems, associated signature and Diffie-Hellman variants. The research motivation is well known as below:

1. The complicated mathematical operations in asymmetric constructions are often too resource hungry for lightweight applications such as IoT nodes.
2. Quantum computers are known to break the most popular public-key cryptosystems [15]. Moreover, our knowledge of what quantum computers can solve is still poor. It is commonly believed that hash function and symmetric-key primitives are relatively resistant to quantum attacks. Thus, it is very attractive to relying the post quantum security solely on hash function and symmetric-key primitives. While cryptographers are devising new public-key cryptosystems for post-quantum security, it is possible that these new post-quantum cryptosystem would be vulnerable to novel quantum algorithms. Moreover, these post-quantum cryptosystems have generally turned out to be less efficient in computation and space than Diffie-Hellman, RSA etc., re-emphasising the first point above.

Both of these provide us with good reason for following the approach adopted in this paper.

In other words we want to build asymmetric encryptions, secret key exchange and efficient signature mechanisms using protocols created from generic and sufficiently long cryptographic hash functions, and sufficiently secure symmetric encryptions. However, itt is seemingly impossible to achieve these goals within standard models of how protocols and their implementations are constructed.

It seems that we need some clever idea or *deus ex machina* to help us. The one we choose is that we rely on hardened physical security of the devices the protocols are implemented on. Specifically we assume we can create devices meeting the following specifications.

(a) They provide a limited range of customised cryptographic protocol services, identical for all devices.
(b) They contain a secret key, identical in all devices, that is available to the above services to use.
(c) The key in the devices cannot be extracted by an attacker
(d) No unadvertised functionality of the devices is obtainable by an attacker.

Conditions (c) and (d) amount to a pretty strong assumption of the device not being vulnerable to reverse engineering. In this paper we do not comment on how easy or difficult it may be to attain these goals, other than to say that one would naturally expect that the more expensive and customised the manufacturing technology is, the better the resistance will be. Even if the individual devices are moderately costly, the benefit of having them all identical and not requiring the post-manufacture or individual initialisation and management of keys will be considerable.

The possibly lower security threshold and certainly low energy threshold for IoT makes this the most likely initial application, in the authors' opinion. For the purposes of the present paper the reader is asked to put this sort of question on one side and treat the core problem as an intellectual exercise. In essence, in a long mathematical tradition, we are reducing one difficult problem to another.

Our assumptions imply that no *priori* key management mechanisms are required. We can rely on them working out their own keys *in situ*. This is a huge and attractive simplification.

2 Background

Asymmetric cryptography provides the core that supports most of modern security by establishing secret keys and implementing signature. Unfortunately the two problems highlighted in the introduction mean we have to look elsewhere than the traditional methods which become expensive as the power of the conventional attacker grows and the ero of quantum computers that can run Shor's and Grover's algorithms on large values get closer.

The second of these has generated a great deal of research on models of signature and asymmetric cryptography that are not thought to be vulnerable to quantum computers. It is generally believed that standard means of cryptographic hashing are or can be made invulnerable, and strong enough symmetric cryptography such as AES similarly, provided a small multiple (typically 1.5 or 2 depending on the detail) is applied to the number of bits involved. However these do not obviously solve the problem since they do not obviously provide an alternative. Much of the work is devoted to lattice-based cryptography, seen by some as the most promising asymmetric prospect. This paper concentrates on uses of conventional primitives in non-standard ways.

The methods we describe are extremely efficient in the amount of cryptographic calculation required and therefore offer prospects of security to applications such as IoT where asymmetric cryptography is barred on cost grounds rather than only because of the worry of future quantum computers.

3 Key Agreement

The concepts below were developed from one of the key ideas underpinning quantum key exchange [2], namely that it is impossible to clone a particle passed from one party to another without disturbing the system, thereby making it and similar activity by an attacker discoverable. This led to the question of how you might create, and exploit, non-clonable transmissions in the classical world.

We imagine that the world is populated by *widgets* that communicate at two levels: with their local users over secure channels (i.e. ones that we do not have to make secure), and through the ether (such as internet or radio waves) which we suppose to be run on Dolev-Yao lines where messages can be copied, blocked or faked at will. To counter this we imagine that the widgets are built to resist reverse engineering and out-of-spec use and so will not reveal their internal secrets.

All these widgets are identical. If Alice and Bob hold one each and want to exchange a key secretly with each other via their widgets, how can they do so and be sure they have not been talking to Eve instead, and know that Eve cannot have acted like a man-in-the-middle or have used one of more of her own widgets to obtain their key?

We are trying to design ones that allow a pair of nodes that own them the ability to run a protocol that gives them the equivalent of running Diffie-Hellman in the conventional pre-quantum world.

We must make widgets able to talk in a way which is secret (to all but other suitably prepared widgets) and such that they guarantee no cloning of messages. This solves some of the problems above.

To do this we will assume they use a secret ms (master secret) that is known to all widgets and no-one else. We could use this to encrypt things X they want to send to each other as $\{X\}_{ms}$. However this would mean that there was a lot of traffic encrypted under ms creating the danger of it being revealed by cryptanalysis. We will therefore use it in more subtle ways.

Because all widgets are identical, Alice cannot tell whether she is talking to Bob's or Eve's. There is no need for us to worry about this, because this is a familiar situation. If Alice was using Diffie-Hellman then that would not of itself tell her who she was running it with. With Diffie-Hellman we need to use authentication so Alice and Bob can confirm that they were talking with each other, and the same will be true here. What we need to confirm is that if Alice and Bob do share a key through use of the widgets, then no-one else shares it. What we want, in effect, is that our widget provides, in a post-quantum world, the same guarantees that doing Diffie-Hellman computation provides in a classical one.

In the world of Diffie-Hellman, this can be achieved by having Alice and Bob agree over an authentic but not private channel on the hash of the key they have developed. A belt-and-braces approach would for be for them to include not only the key but also their g^x and g^y and p and g in this hash. We can clearly adopt an analogous approach here, or use some (perhaps hash-based) cryptographic signature to authenticate common ownership.

Imagine first that Alice simply wishes to create a new key X and send it securely to partner Bob via such widgets A and B (which do not have actual identities, but are the ones they own).

Protocol L1

```
0. Alice -> A: X
1. A -> B    : go
2. B -> A    : {NB}_ms           NB is a fresh random nonce
3. A -> B    : {X,NB}_ms
4. B -> Bob  : X
```

Here X_K means the symmetric encryption of X under key K.

This would be followed by a phase in which Alice and Bob agree over another authentic channel that they have both got, say `hash(X)`. (This confirms but does not reveal `X`).

Here messages 0 and 4 are the message being communicated from A's user Alice to A, and B to its user Bob. `go` is just a signal to B to start. The latter then sends NB, a random fresh nonce, which is included by A with X in Message 3, with B refusing to accept this message unless its own nonce is included. (The names A and B are included here for clarity to us: they do not really exist and the widgets do not know them, at least in any secure sense). All communications between a user and his/her widget are assumed to be secure.

Depending on the implementation, the widgets A and B might communicate directly via the Dolev-Yao medium or might have Alice and Bob do so for on their behalves.

We assume that as soon as the value X or NB has performed its role in the protocol for A or B, the widget forgets it, and will not perform any other series of messages than those required to perform the sender or receiver role in the above. In particular Alice's will never re-use NB and Bob's will accept at most one Message 3 for each NB it generates.

For any such protocol we require that the sender A only sends X on once it has received an entropy from the receiver B, and that this send of X is both confidential and only successful when this entropy is bound up with X in some chosen way. The above is one way of achieving this; we will see more later. The entropy must be fresh and unguessable, and the data must be forgotten by the nodes as soon as possible, and not re-used.

The above protocol is not ideal because encryption under ms is over-used. One way of fixing this is

Protocol L2

```
0. Alice -> A: X
1. A -> B     : NA              NA is a fresh random nonce
both widgets compute ks = hash(NA,ms)
2. B -> A     : {NB}_{ks}       NB is a fresh random nonce
3. A -> B     : {X,NB}_{ks}
4. B -> Bob   : X
```

The guarantee provided by such a protocol is that any X a node sends reaches the user of at most one other widget. Eve can divert the messages from B to E, which will lead to her receiving X. But she cannot persuade both B and E to reveal X, because to do this she would need to get X paired with two different nonces NB and NE. And A pairs X with one and forgets it. Note that this contributes towards the no-cloning of X.

Thus using these, Alice knows that any X she sends reaches at most one party, who might be Bob, and Bob knows that any he received came from someone, who might be Alice. This is very like the logical properties of Diffie-Hellman: anyone who runs the interchange through their widget knows they share a secret X with someone, but does not know who.

Crucial to understanding these protocols is that the widget B generates a unique ticket for each session, namely NB. It will never accept more than one message with any given ticket, and no widget will accept a message with any ticket other than the one it has itself generated.

If we assume that Alice and Bob have an authentic but not secret channel between them, namely one that can be overheard but where they know conclusively that they are talking to each other, they can compare the hashes of an X sent by Alice and one received by Bob to check they are the same. Does this prove that no-one else other than the two of them knows X (on the assumption that it is an entropy created by Alice that is unguessable)?

The answer to this is "**no**" because we have not eliminated the possibility of a man in the middle (MITM). Eve might own two widgets E and F. She gets E to obtain X from A and then has F send the same X to B. She then knows X even though Alice and Bob agree on it. How can we prevent this? In essence the protocols and our assumptions about widgets ensure that X cannot be copied inside the world of widgets: the above protocols are *linear* in the same sense as linear logic, but they do not prevent copying X outside this realm and passing it on.

It follows that protocols L1 and L2 do not meet our requirements: they do not guarantee secure key exchange.

Again taking a clue from the quantum key exchange world, one solution to this is to have A and/or B degrade X in such a way that the test of agreement assumes a single degrading, but does not permit two.

Two interesting forms of degrading are:

- Hashing: if the protocol is modified so that widget B outputs hash(X) rather than X, then the MITM attack above hashes X twice. If Alice and Bob compare hash(hash(X)) with hash(Y), where Y is B's output, they can easily detect the MITM. The approach to sharing a key could then be that Alice sends a pre-key random value X to A, with the hope that k = hash(X) will be delivered to Bob by B. The actual key is then k. (Alternatively the value X can be hashed just by A or by both widgets. If both then the check would have to be different and the natural key would be hash(hash(X))).
- Delay: node B delays the last message by interval T. Bob only accepts X if received $< 2T$ from Alice's send. This time can be sent authentically from Alice to Bob over the same channel used for comparing the keys at either end as part of the key checking. Note that this mechanism allows any message to passed from Alice to Bob, rather than the scrambled hash(X) of the first.

Both of these provide the opportunity for Alice and Bob to exclude the man in the middle on the assumption that they sent/received their messages via a widget, and that the only thing that can be done with a widget is to use it according to its functional specification.

We are thus relying that, even though Eve may own a number of widgets identical to Alice's and Bob's, she cannot use these to decrypt the messages that go between Alice's, Bob's or anyone else's widgets other than by performing a complete protocol, and she cannot extract anything other than the intended outputs from them.

With the use of hashing as degrading the above protocols become

Protocol KA1

```
0. Alice -> A: X
1. A -> B     : go
2. B -> A     : {NB}_ms          NB is a fresh random nonce
3. A -> B     : {X,NB}_ms
4. B -> Bob   : hash(X)          hash computed by B
                                 Bob has no access to X.
```

The above is sub-optimal because it over uses encryption under ms.

Protocol KA2

```
0. Alice -> A: X
1. A -> B     : NA               NA is a fresh random nonce
both widgets compute ks = hash(NA,ms)
2. B -> A     : {NB}_{ks}        NB is a fresh random nonce
3. A -> B     : {X,NB}_{ks}
4. B -> Bob   : hash(X)          hash computed by B
                                 Bob has no access to X.
```

The KA in these names stands for key agreement. In each case we assume that A is obliged to invent a new fresh entropy X for each key she wants to share.

The delay variant of these protocols is intriguing because it allows secret transmission from Alice to Bob without them even having to know keys. The only problem is that Alice has to check that it really is Bob she has shared the secret with since she cannot be sure in advance.

4   Reducing the Role of the Widget

What is it essential for a widget to do? The ones implied in the previous section need to hold on to a long-term secret, and perform specified calculations utilising that secret. These things appear to be necessary. However they also need to hold a certain amount of state, generate random numbers, and hold onto temporary variables such as the nonce NB. These things do not seem so obviously necessary, and when we are trying to build something that cannot be reverse engineered it is as well to keep it as simple as possible.

Let us first examine the issue of random numbers: NB is generated by B in both protocols and in the second one A also generates NA. NA is used to generate a fresh key for sending NB. Strictly speaking, it does not seem to be necessary to encrypt NB at all in these protocols: its role in the protocols is, in essence, to prevent any other recipient E accepting the message that A sends to B in this protocol. Another E would not have generated this NB.

The following is based on stripping the protocols above to the bone, and leaving all the creation of random numbers and remembering of them to Alice and Bob as opposed to the widgets. The biggest trick here is making sure that NB can still only be used by Bob to obtain the transmission, and never allows any other agent to get at it. (More precisely, it is never usedby trustworthy agent and another agent).

Protocol KA3

```
1. Alice -> Bob: go
3. Bob -> Alice  : hash(NB)
3. Alice -> A:(X,hash(NB))
         ks = hash(hash(NB),ms)
4. A -> B    : {X,hash(NB)}_{ks}
4a: Bob -> B : NB   enabling B to compute ks and decrypt Message 3
         X (in B) := this decryption
5. B -> Bob  : hash(X)        hash computed by B
```

Here is is Bob's duty to ensure the freshness and secrecy of NB: if he re-uses a value then the no-copying property does not hold.

This results in widgets that do not need state, all they have to do is

- At A: Given (X,hash(NB)) compute {X,hash(NB)}_ks in an atomic fashion.
- At B: Given encryption Y and NB, compute decrypt(hash(hash(NB,ms))),Y) in an atomic fashion.
- In both cases with no intermediate calculations or data available.

We are thus getting Alice and Bob to remember the state, not the widgets. The important difference here is that we are making B decrypt the packet under the still-secret NB, which has never been seen by anyone other than Bob before. So here NB is acting as a secret key that Bob retains for himself to unlock the message he has triggered with hash(NB). Because no other widget ever knows NB, no-one else can get at the value hash(X).

The rationale here for degrading X to hash(X) are exactly the same as they were with KA1 and KA2.

The basic rationale for degrading NB to hash(NB) in most of this protocol is essentially the same as the rationale for degrading X to hash(X): it prevents an attack based on copying. This seems to what is required to move from a situation where A or B is trustily generating random values to one where they accept values from their users who might not be so trustworthy in general. One might infer that if we did not let A input a pre-key from Alice ubt instead create it internally, then degrading would not actually be necessary at all.

This is witnessed by the following protocol, which requires no degrading.

Protocol KA4

```
2. B -> A     : NB              NB is a fresh random nonce
      ks := hash(NB,ms)
3. A -> B     : {X,NA}_{ks}     NA freshly created by A
4. B -> Bob   : NA xor NB       (or NA)
4a A -> Alice : NA xor NB       (or NA)
```

This protocol achieves a shared secret key in a simpler way, in some sense, again using NB as a ticket. This seems to work for our purposes with in some sense simpler widget functionality, but where state is needed. We cannot here trust Bob to input NB or Alice to input NA, so random number generation is needed here, unlike in KA3.

We regard KA3 as the most promising key agreement protocol, because the widgets need no state, and do not need to generate random numbers. What they do need to do is to keep the long term secret ms securely, and implement the compound functions implementing the encryption and decryption phases of the calculation, and not provide any of the component functions making these up.

5   Verification

The protocols described in this paper look very much like the ones that we have been putting through protocol verifiers for years. The main novelties are

- The role of widgets as trusted computing cores for whom we do not trust the owners.
- The lack of reliable identities at a level at which the protocols and widgets are meant to work.

The idea of non-reverse-engineerability seems to be completely orthogonal to this analysis other than as relevant to the first of these.

In a CSP/Casper model the natural way to analyse the stateless widgets version of the protocol is to build all of the capabilities of a widget usable for (say) protocol KA3 into the intruder model. Thus if the intruder posesses {X,Y} then we can deduce {X,Y}_{hash(Y,ms)} and if it possesses {X,hash(NB)}_{hash(hash(NB),ms)} and NB then it can deduce hash(X).

All this is, of course, in addition to the usual rules of an intruder. Thus stateless widgets seem to fit in well, simply treating the widgets as what they in effect are, a type of oracle.

Widgets that have internal state really need to be treated as trustworthy participants in the protocol, and we need to allow for an unbounded number of them to be present, reason convincingly that somme small number such as 2 is sufficient, or prove limited results on how many our models allow for. This situation is, or course, very similar to the problem of reasoning about many parallel sessions of a cryptoprotocol as was done in [3,12], for example. We leave the resolution of that case to future research.

The question of whether widgets do or do not have internal state also affects how one programs the actions of the likes of Alice and Bob in the network. Just as in their availability to the intruder discussed above, a stateless widget used by a trustworthy agent does not need a separate process to implement it, whereas a stateful one probably does. We would possibly avoid the last issues if Alice and Bob were assumed to own only one widget each.

6   Conclusions and Further Thoughts

This is at least an interesting thought experiment into how to achieve key exchange in unusual ways. How practical it is will depend on the possibility of resisting reverse engineering.

We have similarly provided approaches to asymmetric cryptography: see [13], where we will go into more detail about reverse engineering. There are existing discussions of this, including [4].

We observed that non-stateful widgets will fit smoothly into the established methods of verifying cryptoprotocols, but that stateful ones might pose more of a challenge.

Resistance to reverse engineering is a popular research topic in areas like digital rights mechanisms, key management and blockchain. There are various technologies that implement degrees of it in general such as Hardware Security Modules, and SGX enclaves on Intel processors.

References

1. Armando, A., et al.: The AVISPA tool for the automated validation of internet security protocols and applications. In: Etessami, K., Rajamani, S.K. (eds.) CAV 2005. LNCS, vol. 3576, pp. 281–285. Springer, Heidelberg (2005). https://doi.org/10.1007/11513988_27
2. Cerf, N.J., Levy, M., Van Assche, G.: Quantum distribution of Gaussian keys using squeezed states. Phys. Rev. A **63**(5), 052311 (2001)
3. Chevalier, Y., Vigneron, L.: Automated unbounded verification of security protocols. In: Brinksma, E., Larsen, K.G. (eds.) CAV 2002. LNCS, vol. 2404, pp. 324–337. Springer, Heidelberg (2002). https://doi.org/10.1007/3-540-45657-0_24
4. Colombier, B., Bossuet, L.: A survey of hardware protection of design data for integrated circuits and intellectual properties. IET Comput. Digit. Tech. Inst. Eng. Technol. **8**(6), 274287 (2014)
5. Cremers, C.J.F.: The scyther tool: verification, falsification, and analysis of security protocols. In: Gupta, A., Malik, S. (eds.) CAV 2008. LNCS, vol. 5123, pp. 414–418. Springer, Heidelberg (2008). https://doi.org/10.1007/978-3-540-70545-1_38
6. Lowe, G.: Breaking and fixing the Needham-Schroeder public-key protocol using FDR. In: Margaria, T., Steffen, B. (eds.) TACAS 1996. LNCS, vol. 1055, pp. 147–166. Springer, Heidelberg (1996). https://doi.org/10.1007/3-540-61042-1_43
7. Lowe, G.: Casper: a compiler for the analysis of security protocols. J. Comput. Secur. **6**(1–2), 53–84 (1998)

8. Meadows, C.: The NRL protocol analyzer: an overview. J. Log. Program. **26**(2), 113–131 (1996)
9. Meadows, C.A.: Formal verification of cryptographic protocols: a survey. In: Pieprzyk, J., Safavi-Naini, R. (eds.) ASIACRYPT 1994. LNCS, vol. 917, pp. 133–150. Springer, Heidelberg (1995). https://doi.org/10.1007/BFb0000430
10. Meadows, C.: Applying formal methods to the analysis of a key management protocol. J. Comput. Secur. **1**(1), 5–35 (1992)
11. Roscoe, A.W.: Modelling and verifying key-exchange protocols using CSP and FDR. In: Proceedings of the Eighth IEEE Computer Security Foundations Workshop. IEEE (1995)
12. Roscoe, A.W., Broadfoot, P.J.: Proving security protocols with model checkers by data independence techniques. J. Comput. Secur. **7**(2–3), 147–190 (1999)
13. Roscoe, A.W., Wang, L., Chen, B.: New approaches to key agreement and public key cryptography. In: preparation
14. Ryan, P., Schneider, S., Goldsmith, M., Lowe, G., Roscoe, A.W.: The Modelling and Analysis of Security Protocols: The CSP Approach. Addison-Wesley Professional, Boston (2001)
15. Shor, P.W.: Polynomial time algorithms for discrete logarithms and factoring on a quantum computer. In: Adleman, L.M., Huang, M.-D. (eds.) ANTS 1994. LNCS, vol. 877, p. 289. Springer, Heidelberg (1994). https://doi.org/10.1007/3-540-58691-1_68

Privacy Protocols

Jason Castiglione, Dusko Pavlovic$^{(\boxtimes)}$, and Peter-Michael Seidel

University of Hawaii, Honolulu, HI, USA
{jcastig,dusko,pseidel}@hawaii.edu

Dedicated to Catherine Meadows

Abstract. Security protocols enable secure communication over insecure channels. Privacy protocols enable private interactions over secure
channels. Security protocols set up secure channels using cryptographic
primitives. Privacy protocols set up private channels using secure channels. But just like some security protocols can be broken without breaking the underlying cryptography, some privacy protocols can be broken
without breaking the underlying security. Such privacy attacks have been
used to leverage e-commerce against targeted advertising from the outset;
but their depth and scope became apparent only with the overwhelming advent of influence campaigns in politics. The blurred boundaries
between privacy protocols and privacy attacks present a new challenge
for protocol analysis. Or maybe they do not, as the novelty is often in
the eye of the observer. Cathy Meadows spearheaded and steered our
research in security protocols. The methods for analyzing privacy protocols arise directly from her work.

1 Introduction: What Is Privacy?

The concept of privacy has been a source of much controversy and confusion,
not only in social and political discourse, but also in research.

The *controversy* arises from the fact that privacy is not a security requirement, like secrecy or authenticity, but a fundamental *social right*. In the US
jurisprudence, justices Warren and Brandeis [45] defined it as the *right to be
left alone*. Privacy is thus not just a technical task of controlling some assets,
but first of all a *political* task, requiring that some policies should be specified
and implemented. Privacy policies are generally designed to balance public and
private interests, assets, and resources. This balancing sometimes comes down
to playing out the political forces against one another.

The *confusion* around privacy also arises from the fact that it is both a
technical and a political problem. The problems of privacy are discussed in
many different research communities, often in different terms, or with the same
terms denoting different concepts. Privacy provides an opportunity for security

J. Castiglione—Supported by NSF.
D. Pavlovic—Partially supported by NSF and AFOSR.

researchers to contribute to political discourse [37]. It also provides politicians an incentive to get involved in the technical discourse about security. The overarching source of confusion are the political narratives constructed the process of shifting and blurring the boundaries public and the private, which has been the driving force behind social transformations for centuries [6,21].

History of Privacy. Social history is first of all the history of shifting demarcation lines between the public sphere and the private sphere [7,29,39]. Communist revolutions usually start by abolishing not only private property, but also private rights. Tyrannies and oligarchies, on the other hand, erode public rights and ownership, and privatize resources and social life. The distinction between the realm of public (city, market, warfare...) and the realm of private (family, household, childbirth...) was established and discussed in antiquity [4,12]. It was a frequent topic in Greek tragedies: e.g. Sophocles' *Antigone* is torn between her private commitment to her brothers and her public duty to the king. The English word *politics* comes from the Greek word πόλις, denoting the public sphere; the English word *economy* comes from the Greek word οἶχος, denoting the private sphere.

Distinguishing Privacy. There are many aspects of privacy, conceptualized in different research communities, and studied by different methods; and perhaps even more aspects that are not conceptualized in research, but arise in practice, and in informal discourse. We carve a small part of the concept, and attempt to model it formally.

As an abstract requirement, privacy is a negative constraint, in the form *"bad things should not happen"*. Note that secrecy and confidentiality are also such negative constraints, whereas authenticity and integrity are positive constraints, in the form *"good things should happen"*. More precisely, authenticity and integrity require that some desirable information flows happen. E.g., a message *"I am Alice"* is authentic if it originates from Alice. On the other hand, confidentiality, secrecy and privacy require that some undesirable information flows are prevented: Alice's password should be secret, her address should be confidential, and her health record should be private.

But what is the difference between privacy, secrecy and confidentiality? Let us first move out of the way the difference between the latter two. In the present paper, we ignore that difference. In the colloquial usage, the terms confidentiality and secrecy allow subtle distinctions: e.g., when a report is confidential, we don't know its contents; but when it is secret, we don't even know that it exists. But this is a paper about privacy as a right. Secrecy and confidentiality are security properties. We bundle them into one and use them interchangeably. (Restricting to just one of them gets awkward).

As for the difference between privacy and secrecy (or confidentiality), it comes in two flavors:

(1) while secrecy is a property of *information*, privacy is a property of any *asset* or *resource* that can be secured[1]; and

---

[1] Information is, of course, a resource, so it can be private.

(2) while secrecy is a *local* requirement, usually imposed on information flowing through a given channel, privacy is a *global* requirement: my right to enjoy my private resource should be valid everywhere.

Let us have a look at some examples.

Ad (1), Alice's password is secret, whereas her bank account is private. Bob's health record is private, and it remains private after he shares some of it with Alice. It consists of his health information, but it may also contain some of his tissue samples for later analysis. On the other hand, Bob's criminal record is in principle not private, as criminal records often need to be shared, to protect the public. Bob may try to keep his criminal record secret, but even if he succeeds, it will not become private. Any resource can be made private if the access to it can be secured. E.g., we speak of a private water well, private funds, private party if the public access is restricted. On the other hand, when we speak of a secret water well, secret funds, or a secret party, we mean that public does not have any information about them. A water well can be secret, and it can be private, but not secret.

Ad (2), to attack Alice's secret password, Mallory eavesdrops at the secure channel to her bank; to attack her bank account, he can of course, also try to steal her credentials, or he can initiate a request through any of the channels of the banking network, if he can access it. Or he can coordinate an attack through many channels. To decipher a secret, a cryptanalyst analyzes a given cipher. To gain access to some private data, a data analyst can gather and analyze data from many surveillance points. To protect secrecy, the cryptographer must assure that the plaintexts cannot be derived from the ciphertexts without the key, for a given cipher. To protect privacy, the network operator must assure that there are no covert channels anywhere in the network.

Defining Privacy. Secrecy is formally defined in cryptography. The earliest definition, due to Shannon [40], says that it is a property of a channel where the outputs are statistically independent of the inputs. It is tempting, and seems natural, to define privacy in a similar way. This was proposed by Dalenius back in the 1970s [14]. A database is private if the public data that it discloses publicly say nothing about the private data that it does not disclose. This *desideratum*, as Dalenius called it, persisted in research for a number of years, before it became clear that it was generally impossible as a requirement. E.g., if everybody knows that Alice eats a lot of chocolate, but there is an anonymized database that shows a statistical correlation between eating a lot of chocolate and heart attacks, then this database discloses that Alice may be at a risk of heart attack, which should be Alice's private information, and thus breaches Dalenius' desideratum. Notably, this database breaches Alice's privacy *even if* Alice's record does not come about in it. Indeed, it is not necessary that Alice occurs in the database either for establishing the correlation between chocolate and heart attack, or for the public knowledge that Alice eats lots chocolate; the two pieces of information can arise independently. Alice's privacy can be breached by linking two completely independent pieces of information, one about Alice and chocolate, the other one about chocolate and heart attack. But since Alice's record does not come about in the database, it cannot be removed from it, or anonymized in it. Making sure that neither Alice nor any other record can be identified closer than up to a set of k other records with the same attributes, as required by the popular k-anonymity approach to privacy [43, 44], would not make any difference for Alice's privacy in this case either, since Alice cannot be identified at all in a database where she does not come about. Since Alice's privacy is not breached by identifying her, but by linking her public attribute (chocolate) with the public statistic correlating that attribute with a private attribute (heart disease), it follows that anonymity cannot assure privacy.

Notation. It is convenient to view each natural number as the set of the numbers preceding it, i.e. $n = \{0, 1, 2, \ldots, n - 1\}$.

2   Resources

Definition 1. *A source element of a set $\mathcal{Y}$ is a function $\beta : \mathcal{Y} \longrightarrow [0, 1]$ such that*

- *the set $\beta^{\#} = \{y \in \mathcal{Y} \mid \beta(y) \neq 0\}$ is finite, and*
- *the sum $\Sigma\beta = \sum_{y \in \mathcal{Y}} \beta(y)$ is not greater than 1.*

The set of all source elements of $\mathcal{Y}$ is denoted by $\mathcal{DY}$. The set $\beta^{\#}$ is called the support of β, and its number of elements $\#\beta$ is called the size of β. The number $\Sigma\beta$ is the total weight of β. The values $\beta(y)$ are weights (or probabilities) of $y \in \mathcal{Y}$.

Ordinary elements $y \in \mathcal{Y}$ correspond to the source elements $\chi_y : \mathcal{Y} \longrightarrow [0, 1]$ where $\chi_y(y) = 1$ and $\chi_y(z) = 0$ for all $z \neq y$. A source element β that happens to be *total*, in the sense that $\sum_{y \in \mathcal{Y}} \beta(y) = 1$, corresponds to what would normally be called a finitely supported probability distribution over $\mathcal{Y}$. The set of all total source elements of $\mathcal{Y}$ is $\Delta\mathcal{Y}$. They are often viewed geometrically, as points of the convex polytope spanned by $y \in \mathcal{Y}$ as vertices. If we adjoin to $\mathcal{Y}$ a fresh element $*$, and thus form the set $\mathcal{Y}' = \mathcal{Y} \cup \{*\}$, then each source element β of $\mathcal{Y}$ (not necessarily total) can be mapped into a total source element β' of $\mathcal{Y}'$, defined

$$\beta'(y) = \begin{cases} \beta(y) & \text{if } y \in \mathcal{Y} \\ 1 - \Sigma\beta & \text{if } y = * \end{cases}$$

It is easy to see that this gives a bijection

$$\mathcal{DY} \cong \Delta\mathcal{Y}'$$

so that the source elements of $\mathcal{Y}$ can be viewed as the points of the convex polytope over $\mathcal{Y}'$. Extended along this bijection, the inclusion $\Delta\mathcal{Y} \subseteq \mathcal{DY}$ becomes the retraction $\Delta\mathcal{Y} \leftrightarrows \Delta\mathcal{Y}'$, which projects the polytope $\Delta\mathcal{Y}'$ to the face where the weight of $*$ is 0.

This geometric view of source elements of $\mathcal{Y}$, as convex combinations from $\mathcal{Y}'$, supports the intuition that they are *"incomplete"* probability distributions, which don't add up to 1. The probability deficiency $1 - \Sigma\beta$ can be thought of as the chance that sampling the source element β does not yield any output.

Definition 2. *A* resource *is a function* $\varphi : \mathcal{X} \longrightarrow D\mathcal{Y}$ *whose support* $\varphi^{\#} = \{x \in \mathcal{X} \mid \varphi_x \neq 0\}$ *is finite. The number of elements of* $\varphi^{\#}$ *is called the* size *of* φ *again, and its* total size *is the number*

$$\#\#\varphi = \sum_{x \in \varphi^{\#}} \#\varphi_x$$

A resource that takes as its values the ordinary elements, i.e. the source elements which take a value 1, is just a partial function from $\mathcal{X}$ to $\mathcal{Y}$. A resource that takes only total source elements as its values can be viewed as a stochastic matrix, i.e. a matrix of numbers from the interval $[0,1]$ where columns add up to 1. Any resource $\varphi : \mathcal{X} \longrightarrow D\mathcal{Y}$ can be viewed as a $\mathcal{X} \times \mathcal{Y}$-matrix of numbers $\varphi_x(y) \in [0,1]$. Although the sets $\mathcal{X}$ and $\mathcal{Y}$ can be infinite, the finiteness of $\#\varphi$ and of all $\#\varphi_x$ implies that only $\#\#\varphi$ many entries of this infinite matrix are different from 0. Any given resources $\varphi : \mathcal{X} \longrightarrow D\mathcal{Y}$ and $\psi : \mathcal{Y} \longrightarrow D\mathcal{Z}$ can thus be composed into a resource $\psi\varphi : \mathcal{X} \longrightarrow D\mathcal{Z}$, obtained by matrix composition

$$(\psi\varphi)_x(z) = \sum_{y \in \psi^{\#}} \varphi_x(y) \cdot \psi_y(z)$$

Notation. Since we will most of the time look at the functions in the form $\mathcal{X} \longrightarrow D\mathcal{Y}$, let us omit the D, and write such functions as $\mathcal{X} \longrightarrow \mathcal{Y}$, denoting by the arrow with full head $\longrightarrow$ a function whose outputs are source elements. Such functions are our resources.

2.1   Examples

While the notion of resource is very general, we begin with some very special cases, to ground the intuitions.

Example 1: A database is a function $\varphi : \mathcal{R} \times \mathcal{C} \longrightarrow \mathcal{O}$, where

- $\mathcal{R}$ is a set of *rows*, or *records*, or *items*,
- $\mathcal{C}$ is a set of *columns*, or *attributes*,
- $\mathcal{O}$ is a set of *values* or *outputs*.

The "row-column" terminology suggests that we think of a database as an $\mathcal{R} \times \mathcal{C}$-matrix of entries from $D\mathcal{O}$. When the attributes $c \in \mathcal{C}$ are expressed using different sets of values $\mathcal{O}_c$, we take $\mathcal{O} = \bigcup_{c \in \mathcal{C}} \mathcal{O}_c$. For ordinary databases, the entries are ordinary elements $\varphi_{rc} \in \mathcal{O}$, or they may be empty, and the resource φ is an ordinary map, or a partial map. For online databases, it can be uncertain what will be returned in response to a query, since the data are updated dynamically, often concurrently; so the entries are stochastic, and we model them as source elements $\varphi_{rc} \in \mathcal{DO}$.

In fact, the whole web can be viewed as a large, dynamic, stochastic database.

Example 2: The **web** is a resource $\omega : \mathcal{X} \longrightarrow \mathcal{Y}$ where

- $\mathcal{X}$ is the set of URLs (or more precisely of all possible HTTP requests),
- $\mathcal{Y}$ is the set of HTML documents (embedded in the HTTP responses, often extended with JavaScript executables, JSON or XML object references, etc.).

The web is, of course, a very complex, very dynamic environment, and when you input a URL $x \in \mathcal{X}$ into your browser, the process that determines what output will the random variable ω_x return to your browser is ongoing nonlocally, and there is a lot of uncertainty and chaos in it, like in any complex natural process, such as weather. The web is a typical source showing why privacy is so hard: it combines politics and thermodynamics.

Example 3: A **search engine** $\gamma : \mathcal{X} \longrightarrow \mathcal{Y}$ (e.g. Google) is an attempt at a map of the web:

- $\mathcal{X}$ is the index of keywords and search terms built from them,
- $\mathcal{Y}$ is the set of indexed web pages.

The distribution of $\gamma_x \in \mathcal{DY}$ over the set of the hits for the search term $x \in \mathcal{X}$ captures the web page *ranking* [30,31]: higher ranked pages are assigned higher probabilities in γ_x.

Example 4: A **social engine** $\zeta : \mathcal{X} \longrightarrow \mathcal{Y}$ (e.g. Facebook) is a shared resource for social networking through posting messages, media, and gestures, and distributing them according to some specified privacy policies along the social channels provided by the platform. In the most basic model,

- $\mathcal{X}$ is the set of identifiers of all users' postings,
- $\mathcal{Y}$ are the contents of the postings, i.e. the set of the posted messages, media, and gestures.

For simplicity, we assume that the identifiers $x \in \mathcal{X}$ contain all needed references to their sources, and that the contents of the postings are either equal (i.e., they can be repeated) or different, but have no intrinsic structure or correlations. A social engine can thus be viewed as an ordinary mapping $\zeta : \mathcal{X} \longrightarrow \mathcal{Y}$ of identifiers as ordinary elements $x \in \mathcal{X}$ into the postings as ordinary elements $\zeta_x \in \mathcal{Y}$. The randomness will emerge from sharing: who sees whose postings. And sharing is determined by running privacy protocols.

2.2   Resource Fusion

Data sources are naturally ordered by the amount of information that they provide: e.g., a database φ may provide Alice's IP address, say 98.151.86.153; a database ψ may provide just the first block: 98. The amount of information is usually quantified by the entropy of its source: e.g., Alice's record φ_A would contain 32 bits of information, whereas Alice's record ψ_A would contain only 8 bits. However, the IP prefix given by ψ_A is different from the IP prefix given φ_A, and we are interested in the actual address, then counting the bits does not suffice. Data analysts do not just *quantify* the amounts of information in the available data, they also *qualify* them, and compare their information contents. To model that practice, we need an ordering $\prec$ where $\psi_A \prec \varphi_A$ only if the information provided by ψ_A is really contained in φ_A, not just more uncertain; and moreover, we need an operation $\psi_A \widehat{\Upsilon} \varphi_A$ for *information fusion*, which will join together the parts of ψ_A and φ_A where they are consistent with each other, and discard the parts where they contradict each other. This may sound like a tall order in theory, but that is what the data analysts do in practice.

The problems of ordering information sources turn out to have been studied, albeit implicitly, in theory of *majorization* [2,25]. The basic techniques go back to [22], where a host of inequalities from different parts of mathematics were derived using majorization, as if by magic. In the meantime, it has been well understood that the power of magic was due to ordering information sources, but the problem of conjoining and reconciling information sources has not yet been directly addressed, although some technical results and conceptual expositions came close to it [3,28].

2.2.1   Preferences and Consistency

Definition 3. *Every source element $\beta \in \mathcal{DY}$ induces the following binary relations:*

- preference: $u \overset{\beta}{\trianglelefteq} v \iff \beta(u) \leq \beta(v);$
- strict preference: $u \overset{\beta}{\triangleleft} v \iff \beta(u) < \beta(v);$
- indifference: $u \overset{\beta}{\diamondsuit} v \iff \beta(u) = \beta(v).$

Clearly, strict preference is transitive, preference is also reflexive, i.e. a preorder, and indifference is moreover symmetric, and thus an equivalence relation, and it is the symmetric closure of preference.

Definition 4. *A finite set of source elements $B \subset \mathcal{DY}$ is said to be* consistent *if the preorder $\overset{B}{\trianglelefteq}$ obtained by taking the transitive closure of the union $\bigcup_{\beta \in B} \overset{\beta}{\trianglelefteq}$ creates no new cycles.*

Example. Source elements $\beta, \delta \in \mathcal{DY}$ will be inconsistent, e.g. if $a \overset{\beta}{\triangleleft} b$ and $c \overset{\beta}{\triangleleft} d$ on one hand, while $b \overset{\delta}{\triangleleft} c$ and $d \overset{\delta}{\triangleleft} a$ on the other hand, which will create the new cycle $a \overset{\beta}{\triangleleft} b \overset{\delta}{\triangleleft} c \overset{\beta}{\triangleleft} d \overset{\delta}{\triangleleft} a$. This cycle brings a, b, c and d all in the same equivalence class with respect to $\overset{\beta,\delta}{\diamondsuit}$, while they would in general be unrelated with respect to $\overset{\beta}{\diamondsuit}$ and $\overset{\delta}{\diamondsuit}$.

Consistent Preference Preorders Have Common Refinements. It is clear from the definition that a set of source elements B is consistent if and only if the equivalence classes with respect to $\overset{B}{\diamondsuit}$ are obtained as the intersections of the equivalence classes with respect to $\overset{\beta}{\diamondsuit}$ for $\beta \in B$. Since all $\overset{\beta}{\trianglelefteq}$ are *total* preorders, in the sense that any two elements of $\mathcal{Y}$ are comparable, and since each of them thus induces a strict total order on its indifference equivalence classes, it follows that the total preorder $\overset{B}{\diamondsuit}$ is least common refinement of all partitions of $\mathcal{Y}$ induced by $\beta \in B$, in the sense that it induces a strict total order on its own of equivalence classes, which are the least common refinement of $\overset{\beta}{\diamondsuit}$ for $\beta \in B$. The task is now to lift the least common refinement $\overset{B}{\trianglelefteq}$ of the preference preorders $\overset{\beta}{\trianglelefteq}$ induced by source elements $\beta \in B \subset \mathcal{DY}$ to a least lower bound $\curlyvee B$ with respect to a suitable information preorder $\prec$. The following theorem suggests this information preorder.

2.2.2   Ordered Source Elements

Definition 5. *An* ordering ϑ *of a source element* $\beta : \mathcal{Y} \longrightarrow [0,1]$ *is a pair of functions* $N \mathrel{\substack{\tilde{\vartheta} \\ \longleftarrow\!\!\!\longrightarrow \\ \vartheta}} \mathcal{Y}$ *such that*

- $N > \#\beta$;
- *for all* $i \in N = \{0, 1, \dots, N-1\}$ *holds* $\tilde{\vartheta}\vartheta(i) = i$;
- *for all* $y \in \beta^{\#}$ *holds* $\vartheta\tilde{\vartheta}(y) = y$,
- $\beta\vartheta(0) \geq \beta\vartheta(1) \geq \cdots \geq \beta\vartheta(\#\beta - 1) > \beta\vartheta(\#\beta) = \cdots = \beta\vartheta(N-1) = 0$.

The set of all orderings of $\beta \in \mathcal{DY}$ *is denoted by* $\Theta(\beta)$.

We hope that this formal definition does not conceal the idea of ordering a source element, which is as simple as it sounds: an ordering ϑ of $\beta : \mathcal{Y} \longrightarrow [0,1]$ enumerates the support $\beta^{\#}$ by the indices from the set $N = \{0, 1, \dots, \#\beta - 1, \#\beta, \dots, N-1\}$ in such a way that $u \in \beta^{\#}$ are ordered by weight, with those with the highest weights $\beta(u)$ coming first. All $y \in \mathcal{Y}$ that are not in the support $\beta^{\#}$ of β because $\beta(y) = 0$ are mapped into $\vartheta(y) \geq \#\beta \in N$. A source element β where for any pair $u \neq v \in \beta^{\#}$ holds $\beta(u) \neq \beta(v)$ has a unique ordering. On the other hand, if $\beta(u) = \beta(v)$, and thus $u \overset{\beta}{\diamondsuit} v$, then u and v are indifferent, and allow 2 different orderings. Any indifference class with k elements induces $k!$ different orderings. However, it is easy to see that any pair of orderings $\vartheta, \xi \in \Theta(\beta)$ satisfy $\beta\vartheta(i) = \beta\xi(i)$ for all $i < \#\beta$, and thus induce the same ordered sequence $\beta\vartheta = \beta\xi$. This unique ordered version of β is usually written $\beta^{\downarrow}$, but we will write $\beta\vartheta$ when an explicit ordering is needed, as it will be the case in Proposition 8. Identifying the set $\beta^{\#} \subseteq \mathcal{Y}$ with the set of numbers $\#\beta = \{0, 1, \dots, \#\beta - 1\} \subset N$ allows writing the source element $\beta : \mathcal{Y} \longrightarrow [0,1]$ as the descending sequence

$$\beta^{\downarrow} = \beta\vartheta = \langle \beta\vartheta(0), \beta\vartheta(1), \dots, \beta\vartheta(\#\beta - 1), 0, 0, 0, \dots \rangle$$

Note that "un-ordering" $\beta\vartheta$ by $\tilde{\vartheta}$ restores β, because for all $y \in \beta^{\#}$ holds $\beta\vartheta\tilde{\vartheta}(y) = \beta(y)$.

The orderings of β that are extended to $N > \beta^{\#}$ just add more indices than there are in $\#\beta$, and thus cover by the enumeration ϑ not only the support $\beta^{\#}$, but also some $y \in \mathcal{Y}$ for which $\beta(y) = 0$. Such extensions are needed when we look for common orderings of $\mathcal{Y}$ induced by different source elements $\beta, \gamma : \mathcal{Y} \longrightarrow [0, 1]$. Two such source elements may have different supports $\beta^{\#}$ and $\gamma^{\#}$, but their orderings may be consistent, in the sense that they both may extend to the same ordering of $\beta^{\#} \cup \gamma^{\#}$. Such an extended ordering ϑ with N enumerating $\beta^{\#} \cup \gamma^{\#}$ would belong both to $\Theta(\beta)$ and to $\Theta(\gamma)$, and would thus be an element of the intersection $\Theta(\beta) \cap \Theta(\gamma)$. It will turn out that this intersection characterizes the situation when β and γ are consistent, and can be conjoined into a single source: see Proposition 8 below.

2.2.3   Majorization Preorder

Sequence Differentials and Integrals. To define joins and meets of source elements, we borrow the following operations from [35]. Let $\mathbb{R}^{*}$ be the set of sequences of reals. The operations $\int, \partial : \mathbb{R}^{*} \longrightarrow \mathbb{R}^{*}$ map any sequence $\langle \alpha(0), \alpha(1), \ldots, \alpha(n-1) \rangle$ to its *integral version* $\langle \int\alpha(0), \ldots, \int\alpha(n-1) \rangle$ and its *differential version* $\langle \partial\alpha(0), \ldots, \partial\alpha(n-1) \rangle$ defined

$$\int\alpha(k) = \sum_{i=0}^{k} \alpha(i) \qquad \partial\alpha(k) = \alpha(k) - \alpha(k-1)$$

for $0 \leq k < n$. We assume $\alpha(-1) = 0$. Note that $\int\partial(\alpha) = \alpha = \partial\int(\alpha)$.

Proposition 6. *For any $\beta, \gamma \in \mathcal{DY}$, and $n = \max(\#\beta, \#\gamma)$ the following conditions are equivalent:*

(a) $\beta = D\gamma$, where D is a doubly substochastic matrix[2];
(b) $\beta = \sum_{i=0}^{m-1} \lambda_i P_i \gamma$ where $\lambda_i \in [0, 1]$, $\sum_{i=0}^{m-1} \lambda_i \leq 1$, and P_i are permutations;
(c) $\int\beta^{\downarrow}(k) \leq \int\gamma^{\downarrow}(k)$ for all $k < n$.

Definition 7. *When source elements β and γ satisfy any of the equivalent conditions of Theorem 6, we say that β is* majorized *by γ and write $\beta \prec \gamma$.*

From Majorization to Fusion. The fact that majorization is a reflexive and transitive relation, i.e. a *preorder* on $\mathcal{DY}$, is just a slight refinement of the classical results of [22] and [10]. In the meantime, the role of majorization as *information* preorder has also been well established in several research communities [28].

---

[2] A $\mathcal{Y} \times \mathcal{Y}$-matrix with finitely many nonzero, nonnegative entries is doubly stochastic if the sums of the entries in each nonzero row and in each nonzero column are 1. Already Garrett Birkhoff considered infinite doubly stochastic matrices, asking for the infinitary generalization of his doubly stochastic decomposition in the problem 111 of his *Lattice Theory*.

Our main interest here is to understand and model the operation of *fusion* of resources, used in the practices of data analysis, and in the attacks on private resources. The usual scenario is that an analyst acquire two or more resources, and fuses them together, in order to extract as much information or value as possible. Intuitively, this corresponds to finding a least upper bound (usually called *supremum*, or *join*) with respect to the majorization preorder of the acquired resources. But a pair of sources may not have any upper bounds with respect to majorization, and therefore cannot always be conjoined together. The following proposition characterizes that situation as inconsistency. Proposition 9, coming right after, describes what can be done to make a set of sources consistent.

Proposition 8. *The following conditions on a finite set $B \subset D\mathcal{Y}$ are equivalent:*

(a) B is consistent (in the sense of Definition 4);
(b) there is a common ordering $\vartheta \in \bigcap_{\beta \in B} \Theta(\beta)$ of B (in the sense of Definition 5);
(c) there is an upper bound γ of B: all $\beta \in B$ satisfy $\beta \prec \gamma$ (see Definition 7).

Proposition 9. *Let $B \subset D\mathcal{Y}$ be a finite set, and $\beta \in B$ any of its elements. Consider the indifference relation $\overset{B}{\diamond}$, as in Definition 3, and define the function $\widehat{\beta} : \mathcal{Y} \longrightarrow [0,1]$ by*

$$\widehat{\beta}(y) = \bigwedge_{u \overset{B}{\diamond} y} \beta(u)$$

Then $\widehat{\beta}$ is the greatest among all source elements $\alpha \prec \beta$ which are consistent with the elements of B. Moreover, the set $\widehat{B} = \left\{ \widehat{\beta} \mid \beta \in B \right\}$ is consistent.

2.2.4 Meets, Joins, and Fusions

Proposition 10. *Let $B \subset D\mathcal{Y}$ be a finite consistent set of source elements and let $M \overset{\widetilde{\vartheta}}{\underset{\vartheta}{\rightleftharpoons}} \mathcal{Y}$ be the ordering that makes all $\beta \in B$ consistent. Then their meet and join with respect to the majorization preorder are respectively*

$$\bigwedge B = \left(\partial \bigwedge_{\beta \in B} \smallint \beta \vartheta \right) \widetilde{\vartheta} \qquad\qquad \bigvee B = \left(\partial \bigvee_{\beta \in B} \smallint \beta \vartheta \right) \widetilde{\vartheta}$$

where $\bigwedge$ and $\bigvee$ are pointwise.

Proof Idea. If $\lambda = \partial \bigwedge_{\beta \in B} \smallint \beta \vartheta$ and $\nu = \partial \bigvee_{\beta \in B} \smallint \beta \vartheta$ are the *ordered* majorization meet and join of the set $B^{\downarrow}$ of the ordered versions $\beta^{\downarrow} = \beta \vartheta$ of $\beta \in B$, then it is easy to see that "un-ordering" them by $\widetilde{\vartheta}$ makes them into the majorization meet and the join of the set B. It is also easy to see that λ and ν are below of the set $B^{\downarrow}$ of ordered versions. The heart of the proof is showing that λ and ν are still ordered by ϑ and that "unordering" them by $\widetilde{\vartheta}$ brings them back under the same preference order.

Corollary 11. *Any finite set of source elements $B \subset \mathcal{DY}$ has a majorization meet $\bigwedge B = \bigwedge \widehat{B}$, where $\widehat{B}$ is the consistent set of source elements constructed as in Proposition 9, whereas its meet is constructed as in Proposition 10.*

Definition 12. *The* source fusion *of a finite set $B \subset \mathcal{DY}$ is the source element $\widehat{\curlyvee} B \in \mathcal{DY}$ defined by*

$$\widehat{\curlyvee} B = \curlyvee \widehat{B}$$

where $\widehat{B}$ is the consistent set constructed as in Proposition 9.

A concrete and familiar **example** of this operation will be described in Sect. 4.2.

Definition 13. *The* resource fusion $\widehat{\curlyvee}\Phi : \mathcal{X} \longrightarrow \mathcal{Y}$ *of a finite set of resources $\Phi \subset \mathcal{X} \longrightarrow \mathcal{Y}$ is defined pointwise along $x \in \mathcal{X}$ by*

$$\left(\widehat{\curlyvee}\Phi\right)_x = \widehat{\curlyvee}\Phi_x$$

where the source fusion on the right-hand side is from Definition 12.

Inconsistent Sources Generate a Higher-Order Source. Another view of the above definition is that the set of resources Φ is the pointwise join of the set of resources $\widehat{\Phi}$, where for each $x \in \mathcal{X}$, the set of sources $\widehat{\Phi}_x$ is the greatest consistent set under Φ_x. The notion of consistency of sources, as imposed in Definition 4 requires a consensus of all sources, wherever they declare their preferences by assigning different weights. This is a very restrictive notion of consistency. Different domains require different notions of fusion. Through centuries, many different forms of preference aggregation have been proposed and are nowadays systematized and analyzed in theories of voting and social choice [11,38,41]. An important aspect not analyzed within that tradition are the *higher-order* source aggregations. While with the preference aggregations and the source fusion operations like the one presented above, inconsistent sources are conjoined into a less informative source, any inconsistencies observed in hypothesis testing are the source of new information within a higher-order source [36]. See Sect. 4.2 for an example.

The only point of even mentioning this vast conceptual area in this constrained space is in support our claim that the rapidly evolving practices of information gathering and analysis require a theory of information that takes into account the information content and quality, and not just the transmission rate measures, and quantity.

3   Privacy Protocol Components and Compositions

3.1   Concepts

Interactions, communication, and resource sharing are usually modeled using networks. A *network* structure is based on a graph, here consisting of

- a set $\mathcal{S} = \{A, B, C, D, \ldots, S, \ldots\}$ of *nodes*, representing subjects or users, often called Alice, Bob, Carol, Dave...; and
- a set of links $A \to B$, representing the channels between Alice and Bob.

In most examples, there will be at most one channel between any pair of subjects, so the network structure boils down to a binary relation on the set $\mathcal{S}$. In any case, channels allow us to model *local* interactions: Alice can interact with Bob only if there is a channel $A \to B$, in which case we say that Bob is Alice's *neighbor*. A network is often assumed to provide routing services, whereby Alice can send a message or object to Dave, who is not her neighbor, from neighbor to neighbor: $A \to B \to C \to D$. The Internet is, of course, a network with routing services.

A network can be viewed as infrastructure for sharing some private resources. The node Alice has a private resource $[\![A]\!] : \mathcal{X}_A \longrightarrow \mathcal{Y}_A$, but she can achieve more if she cooperates with Bob, who has a resource $[\![B]\!] : \mathcal{X}_B \longrightarrow \mathcal{Y}_B$, and can share some of it with Alice, often in exchange for some of hers. Privacy protocols are abstract models of such transactions. Optimizing utility of their private resources, all rational agents engage in such transactions at all network levels. The obvious examples are market transactions, where Alice and Bob trade goods, money, labor; also health care, insurance, rescue missions, regulatory control, search, education. At lower levels of interaction, many basic social phenomena arise from privacy protocols. But in a data-driven society, certain data privacy protocols take a life of their own, while other privacy protocols become invisible, and private.

The basic building block of private interactions is a 2-message protocol pattern, depicted in Fig. 1, where Alice submits to Bob a *request* r^{AB} for some of his private resource $[\![B]\!]$, and Bob responds according to his *policy* p^{AB}, and shares with Alice the part of his resource that results from composing her request and his policy, i.e. $[\![AB]\!] = p^{AB}[\![B]\!]r^{AB}$. Our claim is that all privacy protocols are obtained by composing suitable instances of this pattern. The idea is that these *Request-Policy (RP)*-components are atoms of privacy, just like the *Challenge-Response (CR)*-components are atoms of authentication [13, 16, 32–34]. The incremental approach to protocol design, analysis, taxonomy, and to security proofs [15, 19, 26] seems to extend naturally from authentication and key establishment protocols to privacy protocols.

3.2 Definitions

Bob's private resource $[\![B]\!] : \mathcal{X}_B \longrightarrow \mathcal{Y}_B$ accepts Bob's private inputs from $\mathcal{X}_B$ and produces Bob's private outputs in $\mathcal{Y}_B$. In order to be able to request access to some of Bob's private resource, Alice must be able to reference some of his private inputs, and to observe and utilize some of his private outputs. To allow subjects to address each other's private identifiers, we assume

- sets $\mathcal{X}$ and $\mathcal{Y}$ of *public identifiers*, available globally, at all network nodes; and

– sets $\mathcal{X}_S$ and $\mathcal{Y}_S$ of *private identifiers* for each $S \in \mathcal{S}$, together with the partial functions

$$\mathcal{X}_S \xrightleftharpoons[\underline{\pi}_S]{\overline{\pi}_S} \mathcal{X} \qquad\qquad \mathcal{Y}_S \xrightleftharpoons[\underline{\rho}_S]{\overline{\rho}_S} \mathcal{Y} \qquad (1)$$

such that $\overline{\pi}_S\underline{\pi}_S(x) = x$ and $\overline{\rho}_S\underline{\rho}_S(y) = y$.

The last two equations make $\underline{\pi}_S$ and $\underline{\rho}_S$ total, but $\overline{\pi}_S$ and $\overline{\rho}_S$ can be genuinely partial, in which case the composites $\pi_S = \underline{\pi}_S\overline{\pi}_S$ and $\rho_S = \underline{\rho}_S\overline{\rho}_S$ are also partial. It is easy to see that they are also idempotent, i.e. satisfy $\pi_S\pi_S = \pi_S$ and $\rho_S\rho_S = \rho_S$. The following definition puts together all of the above.

Definition 14. *A resource network consists of*

– *a network $\mathcal{S} = \{A, B, C, \ldots, S, \ldots\}$;*
– *global identifiers $\mathcal{X} = \{x, u, \ldots\}$ for inputs and $\mathcal{Y} = \{y, v, \ldots\}$ for outputs;*
– *for each network node $S \in \mathcal{S}$,*
  - *projectors $\pi_S : \mathcal{X} \rightharpoonup \mathcal{X}$ and $\rho_S : \mathcal{Y} \rightharpoonup \mathcal{Y}$, which are partial idempotents determining*
  - *local identifiers $\mathcal{X}_S = \{x \in \mathcal{X} \mid \pi_S(x) = x\}$ for inputs and $\mathcal{Y}_S = \{y \in \mathcal{Y} \mid \rho_S(y) = y\}$ for outputs, together with the casts from (1);*
  - *a resource $[\![S]\!] : \mathcal{X} \longrightarrow \mathcal{Y}$ such that $[\![S]\!] = \rho_S[\![S]\!]\pi_S$.*

Remark. The requirement $[\![S]\!] = \rho_S[\![S]\!]\pi_S$ is equivalent with $\rho_S[\![S]\!] = [\![S]\!] = [\![S]\!]\pi_S$. In either form, it assures that the resource $[\![S]\!]$ only accepts the elements of $\mathcal{X}_S$, which are fixed by π_S, and only produces the elements of $\mathcal{Y}_S$, fixed by ρ_S.

Definition 15. *A Request-Policy (RP) protocol between Alice and Bob in a resource network S is a pair of partial functions $\Phi = \langle \boldsymbol{r}_\Phi^{AB}, \boldsymbol{p}_\Phi^{AB} \rangle$, where*

– $\boldsymbol{r}_\Phi^{AB} : \mathcal{X} \rightharpoonup \mathcal{X}$ *is Alice's request for Bob's private resource, and*
– $\boldsymbol{p}_\Phi^{AB} : \mathcal{Y} \rightharpoonup \mathcal{Y}$ *is Bob's privacy policy towards Alice.*

The outcome of a run of the privacy protocol is that the part of Bob's private resource that is approved by Bob's policy and referenced by Alice's request is released to her, providing her with the resource:

$$[\![AB]\!] = (\mathcal{X} \xrightarrow{r_\Phi^{AB}} \mathcal{X} \xrightarrow{[\![B]\!]} \mathcal{Y} \xrightarrow{p_\Phi^{AB}} \mathcal{Y})$$

which is then conjoined with Alice's own resource $\mathcal{X} \xrightarrow{[\![A]\!]} \mathcal{Y}$, thus providing Alice with the total resource $[\![A]\!]\widehat{\curlyvee}[\![AB]\!]$, as displayed in Fig. 1.

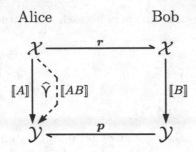

Fig. 1. Basic privacy protocol: Request-Policy (RP)

3.3   Examples

Example 1: Let $\varphi : \mathcal{R} \times \mathcal{C} \longrightarrow \mathcal{O}$ be the data base of a credit rating agency Exavier, presented as a resource in the following format:

- $\mathcal{R} = \mathcal{S}$, i.e. the database rows correspond to the network nodes;
- $\mathcal{C} = \{T_0, T_1, \ldots, T_n\}$ are the types of financial and other relevant transactions;
- $\mathcal{X} = \mathcal{S} \times \mathcal{C}$, i.e. the public identifiers $x \in \mathcal{X}$ are in the form $x = {<}A, T_i{>}$, or T_i^A, denoting a type of Alice's transactions;
- $\mathcal{X}_S = \{T_0^S, T_1^S, \ldots, T_n^S\}$, i.e. $\pi_S(T_i^A) = T_i^A$ if $S = A$ or $S = E$, otherwise it is undefined, meaning that by $[\![A]\!] = [\![A]\!]\pi_A$ Alice can see her own record, and Exavier can see all records;
- $\mathcal{Y} = \coprod_{i=0}^{n} T_i^*$ are the transaction history listings, unencrypted, and
- $\mathcal{Y}_S = \mathcal{Y}$, i.e. $\rho_S(y) = y$ for all $y \in \mathcal{Y}$ makes any released transaction listing readable to anyone.

If Alice is a lender and Bob has requested a loan, then Alice may request access to some of Bob's credit history by submitting $r^{AB} : \mathcal{X} \rightharpoonup \mathcal{X}$ to him, with $r^{AB}(x) = x$ if $x \in \mathcal{X}_B$, otherwise undefined. Bob's privacy policy $p^{AB} : \mathcal{Y} \rightharpoonup \mathcal{Y}$ will then determine which transaction types T_i will be released to Alice by setting $p^{AB}(t) = t$ when $t \in T_i^*$, otherwise undefined. Since Bob has an incentive to modify his private data before releasing them, the integrity of the released data is assured by refining the RP-protocol so that the data are not released by Bob, but by Exavier, upon Bob's approval, which assures Bob's privacy. Besides privacy, this refined RP-protocol also guarantees integrity, *but* it also provides Exavier with an opportunity to record Alice's request as a part of Bob's credit rating. The integrity guarantee increases the utility of the protocol thus, and it also expands Exavier's database; but this last detail also slightly erodes Bob's privacy, since now even his requests for credit get recorded in his credit rating. The large scale of some privacy protocols, such as credit rating and reputation reporting, lends importance to negligibly slow leaks.

In any case, Alice the lender is provided the resource $[\![AB]\!] = \rho^{AB}[\![B]\!]\pi^{AB}$, controlled by Bob and Exavier. If Bob has joint accounts with Carol, Alice may request and Bob and Exavier provide some information about Carol. Alice will then conjoin the obtained information with her own information and resource $[\![A]\!]$ and use the compiled information $[\![A]\!]\widehat{\Upsilon}[\![AB]\!]$, or maybe $[\![A]\!]\widehat{\Upsilon}[\![AB]\!]\widehat{\Upsilon}[\![ABC]\!]$, to make her lending decision. Note that the described Request-Policy protocol is thus embedded within another RP-protocol, where Bob requests from Alice a loan, and Alice requests from Bob some private data, and uses the obtained information resources $[\![A]\!]\widehat{\Upsilon}[\![AB]\!]\widehat{\Upsilon}[\![ABC]\!]$ as the input into her loan policy, which outputs the loan decision. The privacy protocol for credit rating is thus composed with an authentication protocol for data release, and embedded into a privacy protocol for loan provision.

Example 2: The web as a resource $\omega : \mathcal{X} \longrightarrow \mathcal{Y}$ is controlled by Bob through $\pi_B : \mathcal{X} \rightharpoonup \mathcal{X}$, which filters the set of URLs $\mathcal{X}_B$ under Bob's control, locating his web site. The projector $\rho_B : \mathcal{Y} \rightharpoonup \mathcal{Y}$ determines what is published on his web site $[\![B]\!] = \rho_B \omega \pi_B$. If Alice surfs or navigates to Bob's web site, she submits a request $r^{AB} : \mathcal{X} \rightharpoonup \mathcal{X}$ for some of Bob's URLs. Bob may then request some of her identifiers, and maybe some of her private data to authenticate her, and inputs the obtained information into his policy $p^{AB} : \mathcal{Y} \rightharpoonup \mathcal{Y}$ which generates and outputs Bob's web content $[\![AB]\!] = p^{AB}[\![B]\!]r^{AB}$ in response to Alice's request. Alice can now add what she got from Bob to her own resource $[\![A]\!] = \rho_A \omega \pi_A$, and use $[\![A]\!]\widehat{\Upsilon}[\![AB]\!]$ to serve instances of her own web site, when requested in other runs of the web protocol.

Example 3: If Bob owns the search engine $\gamma : \mathcal{X} \longrightarrow \mathcal{Y}$, then his private resource is simply $[\![B]\!] = \gamma$. If anyone can submit any search term from $\mathcal{X}$, and if all pages indexed in $\mathcal{Y}$ are publicly accessible, then $\mathcal{X}_S = \mathcal{X}$ and $\mathcal{Y}_S = \mathcal{Y}$ for all subjects S on the network $\mathcal{S}$. A session of the RP-protocol thus consists of a query, represented as the partial function $r^{AB} : \mathcal{X} \rightharpoonup \mathcal{X}$, undefined everywhere except on some search term $x = r^{AB}(x)$; and a reply according to a policy $p^{AB} : \mathcal{Y} \rightharpoonup \mathcal{Y}$. In modern search engines, the search results are *personalized*, in the sense that our search engine Bob tailors his response especially for Alice. This may mean that Bob's policy p^{AB} is to display just what is of interest for Alice, or what she wants to hear. To achieve this, p^{AB} skews the sample of the source element $\omega_x \in \mathcal{D}\mathcal{Y}$, output by the search engine $\omega : \mathcal{X} \longrightarrow \mathcal{Y}$ in response to the query x; *or* it modifies the induced preference ordering $\overset{\omega_x}{\lhd}$ of the web pages in $\mathcal{Y}$, according to which the search results are displayed to Alice. This preference ordering is based on the ranking of the web content according to relevance and quality of the provided information [30, 31].

In general, Bob does not own the search engine, but only his own web pages: his resource $[\![B]\!] : \mathcal{X} \longrightarrow \mathcal{Y}$ is just a map from $\mathcal{X}_B \subseteq \mathcal{X}$ (which can be thought of as the content menu of his web site, filtered by $\pi_B : \mathcal{X} \rightharpoonup \mathcal{X}$ from the universe of keywords $\mathcal{X}$) to $\mathcal{Y}$, containing the actual content of the pages that he runs. When Alice visits Bob's web page and submits request r^{AB} for some content from his site, he responds according to his policy p^{AB}, and displays $[\![AB]\!] = p^{AB}[\![B]\!]r^{AB}$. Moreover, in addition to providing the content that Alice explicitly requested, Bob can also try to sell a fragment Alice's expressed interest to advertisers, and provide her with some content that she did not explicitly request, but may be related. The search for the advertisers willing to buy a fragment of Alice's interest is a second use that the owner of the search engine, whom we call Gogol[3], will find for his web index $\gamma : \mathcal{X} \longrightarrow \mathcal{Y}$. He will thus extract from γ two different resources:

- the search index $[\![G_{se}]\!] : \mathcal{X} \longrightarrow \mathcal{Y}$, assigning to each search term from $\mathcal{X}$ a source element of web contents from $\mathcal{Y}$, but this time not informative but advertising contents; and on the other hand
- the advertising index $[\![G_{ad}]\!] : \mathcal{Z} \longrightarrow \mathcal{X}$, assigning to each advertising opportunity[4] a source element of related search terms.

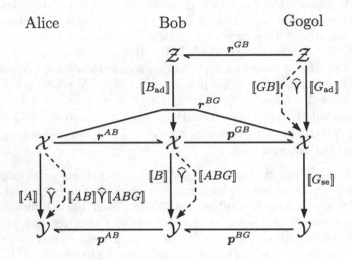

Fig. 2. Composite privacy protocol: Targeted Advertising (TAd)

These two resources are used as follows. Gogol initiates pooling of his and Bob's resources by offering in r^{GB} some advertising opportunities from $\mathcal{Z}$. Bob creates some advertising space $[\![B_{ad}]\!] : \mathcal{Z} \longrightarrow \mathcal{X}$, ready to be inserted into his web site $[\![B]\!] : \mathcal{X} \longrightarrow \mathcal{Y}$, and accepts Gogol's collaboration proposal by p^{GB}. Gogol processes the provided part $[\![GB]\!] = p^{GB}[\![B_{ad}]\!]r^{GB}$ of Bob's resource, and uses $[\![GB]\!]\widehat{\curlyvee}[\![G_{ad}]\!]$ to determine which of the advertising opportunities from $\mathcal{Z}$ will best suit Bob's site. When Bob receives Alice's request r^{AB}, he forwards it to Gogol as his request $r^{GB} = r^{BG}r^{AB}$ for the ad content. Using the current search index $[\![G_{se}]\!]$ of advertising contents and the index $[\![GB]\!]\widehat{\curlyvee}[\![G_{ad}]\!]$ of advertising topics suitable for Bob's site, Gogol provides Bob with the targeted web ad $[\![ABG]\!] = p^{AB}p^{BG}[\![G]\!]r^{BG}r^{AB}$, deemed to be of interest for Alice because of

---

[3] Nikolai Vasilievich Gogol was a XIX century Russian writer. Gogols are also the ape-like enemies in the video game *Xenoblade Chronicles*.

[4] Gogol receives advertising requests in a separate privacy protocol. It will be briefly discussed in the next section.

her interest in Bob's web content. Bob then displays $[\![B]\!]\widehat{\curlyvee}[\![ABG]\!]$, and Alice receives $[\![AB]\!]\widehat{\curlyvee}[\![ABG]\!]$. This composite protocol is displayed in the bottom row of Fig. 2. The protocol component where Gogol pays Bob for displaying the ad is omitted, as is the component where the advertiser pays Gogol, and the one where Alice requests to purchase the advertised goods, and the one where she remits the payment to the merchant, etc. We shall see some such protocols in the next section, but the mosaic of protocols for sharing and trading private resources always spreads beyond the horizon.

Example 4: While Gogol the search engine builds ranked indices of the content existing on the web, and shares these resources with Alice, Bob, and Carol, Zuck the social engine elicits the content from Alice, Bob, and Carol, builds an index of that, and shares their content with them as their social interactions. A bird's eye view of a fragment of this process is displayed in Fig. 3. Zuck's requests r^{ZS} to all $S \in \mathcal{S}$ offer to index and distribute everyone's media and contents. In response he receives $[\![ZS]\!] = p^{ZS}[\![S]\!]r^{ZS}$ from all $S \in \mathcal{S}$, which are some of their private media and content that they want to share with their social network. To better distribute them, Zuck conjoins the shared resources into his main resource, the social engine index

$$\zeta \;=\; [\![Z_{se}]\!] \;=\; \widehat{\curlyvee}_{S\in\mathcal{S}}[\![ZS]\!] \;=\; \widehat{\curlyvee}_{S\in\mathcal{S}}p^{ZS}[\![S]\!]r^{ZS}$$

and shares a part of it with Alice

$$[\![AZ]\!] \;=\; p^{AZ}[\![Z_{se}]\!]r^{AZ} \;=\; p^{AZ}\left(\widehat{\curlyvee}_{S\in\mathcal{S}}p^{ZS}[\![S]\!]r^{ZS}\right)r^{AZ}$$

The idea is that Zuck's resource $[\![AZ]\!]$ shared with Alice consists of Alice's friends' private contents processed by Zuck. As a participant who only relays messages, Zuck plays the role of a legitimate Man-in-the-Middle in this privacy protocol. The Man-in-the-Middle pattern is usually an attack strategy, and not a protocol role. Protocols sometimes use a Trusted Third Party for a particular functionality. However, Zuck is here more than a Trusted Third Party (TTP), because he does not provide a particular functionality, but processes *all* protocol content; but he is also less than a TTP, because he does not originate any content. Most importantly, he fuses all protocol content into his private resource $\zeta = [\![Z_{se}]\!] : \mathcal{X} \longrightarrow \mathcal{Y}$. Like in a search engine, the weights of the source elements $\zeta_x \in \mathcal{DY}$ determine a preference ranking of the content.

Zuck's privacy policy for Carol p^{CZ} determines which of Alice's, Bob's and Dave's postings Carol will see, and in which order. Carol's request r^{CZ} can filter out what she does not want to see; but Carol cannot use r^{CZ} to request what she will see, because Zuck's index is not available to her.

Zuck's resource $[\![Z_{se}]\!]$ and all of his policies p^{SZ} also take into account Alice's and Bob's privacy policies p^{ZA} and p^{ZB}, which may specify whether Carol should have access to their content. However, the existing social engines provide policy languages for p^{ZS} at the expressiveness level of the 1960s operating systems, before the concepts of access control were introduced, where only a

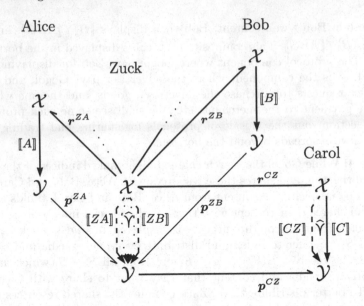

Fig. 3. Composite privacy protocol: Social Networking (SNet)

small number of fixed access control policies are available. The users are usually offered to either make their postings available to general public, or to all of their private contacts ("friends"), and sometimes also to all of their contacts' contacts ("friends' friends"). The option of establishing subgroups and hierarchies of private contacts is not offered. The option of sharing content with specific subgroups is offered as a separate functionality, but the recipients must be reentered with each message, or kept in an address book, which is separate from privacy policies.

While more expressive access control systems, allowing refined privacy policies, would surely vastly enhance usability of the social engine for Alice and Bob, allowing them to manage their content using the access control mechanisms that they got used to while using their computers, this would leave Zuck with narrower choices of his policies. And Zuck, of course, monetizes his services by manipulating the weight biases in his social engine index $[\![Z_{se}]\!]: \mathcal{X} \longrightarrow \mathcal{Y}$, and by selling the choices what to display to each user. These choices are expressed by his policy $p^{SZ}: \mathcal{Y} \longrightarrow \mathcal{Y}$ for each user $S \in \mathcal{S}$. The more privacy choices are made by Alice and Bob as content originators, the fewer privacy choices are left to Zuck as the content aggregator and monetizer.

4   Level-Above: Privacy Protocols as Privacy Attacks

The rapid transformation of the socio-technical context of privacy is an acute socio-political problem, which has been described from many angles [1,5,8,17,47]. The idea of this research is to shed some light on the problem of privacy by analyzing privacy protocol problems. In this section, we attempt to outline the unusual shape of some of the typical privacy protocol problems. They are unusual in that their vulnerabilities are not design flaws that open some attack vectors for outside attackers, as they do in security protocols. Typical privacy protocol vulnerabilities seem inherent to protocols themselves. Not that the protocols always have back doors; but they have transparent roofs. They are not vulnerable to subversions, or level-below attacks, but to sublimations, or level-above applications.

4.1 Man-in-the-Middle Protocols

We have seen that Zuck was an MitM in the SNet protocol on Fig. 3, where his private resource $[\![Z_{se}]\!]$ is inserted in-between everybody else's private resources, as their fusion; and that Bob is an MitM in the TAd-protocol on Fig. 2, where he is inserted in-between Gogol and Alice, and serves Gogol's targeted ads to Alice. A level above SNet and TAd, both Zuck and Gogol are MitMs in the privacy protocols where they monetize their services (social networking and web search, respectively) by inserting themselves in-between the advertisers and their targets (usually voters or consumers). Zuck's protocol for monetizing his social engine through Social Influencing (SInf) is displayed in Fig. 4. This is a level-above protocol in the sense that it is built on top of the SNet protocol, which it uses as an encapsulated procedure. In Fig. 4, we only display a single RP-component of SNet: the rectangle on the left, where Zuck provides Carol her friends' postings. We represent SNet by its single component only because we do not have a good diagrammatic notation to encapsulate a low-level protocol as an atom of a high-level protocol. SInf uses SNet on the left to leverage its business process on the right. Tizer is an advertising campaign manager, and his resource $[\![T_{ad}]\!] : \mathcal{Z} \longrightarrow \mathcal{Z}$ is a campaign strategy, presented as a Markov chain over the a set of campaign messages $\mathcal{Z}$. Tizer initiates an SInf protocol run with r^{TZ}, requesting that Zuck places the campaign messages of interest for Tizer at that moment. Zuck runs the request through his advertising index $[\![Z_{ad}]\!] : \mathcal{Z} \longrightarrow \mathcal{X}$, assigning to each campaign message from $\mathcal{Z}$ a suitable context of recipients and their postings in $\mathcal{X}$, and his social engine $[\![Z_{se}]\!] : \mathcal{X} \longrightarrow \mathcal{Y}$ then inserts the campaign messages among Carol's friends' postings. Zuck's business engine $[\![Z_{bu}]\!] : \mathcal{Y} \longrightarrow \mathcal{Z}$ then generates the service report p^{TZ} and the invoice r^{ZT} for Tizer, who responds with the payment p^{ZT} from his advertising budget $[\![T_\$]\!]$. The payment $[\![ZT]\!]$ is added to Zuck's budget $[\![Z_\$]\!]$.

4.2 Resource Inflation, Privacy Deflation

Dave would like to make pancakes, but he does not have either milk or eggs, so he needs to borrow from Alice, who is his neighbor. But he is shy by nature, and he already borrowed many things. So to avoid intruding into Alice's privacy even more, Dave asks Carol to ask Alice for milk, and he asks Bob to ask her for eggs. If Dave is also short of flour and oil, he can also ask Elizabeth and Frank to knock on Alice's door and ask for that. Then he collects it all, and

Carol   Zuck   Tizer

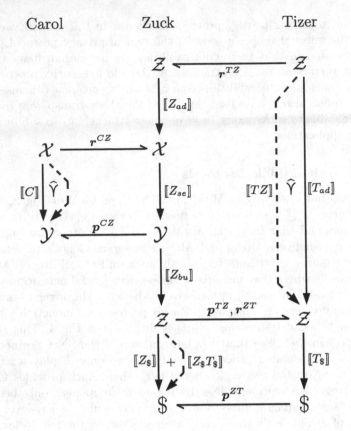

Fig. 4. Level-above privacy protocol: Social Influencing (SInf)

makes pancakes. This *cross-sharing* privacy protocol is displayed in Fig. 5. Dave
developed this protocol when he worked as a police detective. Alice was often
a suspect in his investigations, so whenever he needed to check the details of
Alice's alibi, it turned out to be better to ask Alice's friends, than to ask her
directly. By conjoining the information obtained from others, he would not only
get more details, without drawing attention with too many requests at once,
but he could also *cross-reference* the different details that Alice provided to
different people. If she tells one person one thing, and another person another
thing, then Dave would detect an inconsistency in Alice's alibi. While a fusion
of inconsistent sources eliminates the inconsistent parts, and thus contains less
information than either of the original sources, the inconsistency itself becomes a
higher-order information, as mentioned at the end of Sect. 2. Level-above attacks
and protocols sublimate entire low-level protocol sessions as higher-order information, and manipulate it towards some privacy goals. The loss of a private
resource for Alice is a gain of a private resource for Dave. Having detected an
inconsistency in Alice's alibi by asking around in a cross-referencing protocol,
like the alibi check interpretation of Fig. 5, Dave confronts Alice himself in a

level-above protocol, and requests more higher-order information, to eliminate
the inconsistencies from the acquired resources. An analogous level-above sub-
limation of the cross-sharing protocol in the pancake sources interpretation of
Fig. 5 would be that Dave asks Bob, Carol, Elizabeth and Frank to leave the
milk, egg, flour and oil that they got for him from Alice—to leave it all for him
with Alice. Then he could collect it all simply by asking Alice if the neighbors
by any chance left anything for him.

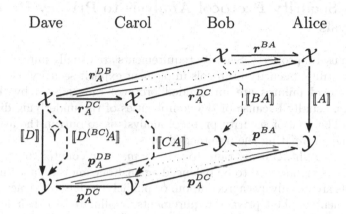

Fig. 5. Resource inflation: cross-referencing and cross-sharing

The problem of cross-referencing is a well-studied privacy problem, because
it arises in statistical databases [24,27,42]. Statistical databases anonymize their
records, and make them publicly available for statistical analyses. The problem
is that Alice's data may be recorded several statistical databases, one owned by
Bob, another one by Carol, another one by Elizabeth, and Frank; and Alice's
data may be anonymized differently in each case: Bob may omit Alice's address,
Carol her date of birth, Elizabeth her phone number. Now Dave may link Alice's
records in Bob's and Carol's databases by the phone number, in Carol's and
Elizabeth's databases by the address, etc. He may then rearrange data according
to a common ordering, and align the anonymized records so that the gap on
each of them is filled by the date in another one. A moment of thought shows
see that this is a special case of the fusion operation described in Sect. 2.2. On
the other hand, the attack is clearly an instance of the privacy protocol in Fig. 5.
Re-identifying someone from statistical databases is similar to borrowing the
pancake ingredients from a neighbor, and to checking an alibi.

Large-scale versions of the cross-sharing protocol are nowadays routinely
launched as level-above attacks over many services and applications. E.g. the
SNet protocol from Fig. 3 is often sublimated into an instance of a cross-sharing
attack from Fig. 5: providers leverage requests for ongoing access to private channels against users' requests for a single service. In a much publicized incident, a
psychology lecturer from Cambridge University, let us call him Dave, designed
a Facebook app to collect user data for research purposes [20,23], which offered

a simple personality quiz, in exchange for full access to users' contact lists. The quiz was taken by 270,000 users, some of them called Bob or Carol, who unwittingly delivered the profiles of 87,000,000 of their contacts, some of them called Alice. The harvested profiles were sold to a political consultancy, Cambridge Analytica [46], and were used it to a great effect in a level-above instance of the SInf protocol from Fig. 4.

5   From Security Protocol Analysis to Privacy Protocol Analysis

Security is a useful property. Security requirements are usually publicly declared, with a clear utility. Security protocols implement explicit security requirements. Security protocol failures are unintended protocol runs missed by the protocol designers, usually because of the complexities of the underlying distributed algorithms. The goal of security protocol analysis is to outrun the attackers in detecting and eliminating the unintended runs.

Privacy is a right. But my right to privacy may run counter to your right to privacy. Private rights need to be balanced against one another, and the privacy requirements are not always agreed upon, or publicly declared. Privacy protocols often implement implicit privacy requirements, sublimated to their level-above deployments. In the realm of privacy, the task of protocol analysis is not just to detect the unintended failures with respect to declared goals, but often also to recognize the intended protocol runs pointing to some undeclared protocol goals, like in SInf and SNet protocols, that may be beneficial for some participants, but detrimental for others. Privacy protocol analysis thus provides a technical underpinning for the process of balancing information and value distributions in network society [9,18,47].

Given a security protocol, we strive to prove that its declared security requirements are enforced, or to uncover any attacks that may exist. Given a privacy protocol, task is to establish whose privacy requirements it implements. Alice's and Bob's privacy requirements often clash, and the boundary between protocols and attacks is blurred. At the level above, though, instead of attacks, there are now deceptions to be uncovered and analyzed.

Summary

Cathy taught us about security protocols. They are rules of interaction intended to assure that some security requirements are met: that some undesired interactions do not happen, and that the desired interactions do happen. They are usually based on cryptographic primitives. Some security protocols can be broken without breaking the underlying cryptographic primitives. We say that they are secure when they can only be broken by breaking the underlying crypto.

In recent years, the problems of privacy came to the forefront. Almost everyone has been a victim of a privacy breach, be it in electronic commerce, or at a social network. Privacy is not a security requirement but a right: right to be left alone, right to control your data and resources. Privacy requirements are met using protocols again: you check in at the doctor's office, and approve which data can be shared with whom; or you login at a web site, upload your photos or music, and choose who can access them. These privacy protocols are based on security protocols, just like security protocols are based on cryptographic primitives. And just like some security protocols can be broken even with perfect crypto, some privacy protocols are broken while perfectly secure. Cathy has solved many problems of the former kind with a smile. We hope her method will crack these new problems as well.

References

1. Acquisti, A., Gritzalis, S., Lambrinoudakis, C., di Vimercati, S.: Digital Privacy: Theory, Technologies, and Practices. CRC Press, Boca Raton (2007)
2. Alberti, P.M., Uhlmann, A.: Stochasticity and Partial Order: Double Stochastic Maps and Unitary Mixing. Mathematics and its Applications. Springer, Heidelberg (1981)
3. Ando, T.: Majorization, doubly stochastic matrices, and comparison of eigenvalues. Linear Algebra Appl. **118**, 163–248 (1989)
4. Angela, A., Conti, G.: A Day in the Life of Ancient Rome. Europa Editions, New York (2009)
5. Angwin, J.: Dragnet Nation: A Quest for Privacy, Security, and Freedom in a World of Relentless Surveillance. Henry Holt and Company, New York (2014)
6. Arendt, H.: The Human Condition. Charles R. Walgreen Foundation Lectures, Second edn. University of Chicago Press, Chicago (1998)
7. Bailey, J.: From public to private: the development of the concept of "private". Soc. Res. **69**(1), 15–31 (2002)
8. Ball, K., Haggerty, K., Lyon, D.: Routledge Handbook of Surveillance Studies. Routledge International Handbooks. Taylor & Francis, Milton Park (2012)
9. Benkler, Y.: The Wealth of Networks: How Social Production Transforms Markets and Freedom. Yale University Press, New Haven (2006)
10. Birkhoff, G.: Tres observaciones sobre el algebra lineal. Univ. Nac. Tucumán Rev. Ser. A **5**, 147–151 (1946)
11. Brandt, F., Conitzer, V., Endriss, U., Lang, J., Procaccia, A.D.: Handbook of Computational Social Choice. Cambridge University Press, Cambridge (2016)
12. Burke, S.: Delos: investigating the notion of privacy within the ancient greek house. Ph.D. thesis, University of Leicester (2000)
13. Cervesato, I., Meadows, C., Pavlovic, D.: An encapsulated authentication logic for reasoning about key distribution protocols. In: Guttman, J. (ed.) Proceedings of CSFW 2005, pp. 48–61. IEEE (2005)
14. Dalenius, T.: Towards a methodology for statistical disclosure control. Statistik Tidskrift **15**, 429–444 (1977)
15. Datta, A., Derek, A., Mitchell, J., Pavlovic, D.: A derivation system and compositional logic for security protocols. J. Comput. Secur. **13**, 423–482 (2005)
16. Datta, A., Derek, A., Mitchell, J.C., Pavlovic, D.: Abstraction and refinement in protocol derivation. In: Focardi, R. (ed.) Proceedings of CSFW 2004, pp. 30–47. IEEE (2004)
17. Diffie, W., Landau, S.: Privacy on the Line: The Politics of Wiretapping and Encryption. MIT Press, Cambridge (2010)

18. van Dijk, J.: The Network Society. SAGE Publications, Thousand Oaks (2012)
19. Durgin, N., Mitchell, J., Pavlovic, D.: A compositional logic for proving security properties of protocols. J. Comput. Security **11**(4), 677–721 (2004)
20. Yearwood, M.H., et al.: On wealth and the diversity of friendships: high social class people around the world have fewer international friends. Personality Individ. Differ. **87**, 224–229 (2015)
21. Habermas, J.: The Structural Transformation of the Public Sphere: An Inquiry into a Category of Bourgeois Society. Studies in Contemporary German Social Thought. MIT Press, Cambridge (1991)
22. Hardy, G.H., Littlewood, J.E., Pólya, G.: Inequalities. The University Press (1934)
23. Kosinski, M., Stillwell, D., Graepel, T.: Private traits and attributes are predictable from digital records of human behavior. Proc. Natl. Acad. Sci. **110**(15), 5802–5805 (2013)
24. Malin, B., Sweeney, L.: Re-identification of DNA through an automated linkage process. In: American Medical Informatics Association Annual Symposium, AMIA 2001, Washington, DC, USA, 3–7 November 2001. AMIA (2001)
25. Marshall, A.W., Olkin, I.: Inequalities: Theory of Majorization and Its Applications. Mathematics in Science and Engineering, vol. 143. Academic Press, Cambridge (1979)
26. Meadows, C., Pavlovic, D.: Deriving, attacking and defending the GDOI protocol. In: Samarati, P., Ryan, P., Gollmann, D., Molva, R. (eds.) ESORICS 2004. LNCS, vol. 3193, pp. 53–72. Springer, Heidelberg (2004). https://doi.org/10.1007/978-3-540-30108-0_4
27. Narayanan, A., Shmatikov, V.: Robust de-anonymization of large sparse datasets. In: Proceedings of the 2008 IEEE Symposium on Security and Privacy, SP 2008, pp. 111–125. IEEE Computer Society, Washington (2008)
28. Nielsen, M.A.: Characterizing mixing and measurement in quantum mechanics. Phys. Rev. A **63**(2), 022114 (2001)
29. Orlin, L.C.: Locating Privacy in Tudor London. Oxford University Press, Oxford (2009)
30. Page, L., Brin, S., Motwani, R., Winograd, T.: The PageRank citation ranking: bringing order to the web. Technical report, Stanford Digital Library Technologies Project (1998)
31. Pavlovic, D.: Network as a computer: ranking paths to find flows. In: Hirsch, E.A., Razborov, A.A., Semenov, A., Slissenko, A. (eds.) CSR 2008. LNCS, vol. 5010, pp. 384–397. Springer, Heidelberg (2008). https://doi.org/10.1007/978-3-540-79709-8_38. arxiv.org:0802.1306
32. Pavlovic, D., Meadows, C.: Deriving authentication for pervasive security. In: McLean, J. (ed.) Proceedings of the ISTPS 2008, 15 p. ACM (2008)
33. Pavlovic, D., Meadows, C.: Actor-network procedures. In: Ramanujam, R., Ramaswamy, S. (eds.) ICDCIT 2012. LNCS, vol. 7154, pp. 7–26. Springer, Heidelberg (2012). https://doi.org/10.1007/978-3-642-28073-3_2. arxiv.org:1106.0706
34. Pavlovic, D., Meadows, C.: Deriving ephemeral authentication using channel axioms. In: Christianson, B., Malcolm, J.A., Matyáš, V., Roe, M. (eds.) Security Protocols 2009. LNCS, vol. 7028, pp. 240–261. Springer, Heidelberg (2013). https://doi.org/10.1007/978-3-642-36213-2_27
35. Pavlović, D., Escardó, M.: Calculus in coinductive form. In: Pratt, V. (ed.) Proceedings of Thirteenth Annual IEEE Symposium on Logic in Computer Science, pp. 408–417. IEEE Computer Society (1998)
36. Popper, K.R.: Conjectures and Refutations: The Growth of Scientific Knowledge. Classics Series. Routledge, Abingdon (2002)

37. Rogaway, P.: The moral character of cryptographic work. IACR Cryptology ePrint Archive 2015:1162 (2015)
38. Saari, D.G.: Basic Geometry of Voting. Basic Geometry of Voting Series. Springer, Heidelberg (1995). https://doi.org/10.1007/978-3-642-57748-2
39. Schoeman, F.D.: Philosophical Dimensions of Privacy: An Anthology. Cambridge University Press, Cambridge (1984)
40. Shannon, C.E.: Communication theory of secrecy systems. Bell Syst. Tech. J. **28**(4), 656–715 (1949)
41. Suzumura, K.: Rational Choice, Collective Decisions, and Social Welfare. Cambridge University Press, Cambridge (2009)
42. Sweeney, L.: Weaving technology and policy together to maintain confidentiality. J. Law Med. Ethics **25**, 98–110 (1997)
43. Sweeney, L.: Achieving k-anonymity privacy protection using generalization and suppression. Int. J. Uncertainty Fuzziness Knowl.-Based Syst. **10**(5), 571–588 (2002)
44. Sweeney, L.: k-anonymity: a model for protecting privacy. Int. J. Uncertainty Fuzziness Knowl.-Based Syst. **10**(5), 557–570 (2002)
45. Warren, S.D., Brandeis, L.D.: The right to privacy. Harvard Law Rev. **4**(5), 193–220 (1890)
46. Wikipedia. Cambridge Analytica. wikipedia.org/wiki/Cambridge_Analytica
47. Zuboff, S.: The Age of Surveillance Capitalism: The Fight for a Human Future at the New Frontier of Power. PublicAffairs, New York (2019)

A Multiset Rewriting Model
for Specifying and Verifying Timing
Aspects of Security Protocols

Musab A. Alturki[1,2], Tajana Ban Kirigin[3], Max Kanovich[4,8], Vivek Nigam[5,6],
Andre Scedrov[7,8], and Carolyn Talcott[9(✉)]

[1] KFUPM, Dhahran, Saudi Arabia
musab@kfupm.edu.sa
[2] Runtime Verification Inc., Urbana, USA
[3] Department of Mathematics, University of Rijeka, Rijeka, Croatia
bank@math.uniri.hr
[4] University College, London, London, UK
m.kanovich@ucl.ac.uk
[5] Federal University of Paraíba, João Pessoa, Brazil
vivek@ci.ufpb.br
[6] fortiss, Munich, Germany
nigam@fortiss.org
[7] University of Pennsylvania, Philadelphia, USA
scedrov@math.upenn.edu
[8] National Research University Higher School of Economics, Moscow, Russia
[9] SRI International, Menlo Park, USA
clt@csl.sri.com

Abstract. Catherine Meadows has played an important role in the
advancement of formal methods for protocol security verification. Her
insights on the use of, for example, narrowing and rewriting logic has
made possible the automated discovery of new attacks and the shaping
of new protocols. Meadows has also investigated other security aspects,
such as, distance-bounding protocols and denial of service attacks. We
have been greatly inspired by her work. This paper describes the use of
Multiset Rewriting for the specification and verification of timing aspects
of protocols, such as network delays, timeouts, timed intruder models and
distance-bounding properties. We detail these timed features with a number of examples and describe decidable fragments of related verification
problems.

1 Introduction

Protocol security verification is one of the best success stories of formal meth-
ods. Indeed a number of attacks and corrections have been discovered since
Lowe found an attack on the Needham-Schroeder protocol [26,30]. Catherine
Meadows' work, particularly her work on the NRL protocol analyzer [27] and
Maude-NPA [12], has played a great role in this success story. She has used

© Springer Nature Switzerland AG 2019
J. D. Guttman et al. (Eds.): Meadows Festschrift, LNCS 11565, pp. 192–213, 2019.
https://doi.org/10.1007/978-3-030-19052-1_13

formal models, such as Rewriting Logic and Narrowing, to advance the use of formal methods in protocol security verification.

However, much of the use of formal methods does not consider the protocols timing aspects. An exception is Meadows' work on Distance-Bounding (DB) Protocols [29,32], which has been an inspiration to our previous work,[1] and her cost-based framework for analyzing DoS attacks [28]. In a sequence of papers [1, 20,23,24], we have developed a number of models based on Multiset Rewriting that investigate different timing aspects of protocols.

A key aspect of Meadows' work is her careful and insightful formalization of important aspects of the assumptions and actions of a protocol. In this spirit, here we describe general Timed Multiset Rewriting (MSR) theories of networks, protocols, and intruders, and show how these theories support representation of diverse timing aspects of protocol execution. We illustrate these aspects with examples. In particular, we model the following timing aspects:

- Network and processing delays, important, *e.g.*, in DB protocol specification and verification;
- Protocol timeouts that have specific applications in a variety of protocols;
- Timed Dolev-Yao intruder, which is similar to the standard Dolev-Yao intruder model in that he can create fresh nonces, compose and decompose messages, for which he possesses the decryption key. However, timed intruder is amended with time features in order to make the physical properties of the system relevant. For example, in contrast to the Dolev-Yao intruder, timed intruder is not able to learn messages immediately, instead, he must obey the restrictions imposed by the physical transmission channel used and wait for a message to reach him.

We illustrate these aspects by specifying DB protocols and protocols with timeouts. The specifications presented here are more general than the ones appearing in our previous work by including all the timing aspects described above.

As an added benefit, we specify verification problems for timed protocol and intruder theories, and obtain some complexity results including the PSPACE-completeness of the secrecy problem. This builds on our past work in which we have developed a rich complexity theory for problems formulated in terms of (Timed) MSR [24]. However, here we focus on specific application of MSR models from [24] to timed protocol specification and verification, for which we build the relevant timed protocol, network and intruder theories, as well as the related verification problems, namely the secrecy problem and the false acceptance and false rejection problems related to DB protocols.

The paper starts with the description of some timing aspects of security protocols in Sect. 2. In Sect. 3, we present the Timed MSR of [24]. In Sects. 4 and 5 we define timed protocol and intruder theories. Section 6 introduces relevant verification problems with examples. We present the related complexity results in Sect. 7. Finally, in Sect. 8 we conclude by discussing related work and pointing to future work.

---

[1] Indeed, it was Cathy that suggested us to investigate DB protocols.

2   Timing Aspects of Security Protocols

We illustrate timing aspects of protocols with two examples. The first one is on distance-bounding protocols and the second is on the use of timeouts.

2.1   Distance-Bounding Protocols

Distance-bounding protocols (DB) [4,15] aim to enhance traditional authentication with additional assurance of users' physical proximity. The goal of a DB protocol is to provide access to some resource only to valid provers that are within a specified distance bound, and, at the same time, reject access to intruders and to provers that are located outside of the distance bound perimeter. By measuring the round trip time of a challenge-response bit exchange, the verifier deduces the upper bound on the distance of a prover.

Attacks on communication protocols, such as relay attacks on DB protocols, can only be analyzed using models with high-resolution timing information representing physical properties of the communication medium. In order to accommodate such requirements, our models for the formalization and verification of timed protocols include *explicit real time* and specific time aspects involving, *e.g.*, comparisons of time variables.

Vulnerabilities of DB protocols, besides cryptographic properties, exploit not only the timing aspects, but also the presence of other honest and dishonest provers, the presence of other verifiers, and colluding intruders, see *e.g.*, [8]. Our model can accommodate such aspects as well. For example, rules of protocol theories (as specified later in Sect. 4) represent the behavior of verifiers and honest provers. Dishonest provers may be represented through intruder theories (as specified later in Sect. 5) with specific initial knowledge. Alternatively, theories representing specific behaviors of dishonest provers can be specified, modeling *e.g.*, early responses and guessing. Consequently, verification of DB protocols using our model can reveal various known types of attacks, including in-between-ticks attack [24], distance hijacking [8], among others, including vulnerabilities in multi-protocol environments.

2.2   Timeouts

Protocol Session Timeouts become relevant when considering timing aspects, such as, network communication delays. Http/Https protocols use timeouts to limit waiting time in multiple situations: idle connections, client waiting for server response, server waiting for client to complete a request. The Session Initiation Protocol (used by VOIP and other communication protocols) uses timers to limit the waiting time during different steps of the protocol. For example if the called party is not available the initialization should not ring forever! The ability to reset such timers provides readily available attack surfaces.

Lifetime/time-to-live is another important time related concept. Networking protocols (for example, TLS, Kerberos) often use *tickets* to control access. These tickets typically have a lifetime after which they are no longer valid. Packets

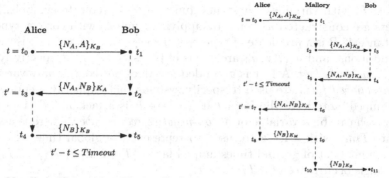

(a) Needham-Schroeder Protocol
with Timeout.

(b) Timed Version of Lowe Attack.

Fig. 1. Adding timeouts to Needham-Schroeder protocol.

traveling through the network (for example TCP/IP) often have a time-to-live
to avoid loops and problems delaying delivery.

As an illustration of the use of timeouts, consider the protocol shown in
Fig. 1a. It is a version of the Needham-Schroeder protocol [30] with timeouts. In
particular, Alice starts the communication with Bob as in the original NS, by
creating a fresh nonce N_A, at time t_0, reaching Bob at time t_1. Bob answers by
creating a fresh nonce N_B and sending it at time t_2, reaching Alice at time t_3.
Then Alice responds at time t_4 reaching Bob at time t_5. The difference is that
Alice waits for Bob's response for a given period, *Timeout*. If expected message
is not received within this period, the protocol session is terminated.

The use of timeouts has implications to an intruder, as shown in the timed
version of the Lowe Attack [26] in Fig. 1b. In particular, the intruder has to be
able to send the response $\{N_A, N_B\}_{K_A}$ to Alice within the period *Timeout*. That
is, for that attack to succeed, $t_7 - t_0 \leq Timeout$ has to hold.[2]

For the traditional Dolev-Yao intruder, this is not a problem as he imperson-
ates the network. Thus he can forward messages instantaneously. This may lead
to false positives, as it is not physically possible to forward messages instantaneously. We propose in Sect. 5, therefore, a refinement of the Dolev-Yao intruder
which takes timing aspects, such communication and processing delays, into
account.

3   Timed Multiset Rewriting

We review Timed Multiset Rewriting of [24] which is the language we use to
specify timed protocol and intruder theories. Assume a finite first-order typed

---

[2] For simplicity, we ammended only the initiator role, Alice, with a timeout. Since
Lowe attack is an attack against both Alice and Bob, the protocol could similary be
enhanced with another timeout in the reponder role that would additionally enable
Bob to detect that something is wrong.

alphabet, Σ, with variables, constants, function and predicate symbols. Terms and facts are constructed as usual by applying symbols with correct type [11]. For instance, if P is a predicate of type $\tau_1 \times \tau_2 \times \cdots \times \tau_n \to o$, where o is the type for propositions, and $u_1, \ldots, u_n$ are terms of types $\tau_1, \ldots, \tau_n$, respectively, then $P(u_1, \ldots, u_n)$ is a *fact*. A fact is grounded if it does not contain any variables.

Timestamped facts are used to specify systems that explicitly mention time. Timestamped facts have the form $F@T$, where F is a fact and T is its timestamp, which can be a variable or a *non-negative real number*. There is a special predicate *Time* with arity zero, used to represent the global time. A configuration is a multiset of ground timestamped facts, $\{Time@t, F_1@t_1, \ldots, F_n@t_n\}$, with a single occurrence of a *Time* fact.

Actions. Actions are multiset rewrite rules and are either time advancement or instantaneous actions. The *Tick* action, $Time@T \longrightarrow Time@(T + \varepsilon)$, where ε can be instantiated by any positive real number, represents the advancement of time. We also write $Tick_\varepsilon$ when we refer to the *Tick* rule for a specific ε. Applying the $Tick_\varepsilon$ rule to the configuration $\{Time@t, F_1@t_1, \ldots, F_n@t_n\}$ yields the configuration $\{Time@(t + \varepsilon), F_1@t_1, \ldots, F_n@t_n\}$ where time advances by ε.

The remaining actions are the Instantaneous Actions, which do not affect the global time, but may rewrite the remaining facts. They have the following form:

$$Time@T, W_1@T_1, \ldots, W_k@T_k, F_1@T_1', \ldots, F_n@T_n' \mid \mathcal{C} \longrightarrow$$
$$\exists \mathbf{X}.[Time@T, W_1@T_1, \ldots, W_k@T_k, Q_1@(T + D_1), \ldots, Q_m@(T + D_m)],$$

where $D_1, \ldots, D_m$ are natural numbers and $\mathcal{C}$ is the guard of the action which is a set of constraints involving the time variables appearing in the pre-condition, *i.e.* the variables $T, T_1, \ldots, T_k, T_1', \ldots, T_n'$. Facts $W_1@T_1, \ldots, W_k@T_k$ are preserved by the rule, while $F_1@T_1', \ldots, F_n@T_n'$ are replaced by $Q_1@(T + D_1), \ldots, Q_m@(T + D_m)$. All free variables appearing in the post-condition appear in the pre-condition. Time constraints are of the form:

$$T \geq T' \pm D, \quad T > T' \pm D \quad \text{and} \quad T = T' \pm D$$

where T and T' are time variables, and D is a natural number. In the above rules we omit the time constraints whenever the set $\mathcal{C}$ of time constraints is empty.

An instantaneous rule of the form $\mathcal{P} \mid \mathcal{C} \longrightarrow \exists \mathbf{X}.\mathcal{P}'$ can be applied to a configuration $\mathcal{S}$ if there is a subset $\mathcal{S}_0 \subseteq \mathcal{S}$ and a matching substitution θ, such that $\mathcal{S}_0 = \mathcal{P}\theta$ and $\mathcal{C}\theta$ evaluates to true. The resulting configuration from the application of this rule is $(\mathcal{S} \setminus \mathcal{S}_0) \cup ((\mathcal{P}'\sigma)\theta)$, where σ is a substitution that maps the existentially quantified variables $\mathbf{X}$ to fresh constants, that is, constants not appearing in $\mathcal{S}$. These fresh values are also called *nonces* in protocol security literature [5,10].[3] For example, the action

$$Time@T, F_1(X, Y)@T_1 \mid T_1 \geq T + 1 \longrightarrow \exists N.[Time@T, F_2(X, Y, N)@(T + 3)]$$

can be applied to configuration $\{Time@5.1, F_1(a, b)@7.5\}$ resulting in configuration $\{Time@5.1, F_2(a, b, n_1)@8.1\}$, where the fact $F_1(a, b)@7.5$ is replaced by

---

[3] Substitution application ($\mathcal{S}\theta$) is defined as usual [11], *i.e.*, by mapping time variables in $\mathcal{S}$ to non-negative real numbers, nonce names to nonce names (renaming of nonces) and term variables to terms.

$F_2(a, b, n_1)$@8.1 with n_1 being a fresh constant. Notice that instantaneous actions do not change the global time. Moreover, the timestamps of the facts that are created by instantaneous actions are in the present or the future.

A trace of timed MSR rules $\mathcal{R}$ from a given initial configuration $\mathcal{S}_0$ is a sequence of configurations $\mathcal{S}_0 \longrightarrow_{r_1} \mathcal{S}_1 \longrightarrow_{r_2} \cdots \longrightarrow_{r_n} \mathcal{S}_n$, such that for all $0 \le i \le n - 1$, $\mathcal{S}_{i+1}$ is a configuration obtained by applying $r_{i+1} \in \mathcal{R}$ to $\mathcal{S}_i$.

Goal Configurations. Among all the possible traces we will be interested in traces that reach some goal. A goal configuration is specified by a *goal* $\mathcal{GS}$ which is a set of pairs $\{\langle \mathcal{S}_1, \mathcal{C}_1 \rangle, \dots, \langle \mathcal{S}_n, \mathcal{C}_n \rangle\}$. Each pair $\langle \mathcal{S}_j, \mathcal{C}_j \rangle$ is of the form: $\langle \{F_1@T_1, \dots, F_p@T_p\}, \mathcal{C}_j \rangle$, where $T_1, \dots, T_p$ are time variables, $F_1, \dots, F_p$ are facts and $\mathcal{C}_j$ is a set of time constraints involving only variables $T_1, \dots, T_p$. A configuration $\mathcal{S}$ is a *goal configuration w.r.t.* $\mathcal{GS}$ if for some $1 \le i \le n$, there is a grounding substitution, σ, such that $\mathcal{S}_i \sigma \subseteq \mathcal{S}$ and $\mathcal{C}_i \sigma$ evaluates to true.

For example, the configuration $\{Time@10.5, F@12.3, G(a)@0.1\}$ is a goal configuration w.r.t. the goal $\{\langle \{Time@T, F@T_1\}, \{T_1 \ge T\} \rangle\}$.

Reachability is one of the main verification problems for MSR systems.

Definition 1. *[Reachability problem] Given a timed MSR $\mathcal{T}$, a goal $\mathcal{GS}$ and an initial configuration $\mathcal{S}_0$, is there a trace, $\mathcal{P}$, that leads from $\mathcal{S}_0$ to a goal configuration?*

Balanced Rules. Balanced rules were introduced in [33]. Systems containing only balanced rules represent an important class of systems for which several reachability problems have been shown to be decidable [17,22,24].

A rule is balanced if the number of facts appearing in its pre-condition is the same as the number of facts appearing in its post-condition. An MSR system is balanced if all its rules are balanced. Balanced systems have the following important property: All the configurations in a trace of a balanced system have the same number of facts.

As described in [17], any unbalanced rule can be made balanced by using so-called *empty facts*. For example, the unbalanced rule: $Time@T, F_1@T_1 \longrightarrow Time@T, F_1@T_1, F_2@T_2$ can be turned into a balanced rule by adding an empty fact to its pre-condition, $Time@T, F_1@T_1, P@T_3 \longrightarrow Time@T, F_1@T_1, F_2@T_2$. However, the obtained balanced system is not equivalent to the original, unbalanced system as the set of reachable states and possible traces is reduced. Notice that the above balanced rule can only be applied if a P fact is available in the enabling configuration. That is not the condition for the application of the original, unbalanced rule. While the number of facts in all reachable configurations of a balanced system is constant, rules in unbalanced systems may add facts, so reachable configurations potentially have unbounded size.

Balanced systems are suitable *e.g.*, for modeling scenarios with a fixed amount of memory. As in [17], empty facts represent available free memory slots. In order to model systems and intruders with bounded memory, we will consider empty facts related to the system including agents, servers and the network, D facts, and additionally consider empty facts related to each specific intruder s, $P(s)$.

For some of our complexity results (in Sect. 7), we will assume an upper-bound on the size of facts. The size, $|F@t|$, of a timed fact $F@t$ is the total number of symbols in F. For example, $|M(a, \{a, b\}_k)@t| = 5$.

4   Timed Protocol Theories

In the traditional "Alice and Bob" protocol notation and specification (such as the one used in Fig. 1, Sect. 2.2) timing aspects of protocols are not formally specified. Necessary assumptions about time, such as the time requirements for the fulfillment of a protocol session, are not included. For example, in the description of distance-bounding protocols it is only informally described that the verifier remembers the time of sending a challenge bit and the time when receiving the response bit, which are then used to make a decision whether of not to grant access. Moreover, from the traditional protocol description, it is not clear which assumptions about the network are used, such as the transmission medium used by the participants. Furthermore, it is not formally specified which properties does the above protocol ensure, in which conditions, and against which intruders. Security verification should include such specifications when checking whether a system is vulnerable to an attack.

Given a timed MSR model and an initial configuration representing the knowledge of participating agents and intruders, their capabilities and behavior (including protocol rules), we look for a trace representing an attack. For that purpose, a goal configuration will denote that a protocol has suffered an attack.

For protocol and intruder theories that obey the physical laws involving time, it is, in particular, important to consider network delays and processing time. Non-zero processing time can be formalized by adding time constraints to rules, e.g., $Time@T, M(m)@T' \mid \{T > T'\} \longrightarrow Time@T, M(m)@T', \mathsf{N}_S(m')@T$.

Similarly, faithful timing of message transmission for a given network topology between agents can be obtained by adding to transmission rules constraints that involve relevant distances, e.g.: $Time@T, \mathsf{N}_S(A, X)@T' \mid \{T \geq T' + D(A, B)\} \longrightarrow Time@T, \mathsf{N}_R(B, X)@T$, where $D(A, B)$ denotes the time required for messages to travel the distance from agent A to agent B.

4.1   Network Theory

We enhance the traditional network models used for protocol execution. A suitable network model used for communication during protocol execution should take care of distances between agents. More specifically, it should not only take care of physical distances between protocol participants, but also represent various available transmission media and the corresponding network distances, i.e., transmission speed, as well as availability of some transmission channel to a particular agent for sending or receiving messages.

We assume that a topology of participating agents, including intruders, representing communicating distances (network distances) between agents, is given. We also assume that agents' and intruder's capabilities of using transmission

NET-1: $Time@T, Cap_S(A, C)@T_1, Cap_R(B, C, 1)@T_2, \mathsf{N}_S(A, C, X)@T_3$
$$| \; T \geq T_3 + D(A, B, C) \longrightarrow$$
$$Time@T, Cap_S(A, C)@T_1, Cap_R(B, C, 1)@T_2, \mathsf{N}_R(B, C, X)@T$$

NET-2: $Time@T, Cap_S(A, C)@T_1, Cap_R(B, C, 2)@T_2, \mathsf{N}_S(A, C, X)@T_3$
$$| \; T \geq T_3 + D(A, I, C) \longrightarrow$$
$$Time@T, Cap_S(A, C)@T_1, Cap_R(B, C, 2)@T_2, \mathsf{N}_S(A, C, X)@T_3,$$
$$\mathsf{N}_R(B, C, X)@T$$

Fig. 2. Network theory

channels, are given.[4] We model capabilities of agents of sending and receiving messages on some particular transmission media and the corresponding time distances between agents per specific media. Hence, network distances are specified per pair of participants on a specific transmission channel.

We assume that agents do not move. This is also suitable for scenarios where agents may move at a speed that is negligible w.r.t. transmission speed.

Our signature is based on the signature used to model protocols and the Dolev-Yao intruder model in [9,10] and timed Dolev-Yao intruders in [24,31]. In order to provide a finer formalization of the network that supports the timing aspects, we add the following predicate and constant symbols to the signature:

$D(A, B, C)$, natural number denoting the network delay time in communication from agent A to agent B when using transmission media C;

$\mathsf{N}_S(A, C, m)@t$, denoting that message m was sent by agent A on transmission medium C at moment t;

$\mathsf{N}_R(A, C, m)@t$, denoting that message m may be received by agent A on transmission medium C;

$Cap_S(A, C)$, denoting that the agent A is capable of sending messages on transmission medium C;

$Cap_R(A, C, k)$, denoting that the agent A is capable of receiving messages on transmission medium C, where for $k = 1$ the message is removed from the network, while for $k = 2$ reading does not remove messages from the network.

Network rules are shown in Fig. 2. Transmission of messages is encoded as the transformation of N_S facts to N_R facts, *i.e.*, network delivers sent messages according to the receipt capabilities and time distances between participants.

Network theory rules ensure that a message may be received, only after the corresponding message transmission time, so-called "time of flight", has passed. These rules also ensure that agents and intruders only send and receive messages on communication channels they are connected to, *i.e.*, for which they have capabilities of sending or receiving messages. Rule NET-1 models message receipt that removes messages from the network, while NET-2 models non-consumption

---

[4] Instead of such fixed connections of agents to particular channels it is possible to represent agents establishing or dropping connections by additional rules in the model.

message receipt, so that the same message X may additionally be received by other agents without re-sending (as in *e.g.*, radio transmission). Which of the two rules is used depends on the nature of the transmission media modeled, which is specified through $Cap_R(X, Y, k)$ facts by having $k = 1$ or $k = 2$.

4.2   Protocol Theories

In the verification of protocols for which time plays a prominent role, such as distance-bounding protocols and cyber-physical systems in general, *explicit real time* is needed for representation of continuity of time in the real physical world.

Our timed MSR model presented in Sect. 3 is suitable for this purpose. In addition, our model is also suitable for expressing protocols with *timeouts*.

Since the execution and verification of security protocols may be affected by processing time, we add *duration* to the rules specified by DUR function. The arguments and the value of this function are specific to each rule. For example, the length of the plaintext and the key may effect the duration of the encryption. Duration of a rule execution, *i.e.*, DUR function, may be used when suitable, *e.g.*, in verification of attacks that involve the variance of execution time, such as passport traceability attacks in [7]. Rules for which the DUR function is not explicitly mentioned, have zero execution time.

Similarly, protocol states may or may not have timeouts. Once a timeout of a protocol state has passed, the protocol session changes its state.

A general theory of security protocols involving time is specified below. It includes the following predicate symbols:

$E@t$, denoting empty memory slots available for the network and the agents (different from intruders) from the moment t;

$S_i^A(n, \mathbf{X})$, denoting the protocol state predicate of the role A in the session with identifier n;

$T_i^A(n)@t$, denoting that the protocol state $S_i^A(n, \mathbf{X})$ times out at moment t.

A protocol state S_i associated with a timeout will be accompanied by the corresponding T_i fact, created by the rule leading to that protocol state.

In protocol theories related to traditional security protocols formalized in [10], a protocol execution rule represents an event of a message being received, followed by an immediate message reply. In order to model a variety of protocols, we allow protocol theories where at some protocol state, sending of a message may not be necessarily triggered by a message receipt. Similarly, a receipt of a message at some protocol state, may not be immediately followed by a reply message being sent. As in [10,17] protocols involve a number of roles that can be played by the participants, such as initiator, responder, client or server role.

Definition 2 (Protocol Theory). *A protocol theory $\mathcal{P}$ is specified by a number of roles, $A_1, \ldots, A_m$, and a set of state predicates, $S_0^{A_i}, \ldots, S_{n_i}^{A_i}$, and rules of the following form for each role A_i:*

- *protocol initialization rule:*

$Time@T, \mathcal{W} \longrightarrow$

$\quad \exists S_{id}.[Time@T, \mathsf{S}_0^{A_1}(S_{id}, \mathbf{X_1})@(T+t_i), \ldots, \mathsf{S}_0^{A_m}(S_{id}, \mathbf{X_m})@(T+t_i), \mathcal{W}'],$

where S_{id} is a fresh protocol session identification token, $\mathsf{S}_0^{A_i}$ is the initial state of role A_i, $t_i = \mathrm{DUR}_{INIT}$ is a natural number specifying the time it takes to initialize a protocol session, $\mathcal{W}$ is an arbitrary multiset of facts, $\mathcal{W}' = \mathcal{W} \cup \{ \mathsf{T}_0^{A_k}(S_{id})@(T+b_k) \mid \text{if } \mathsf{S}_0^{A_k} \text{ timeouts in } b_k \text{ time units}\}$, and $\mathbf{X_i}$ are variables from $\mathcal{W}$;

- *protocol execution rules* for protocol states $\mathsf{S}_i^{A_k}$ with no timeout:

$\quad Time@T, \mathsf{S}_i^{A_k}(S, \mathbf{X})@T_1, \mathcal{W}_1, \ \mathcal{W} \ \mid \ T_1 \leq T, \longrightarrow$

$\qquad \exists \mathbf{N}.[Time@T, \mathsf{S}_j^{A_k}(S, \mathbf{Y})@(T+t), \mathcal{W}_2, \mathcal{W}]$

and for protocol states $\mathsf{S}_i^{A_k}$ with associated timeout:

$\quad Time@T, \mathsf{S}_i^{A_k}(S, \mathbf{X})@T_1, \mathsf{T}_i^{A_k}(S)@T_2, \mathcal{W}_1, \ \mathcal{W} \ \mid \ T_1 \leq T, T_2 \geq T \longrightarrow$

$\qquad \exists \mathbf{N}.[Time@T, \mathsf{S}_j^{A_k}(S, \mathbf{Y})@(T+t), \mathcal{W}_2, \mathcal{W}],$

where for $i, j \in \{0, \ldots, k\}^5$ $t = \mathrm{DUR}_{i,j}(X)$ is a natural number specifying the processing time needed when moving from protocol state $S_i^{A_k}$ to protocol state $S_j^{A_k}$, $\mathbf{N}$ are fresh values, $\mathbf{X}$ and $\mathbf{Y}$ are variables, where variables in $\mathbf{Y}$ either appear in facts on the left side of the rule or are freshly generated variables from $\mathbf{N}$, and $\mathcal{W}, \mathcal{W}_1, \mathcal{W}_2$ are arbitrary multisets of facts, possibly containing facts N_S or N_R denoting messages being sent and received, where in particular $\mathcal{W}_2$ contains the fact $\mathsf{T}_j^{A_k}(S)@(T+b_j)$ if the protocol state $\mathsf{S}_j^{A_k}$ has the associated timeout (set to expire at moment $T+b_j$);

- *protocol timeout rules* for a protocol state $\mathsf{S}_j^{A_k}$ with associated timeout:

$\quad Time@T, \mathsf{S}_j^{A_k}(S, \mathbf{X})@T_1, \mathsf{T}_j^{A_k}(S)@T_2 \mid T_2 = T \longrightarrow$

$\qquad Time@T, \mathsf{S}_i^{A_k}(S, \mathbf{X})@(T+t),$

where $\mathsf{S}_i^{A_k}$ is a protocol state of the role A_k with no associated timeout, or

$\quad Time@T, \mathsf{S}_j^{A_k}(S, \mathbf{X})@T_1, \mathsf{T}_j^{A_k}(S)@T_2 \mid T_2 = T \longrightarrow$

$\qquad Time@T, \mathsf{S}_i^{A_k}(S, \mathbf{X})@(T+t), \mathsf{T}_i^{A_k}(S)@(T+t),$

where $\mathsf{S}_i^{A_k}$ is a protocol state of the role A_k associated with a timeout, and in both cases $t = \mathrm{DUR}_{i,j}^{timeout}$ is a natural number specifying transition from state $\mathsf{S}_j^{A_k}$ to state $\mathsf{S}_i^{A_k}$ due to a timeout;

- *protocol finalization rule:*

$\quad Time@T, \mathsf{S}_{n_k}^{A_k}(\mathbf{X})@T_1 \mid T_1 \leq T \longrightarrow Time@T,$

where n_k is natural number specifying the final protocol state $\mathsf{S}_{n_k}^{A_k}$ or role A_k.

All rules of a protocol session are initialized with the same session identifier. Protocol execution rules involve execution time and may also relate to a timeout and network communication. Timeout rules force protocol state change once a timeout has passed, which may result, *e.g.*, in a retry or session termination. Finished sessions are removed by the finalization rule.

For our complexity results we will consider balanced versions of protocol theories that are obtained by adding empty facts on left or right side of the

---

^{5} In our generalization of protocol theories we might omit the condition $i \leq j$ that was the condition in [10] forcing that protocols proceed in execution.

rule, where needed. Such empty facts have timestamps denoting availability or execution time. For example, the balanced version of the protocol finalization rule: $Time@T, S_{n_k}^{A_k}(\mathbf{X})@T_1 \mid T_1 \geq T \longrightarrow Time@T, E@(T+t)$, involves the value t given by the DUR_{FIN} function denoting duration of the finalization rule. Such empty memory slots, $E@(T+t)$, are available only when the global time reaches moment $T+t$.

5 Timed Intruder Models

The standard Dolev-Yao intruder (DY) [9] is able to intercept and send messages anywhere at anytime, appearing, hence, faster than the speed of light. For the verification of timed protocols we, therefore, introduce a more adequate, less powerful intruder theories. Our timed intruders still share the capabilities of the standard DY intruder related to composition and decomposition of messages, including encryption and generation of nonces, but in doing so, they respect the physical laws related to time. As in [17], we will also consider intruders with bounded memory.

In order to model the presence of multiple intruders, we associate an identification id to each of the intruders. This id is used to model the knowledge and the memory of a particular intruder through facts $M(id, X)$ and $P(id)$ where:

$M(id, x)@t$ denotes that term x is known to intruder id from the moment t;
$P(id)@t$ denotes that a memory slot (empty fact) is available to the bounded memory intruder id from the moment t.

As already mentioned, in order to model processing time, each of the intruder rules has an associated time cost. This is specified by the associated function DUR, returning the time needed to carry out the action (as detailed below). This allows us to model the standard message processing time where *e.g.*, encryption takes much more time than composition of a pair of messages.

5.1 Bounded Memory Timed Dolev-Yao Intruder

Intruder rules of a *Bounded Memory Timed DY Intruder* are balanced and contain empty facts representing memory available to the intruder, see Fig. 3.

The general timed DY intruder theory with unbounded memory is obtained by dropping the empty facts and the memory management rule from the theory in Fig. 3.

At the time T intruder I can access only known terms, $M(I, X)@T'$, and empty memory slots, $P(I)@T'$, only All empty facts, $P(I)@T'$, that appear on the left side of a rule have the associated time constraint, $T' \leq T$, to ensure that a memory slot is available at current time, $Time@T$.

Deleting facts from the memory (denoted by the DELM rule) may also take time. The COMP rule has two associated time constants through DUR function, one denoting the time it takes to produce a pair of messages, and the other

I/O Rules:

REC: $Time@T, \mathsf{N}_R(I, C, X)@T_1, P(I)@T_2 \mid T_2 \leq T \longrightarrow$
$\qquad Time@T, M(I, X)@(T+t), E@(T+t),$ where $\text{DUR}_{REC}(X, I) = t$

SND: $Time@T, M(I, X)@T_1, E@T_2 \mid T_1 \leq T, T_2 \leq T \longrightarrow$
$\qquad Time@T, \mathsf{N}_S(I, C, X)@(T+t), P(I)@(T+t),$ where $\text{DUR}_{SND}(X, I) = t$

Message Composition and Decomposition Rules:

COMP: $Time@T, M(I, X)@T_1, M(I, Y)@T_2 \mid T_1 \leq T, T_2 \leq T \longrightarrow$
$\qquad Time@T, M(I, \langle X, Y \rangle)@(T+t), P(I)@(T+t'),$
$\qquad$ where $\text{DUR}_{COMP}(X, Y, I) = \langle t, t' \rangle$

DCMP: $Time@T, M(I, \langle X, Y \rangle)@T_1, P(I)@T_2 \mid T_1 \leq T, T_2 \leq T \longrightarrow$
$\qquad Time@T, M(I, X)@(T+t), M(I, Y)@(T+t),$
$\qquad$ where $\text{DUR}_{DCMP}(\langle X, Y \rangle, I) = t$

USE: $Time@T, M(I, X)@T_1, P(I)@T_2 \mid T_1 \leq T, T_2 \leq T \longrightarrow$
$\qquad Time@T, M(I, X)@T_1, M(I, X)@(T+t),$ where $\text{DUR}_{USE}(X, I) = t$

ENC: $Time@T, M(I, K)@T_1, M(I, X)@T_2, P(I)@T_3 \mid T_1 \leq T, T_2 \leq T, T_3 \leq T \longrightarrow$
$\qquad Time@T, M(I, K)@T_1, M(I, X)@T_2, M(I, \{X\}_K)@(T+t),$
$\qquad$ where $\text{DUR}_{ENC}(K, X, I) = t$

DEC: $Time@T, M(I, K^{-1})@T_1, M(I, \{X\}_K)@T_2, P(I)@T_3 \mid T_1 \leq T, T_2 \leq T, T_3 \leq T$
$\qquad \longrightarrow Time@T, M(I, K^{-1})@T_1, M(I, \{X\}_K)@T_2, M(I, X)@(T+t),$
$\qquad$ where $\text{DUR}_{DEC}(K^{-1}, \{X\}_K, I) = t$

GEN: $Time@T, P(I)@T_1 \mid T_1 \leq T \longrightarrow \exists N.Time@T, M(I, N)@(T+t),$
$\qquad$ where $\text{DUR}_{GEN}(I) = t$

Memory Maintenance Rule:

DELM: $Time@T, M(I, X)@T_1 \mid T_1 \leq T \longrightarrow Time@T, P@(T+t),$
$\qquad$ where $\text{DUR}_{DEL}(X, I) = t$

Fig. 3. Bounded memory timed Dolev-Yao intruder theory $\mathcal{I}$

denoting the time it takes to make an empty fact available. The REC and SND rules are related to receiving and sending messages on transmission media that is available to some intruder. Notice that intruders obey physical laws related to message delivery and transmission media availability, which are enforced through network theory, given in Fig. 2, for all agents, including intruders. Notice as well that send and receive rules maintain the total memory of intruder and the total memory of the system, by consuming or creating P and E facts.

An adversary can also jam a channel by sending a large number of messages, exhausting the system's network by consuming E facts through the SND rule. For the representation of specific channel capacities, special empty facts representing the network bandwidth could be added and associated to each channel.

For specific scenarios, other intruder capabilities may be relevant, such as intruder capabilities of message manipulation on the wireless channels, modeled, e.g., in [8]. This includes overshadowing parts of a message, as well as flipping some bits of a message. Such capabilities, we believe, could be formalized in our model as well, by adding the Xor function to the signature and by adding the corresponding intruder rules.

6   Verification Problems

Reachability and the related problems for MSR are undecidable in general [22]. By imposing some restrictions, such as using only balanced rules and bounding the size of facts, these problems become decidable, even in timed models with fresh values [18,24]. Balanced systems used for protocol verification, as the ones in [17,24], implicitly bound the number of protocol sessions that can be executed concurrently. However, the number of sessions in a trace is unbounded.

Various problems can be considered in the verification of security protocols. Here we state some of them.

Definition 3 (Secrecy Problem). *Given a protocol theory $\mathcal{P}$, network theory $\mathcal{N}$, intruder theories $\mathcal{I}_1, \ldots \mathcal{I}_k$ and an initial configuration $\mathcal{S}_0$ denoting the initial protocol setting including key distribution, communication capabilities, network distances and a constant s known only to some agent, the* secrecy problem of a protocol theory $\mathcal{P}$ *is the problem of determining whether or not a configuration containing the fact $M(I,s)$, for some intruder identifier I, is reachable from $\mathcal{S}_0$ using rules in $\mathcal{N}, \mathcal{I}_1, \ldots, \mathcal{I}_k$ and $\mathcal{P}$.*

In other words, the secrecy problem is the problem of determining whether or not an intruder can learn the secret s, initially known to some honest agent.

A more general version of the secrecy problem involving several different protocol theories, $\mathcal{P}_1, \ldots, \mathcal{P}_k$, suitable for verification of multi-protocol environments, is analogously defined.

Next, we define verification problems related to DB protocols.

Definition 4 (False Acceptance Problem). *Given a DB protocol theory $\mathcal{P}$ with a distance bound R, network theory $\mathcal{N}$, intruder theories $\mathcal{I}_1, \ldots \mathcal{I}_k$ and an initial configuration $\mathcal{S}_0$ denoting the initial protocol setting including key distribution, communication capabilities etc., the* false acceptance problem *is the problem of determining whether or not a configuration denoting that a verifier has granted access to an intruder or to a prover that is outside the perimeter R, is reachable from $\mathcal{S}_0$ using rules in $\mathcal{N}, \mathcal{I}_1, \ldots, \mathcal{I}_k$ and $\mathcal{P}$.*

A dual problem related to decision errors for DB protocols, is the following.

Definition 5 (False Rejection Problem). *Given a DB protocol theory $\mathcal{P}$ with a distance bound R, network theory $\mathcal{N}$, intruder theories $\mathcal{I}_1, \ldots \mathcal{I}_k$ and an initial configuration $\mathcal{S}_0$ denoting the initial protocol setting including key distribution, communication capabilities etc., the* false rejection problem *is the problem of determining whether or not a configuration denoting that a verifier has denied access to an honest prover that is within the perimeter R, is reachable from $\mathcal{S}_0$ using rules in $\mathcal{N}, \mathcal{I}_1, \ldots, \mathcal{I}_k$ and $\mathcal{P}$.*

By including several DB protocol theories, multi-protocol environments, as in [8], can be verified. In our recent work [1] on DB protocols we have also investigated Attack Detection Problem. We believe other problems such as Denial of Service, as well as other classes of problems involving *e.g.*, privacy and traceability could also be formulated in our model. We leave this for future work.

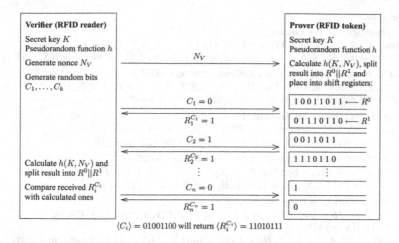

Fig. 4. The Hancke-Kuhn protocol (taken from [15])

6.1   Example: The Hancke-Khun Protocol Theory

We now illustrate the expressiveness of timed protocol theories introduced in Sect. 4 by formalizing the Hancke-Khun (HK) distance-bounding protocol [15].

The HK protocol, shown in Fig. 4, aims to ensure that the prover, P, is in the vicinity of the verifier, V. It is assumed that the prover and the verifier share a long-term secret key, K, and a public hash function, h.

In the initial phase of the protocol the verifier and the prover generate nonces N_V and N_P which are used to calculate a sequence of $2n$ bits using K and h: $\mathbf{h} = h(K, N_V, N_P) = R_1^0, \ldots, R_n^0 \| R_1^1, \ldots, R_n^1$, $R_i^j \in \{0, 1\}$. Let $\mathbf{s} = \langle K, h, N_V, N_P \rangle$ denote data that, together with $\mathbf{h}$, is known to both participants after the initial phase of a particular protocol session.

The setup phase of HK protocol is followed by a series of n single-bit exchanges, defined by the following procedure: To a random challenge bit C_i sent by the verifier in the ith round, the prover instantly replies with either R_i^0, in case $C_i = 0$, or R_i^1, in case $C_i = 1$. We formalize verifier's random bit generation of challenge bits using nonce generation and a function b that returns a bit, i.e., $b(x) \in \{0, 1\}$. Comparison of received responses with the correct bits in $\mathbf{h}$, precalculated in the initial phase of the protocol, is obtained using a function r that returns the bit $R_i^{C_i}$ based on bit C_i and $\mathbf{h}$ for ith round, as per H-K protocol specification, i.e., $r(i, \mathbf{h}, x) = \begin{cases} h_i, & x = 0, \\ h_{n+i}, & x = 1. \end{cases}$

For each round, the verifier marks the time when a challenge bit is sent, and the time the response is received. In the last phase of the protocol, the verifier computes his distance from the prover and checks that the responses are correct.

The verifier grants access to the prover if all time tests for bit exchanges are successful, i.e., do not exceed the predefined distance bound, R, and if all n bits are correctly exchanged. Keeping in mind potential errors, due to e.g., noise, the

Verifier role

Send challenge bit for round j :
$Time@T, S_0^V(S, A, C, \mathbf{s}, \mathbf{h}, j)@T_1, E@T_2, E@T_3 \mid \{ T \geq T_2, T \geq T_3 \} \longrightarrow$
    $\exists x. Time@T, S_1^V(S, A, C, \mathbf{s}, \mathbf{h}, \text{pending}, b(x), j)@T, \mathsf{N}_S(A, C, b(x))@T, Start(S, j)@T$

Mark the time of sending the challenge bit in round j :
$Time@T, S_1^V(S, A, C, \mathbf{s}, \mathbf{h}, \text{pending}, B_j, j)@T_1, E@T_2 \mid \{ T > T_1, T \geq T_2 \} \longrightarrow$
    $Time@T, S_1^V(S, A, C, \mathbf{s}, \mathbf{h}, \text{start}, B_j, j)@T, Start_V(S, j)@T$

Receive the response bit in round j :
$Time@T, S_1^V(S, A, C, \mathbf{s}, \mathbf{h}, \text{start}, B_j, j)@T_1, \mathsf{N}_R(A, C, X)@T_2 \longrightarrow$
    $Time@T, S_2^V(S, A, C, \mathbf{s}, \mathbf{h}, \text{pending}, B_j, j, X)@T_1, Stop(S, j)@T$

Mark the time of receiving the response bit in round j :
$Time@T, S_2^V(S, A, C, \mathbf{s}, \mathbf{h}, \text{pending}, B_j, j, X)@T_1, E@T_2 \mid \{ T > T_1 \} \longrightarrow$
    $Time@T, S_2^V(S, A, C, \mathbf{s}, \mathbf{h}, \text{stop}, B_j, j, X)@T_1, Stop_V(S, j)@T$

Check the round trip time for round j :
$Time@T, Start_V(S, j)@T_1, Stop_V(S, j)@T_2, S_2^V(S, A, C, \mathbf{s}, \mathbf{h}, \text{stop}, B_j, j, X)@T_3,$
    $Test(S, m)@T_4 \mid \{ T_2 - T_1 \leq 2R \} \longrightarrow$
    $Time@T, S_2^V(S, A, C, \mathbf{s}, \mathbf{h}, \text{bit}, B_j, j, X)@T, TimeCheck(S, j, \text{ok})@T, Test(S, m + 1)@T, E@T$

$Time@T, Start_V(S, j)@T_1, Stop_V(S, j)@T_2, S_2^V(S, A, C, \mathbf{s}, \mathbf{h}, \text{stop}, B_j, j, X)@T_3,$
    $Test(S, m)@T_4 \mid \{ T_2 - T_1 > 2R \} \longrightarrow$
    $Time@T, S_2^V(S, A, C, \mathbf{s}, \mathbf{h}, \text{bit}, B_j, j, X)@T, TimeCheck(S, j, \text{not-ok})@T, Test(S, m)@T_4, E@T$

Check the bit correctness in round j :
$Time@T, S_2^V(S, A, C, \mathbf{s}, \mathbf{h}, \text{bit}, B_j, j, r(j, \mathbf{h}, B_j))@T_1, Bit(m)@T_2, E@T_3 \mid \{T_3 \leq T \}$
    $\longrightarrow Time@T, S_3^V(S, A, C, \mathbf{s}, \mathbf{h})@T, Bit(m + 1)@T, BitCheck(S, j, \text{ok})@T$

$Time@T, S_2^V(S, A, C, \mathbf{s}, \mathbf{h}, \text{bit}, B_j, j, y \neq r(j, \mathbf{h}, B_j))@T_1, Bit(m)@T_2, E@T_3 \mid \{T_3 \leq T \}$
    $\longrightarrow Time@T, S_3^V(S, A, C, \mathbf{s}, \mathbf{h}, j)@T, Bit(m)@T_2, BitCheck(S, j, \text{not-ok})@T$

Starting a new round or finishing the last round :
$Time@T, S_3^V(S, A, C, \mathbf{s}, \mathbf{h}, j \neq n)@T_1 \longrightarrow Time@T, S_0^V(S, A, C, \mathbf{s}, \mathbf{h}, j + 1)@T$

$Time@T, S_3^V(S, A, \mathbf{s}, \mathbf{h}, n)@T_1 \longrightarrow Time@T, S_4^V(S, A, C, \mathbf{s}, \mathbf{h})@T$

Allowing or rejecting the access :
$Time@T, S_4^V(S, A, C, \mathbf{s}, \mathbf{h})@T_1, Test(S, X \geq k_1)@T_2, Bit(S, Y \geq k_2)@T_3 \longrightarrow$
    $Time@T, S_5^V(S, A, C, \mathbf{s}, \mathbf{h})@T, Decision(S, \text{ok})@T, E@T$

$Time@T, S_4^V(S, A, C, \mathbf{s}, \mathbf{h})@T_1, Test(S, X < k_1)@T_2, Bit(S, Y < k_2)@T_3 \longrightarrow$
    $Time@T, S_5^V(S, A, C, \mathbf{s}, \mathbf{h})@T, Decision(S, \text{reject})@T, E@T$

Prover role

Responding to a challenge bit in round j :
$Time@T, S_0^P(S, A, C, \mathbf{s}, \mathbf{h}, j \neq n)@T_1, \mathsf{N}_R(A, C, X)@T_2 \longrightarrow$
    $Time@T, S_0(S, A, C, \mathbf{s}, \mathbf{h}, j + 1)@T, \mathsf{N}_S(A, C, r(i, \mathbf{h}, X))@T$

Responding to a challenge bit in the last round :
$Time@T, S_0^P(S, A, C, \mathbf{s}, \mathbf{h}, n)@T_1, \mathsf{N}_R(A, C, X)@T_2 \longrightarrow$
    $Time@T, S_1(S, A, C, \mathbf{s}, \mathbf{h})@T, \mathsf{N}_S(A, C, r(i, \mathbf{h}, X))@T$

Receiving the decision :
$Time@T, Decision(S, X)@T_1, S_1^P(S, \mathbf{Y})@T_2 \longrightarrow Time@T, Decision(S, X)@T_1, S_2^P(S, \mathbf{Y})@T$

Fig. 5. Protocol theories for bit exchange phase of Hancke-Kuhn protocol with n rounds

verifier's decision can be parameterised so that access is granted if the time-test is satisfied in a number of rounds, k_1 out of n, e.g., in a simple majority of rounds, and if a certain number of response bits, k_2 out of n, are correct.

For illustration purposes we only formalize the bit exchange phase of the HK protocol with n challenge-response rounds, see Fig. 5. The initial phase of the HK protocol could be similarly formalized. Here, we assume that the initial phase of HK protocol session S has already been completed, denoted by the facts $S_0^V(S, \mathbf{s}, \mathbf{h}, 1)$ and $S_0^P(S, \mathbf{s}, \mathbf{h}, 1)$, representing the initial protocol states for the verifier and the prover roles, respectively. Completion of n rounds of bit exchanges is denoted by the fact $S_4^V(S, \mathbf{s}, \mathbf{h})$.

Besides agents' capabilities of using transmission media, keys etc., the initial configuration additionally includes the following auxiliary facts: $Bits(S, 0)@0$ denoting the number of rounds with correct bit responses, $Test(S, 0)$ denoting the number of rounds successfully passing the time-test.

Since this distance measuring phase of the protocol is technically performed with negligible processing time related to reading and responding with bits, we set the related processing time to zero.

However, in order to model actual verifiers that are usually not very powerful processors operating at some clock rate, the formalization distinguishes between the actual time of sending challenge bits or receiving response bits and the recorded time. This is accomplished using time constraints of the form $T > T_1$, where T is the global time and T_1 the actual time of sending or receiving the bit. Alternatively, function DUR could be used for specific time delays.

Checking whether a sufficient number of rounds have passed the time-test and the bit correctness test is part of the final phase of HK protocol. In our formalization we have included these rules in each round, but with no time cost.

For the HK protocol specification given in Fig. 5, with the protocol distance bound R, the false acceptance problem representing an attack-in-between ticks is specified as a reachability problem with the following goal configuration:

$$\{Start(S, X_1)@T_1^1, Stop(S, X_1)@T_2^1, \ldots, Start(S, X_{k_1})@T_1^{k_1}, Stop\ (S, X_{k_1})@T_2^{k_1},$$
$$Decision(S, \mathrm{ok})@T, \} \mid \{T_2^1 - T_1^1 > R, \ldots T_2^{k_1} - T_1^{k_1} > R\},$$

for some protocol session S and k_1 rounds X_i. Similarly, a more general false acceptance can be formalized with the goal configuration:

$$S_5^V(S, A, C, \mathbf{X})@T, S_2^P(S, B, C, \mathbf{Y})@T_1, Decision(S, \mathrm{ok})@T_2,$$

where $D(A, B, C) > R$. This goal denotes a false positive of the time test, $i.e.$, the verifier allows access to a prover that is outside the perimeter R.

False rejection can similarly be represented with the following goal:

$$S_5^V(S, A, C, \mathbf{X})@T, S_2^P(S, B, C, \mathbf{Y})@T_1, Decision(S, \mathrm{reject})@T_2,$$

where $D(A, B, C) \leq R$, for the protocol distance bound R.

Guessing ahead attacks could also be captured by checking whether response bits are received before the necessary traversal time, as specified by the goal:

$$Decision(S, \mathrm{ok})@T, S_5^V(S, A, C, \mathbf{X})@T, S_2^P(S, B, C, \mathbf{Y})@T_1,$$
$$Start(S, i)@T_2, Stop\ (S, i)@T_3 \mid T_3 - T_2 < 2D(A, B, C).$$

ROLES : $Time@T, Guy(K_e, K_d)@T_1, Guy(K'_e, K'_d)@T_2, E@T_3, E@T_4$
$\qquad | \ T_3 \leq T, T_4 \leq T \ \longrightarrow \ \exists X.Time@T, Guy(K_e, K_d)@T_1, Guy(K'_e, K'_d)@T_2,$
$\qquad\qquad S_0^A(X, K_e)@(T + d_0), T_0^A(X)@(T + b_0), S_0^B(X, K'_e)@(T + d_0)$
FINA : $\quad Time@T, S_2^A(\mathbf{X})@T_1 \to Time@T, E@T$
FINB : $\quad Time@T, S_2^B(\mathbf{X})@T_1 \to Time@T, E@T$
A1 : $Time@T, S_0^A(S, K_e)@T_1, T_0^A(S)@T_2, Agent(K'_e)@T_3 \ | \ T_2 \geq T, T_1 \leq T$
$\qquad \to \exists X.Time@T, S_1^A(S, K_e, K'_e, X)@(T + d_1), Agent(K'_e)@T_3,$
$\qquad\qquad N_S(K_e, C, enc(K'_e, \langle X, K_e \rangle))@(T@d_1)$
A2 : $Time@T, S_1^A(S, K_e, K'_e, X)@T_1, N_R(K_e, C, enc(K_e, \langle X, Y \rangle))@T_2 \ | \ T_1 \leq T$
$\qquad \to Time@T, S_2^A(S, K_e, K'_e, X, Y)@(T + d_2), N_S(K_e, C', enc(K'_e, Y))@(T + d_2)$
AT : $Time@T, S_0^A(S, X)@T_1, T_0^A(S)@T_2 \ | \ T_2 = T \longrightarrow \ Time@T, S_2^A(S, X, *, *, *)@T_1$
B1 : $Time@T, S_0^B(S, K_e)@T_1, Agent(K'_e)@T_2, N_R(K_e, C, enc(K_e, \langle X, K'_e \rangle))@T_3$
$\qquad | \ T_1 \leq T \ \to \exists Y.Time@T, S_1^B(S, K_e, K'_e, X, Y)@(T + d_3), Agent(K'_e)@T_2,$
$\qquad\qquad N_S(K_e, C', enc(K'_e, \langle X, Y \rangle))@(T + d_3)$
B2 : $Time@T, S_1^B(S, K_e, K'_e, X, Y)@T_1, N_R(K_e, C, enc(K_e, Y))@T_2 \ | \ T_1 \leq T$
$\qquad \to Time@T, S_2^B(S, K_e, K'_e, X, Y)@(T + d_4), E@T$

Fig. 6. Timed protocol theory of Needham-Schroeder protocol with timeouts.

This indicates that the response bit has been sent in advance, before the receipt of the challenge bit, representing, hence, guessing in advance, *i.e.*, involvement of a dishonest prover or an intruder.

6.2   Example: The Needham-Schroeder Protocol with Timeouts

We specify the Needham-Schroeder (NS) protocol with timeouts detailed in Sect. 2.2. Initiator role A has the associated timeout. Only if the expected reply message is received within the timeout time bound, the final protocol message is sent. Otherwise, the session ends.

A balanced timed protocol theory of NS with timeouts is given in Fig. 6. The protocol state S_0^A has the associated timeout. Here, $*$ denotes a dummy constant, d_i are constants denoting action duration and b_0 is the constant denoting the timeout. For simplicity, we use public keys to denote names of agents, where *Agent* predicate is used to specify public keys, while key pairs of public and private keys that belong to an honest participant are denoted by *Guy* facts.

Protocol security is considered in the usual sense, *i.e.*, if the "accepted" nonces N_A and N_B are never revealed to anybody else except Alice and Bob executing the protocol. The protocol is still vulnerable to the timed version of Lowe attack [26], see Fig. 1b, but a well-chosen timeout may enhance protocol security.

For illustration, let $d_0 = d_1 = d_2 = d_3 = d_4 = 1$, *i.e.*, all actions take one time unit to be executed. Let $b_0 = 10$, *i.e.*, state S_0^A timeouts after 10 time units. Let $D(k_A, k_B, c) = D(k_B, k_A, c) = 3$. In this setting, execution of rules ROLES, A1, B1 and network rules takes at least $(1 + 1 + 3 + 1 + 3 = 9)$ 9 time units, *i.e.*, Alice can expect to receive the reply within the set timeout and proceed protocol execution with rule A2.

Consider now the setting with Mallory positioned optimally, inbetween Alice and Bob, as illustrated in Fig. 1b, with $D(k_A, k_M, c) = D(k_M, k_A, c) = 2$ and $D(k_B, k_M, c) = D(k_M, k_B, c) = 1$. Let Mallory intruder rules also have associated time cost of one time unit, for simplicity. Mallory will need to intercept, decrypt, encrypt and send messages which will take some additional time. Now, protocol, intruder and network execution of rules from ROLES up to A2 rule take at least 15 time units (Mallory has to use the sequence of REC, DEC, ENC, SND rules, and later REC and SND rules), by which time the protocol session timeouts and, hence, Lowe type attack fails. In case the timeout is set to a high enough value, e.g., $b_0 = 20$, there is a trace in the model representing the Lowe attack.

7   Complexity Results

Timed MSR theories containing network, protocol and intruder theories defined in Sects. 4 and 5 represent a segment of general timed MSR for specification and verification of security protocols. By relying on our previous complexity results for the secrecy problem and for the reachability problem for timed MSR, we obtain the complexity result for the timed version of secrecy problem described in Sect. 6. We point out that this verification relates to traces with a bounded number of concurrent protocol sessions, but to an unbounded number of protocol sessions in total.

Theorem 1. *The secrecy problem with respect to the memory bounded timed Dolev-Yao intruders, balanced network and protocol theories is PSPACE-complete when assuming a bound on the size of facts.*

Proof. For the upper bound we rely on the PSPACE-completeness of the reachability problem for general MSR with real time [24], since the secrecy problem is an instance of the reachability problem. The rules of the timed MSR contain network, protocol and intruder theories. The goal of the reachability problem is specified as a configuration containing $M(I, s)@T$, for some intruder identifier I, with no time constraints attached. Therefore, it follows from [24] that the secrecy problem is in PSPACE when considering balanced timed network, protocol and intruder theories with a bound on the size of facts.

The lower bound follows from PSPACE-completeness of the secrecy problem for untimed version of bounded memory intruder and balanced MSR protocol theories [17]. It can be encoded as timed secrecy simply by adding timestamps to facts, by adding time constraints to the rules of protocol and intruder theories, as per Definition 2 and Fig. 3, and by considering some arbitrary network topology and a single transmission channel, accessible to all agents and intruders both for sending and receiving messages. In particular, the protocol states of timed protocol theories have no timeouts attached. Exact values of timestamps, duration of rules, just like the message traversal time (specified by the topology) have no impact to the encoding. Indeed, the goal involves the secret being discovered by an intruder, taking any amount of time, as the goal involves no related time constraints, and all constraints attached to rules of network, intruder and protocol theories (since no timeouts are present) are of the form $T' \leq T$, *i.e.*, require only advancement of global time T, which is always applicable.

False acceptance and false rejection problems could also be formalized as reachability problems, as in Sect. 6.1, hence the PSPACE membership of these problems can also be deduced.

Theorem 2. *The false acceptance and the false rejection problems with respect to the memory bounded timed Dolev-Yao intruders, balanced network and distance-bounding protocol theories is in PSPACE when the size of facts is bounded.*

Similarly to the bounded-time problems introduced in [21], we could consider bounded time version of the secrecy problem, *e.g.*, by bounding the total time in a trace or bounding the total number of protocol sessions. We expect that such restrictions would improve the complexity of the problem. We leave this investigation for future work.

8   Conclusions and Related Work

This paper builds on [1,20,23,24] and introduces a uniform and extensible framework for expressing a wide range of timing properties of protocols enabling the investigation of the complexity of different verification problems. Thus, this work is complementary to the related works that focus on more limited languages in order to automate analyses.

The first full-scale formal representation and analysis of a distance-bounding protocol is the work of Meadows and collaborators [29] formalizing distance-bounding protocols in Protocol Derivation Logic (PDL). This work provided the basis for practical improvements, new insights, and inspirations for other researchers including ourselves. Like our work that is founded on an existing general model (Timed MSR), the formalization started with an existing formal logic, PDL.

The paper [31] introduces a timed protocol language and addresses the issue of timed intruder models, showing that one DY intruder per honest player is sufficient. This formal system is implemented in Maude to automate analysis. This work built on earlier formalizations in Timed MSR [19,23] and in turn has suggested new modeling challenges addressed in the present paper.

Timing aspects of security protocols in the presence of the DY intruder, but related to different verification problems, are investigated in [16]. Timed authentication properties are investigated, based on expected time intervals for completion of successful protocol sessions. Differently from [16], we consider more general protocol theories w.r.t. protocol message flow, allowing even loops in correct protocol executions. Consequently, combined with the use of timeouts, in our investigation and results we also include protocols for which the execution time of correct sessions varies. Hence, the approach used in [16] may not be adequate for our protocol theories. Also, our model has finer grading of timing, *i.e.*, duration of actions specified through DUR function parameters, and furthermore, we investigate the computational complexity related to the verification.

A number of other frameworks have been developed for the verification of timing properties of systems. Early examples include [3,13,14]. Basin et al. [2] and Cramers et al. [8] present a formalism for representing and analyzing cyber-physical security protocols that is implemented in Isabel/HOL. They model physical properties of communication, location, and time. Similar to our approach both honest players and intruders are subject to physical constraints. Cheval et al. [6] present a decidability result relating to timing attacks in security protocols. The result is based on the reduction of time-trace equivalence to length-trace equivalence, and is applied, in particular, on verification of privacy properties. It remains to be investigated whether such an approach may be applicable to protocol theories with varied correct executions, as already discussed above. A benefit of formalization in our Timed MSR is the ability to leverage a variety of complexity results developed for different fragments as illustrated in the previous section.

Verification in this paper assumes that a concrete topology of agents and intruders is specified. We believe it may be possible to consider verification of general topologies by combining our models with SMT solvers, similarly to [31].

For a close formalization of DB protocols probabilities involving various guessing strategies as given in [1], we intend to investigate ways of extending our models with probabilities. One of the ways of such probabilistic extensions of our models might involve branching actions introduced in [25].

Acknowledgments. We thank Cathy for her inspiring work, insightful and motivating discussions and for her friendship. Part of this work was done during the visits to the University of Pennsylvania by Alturki, Ban Kirigin, Kanovich, Nigam, and Talcott, which were partially supported by ONR and by the University of Pennsylvania. Ban Kirigin is supported in part by the Croatian Science Foundation under the project UIP-05-2017-9219. Scedrov is partially supported by ONR. Talcott is partly supported by ONR grant N00014-15-1-2202 and NRL grant N0017317-1-G002. Nigam is partially supported by NRL grant N0017317-1-G002, and CNPq grant 303909/2018-8.

References

1. Alturki, M.A., Kanovich, M., Ban Kirigin, T., Nigam, V., Scedrov, A., Talcott, C.: Statistical model checking of distance fraud attacks on the Hancke-Kuhn family of protocols. In: Proceedings of the 2018 Workshop on Cyber-Physical Systems Security and PrivaCy, pp. 60–71. ACM (2018)
2. Basin, D.A., Capkun, S., Schaller, P., Schmidt, B.: Formal reasoning about physical properties of security protocols. ACM Trans. Inf. Syst. Secur. **14**(2), 16 (2011)
3. Bella, G., Paulson, L.C.: Kerberos version IV: inductive analysis of the secrecy goals. In: Quisquater, J.-J., Deswarte, Y., Meadows, C., Gollmann, D. (eds.) ESORICS 1998. LNCS, vol. 1485, pp. 361–375. Springer, Heidelberg (1998). https://doi.org/10.1007/BFb0055875
4. Brands, S., Chaum, D.: Distance-bounding protocols. In: Helleseth, T. (ed.) EUROCRYPT 1993. LNCS, vol. 765, pp. 344–359. Springer, Heidelberg (1994). https://doi.org/10.1007/3-540-48285-7_30

5. Cervesato, I., Durgin, N.A., Lincoln, P., Mitchell, J.C., Scedrov, A.: A meta-notation for protocol analysis. In: CSFW, pp. 55–69 (1999)
6. Cheval, V., Cortier, V.: Timing attacks in security protocols: symbolic framework and proof techniques. In: Focardi, R., Myers, A. (eds.) POST 2015. LNCS, vol. 9036, pp. 280–299. Springer, Heidelberg (2015). https://doi.org/10.1007/978-3-662-46666-7_15
7. Chothia, T., Smirnov, V.: A traceability attack against e-passports. In: Sion, R. (ed.) FC 2010. LNCS, vol. 6052, pp. 20–34. Springer, Heidelberg (2010). https://doi.org/10.1007/978-3-642-14577-3_5
8. Cremers, C., Rasmussen, K.B., Schmidt, B., Capkun, S.: Distance Hijacking attacks on distance bounding protocols. In: 2012 IEEE Symposium on Security and Privacy, pp. 113–127 (2012). https://doi.org/10.1109/SP.2012.17
9. Dolev, D., Yao, A.: On the security of public key protocols. IEEE Trans. Inf. Theory **29**(2), 198–208 (1983)
10. Durgin, N.A., Lincoln, P., Mitchell, J.C., Scedrov, A.: Multiset rewriting and the complexity of bounded security protocols. J. Comput. Secur. **12**(2), 247–311 (2004)
11. Enderton, H.B.: A Mathematical Introduction to Logic. Academic Press, Cambridge (1972)
12. Escobar, S., Meadows, C., Meseguer, J.: Maude-NPA: cryptographic protocol analysis modulo equational properties. In: Aldini, A., Barthe, G., Gorrieri, R. (eds.) FOSAD 2007–2009. LNCS, vol. 5705, pp. 1–50. Springer, Heidelberg (2009). https://doi.org/10.1007/978-3-642-03829-7_1
13. Evans, N., Schneider, S.: Analysing time dependent security properties in CSP using PVS. In: Cuppens, F., Deswarte, Y., Gollmann, D., Waidner, M. (eds.) ESORICS 2000. LNCS, vol. 1895, pp. 222–237. Springer, Heidelberg (2000). https://doi.org/10.1007/10722599_14
14. Gorrieri, R., Locatelli, E., Martinelli, F.: A simple language for real-time cryptographic protocol analysis. In: Degano, P. (ed.) ESOP 2003. LNCS, vol. 2618, pp. 114–128. Springer, Heidelberg (2003). https://doi.org/10.1007/3-540-36575-3_9. http://dl.acm.org/citation.cfm?id=1765712.1765723
15. Hancke, G.P., Kuhn, M.G.: An RFID distance bounding protocol. In: First International Conference on Security and Privacy for Emerging Areas in Communications Networks, SECURECOMM 2005, pp. 67–73 (2005). https://doi.org/10.1109/SECURECOMM.2005.56
16. Jakubowska, G., Penczek, W.: Modelling and checking timed authentication of security protocols. Fundamenta Informaticae **79**(3–4), 363–378 (2007)
17. Kanovich, M., Ban Kirigin, T., Nigam, V., Scedrov, A.: Bounded memory Dolev-Yao adversaries in collaborative systems. Inf. Comput. **238**, 233–261 (2014)
18. Kanovich, M., Ban Kirigin, T., Nigam, V., Scedrov, A., Talcott, C.: Compliance in real time multiset rewriting models. https://arxiv.org/abs/1811.04826
19. Kanovich, M., Kirigin, T.B., Nigam, V., Scedrov, A., Talcott, C.: Discrete vs. dense times in the analysis of cyber-physical security protocols. In: Focardi, R., Myers, A. (eds.) POST 2015. LNCS, vol. 9036, pp. 259–279. Springer, Heidelberg (2015). https://doi.org/10.1007/978-3-662-46666-7_14
20. Kanovich, M., Ban Kirigin, T., Nigam, V., Scedrov, A., Talcott, C.: Can we mitigate the attacks on distance-bounding protocols by using challenge-response rounds repeatedly? In: FCS (2016)
21. Kanovich, M., Ban Kirigin, T., Nigam, V., Scedrov, A., Talcott, C.: Timed multiset rewriting and the verification of time-sensitive distributed systems. In: Fränzle, M., Markey, N. (eds.) FORMATS 2016. LNCS, vol. 9884, pp. 228–244. Springer, Cham (2016). https://doi.org/10.1007/978-3-319-44878-7_14

22. Kanovich, M., Rowe, P., Scedrov, A.: Policy compliance in collaborative systems. In: Proceedings of the 2009 22nd IEEE Computer Security Foundations Symposium, CSF 2009, pp. 218–233. IEEE Computer Society, Washington, DC (2009). https://doi.org/10.1109/CSF.2009.19

23. Kanovich, M.I., Ban Kirigin, T., Nigam, V., Scedrov, A., Talcott, C.L.: Towards timed models for cyber-physical security protocols (2014). Available in Nigam's homepage

24. Kanovich, M.I., Ban Kirigin, T., Nigam, V., Scedrov, A., Talcott, C.L.: Time, computational complexity, and probability in the analysis of distance-bounding protocols. J. Comput. Secur. **25**(6), 585–630 (2017). https://doi.org/10.3233/JCS-0560

25. Kanovich, M.I., Ban Kirigin, T., Nigam, V., Scedrov, A., Talcott, C.L., Perovic, R.: A rewriting framework and logic for activities subject to regulations. Math. Struct. Comput. Sci. **27**(3), 332–375 (2017). https://doi.org/10.1017/S096012951500016X

26. Lowe, G.: Breaking and fixing the Needham-Schroeder public-key protocol using FDR. In: TACAS, pp. 147–166 (1996)

27. Meadows, C.: The NRL protocol analyzer: an overview. J. Logic Program. **26**(2), 113–131 (1996). https://doi.org/10.1016/0743-1066(95)00095-X. http://www.sciencedirect.com/science/article/pii/074310669500095X

28. Meadows, C.: A cost-based framework for analysis of denial of service in networks. J. Comput. Secur. **9**(1–2), 143–164 (2001). http://dl.acm.org/citation.cfm?id=374742.374757

29. Meadows, C.A., Poovendran, R., Pavlovic, D., Chang, L., Syverson, P.F.: Distance bounding protocols: authentication logic analysis and collusion attacks. In: Poovendran, R., Roy, S., Wang, C. (eds.) Secure Localization and Time Synchronization for Wireless Sensor and Ad Hoc Networks. ADIS, vol. 30, pp. 279–298. Springer, Boston (2007). https://doi.org/10.1007/978-0-387-46276-9_12

30. Needham, R.M., Schroeder, M.D.: Using encryption for authentication in large networks of computers. Commun. ACM **21**(12), 993–999 (1978). https://doi.org/10.1145/359657.359659

31. Nigam, V., Talcott, C., Aires Urquiza, A.: Towards the automated verification of cyber-physical security protocols: bounding the number of timed intruders. In: Askoxylakis, I., Ioannidis, S., Katsikas, S., Meadows, C. (eds.) ESORICS 2016, Part II. LNCS, vol. 9879, pp. 450–470. Springer, Cham (2016). https://doi.org/10.1007/978-3-319-45741-3_23

32. Pavlovic, D., Meadows, C.: Bayesian authentication: quantifying security of the Hancke-Kuhn protocol. Electron. Notes Theoret. Comput. Sci. **265**, 97–122 (2010)

33. Rowe, P.: Policy compliance, confidentiality and complexity in collaborative systems. Ph.D. thesis. University of Pennsylvania (2009)

Belenios: A Simple Private and Verifiable Electronic Voting System

Véronique Cortier[✉], Pierrick Gaudry, and Stéphane Glondu

CNRS, Inria, Univ. Lorraine, Lorraine, France
veronique.cortier@loria.fr

Abstract. We present the electronic voting protocol Belenios together with its associated voting platform. Belenios guarantees vote privacy and full verifiability, even against a compromised voting server. While the core of the voting protocol was already described and formally proved secure, we detail here the complete voting system from the setup to the tally and the recovery procedures.

We comment on the use of Belenios in practice. In particular, we discuss the security choices made by election administrators w.r.t. the decryption key and the delegation of some setup tasks to the voting platform.

1 Introduction

Electronic voting facilitates counting and enables elections with multiple questions or sophisticated tally functions like approval voting or single transferable vote. Ballots may be quite complex since voters may have to give a score to each candidate or rank them according to their preference. Tallying such complex ballots is a tedious job if done by hand while it is an easy task for a computer. Electronic voting also provides flexibility: an election may last from a few minutes to several weeks and voters may vote from any place. Consequently, e-voting is now often used at least as a replacement for postal voting.

Besides, electronic voting is subject to heavy controversy. The main reason is that existing systems are not sufficiently secure, as exemplified by several severe attacks. For example, the Washington, D.C., Internet voting system has been attacked [40], during a trial just before the election. The research team successfully replaced existing ballots, modified the code, and retrieved the login and passwords of all (real) voters. Similarly, important security concerns have been raised in the voting systems used respectively in Estonia [38] and Australia [28].

Modern electronic voting systems aim at two main properties: vote privacy (no one should know my vote) and verifiability (it is possible to check that the votes are correctly counted). Verifiability is often divided into three subproperties:

- individual verifiability: a voter can check that her vote has been properly counted;

J. D. Guttman et al. (Eds.): Meadows Festschrift, LNCS 11565, pp. 214–238, 2019.
https://doi.org/10.1007/978-3-030-19052-1_14

- universal verifiability: everyone can check that the result corresponds to the ballots on the public bulletin board;
- eligibility verifiability: ballots come from legitimate voters.

Privacy and verifiability are difficult to achieve simultaneously.

Many e-voting systems have been proposed in the literature. Each protocol solves some security issues. They are either designed to vote in polling stations or remotely. We focus here on Internet voting, although the models and techniques developed in this context also apply to on-site systems whose security does not assume trusted machines (e.g. STAR-vote [7], Prêt-à-voter [35]).

Systems like CHVote [27] and the Neuchâtel protocol [24] protect voters against a corrupted device. Even if a voter uses a corrupted computer or smartphone, she should be able to check that her *intended vote* has been correctly recorded on the voting platform thanks to return codes: after casting a vote, a voter receives a code (a short sequence of characters) and checks using a previously received sheet of paper that the code corresponds to her vote intent. Such protocols rely on a rather heavy infrastructure and for the Neuchâtel protocol, voters cannot check that the election result corresponds to the received ballots. In a contrast, Helios [3] is a simple protocol that aims at privacy and end-to-end verifiability in low coercion environment. A voter may audit her voting device by generating mock ballots and sending them to a third (trusted) party. Another simple system is sElect [31], where voters can easily check that their vote has been counted as intended thanks to a tracking number displayed next to their vote, once the election result is published. A drawback is that vote buying is then straightforward. Selene [36] also uses tracking numbers to ease verifiability, together with a cryptographic mechanism that provides receipt-freeness: voters cannot prove for whom they voted. Demos [30] also aims at both verifiability and receipt-freeness. Actually, all the aforementioned systems admit a way for a voter to sell her vote to a buyer (or a coercer). Civitas [15] is the only system that provably achieves both verifiability and coercion-resistance. The idea is that voters may produce fake voting credentials such that the corresponding ballots will eventually be deleted without the coercer noticing. Other systems aim at everlasting privacy [22] (will my vote remain secret if the underlying cryptography is broken?) or accountability [32].

We present here the Belenios system. It offers a good compromise between simplicity and security. Belenios has been deployed on an online platform [1] that has already been used in more than 200 elections, in academia, education, and in sport associations. Belenios is built upon Helios. Like in Helios, the voters can check that their ballots appear on the bulletin board, and that the result corresponds to the ballots on the board, while vote secrecy is guaranteed. In addition, Belenios provides eligibility verifiability: anyone can check that ballots come from legitimate voters, whereas in Helios, a dishonest bulletin board could add ballots without anyone noticing. Helios is thus vulnerable to ballot stuffing. Eligibility verifiability can be added to voting systems through a signature mechanism and additional credentials [18]. Belenios is an instance of this generic construction, applied to Helios. Note that, like in Helios, Belenios is not coercion-resistant:

voters may prove for whom they voted by providing the randomness used to produce their ballot or they may simply sell their voting material. Therefore Belenios should not be used in high stake elections. More generally, we believe that electronic voting systems still do not achieve an appropriate security level for high stake elections, such as politically binding national elections. At least, we believe that e-voting does not yet achieve the same level of security as paper-based elections, organized in physical polling stations, where people may watch the ballot box and manually count the ballots. A more detailed security comparison needs to be carried out for paper-based elections where the ballot box cannot be properly monitored or when ballots are counted through electronic devices.

As it is often the case for protocols, the specification of Belenios can be retrieved only by expanding a series of papers [3,11,17,18] that still omit many implementation choices. Alternatively, one may dive directly in the code specification [26]. To fill the gap between these two highly technical (in a different way) descriptions, in the first part of this article, we provide a detailed presentation of Belenios, from the setup to the tally and the recovery procedures. We discuss practical implementation choices. For example, Belenios involves several entities: voters, of course, but also a registrar, and decryption trustees. None of these roles require special cryptographic skills. We therefore describe here which adaptions had to be made for our system to be usable. Moreover, our voting platform offers several levels of security: the registration may be done directly by the voting server, the decryption key may or may not be split into several shares. This yields different tradeoffs between security and simplicity. We discuss these choices and we report on Belenios usage in various elections.

The security of Belenios has been formally proved in [16] w.r.t. vote privacy and verifiability. We do not reproduce here the formal security models but we provide a detailed overview of the properties that have been proved and the associated security assumptions. In particular, these high security guarantees are provided when the decryption key as well as the setup phase are distributed among several entities. Yet, the voting platform still offers some guarantees when the server is entrusted with more tasks.

2   Description of Belenios

The full description of Belenios can be found in the specification document [26], and this article refers to the version 1.6. We provide here a high level description where some cryptographic details are omitted.

2.1   Preliminaries: Cryptographic Tools

Belenios relies on a couple of rather standard cryptographic primitives, namely hash functions, encryption, signature, and zero-knowledge proof. For the public-key part, we work in a cyclic group G of order q for which a generator g is given, and we assume that the decisional Diffie-Hellman problem is hard in G. In the current implementation, the only choice for G is a subgroup of a multiplicative group of a prime finite field. Everything is in place to implement other instances of G, for instance elliptic curves, if needed for efficiency or security reasons.

Encryption. In Belenios, votes are encrypted using El Gamal encryption. To generate a private key, one simply picks x uniformly (as always in this paper) at random in $\mathbb{Z}_q$. The associated public key is $y = g^x$.

Given a vote v encoded as an integer in $\{0, \ldots, q-1\}$ and a public key y, the encryption of v is defined as follows: pick r at random in $\mathbb{Z}_q$ and compute

$$\mathsf{enc}(v, y, r) = (g^r, y^r g^v).$$

Note that compared to the textbook El Gamal encryption where the message is a group element, the vote v is encrypted as g^v. So, to decrypt a ciphertext $c = (a, b)$ using the private key x, we should first compute $b/a^x = g^v$ and then retrieve v by a discrete logarithm computation. This is possible only if v is taken from a small subset and not the entire interval $\{0, \ldots, q-1\}$.

This encryption enjoys an homomorphic property, which is particularly useful in the context of voting, namely:

$$\prod_{i=1}^{n} \mathsf{enc}(v_i, y, r_i) = \mathsf{enc}\Big(\sum_{i=1}^{n} v_i, \; y, \; \sum_{i=1}^{n} r_i\Big),$$

where the product of encrypted messages is defined coordinate-wise as $(a_1, b_1) \cdot (a_2, b_2) = (a_1 a_2, b_1 b_2)$. This property is used in Belenios to compute the encrypted sum of the votes directly from the encrypted ballots.

Hash Function. A hash function is used in several places, including as an internal operation for signatures and zero-knowledge proofs. We denote by $h(m)$ the hash of m. To avoid any collision when the hash function is used in different contexts, a message m is actually prefixed by a tag indicating the context and no tag is a prefix of another tag. For example, if m is hashed inside the signature function then $h(\mathsf{sigmsg} \mid m)$ is computed instead of $h(m)$. These tags will be omitted in the rest of the paper for the sake of readability but they are important for the security analysis to be valid.

Signature. Each voter signs her encrypted ballot with a Schnorr signature to avoid any ballot stuffing. A private signing key sk can be generated as a random element of $\mathbb{Z}_q$ and the associated verification key is $\mathsf{vk} = g^{\mathsf{sk}}$. The signature of a message m with signing key sk is denoted $\mathsf{sign}(m, \mathsf{sk})$ and is computed as follows:

- pick a random $w \in \mathbb{Z}_q$;
- compute $c = h(m \mid g^w)$ and $r = w - \mathsf{sk} \cdot c \mod q$;
- return (r, c).

Given a message m, a signature (r, c), and a verification key vk, the verification algorithm $\mathsf{verifsign}$ computes $A = g^r \mathsf{vk}^c$ and checks that $c = h(m \mid A)$.

Zero-Knowledge Proofs. Zero-knowledge proofs are used in several places in Belenios. First, voters must show that they encrypt a valid vote (e.g. they prove that they selected at most 4 candidates, as allowed by the election). Second, the decryption trustees must prove that they correctly decrypted the result of the election. All the zero-knowledge proofs are made non-interactive using the Fiat-Shamir technique.

A basic zero-knowledge proof is a proof of knowledge of a discrete logarithm. For example, a voter may need to prove that she knows the randomness r used to encrypt her vote v as $(g^r, y^r g^v)$. Given g^r and r, she proceeds, as a prover, as follows:

- pick a random $w \in \mathbb{Z}_q$;
- compute $c = h(g^r \mid g^w)$ and $s = w - r\,c \mod q$;
- return (s, c).

The verifier, given the proof (s, c) and the message $z = g^r$, checks that $c = h(z \mid A)$ where $A = g^s\,z^c$.

Given a finite set $\mathcal{V}$ of valid votes, a voter may similarly prove that her encrypted vote v belongs to $\mathcal{V}$, providing a proof $\mathsf{proofv}(v, r, \mathsf{enc}(v, \mathsf{pk}, r), \mathsf{pk}, \mathsf{vk})$. In particular, the associated verification algorithm $\mathsf{verifproofv}$ is such that $\mathsf{verifproofv}(\mathsf{proofv}(v, r, \mathsf{enc}(v, \mathsf{pk}, r), \mathsf{pk}, \mathsf{vk}), \mathsf{enc}(v, \mathsf{pk}, r), \mathsf{pk}, \mathsf{vk})$ returns true if $v \in \mathcal{V}$ and false in any other situation. Note that in Belenios, we chose to make the zero-knowledge proof depend also on the verification key vk of the voter. We will explain why in Sect. 3.2.

Zero-knowledge proofs are also used by the decryption trustees. First, during the setup, they prove knowledge of their secret key. Second, during the tally, they produce a proof of correct decryption.

The reader is referred to [25, 26] for the precise description of the corresponding algorithms and e.g. to [8] for more scientific background on zero-knowledge proofs.

2.2   Participants

Belenios includes four main participants: the server, the voters and their voting device, the registrar, and the decryption trustees. We describe them informally. The role of each participant is explained in more details in the next section.

Registrar. The registrar, also called credential authority on the voting platform, generates and sends privately a signing key to each voter. This key is used by voters to sign their ballot. The registrar also sends the corresponding verification keys to the voting server.

Voters. The voters select their vote. Their voting device encrypts and signs their vote. The resulting ballot is sent on an authenticated channel to the voting server (thanks to a login and password mechanism). Voters may check at any time that their ballot is present on the bulletin board. They may also revote, in which case only the last ballot is retained. In Belenios, voting devices are assumed to be honest, hence we will not distinguish between a voter and her voting device in the rest of the paper.

Voting Server. The voting server is in charge of maintaining the bulletin board, that is, the list of accepted ballots. Upon receiving a ballot from a voter, the voting server checks that the ballot is valid (e.g. the signature is valid) and adds it to the bulleting board.

Decryption Trustees. No single authority detains the private key of the election. Instead, a set of m decryption trustees are selected, out of which $t + 1$ are needed to decrypt the result of the election. For example, if 5 out of 7 trustees are needed to decrypt the election then 2 trustees may lose their key without having to cancel the whole election.

2.3   Protocol

The voting protocol Belenios is divided in three main phases. During the setup, the election material is sent to the voters and the election public key is computed. During the voting phase, voters may cast their vote. Once the voting phase is over, the result is tallied thanks to the decryption trustees. For simplicity, we present Belenios in a simplified version, where voters simply express their vote as a number. For example, in the context of a single-question referendum, 1 means "yes" while 0 means "no". We explain later how to use Belenios for more complex elections.

Election Material Generation. For each voter id, the registrar generates a signing key $sk_{id} \in \mathbb{Z}_q$ and sends it privately (in practice, by email) to the voter. The registrar transmits the corresponding list of verification keys $vk_{id_1}, \ldots, vk_{id_n}$ to the voting server, in some random order, where $vk_{id} = g^{sk_{id}}$.

   The voting server publishes the list of verification keys, that is, this list is part of the public election data. Moreover, the voting server generates a password for each voter and sends it privately (in practice, again by email) to the voter.

   This phase is depicted in Fig. 1.

Key Generation. The decryption key of the election is never computed in any form. Instead, m decryption trustees are selected, out of them a threshold of $t + 1$ suffices to decrypt the election. In case $t + 1 = m$, that is, all trustees need to contribute to the decryption, the key generation phase can be simplified. We present here the general case, following the scheme proposed by Pedersen [34] and proved to yield a secure encryption scheme when combined with ElGamal encryption in [17].

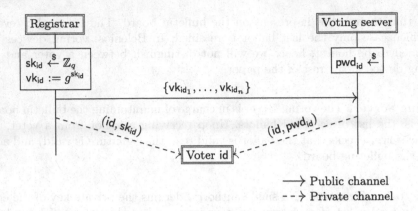

—→ Public channel
- - → Private channel

Fig. 1. Election material generation.

Each decryption trustee i chooses at random a polynomial $f_i(x) = a_{i0}+a_{i1}x+ \cdots+a_{it}x^t$ of degree t and sends privately the value of the polynomial $s_{ij} = f_i(j)$ to the trustee j. Intuitively, the secret of the trustee i is a_{i0} and any $t+1$ evaluations of the polynomial will allow to reconstruct the polynomial by Lagrange interpolation and hence a_{i0} (even if it is not done this way). The public key of the election is set to $pk = \prod_{i=1}^{m} g^{a_{i0}}$. To avoid potentially malicious trustees to corrupt the election key, the key generation includes further checks: each trustee i commits to her polynomial by publishing $A_{i0} = g^{a_{i0}}, \ldots, A_{it} = g^{a_{it}}$. This way, the trustee i can verify the consistency of each received private contribution s_{ji} by checking that $g^{s_{ji}} = \prod_{k=0}^{t}(A_{jk})^{i^k}$. Finally, each trustee i computes her public key $pk_i = g^{dk_i}$ with associated decryption key $dk_i = \sum_{j=1}^{m} s_{ji}$ and sends pk_i to the server, together with a proof of knowledge pok of dk_i.

This protocol is depicted in Fig. 2. The last consistency checks made by the server are omitted and can be found in [17].

Voting Phase. The list BB of accepted ballots, the *public board*, is public and can be accessed at any time. Of course, BB is initially empty. The voting server also displays the election data, namely:

– the set of verification keys $\{vk_{id_1}, \ldots, vk_{id_n}\}$,
– the public key of the election pk.

The voting server initially does not know the link between a verification key and the corresponding voter. It will memorize this link in a private database log.

To vote, a voter simply encrypts her vote yielding a ciphertext $c = enc(v, pk, r)$, produces a proof $\pi = proofv(v, r, enc(v, pk, r), pk, vk)$ that the vote belongs to the set of valid votes, and signs c, yielding a signature $s = sign(c, sk)$. The ballot $(c, \pi, s), vk$ is sent to the voting server over an authenticated channel thanks to a login and password mechanism.

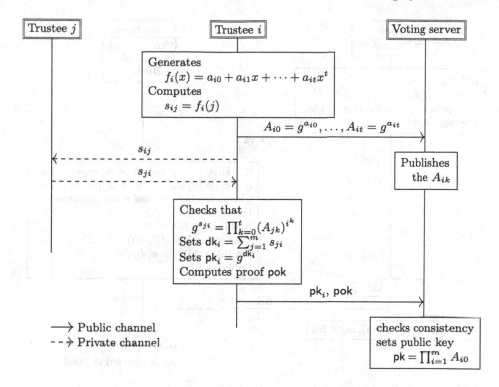

Fig. 2. Election key generation.

Upon receiving a ballot b, vk from voter id, the server checks whether id already voted, by looking for an entry of the form $(\text{id}, \text{vk}') \in \text{log}$. If $\text{vk}' \neq \text{vk}$, the ballot is rejected: a voter cannot use different verification keys. The server also checks that no other voter used vk as signing key, otherwise the ballot is also rejected. Then the server checks the consistency of the signature and the proof and rejects the ballot if one of the checks fails. If no such entry exists, the server adds (id, vk) to log. Then, if there is already a ballot of the form (b', vk) in BB then this ballot is removed: $\text{BB} := \text{BB} \setminus \{(b', \text{vk})\}$ (only the last ballot is kept for each voter). Finally, the new ballot is added: $\text{BB} := \text{BB} \| (b, \text{vk})$.

At any time, voters may check that their last submitted ballot appears in the public board BB.

The voting phase is depicted in Fig. 3.

Tally Phase. Once the voting phase is over, the list BB of accepted ballots is of the form

$$((c_1, \pi, s_1), \text{vk}_1), \ldots, ((c_p, \pi_p, s_p), \text{vk}_p),$$

where the vk_j are all distinct, the proofs and the signature are valid. Anyone can compute the encrypted result $\text{res}_e = \prod_1^p c_i$. Since each c_i is the encryption of a

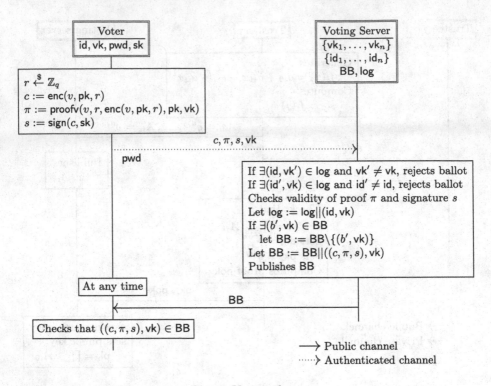

Fig. 3. Voting phase.

vote $c_i = \mathsf{enc}(v_i, \mathsf{pk}, r_i)$, we have that res_e corresponds to the encryption of the result: $\mathsf{res}_e = \mathsf{enc}(\sum_{i=1}^{p} v_i, \mathsf{pk}, \sum_{i=1}^{p} r_i)$.

Then each trustee i (or at least $t + 1$ trustees) contributes to the decryption by providing $\mathsf{res}_e^{\mathsf{dk}_i}$ together with a proof pok of correct decryption. As explained in [17,26], from these contributions, it is possible to compute the decryption of res_e, that is $\sum_{i=1}^{p} v_i$. The tally phase is depicted in Fig. 4.

2.4   Elections with Several Candidates

For simplicity, we have presented Belenios when voters express their vote as a (small) integer. Actually, in Belenios, voters have to select between k_1 and k_2 candidates out of l. A vote is represented by a vector in $\{0,1\}^l$. For example, if there are 5 candidates, the vote $(0, 1, 1, 0, 0)$ means that the voter has selected the second and third candidates. Then the encryption of a vote $v = (v_1, \ldots, v_l)$ with the public key pk is simply

$$\mathsf{enc}(v_1, \mathsf{pk}, r_1), \ldots, \mathsf{enc}(v_l, \mathsf{pk}, r_l),$$

and the associated zero-knowledge proof guarantees that:

– each v_i is either 0 or 1;

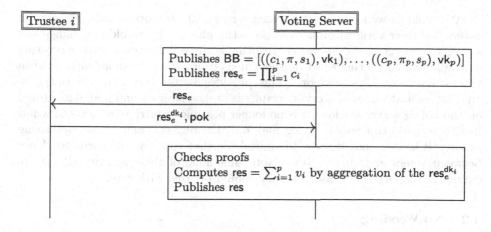

Fig. 4. Tally phase.

- the voter has selected at least k_1 and at most k_2 candidates, that is, $k_1 \leq \sum_{i=1}^{l} v_i \leq k_2$.

Then, during the tally, the final ballot box BB contains ballots b_i of the form

$$b_i = ((c_i^1, \ldots, c_i^l), \pi, s_i, \mathsf{vk}_i).$$

An encrypted result $\mathsf{res}_e^j = \prod_{i=1}^{p} c_i^j$ is computed for each candidate j. Each res_e^j is then decrypted by the decryption trustees, yielding the sum of the votes received by each candidate.

3   Design Choices and Variants

3.1   The Log File

One of the security goals of Belenios is to prevent ballot stuffing. Intuitively, the authentication of a voter is split into two parts: the login and password authentication on the one hand, and the signature of the ballot on the other hand. Belenios guarantees that no ballot can be added unless both the registrar and the voting server are corrupted.

In the case where revoting is allowed (which is the case in Belenios), then the voting server needs to store the correspondence between a voter and her verification key. This correspondence is used to enforce that a voter does not vote with two distinct verification keys and that no two voters use the same key. This is absolutely necessary to avoid the following attack. Assume the registrar is dishonest, as well as one voter C. Assume also that the voters who received the verification keys $\mathsf{vk}_{i_1}, \ldots, \mathsf{vk}_{i_m}$ from the registrar will not vote (in many elections, the turnout is low). Then, using the login and password of the corrupted voter C, the registrar may cast m ballots using successively $\mathsf{vk}_{i_1}, \ldots, \mathsf{vk}_{i_m}$, pretending C is re-voting. This way, the registrar would insert m ballots instead of one.

We could as well provide the voting server with the correspondence between voters and their verification keys at the setup phase. This would not change any security property in the case where revoting is allowed. However, in case revoting is disallowed, the voting sever does not need to log the correspondence between voters and their keys anymore. This provides better *everlasting privacy* [33] guarantees. Indeed, even if cryptography is broken later on and if all data stored on the voting server are lost, it is no longer possible to retrieve who voted what. In this scenario (no revote, no log file), only the registrar may break everlasting privacy if he does not destroy his initial file that contains the correspondence between voters and signing keys. Note that none of these security claims are currently supported by proofs so they should be used with care.

3.2   No Weeding

An expert reader may know that Helios (on which Belenios elaborates) requires weeding: the voting server must check that no ciphertext is submitted twice. This is to avoid copy attacks [21]. Imagine that Alice is voting 1 and casts ballot b_1, Bob is voting 0, and casts ballot b_2. Then, if a dishonest voter Charlie (re)casts b_1 pretending it is his own ballot, in the end, the result of the election would be 2 and Charlie deduces that Alice voted 1.

This ballot privacy attack is no longer possible in Belenios thanks to the zero-knowledge proofs. Remember that a ballot is of the form $b = (c, \pi, s), \mathsf{vk}$ where $c = \mathsf{enc}(v, \mathsf{pk}, r)$, $\pi = \mathsf{proofv}(v, r, \mathsf{enc}(v, \mathsf{pk}, r), \mathsf{pk}, \mathsf{vk})$, and $s = \mathsf{sign}(c, \mathsf{sk})$. Assume a dishonest voter id' wishes to copy the ciphertext c already submitted by a voter id. Then he also needs to use the same proof π (since he does not know the randomness r). However, since π embeds the verification key vk of voter id, he also needs to include the signature s. Now, if voter id' submits b, the ballot would be rejected since $(\mathsf{id}, \mathsf{vk}) \in \mathsf{log}$ with $\mathsf{id} \neq \mathsf{id}'$.

In other words, the zero-knowledge proof guarantees that the ballot has been produced by the voter that received the signing key sk.

3.3   The BeleniosRF Variant

In Belenios (as in Helios), a voter may prove for whom she voted. Indeed, if Alice publishes the randomness r used to form the encryption of her vote, anyone can re-encrypt using this randomness and check the value of the vote. Note that, of course, our implementation does not provide the voter with a direct tool to obtain her randomness. However, it would be easy for a malicious voter to write her own voting client.

To avoid this issue, a variant of Belenios has been proposed, named BeleniosRF [14], that offers both receipt-freeness and verifiability. It is receipt-free in the sense that even dishonest voters cannot prove how they voted. It relies on re-randomizable signed encryption [13]. Namely, given an (ElGamal) encryption and its signature, anyone can produce a re-randomized encryption together with a valid signature (without knowing the signing key). Then the key ingredient of

BeleniosRF is that the voting server re-randomizes the ballots before publishing them on the ballot box. This way, no voter can provide the corresponding randomness since part of it has been generated by the voting server. Hence the randomness is not known to the voter nor to her voting client. Therefore BeleniosRF prevents behaviours where voters may e.g. tweet for whom they voted. Note however that this is not sufficient to prevent vote buying. Indeed, a voter may still sell her credentials (password and signing key) to an attacker.

3.4 The BeleniosVS Variant

Another limitation of Belenios is that the voting device of the voter (typically her computer) needs to be trusted. Indeed, a malicious voting device may learn the vote of a voter or even modify it. Building upon BeleniosRF, another variant, BeleniosVS [23], has been proposed, in which the voter receives a voting sheet as part of her voting material. This sheet is generated by the registrar and contains the list of candidates together with a corresponding, signed, encrypted vote next to each candidate. A voter then simply provides her encrypted ballot to her voting device by scanning exactly this ballot and nothing else. This way, the voting device cannot learn the value of the vote (since it is encrypted) nor modify it (since it does not have the signing key). Both the voting device and the voting server re-randomize the ballot in order to break the correspondence between the initial ballot and the vote. Moreover, a voter may audit the voting sheet using another device (e.g. her smartphone) or delegate this audit to a third party, to check that each encrypted ballot does actually correspond to the vote written next to it. For the sake of auditing, the randomness used for encryption is also provided on the voting sheet.

BeleniosVS guarantees both privacy and verifiability even against a dishonest voting device.

4 Security Proofs

The design of security protocols in general is known to be error-prone and voting protocols make no exception to this rule. For example, the well-known Helios protocol, from which Belenios builds upon, was first proposed in [9] in 2006 and implemented as Helios in 2008 [3]. In 2011, it was found [21] to be subject to a replay attack, which compromises privacy. Namely, dishonest voters can collude and can all vote as Alice (without knowing Alice's vote). Then dishonest voters may infer information on Alice's vote from the result of the election.

Therefore, the state-of-the-art practice consists in *proving* the security of protocols. A security proof identifies in particular what are the security guarantees and the trust assumptions. For example, the Swiss Chancellerie requires [2] that "there exists a cryptographic proof and a symbolic proof [of the voting protocol]". What does this mean? Two distinct approaches have been developed for analysing and proving security protocols, developed by two distinct communities (resp. logic and cryptography): symbolic and computational models. Symbolic models analyse the logical flow of protocols, with an abstract representation of the cryptographic primitives, based on rewriting or logic. Mature push-button tools such as ProVerif [12] or Tamarin [37] can automatically find flaws or formally prove security in symbolic models, possibly with some user guidance for Tamarin. Computational models are based on complexity theory. Namely, the security of a protocol is reduced to some algorithmically hard problem such as discrete logarithm or factorisation. The execution model is specified down to the bitstring level, yielding higher guarantees but also more complex proofs. Computational proofs of protocols are typically done by hand (e.g. [3, 29] for voting protocols) with a recent attempt of a machine-checked framework [6] using the EasyCrypt tool [6]. EasyCrypt is an interactive theorem prover specialized in proofs of probabilistic equivalence of programs and well adapted to cryptographic security proofs. Reading hand-written proofs in this domain requires a lot of expertise and spotting mistakes is difficult. Therefore using a tool like EasyCrypt provides a higher level of confidence in the proofs.

Both symbolic and computational proofs have been conducted for Belenios. However, the existing symbolic proofs of Belenios have been developed as an illustration of a proof technique and remain quite abstract. For example, [5] shows that Belenios preserves vote privacy in a simplified model where the registrar is not represented explicitly. There is no proof of verifiability. Since BeleniosVS has been proved verifiable, the corresponding symbolic proof could probably be adapted to Belenios but this has not been done yet.

Therefore, in the rest of this section, we will focus on the proof of both privacy and verifiability, conducted in a cryptographic model [16]. These proofs have been established with the aforementioned EasyCrypt tool. In the remainder of this section, we first sketch the formal definitions of privacy and verifiability and we then detail the security guarantees and the corresponding trust assumptions for Belenios.

4.1   Overview of the Privacy and Verifiability Definitions

In cryptographic models, messages are bitstrings and the adversary is any probabilistic polynomial time Turing machine. This represents the fact that an adversary may use any algorithm, provided it runs in a reasonable amount of time. Of course, the adversary controls all public communications and may send any message it can compute. Security proofs work by reduction: breaking the security of a (voting) protocol should be as hard as breaking some well known algorithmic problems. For example, Belenios uses ElGamal encryption and its security relies on the difficulty of solving the decisional Diffie-Hellman problem.

Vote Privacy. There is no well established consensus on how to define vote privacy. Several definitions have been proposed, often through games: the attacker should not observe any difference when Alice is voting 0 or 1. We chose here to consider the privacy definition BPRIV [10].

Intuitively, BPRIV defines an experiment where the adversary tries to distinguish between two worlds: a "real world" and a "simulated world". For this, we give to the adversary the power to ask the (honest) voters to vote differently in both worlds, and all the votes in both worlds are known to the adversary (they can actually be chosen by him). At any time in the experiment, the adversary can look at the public board of the world he is in. In a secure scheme, the public board contains only the encrypted ballots, so there is no direct way for the adversary to deduce in which world he is, even if the votes are different.

At any time in the experiment, the adversary can also emulate a dishonest voter and cast any ballot, not necessarily coming from the legitimate voting algorithm. For instance, he can attempt to forge a ballot from what he has previously seen in the public board of his world. As long as it is recognized as a valid ballot by the validation algorithm of the protocol, it will be cast in both worlds.

In the end of the experiment, the adversary gets the result of the election. To avoid a trivial attack, the adversary is always given the tallying function applied to the public board of the real world, even if he is in the simulated world (otherwise, this would immediately reveal the answer to the adversary, since he knows the votes and they can be different in both worlds). The additional data, for instance, the proof of correct decryption, is computed by the legitimate algorithm in the real world, or is computed by a simulator (an algorithm to be defined in the security proof) in the simulated world. If it can be proven that no polynomial-time adversary can guess with a non-negligible advantage in which world he is, then the scheme respects privacy.

This definition is meant to capture the fact that, besides the result of the election, no other data should leak information about the votes.

Verifiability. Again, several notions of verifiability have been proposed in the literature, surveyed for example in [19]. Intuitively, verifiability ensures that votes are correctly reflected in the result of the election. We distinguish between three types of voters:

- Honest voters that follow the voting protocol exactly as expected. In particular, they perform the required checks. In Belenios, honest voters are supposed to check that their ballot is included in the (public) ballot box.
- Honest voters that do not check. Unfortunately this corresponds to the majority of voters: voters follow the protocol but not entirely, they stop once they have cast their ballot.
- Dishonest voters are fully controlled by the attacker and may submit anything as their own ballot (if they wish to).

In what follows, we will say that a protocol is *verifiable* if the result of the election corresponds to:

- all the votes from voters who checked;
- a subset of the votes from voters who did not check;
- an arbitrary set of valid votes, of size smaller than the number of corrupted voters. This last part guarantees that there is *no ballot stuffing*: the attacker cannot control more votes than the number of dishonest voters.

We refer the reader to [18] for a formal definition. Since the attacker controls all the public communications, Belenios cannot guarantee that votes of voters that did not check will be counted. Indeed, the corresponding ballots may have been dropped by an attacker. However, Belenios guarantees that these votes cannot be modified by the attacker.

4.2 Security Guarantees of Belenios

As mentioned earlier, the security definitions as well as the corresponding proofs have been fully developed through the EasyCrypt tool, forming the first machine-checked proof of both verifiability and privacy of a deployed voting protocol. We now spell out our trust assumptions, summarised in Fig. 5.

	Number of dishonest authorities							
Decryption trustees	$\leq t$	$\leq t$	$\leq t$	$\leq t$	$> t$	$> t$	$> t$	$> t$
Registrar	0	0	1	1	0	0	1	1
Voting Server	0	1	0	1	0	1	0	1
Verifiability	✓	✓	✓	✗	✓	✓	✓	✗
Privacy	✓	.	.	.	✗	✗	✗	✗

✓ indicates that the property is satisfied. ✗ indicates that the property is not satisfied. . indicates that there is no formal proof, yet no attack is known. As in Section 2.3, t is the threshold decryption parameter, *i.e.* at least $t + 1$ contributions are required to be able to decrypt.

Fig. 5. Trust assumptions for Belenios.

Verifiability. Belenios is verifiable provided that the registrar or the voting server are honest and the voting device of the voter is honest. The decryption trustees may all be corrupted.

Privacy. Belenios guarantees vote privacy provided that both the registrar and the voting server are honest, that the voting device of the voter is honest, and that at most t decryption trustees are corrupted (where t is the threshold used to generate the key, as explained in Sect. 2.3).

Discussion. Why do we need to assume that both the registrar and the voting server are honest for privacy? Intuitively, there is no reason for that. On the contrary, Belenios is designed to preserve vote privacy even if both the registrar and the voting server are corrupted since these two authorities are rather in charge of ensuring that only legitimate voters can vote. The first reason is that existing definitions of privacy in a computational setting all implicitly assume an honest voting server. Thus we cannot prove privacy in a setting that has not been defined yet. The second, deeper, reason is that there are subtle relations between verifiability and privacy. In a scenario where an attacker may selectively drop votes, he can thereby learn information from the result. In particular, it has been recently shown that the current definitions of privacy imply individual verifiability, that is, they imply that all honest votes are counted (including votes from voters that do not check) [20]. These limitations apply to the other voting schemes as well.

Note that as stated in the description of Belenios, we also assume, for both properties, that the voting device is honest. Indeed, since the voter selects her voting choice thanks to her voting device, the voting device automatically learns the vote. Moreover, a corrupted voting device may easily change the vote by encrypting 1 when a voter selects 0 for example. Helios includes a cast-or-audit mechanism. Indeed, a voter can interact with her voting device to check that it behaves as expected. When she is satisfied, she can then use her device for the actual vote. This mechanism could easily be added to Belenios. We chose not to include it as it is not really used in practice and it is easy to target attacks to voters that are more likely to avoid checks.

5 Implementation and Deployment of the Public Platform

5.1 Source Code and System Aspects

We have written a full implementation of the Belenios protocol following the specification. The current version is 1.8 and corresponds to the version 1.6 of the specification (the versioning numbers are independent). The source code is written in OCaml and is regularly checked and updated if necessary to work with the latest version of OCaml. The few non-OCaml dependencies (`wget`, `zip`, `openssl`) are standard tools easily available, for instance in a Debian Linux distribution. The implementation provides a command-line tool called `belenios-tool` that allows to perform all the algorithmic steps required in the protocol. It can be compiled separately from the other part which contains a web server allowing the deployment of elections. For this web part, the same back-end is called for the algorithmic operations of the protocol, the `http` server is the OCaml `ocsigen` server, and the web application is programmed within the `eliom` OCaml package. This use of a consistent framework for the whole code of the platform allows to share several parts of the code between the server (for which the OCaml code is compiled to the native machine language of the host) and the web browser on the client side for which the OCaml code is compiled to Javascript. These Javascript clients depend on the classical libraries `jsbn` and `sjcl` for low-level big integer arithmetic and cryptographic functions.

The command-line program `belenios-tool` is available as a Debian package, but the web part is not, due to difficulties with some OCaml dependencies within the Debian distribution.

The web interface allows an election administrator to setup a new election, in interaction with the registrar and the decryption trustees. She is responsible in providing the list of e-mail addresses of voters, to which a login/password is sent by the server. The signing keys are sent to the voters by the registrar; usually this is also done by e-mail, but it could be sent via any other channel. This use of e-mail as an implementation of the private channels in Fig. 1 is certainly a weakness of our on-line platform. For a high-stake election, the way to send the election material must be adapted, taking into account what is realistically feasible (postal mail, use of existing e-IDs, . . .). In a context where all the voters belong to a same entity that provides a single-sign-on solution, this can be a replacement to the login/password authentication. There is actually support for the CAS protocol in our implementation.

On the voting side, the easiest way to vote is to use the web-interface, following the URL of the election. Then, the ballot is prepared entirely on the client side with a Javascript code sent by the server. Since it is not easy to provide guarantees that the Javascript code is really the one that it is supposed to be, there is, in principle, a safer way to prepare the ballot. Indeed, the interface proposes to upload directly an encrypted ballot prepared externally from the browser, for instance with `belenios-tool`. This tool can be installed from a Debian distribution, with the standard package signature mechanism, which gives guarantees on the authenticity of the code. Yet another possibility is to download the sources of Belenios, compile them, and use the generated Javascript code directly instead of the one provided by the server.

The online platform [1] which is available freely for anyone who wants to run an election, with a limitation on the number of voters, is running on a machine that is hosted in our research laboratory. The software deployed is exactly the same as the Belenios package that is freely distributed. The additional features that had to be added are the configuration for the network (a reverse proxy) and the e-mail, some backup mechanism, and monitoring and statistics tools. Although the platform is reasonably monitored for suspicious behaviours, we do not provide a strong hardening, for instance against denial of service, and we do not guarantee 24/7 uptime. Therefore, our online platform does not claim the robustness that one could expect for a high stake election.

5.2   Implementation Issues Related to Voters

While working on Belenios, both as a protocol specification and as an online platform, we took into account the usability for the voters as a strong criterion. Some of the features that we list here were actually implemented after feedback from our users.

Size of the Voting Material. A first important issue for the voters is the size of the voting material. In the current setting of our platform where it is sent by e-mail, everything can be copy-pasted. So limiting the size of the material is not such a strong requirement. But we keep in mind that, in some context, the voter might have to type their voting material. Therefore, the registrar does not send the signing key itself to the voter but a 15-character string that includes a checksum. The corresponding 88 bits of entropy are used to derive the signing key with the PBKDF2 primitive. In the same spirit, the encrypted ballot is not presented as such to the voter, but only its hashed version is shown during the preparation, sent by e-mail, and printed in the ballot-box (of course, the raw ballots are also easily available for verifiability).

Multilingual Support. Since our first users were from the academic world which is highly international, we quickly felt the need to have multilingual support for the part of the interface that is exposed to the voters. Indeed, although most of them are comfortable with the basic English used in scientific articles, the vocabulary of an election (voting booth, credential, ballot, tally, . . .), is not well known to non-native speakers. We currently support English, French, German, Italian, Romanian, and adding a new language is not difficult. For the moment, the web interfaces for the election administrator, the registrar, and the decryption trustees are in English only.

Re-sending the Voting Material. Another predictable request from users is to have a way to receive their voting material again, in case they have lost it. It is even more important in the setting of our platform, where the material is sent by e-mail and the messages are considered as spam by some automatic filters due to the presence of URLs and the key-words login/password. There is no difficulty on the voting server side which can easily generate a new password and send it to the voter. For the registrar, there is no need to keep the list of signing keys once they have been sent to the voters, except if a voter loses her key. Since we did not want to impose to the registrar the need to keep secrets for a long time, the specification contains a protocol of credential recovery (see Sect. 3.3 of [26]) in which the registrar generates a new signing key and sends the corresponding updates to the server, to ensure that the old key had not been used in the past and will not be used in the future. We remark however that, in practice, the registrars usually prefer keeping the list of signing keys to be able to send them again instead of running this credential recovery protocol with the server.

5.3   Other Features of Belenios

Counting the Blank Votes. In an early version of the Belenios specification, the only elections that could be setup were the one described in Sect. 2.4, namely choosing k candidates among l, where k lies in a prescribed set of values. Allowing k to be 0 was a way for voters to express a blank vote. The problem with this easy solution is that counting the number of blank votes is not always possible. This was a major missing feature for some potential users, who complained. Therefore we added a bit for encoding a blank vote in the ballots, together with the corresponding zero-knowledge proof that, if this bit is activated, no other one is (see Sect. 4.10 of [26] or [25]). Other frequent requests include various advanced counting functions, but most of them are not compatible with the homomorphic decryption, and we postpone their support to a future inclusion of verifiable mixnets in Belenios.

Secure Channels Between Different Parties. In the formal protocol description, some messages are sent via a secure channel from one authority to another, in particular for the election key setup, in the threshold mode (Fig. 2). In practice, everything is organized around the web server that plays the role of a hub through which all the messages are transmitted. Unfortunately, it is not realistic in our setting to assume that all the decryption trustees possess signing and encryption keys that can be used for ensuring secure channels to and from them. Therefore, in a first step of the key generation protocol, each decryption trustee starts by generating a random secret seed from which she derives cryptographic keys that are the basis of a custom PKI (see Sect. 4.5.1 of [26]). Then, the messages from one trustee to another go through the server, and thanks to the PKI, the server is just part of the (untrusted) network in the abstract model.

Although the support for threshold decryption has been implemented for more than a year, it has been only recently added to the web interface of the online platform. We have tried to keep the tasks of the decryption trustees as easy as possible, and the PKI is part of this effort, but we do not have feedback yet from users. To our knowledge, this state-of-the-art threshold decryption protocol is the first one to be implemented on a public voting platform.

Degraded Mode for Testing Purpose. For very low stake elections (which pizza for tonight?) or for testing purposes, the web server can emulate the roles of the registrar and of the decryption trustees. This mode is tempting for election administrators since it makes their life simpler. However, in this mode, the system administrators of the machine that runs the web server become powerful attackers. If we do not assume that they can be trusted, almost no security property is preserved, apart from some verifiability. Namely, as in Helios, voters who check the presence of their ballot are guaranteed that their vote is counted but extra ballots may have been added, taking advantage of abstention. To mitigate the danger of the presence of such a degraded mode, the server forgets the signing keys once they are sent to the voters. As a consequence, ballot-stuffing by the system administrators must be planned in advance to be successful. Also, the voters can not ask the server to send this signing key again if they lose it. This last part is actually a strong incentive not to use the degraded mode for real elections. Unfortunately, we still observe many elections being run in degraded mode while not of so low stake as we would expect. When asked, the users simply answer that they are happy to trust the system administrators.

Auditing and Monitoring. A strong assumption in the security analysis of Belenios is that all the process is monitored and audited by sufficiently many independent participants. For this, tools are needed and ideally, they should be written by developers different from the one of Belenios, directly from the specification document. For the moment, the only available program is `belenios-tool` which provides two auditing commands: `verify` and `verify-diff`. The first one checks the consistency of all the public data at a given time during an election, including the decrypted tally if the election if finished. All the zero-knowledge proofs and all the signatures are checked; no two ballots can be signed by the same key. The `verify-diff` command takes as input two snapshots of the public data and checks that the second one is a valid future state of the first one. This includes checking that the size of the ballot box is increasing, and more precisely that if a ballot has disappeared, another one has been cast with the same signature key (i.e. someone can re-vote, but the voting server did not drop ballots). This command is also aware of the credential recovery protocol and will check that if the list of verification keys is modified, everything is consistent with the protocol.

5.4 Usage Statistics

After a long test period of more than one year in 2016–2017 where various elections were organized with a big help from us, we have now reached a point where the organizers are autonomous and most elections are done without interaction with us. In the rest of this section, all the data and comments are related to the year 2018 and refer to this period where our on-line platform was no longer considered in test. General statistics for this 2018 year are:

Number of elections	142
Total number of voters	17 650
Total number of tallied ballots	5 579

Type of Elections. Given the academic nature of the Belenios project, it is not a surprise that most of the elections organized on the platform are related to (mostly French) academia. This includes elections for representatives in councils of research laboratories, elections for the head or for representatives of scientific working groups or learned societies, or elections during committees for promotions. A few not-so-small elections are for representatives in associations that are unrelated to academia. For numerous small elections we are not aware of the context at all.

Sizes. We have a limit to 1000 voters for a single election. Occasionally, upon request, we increase this limit for a larger election to be held on our platform. The picture in Fig. 6 shows how the sizes of the 142 elections held in 2018 are distributed and the turnout for them. Statistics for five intervals of the logarithm of the number of voters are given in the following table:

Number of voters	Number of elections	Average turnout	Elections with external trust party
$\cdot < 12$	15	84.5%	46.7%
$12 \leq \cdot < 50$	62	62.9%	29.0%
$50 \leq \cdot < 200$	45	41.6%	51.1%
$200 \leq \cdot < 800$	14	25.6%	21.4%
$800 \leq \cdot$	6	22.5%	67.7%
Total	142	31.6%	38.7%

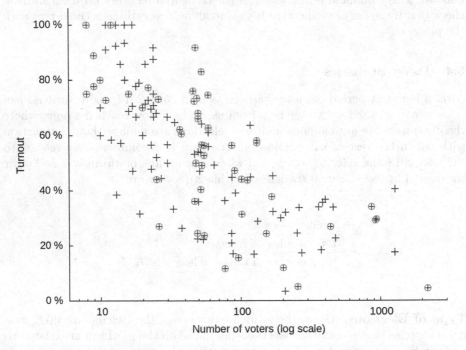

Fig. 6. Elections run on the Belenios platform in 2018. Each + symbol corresponds to an election. When a red circle ○ surrounds it, it means that at least one of the roles (registrar or decryption trustee) was not emulated by the server but was held by a third party. (Color figure online)

Use of the Degraded Mode. In Fig. 6, we see that the majority of the elections are configured in such a way that the server plays all the roles, so that the security is severely degraded: the trust on the administrators of the server is almost total.

We summarize the number of elections that were run for various security configurations.

Security configuration	# elections	Comment
Server plays all the roles (no circle on Fig. 6)	87	Organizer made no effort regarding security
Other configurations with a unique decrypt. auth.	27	Privacy issue
At least 2 decrypt. auth. and server is cred. auth.	4	Ballot stuffing issue
At least 2 decrypt. auth. and external cred. auth.	24	Scenario corresponding to security proofs

We noticed that for elections where the administrators "have to" care about security due to the regulations, they usually do it. This is especially the case for the administrators who have been using the platform during the testing phase where we had a lot of interaction with them: now that they use it by themselves, they continue to follow our advices. This corresponds to the cluster of circles for elections of about 50 voters on Fig. 6. Some of them have a high turnout, which might indicate that they are indeed considered important and deserve a high level of security.

6   Further Possible Developments

Public Board in Practice. Belenios, like several e-voting protocols, relies on the notion of public board were the ballots are recorded. In the current platform, it is implemented in the most naive way, as a public web page, and it is assumed that enough parties will monitor it, so that it is consistent. A more advanced decentralized public board, together with a state-of-the-art consensus protocol would certainly be preferable. Since this is not specific to Belenios, it makes no sense to develop a specific tool, though. In the meantime, providing better tools for monitoring and auditing the public board would be useful to push more users to contribute to the security of their election.

More Trust in the Software. All the parties, the voters, the registrar, the decryption trustees, use software during their participation to the protocol. The easiest way for the voters and the decryption trustees is to use the Javascript code that is provided by the web platform and do everything in the browser (for the registrar, this is not possible, since she must send e-mails to the voters). A cast-or-audit (or more generally compute-or-audit) mechanism could be added. But we still need to find the appropriate mechanism to ensure that the users will really perform the checks. It might then be better to allow ourselves to modify the protocol, and, for instance, design a practical variant of BeleniosVS that would be robust in the case of a corrupting device.

An easier, but less elegant approach, would be to provide standalone applications that work outside the browser and rely on the security mechanisms of the application store of the operating system for ensuring the traceability of the software that has been installed and run.

Another possible direction to enhance the amount of trust in the software is to formally prove part of it with tools like F* [39]. The difficulty might be to get a proof that goes all along to the GUI (and ensures that "yes" and "no" are not swapped on the screen of the voter).

More Types of Elections via Mixnets. The use of homomorphic encryption does not allow complex counting functions. Switching to verifiable mixnets is not a problem from a theoretical point of view, and in fact, the security proofs mentioned in Sect. 4 have also been done in this context. The implementation is work in progress, and the list of counting functions that we plan to support in the platform is not yet decided.

We had also demands from users for votes with weights. Depending on the situation, it might be necessary to include some weight randomization to avoid privacy issues due to underlying Knapsack problems [4]. Adding this kind of feature on an online platform requires great care, because it can lead to confusion of the users.

References

1. Belenios – Verifiable online voting system. http://www.belenios.org/
2. Exigences techniques et administratives applicables au vote électronique. Chancellerie fédérale ChF (2014). Swiss recommendation on e-voting
3. Adida, B.: Helios: web-based open-audit voting. In: 17th USENIX Security Symposium (Usenix 2008), pp. 335–348 (2008)
4. Adida, B., de Marneffe, O., Pereira, O., Quisquater, J.-J.: Electing a university president using open-audit voting: analysis of real-world use of Helios. In: Electronic Voting Technology Workshop/Workshop on Trustworthy Elections. USENIX, August 2009
5. Arapinis, M., Cortier, V., Kremer, S.: When are three voters enough for privacy properties? In: Askoxylakis, I., Ioannidis, S., Katsikas, S., Meadows, C. (eds.) ESORICS 2016. LNCS, vol. 9879, pp. 241–260. Springer, Cham (2016). https://doi.org/10.1007/978-3-319-45741-3_13
6. Barthe, G., Dupressoir, F., Grégoire, B., Kunz, C., Schmidt, B., Strub, P.-Y.: EasyCrypt: a tutorial. In: Aldini, A., Lopez, J., Martinelli, F. (eds.) FOSAD 2012-2013. LNCS, vol. 8604, pp. 146–166. Springer, Cham (2014). https://doi.org/10.1007/978-3-319-10082-1_6
7. Bell, S., et al.: STAR-vote: a secure, transparent, auditable, and reliable voting system. In: Electronic Voting Technology Workshop/Workshop on Trustworthy Elections (EVT/WOTE 2013) (2013)
8. Bellare, M., Rogaway, P.: Random oracles are practical: a paradigm for designing efficient protocols. In: ACM CCS 1993 (1993)
9. Benaloh, J.: Simple verifiable elections. In: USENIX Security Symposium (EVT 2006) (2006)

10. Bernhard, D., Cortier, V., Galindo, D., Pereira, O., Warinschi, B.: A comprehensive analysis of game-based ballot privacy definitions. In: 36th IEEE Symposium on Security and Privacy (S&P 2015), pp. 499–516. IEEE Computer Society Press, May 2015

11. Bernhard, D., Pereira, O., Warinschi, B.: How not to prove yourself: pitfalls of the Fiat-Shamir heuristic and applications to Helios. In: Wang, X., Sako, K. (eds.) ASIACRYPT 2012. LNCS, vol. 7658, pp. 626–643. Springer, Heidelberg (2012). https://doi.org/10.1007/978-3-642-34961-4_38

12. Blanchet, B.: Automatic verification of security protocols in the symbolic model: the verifier ProVerif. In: Aldini, A., Lopez, J., Martinelli, F. (eds.) FOSAD 2012-2013. LNCS, vol. 8604, pp. 54–87. Springer, Cham (2014). https://doi.org/10.1007/978-3-319-10082-1_3

13. Blazy, O., Fuchsbauer, G., Pointcheval, D., Vergnaud, D.: Signatures on randomizable ciphertexts. In: Catalano, D., Fazio, N., Gennaro, R., Nicolosi, A. (eds.) PKC 2011. LNCS, vol. 6571, pp. 403–422. Springer, Heidelberg (2011). https://doi.org/10.1007/978-3-642-19379-8_25

14. Chaidos, P., Cortier, V., Fuchsbauer, G., Galindo, D.: BeleniosRF: a non-interactive receipt-free electronic voting scheme. In: 23rd ACM Conference on Computer and Communications Security (CCS 2016), Vienna, Austria, pp. 1614–1625 (2016)

15. Clarkson, M.R., Chong, S., Myers, A.C.: Civitas: toward a secure voting system. In: IEEE Symposium on Security and Privacy (S&P 2008), pp. 354–368. IEEE Computer Society (2008)

16. Cortier, V., Dragan, C.C., Strub, P.-Y., Dupressoir, F., Warinschi, B.: Machine-checked proofs for electronic voting: privacy and verifiability for Belenios. In: 31st IEEE Computer Security Foundations Symposium (CSF 2018), pp. 298–312 (2018)

17. Cortier, V., Galindo, D., Glondu, S., Izabachene, M.: Distributed ElGamal à la Pedersen - application to Helios. In: Workshop on Privacy in the Electronic Society (WPES 2013), Berlin, Germany (2013)

18. Cortier, V., Galindo, D., Glondu, S., Izabachène, M.: Election verifiability for Helios under weaker trust assumptions. In: Kutyłowski, M., Vaidya, J. (eds.) ESORICS 2014. LNCS, vol. 8713, pp. 327–344. Springer, Cham (2014). https://doi.org/10.1007/978-3-319-11212-1_19

19. Cortier, V., Galindo, D., Küsters, R., Müller, J., Truderung, T.: SoK: verifiability notions for e-voting protocols. In: 36th IEEE Symposium on Security and Privacy (S&P 2016), pp. 779–798, San Jose, USA, May 2016

20. Cortier, V., Lallemand, J.: Voting: you can't have privacy without individual verifiability. In: 25th ACM Conference on Computer and Communications Security (CCS 2018), pp. 53–66. ACM (2018)

21. Cortier, V., Smyth, B.: Attacking and fixing Helios: an analysis of ballot secrecy. J. Comput. Secur. **21**(1), 89–148 (2013)

22. Cuvelier, E., Pereira, O., Peters, T.: Election verifiability or ballot privacy: do we need to choose? In: 18th European Symposium on Research in Computer Security (ESORICS 2013), pp. 481–498 (2013)

23. Filipiak, A.: Design and formal analysis of security protocols, an application to electronic voting and mobile payment. Ph.D. thesis, Université de Lorraine, March 2018

24. Galindo, D., Guasch, S., Puiggalí, J.: 2015 Neuchâtel's cast-as-intended verification mechanism. In: Haenni, R., Koenig, R.E., Wikström, D. (eds.) VOTELID 2015. LNCS, vol. 9269, pp. 3–18. Springer, Cham (2015). https://doi.org/10.1007/978-3-319-22270-7_1

25. Gaudry, P.: Some ZK security proofs for Belenios (2017). https://hal.inria.fr/hal-01576379
26. Glondu, S.: Belenios specification - version 1.6 (2018). http://www.belenios.org/specification.pdf
27. Haenni, R., Koenig, R.E., Locher, P., Dubuis, E.: CHVote system specification. Cryptology ePrint Archive, Report 2017/325 (2017)
28. Halderman, J.A., Teague, V.: The New South Wales iVote system: security failures and verification flaws in a live online election. In: Haenni, R., Koenig, R.E., Wikström, D. (eds.) VOTELID 2015. LNCS, vol. 9269, pp. 35–53. Springer, Cham (2015). https://doi.org/10.1007/978-3-319-22270-7_3
29. Juels, A., Catalano, D., Jakobsson, M.: Coercion-resistant electronic elections. In: Workshop on Privacy in the Electronic Society (WPES 2005), pp. 61–70. ACM (2005)
30. Kiayias, A., Zacharias, T., Zhang, B.: DEMOS-2: scalable E2E verifiable elections without random oracles. In: ACM Conference on Computer and Communications Security (CCS 2015) (2015)
31. Küsters, R., Müller, J., Scapin, E., Truderung, T.: sElect: a lightweight verifiable remote voting system. In: 29th IEEE Computer Security Foundations Symposium (CSF 2016), pp. 341–354 (2016)
32. Küsters, R., Truderung, T., Vogt, A.: Accountabiliy: definition and relationship to verifiability. In: 17th ACM Conference on Computer and Communications Security (CCS 2010), pp. 526–535 (2010)
33. Moran, T., Naor, M.: Receipt-free universally-verifiable voting with everlasting privacy. In: Dwork, C. (ed.) CRYPTO 2006. LNCS, vol. 4117, pp. 373–392. Springer, Heidelberg (2006). https://doi.org/10.1007/11818175_22
34. Pedersen, T.P.: Non-interactive and information-theoretic secure verifiable secret sharing. In: Feigenbaum, J. (ed.) CRYPTO 1991. LNCS, vol. 576, pp. 129–140. Springer, Heidelberg (1992). https://doi.org/10.1007/3-540-46766-1_9
35. Ryan, P.: Prêt à Voter with Paillier encryption. Math. Comput. Model. **48**(9–10), 1646–1662 (2008)
36. Ryan, P.Y.A., Rønne, P.B., Iovino, V.: Selene: voting with transparent verifiability and coercion-mitigation. In: Clark, J., Meiklejohn, S., Ryan, P.Y.A., Wallach, D., Brenner, M., Rohloff, K. (eds.) FC 2016. LNCS, vol. 9604, pp. 176–192. Springer, Heidelberg (2016). https://doi.org/10.1007/978-3-662-53357-4_12
37. Schmidt, B., Meier, S., Cremers, C., Basin, D.: Automated analysis of Diffie-Hellman protocols and advanced security properties. In: 25th IEEE Computer Security Foundations Symposium (CSF 2012), pp. 78–94 (2012)
38. Springall, D., et al.: Security analysis of the Estonian Internet voting system. In: 11th ACM Conference on Computer and Communications Security (CCS 2004), pp. 703–715 (2004)
39. Swamy, N., et al.: Dependent types and multi-monadic effects in F*. In: 43rd ACM SIGPLAN-SIGACT Symposium on Principles of Programming Languages (POPL 2016), pp. 256–270. ACM (2016)
40. Wolchok, S., Wustrow, E., Isabel, D., Halderman, J.A.: Attacking the Washington, D.C. internet voting system. In: Keromytis, A.D. (ed.) FC 2012. LNCS, vol. 7397, pp. 114–128. Springer, Heidelberg (2012). https://doi.org/10.1007/978-3-642-32946-3_10

Author Index

Printed in the United States
By Bookmasters